Oratorical Encounters

Recent Titles in
Contributions to the Study of Mass Media and Communications

News of Crime: Courts and Press in Conflict
J. Edward Gerald

As Good As Any: Foreign Correspondence on American Radio, 1930-1940
David H. Hosley

Freedom for the College Student Press: Court Cases and Related
Decisions Defining the Campus Fourth Estate Boundaries
Louis E. Ingelhart

The Press and the Decline of Democracy: The Democratic Socialist
Response in Public Policy
Robert G. Picard

Innovators and Preachers: The Role of the Editor in Victorian England
Joel H. Wiener, editor

Press Law and Press Freedom for High School Publications: Court Cases and
Related Decisions Discussing Free Expression Guarantees and Limitations for
High School Students and Journalists
Louis E. Ingelhart

Free Flow of Information: A New Paradigm
Achal Mehra

Shared Vulnerability: The Media and American Perceptions of the Bhopal Disaster
Lee Wilkins

Communications and History: Theories of Media, Knowledge, and Civilization
Paul Heyer

Oratorical Encounters

Selected Studies and Sources
of Twentieth-Century
Political Accusations and Apologies

Edited by
Halford Ross Ryan

Foreword by Edward P. J. Corbett

Contributions to the Study of Mass Media and Communications, Number 9

Greenwood Press
New York • Westport, Connecticut • London

Library of Congress Cataloging-in-Publication Data

Oratorical encounters.

(Contributions to the study of mass media and
communications, ISSN 0732-4456 ; no. 9)
  Bibliography: p.
  Includes index.
  1. Political oratory—United States—History—
20th century.   2. Speeches, addresses, etc.,
American—History and criticism.   I. Ryan, Halford
Ross.   II. Series.
PN4193.P6068   1988   808.5'1'0973   87-23662
ISBN 0-313-25568-7 (lib. bdg. : alk. paper)

British Library Cataloguing in Publication Data is available.

Library of Congress Catalog Card Number: 87-23662
ISBN: 0-313-25568-7
ISSN: 0732-4456

First published in 1988

Greenwood Press, Inc.
88 Post Road West, Westport, Connecticut 06881

Printed in the United States of America

The paper used in this book complies with the
Permanent Paper Standard issued by the National
Information Standards Organization (Z39.48-1984).

10 9 8 7 6 5 4 3 2 1

Copyright Acknowledgments

The author and publisher gratefully acknowledge permission to reprint material from the
following copyrighted sources.

Halford R. Ryan, "Baldwin vs. Edward VIII: A Case Study in *Kategoria* and *Apologia*,"
Southern Speech Communication Journal 49 (1984):125-34.

Halford R. Ryan, "*Kategoria* and *Apologia*: On Their Rhetorical Criticism as a Speech Set,"
Quarterly Journal of Speech 68 (1982):254-61.

Contents

Foreword

Edward P. J. Corbett

The tradition of *kategoria* (accusation) and *apologia* (defense) must be as old as human language. For surely as soon as people began to fight with words rather than with clubs or fists, they must have tried to defend themselves verbally against the slings and arrows of outrageous verbal assault. It is certain that, after such encounters, each one felt that he had scored a victory.

Perhaps that is the most characteristic feature of the speech set: the smug feeling on the part of the participants in the verbal exchange that each has scored points against the other. It may be only the audience—the listeners or the readers of the verbal contention—that can discriminate the winners and the losers. For that reason, in the most formal manifestation of this age-old speech act, the courtroom trial, a judge or a jury is always engaged to decide what the verdict will be. But as we all know, even judges and juries sometimes get hung up on whether to hang a man or not.

I seem already to have decided that the speech set of *kategoria* and *apologia* should be classified as an instance of forensic discourse. Would Aristotle have so classified it? According to what Aristotle said in the third chapter of Book I of his *Rhetoric*, where he first classified the three kinds of persuasive discourse—deliberative, forensic, epideictic—the lawcourts would indeed seem to be the place where accusatory and defensive discourse had its main arena. In fact, Aristotle himself used the terms *kategoria* and *apologia* in connection with forensic oratory. Moreover, the time province that Aristotle assigned to forensic discourse is the past, because this kind of discourse deals primarily with the question of what was done or not done in the past rather than with what needs to be done in the future (the main province of deliberative discourse) or with what prevails in the present (the main province of epideictic discourse). The end, the objective, the *telos* of forensic discourse is the determination of what is just or unjust (*dikaison* or *adikon*). So all of Aristotle's characterizations of forensic discourse (*dikanikon*) seem to fit the kind of public discourse that this collection deals with.

And yet there is a hint, even in Aristotle's *Rhetoric*, that apology and accusation partake of some of the characteristics of epideictic or ceremonial discourse. The epideictic orator engages primarily in praising or blaming someone or something. And in the kind of discourse featured in this book, there is a great deal of praising and blaming going on. Although epideictic orators focus mainly on the present, they sometimes slip over into the past, if only to recall it, or even into the future, if only to anticipate it. And the *telos* of epideictic discourse is the determination of the noble and the ignoble, of the virtuous and the vicious. When accusatory and defensive discourse concerns moral issues, it seems to be encroaching on the province of epideictic discourse.

What all of this discussion of the proper classification of accusatory and apologetic discourse confirms, once again, is that all classifications of kinds of discourse ultimately leak or overlap. Maybe it is futile and unnecessary to try to fit this kind of discourse into an airtight compartment. Let us be content to say that *kategoria* charges someone with a crime or a moral lapse or an act of indiscretion, negligence, incompetence, or stupidity and that *apologia* attempts to exonerate or exculpate the accused. The two kinds of discourse are linked and ultimately become a pair or a series of discourses. The *kategoria* usually occurs first and prompts the *apologia*. Although there have been some instances of a *kategoria* that did not prompt an apologetic response, I do not know of a single instance where the *apologia* occurred first. Nobody seems to be interested in listening to someone getting up, unprovoked, and exclaiming "Oh, what a good boy (or girl) am I."

But since the beginning of civilization, society has always been interested in listening to a publicly accused citizen defend himself or herself—especially if that citizen occupies a prominent or sensitive position in the polity. The most noted classical example of the genre is the *Apology*, in which Plato recreated the public trial of Socrates, who was accused, among other things, of having "corrupted the youth" of the Athenian polis. Students of English literature may recall *The Epistle to Dr. Arbuthnot* (1735), in which Alexander Pope responded, in brilliant heroic couplets, to a versified broadside that attacked, as Pope said, "not only my writings . . . but my person, my morals, and my family." Students of the literature of the eminent Victorians have certainly read the whole or substantial parts of John Henry Newman's *Apologia Pro Vita Sua* (1864), in which this clergyman eloquently defended himself against Charles Kingsley's aspersions on his intellectual and religious integrity.

But the beat goes on. *Kategoria* and *apologia*, as a matched set, are still with us, persistently and recurrently. We all have our favorite example or examples, written or spoken. Many of those examples probably involve public figures—presidents, generals, scholars, candidates for public office—who came into national prominence sometime after the mid-twentieth century. Many of those favorite examples are probably discussed in the essays included in this collection. After reading this set of essays, we may acquire other favorites.

What perversity is there in the human psyche that makes us enjoy the spectacle of human beings desperately trying to answer the charges leveled against them? Maybe secretly, as we read or listen, we say to ourselves, "Ah, there but for the grace of God go I." We soon learn that not only can sticks and stones break our bones, but words can break them too.

Edward P. J. Corbett
Columbus, Ohio

Preface

At Springfield, Illinois, on June 1858, Abraham Lincoln opened his senatorial campaign against Stephen A. Douglas by prefacing his "House Divided" speech with these words: "If we could first know where we are, and whither we are tending, we could then better judge what to do, and how to do it."

This book is about oratorical encounters. It explicates eighteen studies on some of the most significant accusations and apologies in the twentieth century. Focusing on the role of persuasion in destroying or saving numerous public careers in the United States and Great Britain—in the case of Prime Minister Stanley Baldwin vs. King Edward VIII in 1936—the book assays the value of treating charges and defenses as a rhetorical set.

It tends to support in most respects the tenets of the theory, and refines the construct so that rhetorical insights, hitherto unrealized, may be opened for further scrutiny by students of human communication.

Nineteen writers in the field of speech consented to "build, revise, extend, or amend the tenets" of the theory with regard to their respective communicators. The product of their research is the core of this book.

They accomplished their tasks by using the methodology of the case study. Explaining the historical and political situations in which the encounters arose, each contributor plumbs the significance of the exchange with regard to the orators' lives and their causes. Explicating the persuasions in terms of the theory, each essayist offers a reasoned critical analysis of why and how each rhetorical combatant sustained or lost his or her persuasive goal. Each author closes with information sources that list authoritative texts for the confrontations as well as a selected bibliography, culled from books, articles, essays, and presidential libraries, that would aid a researcher in the further study of accusations and apologies.

In a technical sense, three of the case studies do not narrowly conform to the title of oratorical encounters. One was played out entirely in the media, although spokespersons were involved; one was a hearing, although there were oral arguments presented; and one apologia was written from a jail cell. Yet to exclude studies on the basis that they were not comprised of oratorical encounters of the kind Lincoln engaged in with Douglas in 1858 would be a disservice to the theory and a suppression of the valuable insights offered in these three essays. For while the ideal model may be one person's confronting another in oral combat, a fact of life is that the media often intervenes in contemporary persuasions. As two studies clearly demonstrate, and others tangentially illustrate, newspapers and television not only mediate the encounters, they can initiate them as well as judge their outcome.

As this book implies, the study of encounters is ongoing and more will occur as long as men and women talk. Although the book is not meant to be prescriptive, the critical mind will find in it what to do and how to do it.

Acknowledgments

Along the way, I have received help and encouragement from numerous individuals and I wish to thank them.

To Edward P. J. Corbett, director of the National Endowment for the Humanities (NEH) Summer Seminar "Rhetoric and Public Address," Ohio State University, 1981, and to the seminar's twelve disciples, as the group styled itself, I owe a special obligation for assistance. Corbett kindly consented to compose a Foreword. He also responded to a panel of papers, culled from the contributions herein, at the 1987 annual meeting of the Speech Communication Association in Boston.

My original essay, "*Kategoria* and *Apologia*: On Their Rhetorical Criticism as a Speech Set," a product of the NEH Summer Seminar, and a subsequent piece, "Baldwin vs. Edward VIII: A Case Study in *Kategoria* and *Apologia*," were respectively guided through the publication process by Hermann Stelzner, editor of the *Quarterly Journal of Speech*, and Howard Dorgan, editor of *Southern Speech Communication Journal*.

Without the scholars who applied my theory and their expertise to the oratorical encounters, this book would not exist. Their help in contributing to it is deeply appreciated. I note that Bernard Duffy, my coeditor of *American Orators Before 1900: Critical Studies and Sources* and *American Orators of the Twentieth Century: Critical Studies and Sources*, was the first person to pledge support for the book's mission.

John Elrod, dean of the college, Washington and Lee University, supported subvention for the book by an award from the Glenn Grant Publication Fund, and granted a leave, part of which was devoted to editing the book.

This is the third book on which Marilyn Brownstein, humanities editor at Greenwood Press, has helped me. Her sound advice is reflected herein. William Neenan, production editor, guided the book to completion.

I thank the Speech Communication Association (SCA) for carrying a call for contributors; William Work, executive secretary of SCA, for granting permission to use my article from the *Quarterly Journal of Speech*; and Howard Dorgan, executive secretary of Southern Speech Communication Association, for giving permission to use my essay from *Southern Speech Communication Journal*.

Introduction

As I was casting about for an idea that could be the basis for a viable proposal for a National Endowment for the Humanities Summer Seminar on "Rhetoric and Public Discourse" in 1981, directed by Edward P. J. Corbett, a thesis became apparent. Although a number of contemporary scholars had defined the apologia as a speech of defense, no one had treated the kind of address that motivated an apology. Scholars had, in effect, judged a debate in which only the negative's defense was significant, or explicated the transcript of a trial in which only the defense's motions, objections, and arguments were salient. This concept was developed as a paper delivered at the seminar, and then published as "*Kategoria* and *Apologia*: On Their Rhetorical Criticism as a Speech Set" in the *Quarterly Journal of Speech* in 1982.

That essay is the basis for this book, and its central idea is simple. Accusatory discourse motivates apologetic discourse. Although the point was overlooked by modern theorists, the ancients recognized the existence of accusatory and apologetic rhetoric. Plato divided oratory into two genres of accusation and apology and Isocrates included them in his fourpart division of speeches. Aristotle divided forensic oratory into accusation and apology, and observed the motivational relationship in the speech set: "One man accuses the other, and the other defends himself, with reference to things already done." Isocrates observed the same motivational relationship: "for a plea in defense is appropriate only when the defendant is charged with a crime." Quintilian also appreciated the nature of accusation and defense:

> I cannot understand why some hold that the elaboration of speech originated in the fact that those who were in peril owing to some accusation being made against them, set themselves to speak with studied care for the purpose of their own defense. This however, though a more honourable origin, cannot possibly be the earlier, for accusation necessarily precedes defense. You might as well assert that the sword was invented for the purpose of self-defense and not

for aggression.
The ancient Greeks had two terms for the kind of oratorical encounters discussed in this book. *Kategoria*, a noun, denoted "an accusation, charge" and
apologia, a noun, meant "a speech in defense."[1]

Although my original essay seemed to rely extensively on the forensic
characteristics of the speech set, it did offer examples of encounters in
Aristotle's epideictic and deliberative categories. In truth, as some of the
essayists here demonstrate, a speech set can inhere in one or more of the
Aristotelian genres as well as concomitantly transcend them. Susan Huxman and Wil Linkugel argue that the set of General Hugh Johnson vs.
Father Charles Coughlin and Senator Huey Long over the New Deal had
elements of forensic and epideictic oratory in it, but that neither category
cleanly characterized the set. Carl Burgchardt shows that, concerning the
issue of free speech in World War I, Senator Robert La Follette defended
his past actions and speeches against the Wilson administration with the
clear intention, in a deliberative sense, to continue his attacks; whereas,
Senator Joseph Robinson, taking the floor to attack La Follette, scored his
adversary's past policies as well as their future implications to the United
States war effort. In fact, Burgchardt notes that the Senate sat as a judicial
and deliberative body, that the form of Robinson's speech was deliberative
and defensive but his intent was forensic and offensive, and that La
Follette's form was deliberative and offensive but his motive was forensic
and defensive. Thomas Lessl reads the Scope Trial as a forensic situation—
but the trial itself was incidental to the rhetorical encounter—in which
William Jennings Bryan came to Dayton, Tennessee, to praise fundamental Christianity whereas Clarence Darrow came to blame Bryan's brand of
religion; moreover, they both had a keen interest in shaping Tennessee with
or without an anti-evolution law. The point is, as other essayists show, that
speech sets cannot be conceived of as one or more of Aristotle's three
categories of oratory without doing a grave disservice to both constructs.
The authors who use Aristotle's generic schema clearly caution the extent
to which the critic can apply his contrived categories to the encounters, and
they, in company with those writers who eschewed Aristotle's tripartite
division of oratory, rely instead on their close and careful understandings
of the rhetorical situations in which the sets occurred.

The accuser is the persuasive prime-mover in the speech set. The attacker perceives an evil, is motivated to expose it, and the rhetorical
response is a *kategoria*. An accusation always begins with, but is not necessarily limited to, the accusee's policy, a term denoting a wide range of
actions or practices: vice, theft, sexual misconduct, libel, treason, illegal activities, future proposals, and so on. An accusation against policy always
begins with Cicero's stasis of fact, *conjecturalis*, that focuses on whether an
action was done. In some cases, accusers easily established the actuality of

a practice because it was public information. Senator Edward Kennedy's leaving the scene of an accident at Chappaquiddick, General Douglas MacArthur's insubordination in 1951, Senator Richard Nixon's campaign fund in 1952, and President Ronald Reagan's announced visit to Bitburg cemetery in 1985 were incontrovertible facts. Yet, accuser's persuasive arguments are not always so easily established. Larry Haapanen explains the rhetorical craft that Premier Nikita Khrushchev used to trap President Dwight Eisenhower into confronting the fact of secret U.S. U-2 airplane flights over the Soviet Union in 1960. Moreover, Haapanen details Khrushchev's devious cleverness in creating a rhetorical situation distinctly disadvantageous to the Eisenhower administration. Craig Allen Smith unravels the rhetorical Gordian knot that President Richard Nixon and members of his staff wove to contain his illegal cover-up in the Watergate affair. Smith demonstrates that Nixon used different strategies, sometimes inappropriately and unwisely, to persuade separate audiences — the courts, Congress, the press, and the American people — that he had not participated in a cover-up. As the accusations shifted from arena to arena, Smith demonstrates that Nixon helped create his own rhetorical demise by delivering apologies that raised more questions than they answered.

The accuser may move to other stases to bolster the accusation. Definition, *definitiva*, and/or quality, *generalis* (see Glossary) may be used to heighten the exigence of a policy. To that point, Robert Friedenberg explicates Elie Wiesel's accusations against President Ronald Reagan for his handling of the Bitburg controversy. Wiesel defined the president's policy as insensitive to the sufferers and survivors of the holocaust and as homage to Nazi Germany; as for quality, Wiesel contended it was a question of good or evil. Senator Nixon's accusers defined his fund as immoral and unethical, and Prime Minister Stanley Baldwin declared that Edward VIII's morganatic marriage proposal to Wallis Simpson was unconstitutional and allowed that the king's policy was selfish. As Friedenberg explains, the way Wiesel defined and characterized the symbolism of Reagan's proposed visit to Bitburg was more telling than the act itself. Many of the authors note that although it is true a critic can distinguish the stases of fact from definition and quality for critical purposes, in the realm of human communication, the critic often finds these stases so interdependent in an accusation that the persuasive power of the charge derives from their functioning as a troika and not separately.

Posited on a policy, an accusation can address the accusee's character by stressing ethical materials. For instance, accusations against Senator Nixon's fund scored it but also arraigned his character as an example of loose conduct and corruption in government, as a loss of public morals. Turning to Nixon two decades later, Smith demonstrates that President Nixon was attacked not only for his cover-up in the Watergate fiasco, but more importantly for the obvious character flaws attendant to that act. Character charges also played an important role in the accusations against Senator Edward Kennedy and King Edward VIII.

My original theory allowed for the possibility that the critic may find in accusations (and apologies) elements of both policy and character. In cases where both elements inhere in an accusation, it maintained, one element will tend to dominate the rhetorical situation. Concerning these holdings, some authors have made significant contributions to the theory by advancing a "yes, but" argument. Huxman and Linkugel show that Johnson delivered an accusation against Long and Coughlin, by so skillfully weaving together their respective policies and characters, that for the critic to unravel the warp from the woof runs the risk of destroying the tapestry of the speech. In the matter of J. Robert Oppenheimer, the father of the atomic bomb, Rachel Holloway reveals how Major General Kenneth Nichols of the Atomic Energy Commission accused Oppenheimer of being disloyal and a security risk in 1954. Nichols assailed the scientist's past associations and then argued his actions revealed substantial flaws in his character. Holloway notes that the intricate fusing of policy to character in Nichol's charge presented a formidable *kategoria*. Smith notes the same interconnection between how President Nixon's policy revealed his character and how his character informed his policy in the Watergate scandal. In other words, these writers kindly imply that for the future study of significant speech sets, the critic should forego attempting to isolate, sometimes futilely, whether policy or character dominates an accusation; instead, the critic may focus more productively on how policy and character are interrelated in a *kategoria*.

In reaction to the accusation, the apologist is motivated to deny, mitigate, or purify the resultant image. The rhetorical response to that motivation is a speech in apology, an *apologia*. As a counterpart to the accuser, the apologist can deny the fact, redefine the allegation, justify the quality, and appeal to a different jurisdiction. If the apologist claims that she or he did not practice the policy under attack, then the apologist cannot logically redefine the act nor seek to justify it; conversely, if the apologist argues the stases of definition, quality, or jurisdiction, then he or she must at least tacitly admit the stasis of fact. Thus, Senator Nixon admitted he had the fund, but sought to redefine it and to justify his character in maintaining it. Similarly, Haapanen explains that Dwight Eisenhower sought only to redefine the U-2 overflights as national security precautions and this was viable, partially at least, because Nikita Khrushchev refrained from attacking the president's character; likewise, Friedenberg finds that Ronald Reagan's strategy was to redefine his actions at Bitburg.

Whereas my original theory tended to separate apologies for policy from those for character, although it did allow that apologists might respond to an accusation against policy with a defense of character or respond to a charge against character with a defense of policy, several contributors amend the theory by noting that apologies cannot always be cast into one or the other compartments. The interrelationship between policy and character that can inhere in accusations often occurs in apologies. William Benoit makes the insightful point that because there was no formal accusation against Senator Kennedy's actions at Chappaquiddick—he was reacting to a climate of accusation—Kennedy had some leeway in responding. Benoit believes the senator subtly displaced the charge from one of policy to character, and then shifted the blame away from his character to the scene of the tragedy. Thus, as a victim, the lack of culpability in policy could not taint Kennedy's character. Benoit also reveals the senator's sophistication in shifting the jurisdiction from the judiciary to his most favorable jurors—his constituents in Massachusetts. Ronald Burke holds in the case of eight Alabama clergymen vs. the Reverend Martin Luther King, Jr., that King constructed an apologia that was grounded soundly in an inseparable policy-character nexus. King defended his policy by explaining his character motives and his righteous actions revealed his moral stature. Thus, when King denied the clergymen's allegations by redefining and transcending them, he concomitantly, and successfully, defended himself and civil disobedience in one of the most eloquent statements on civil rights in contemporary United States history.

Seven studies speak to issues concerning the construct of the rhetorical presidency in the context of accusation and apology. How the chief executive persuades the people and the Congress is of general interest to students of the presidency and how the first orator attacks enemies and responds to critics is of special interest in this book. In addition to the three essays already discussed, four other essays examine presidential rhetoric in conflict.

In Franklin D. Roosevelt's ill-fated 1938 purge attempt, Jack Gravlee reveals some findings that contribute to both constructs. He argues that the press conference format in FDR's era was a better way to attack Representative John O'Connor's character than by public address because the absence of direct quotation by reporters and the fanfare for a major speech were not inflammatory. (However, a political generation later, Friedenberg demonstrates that the press conference situation, especially in Ronald Reagan's less skilled hands, can be devastating.) Conversely, Gravlee contends that Roosevelt should have concentrated on policy attacks, while eschewing character concerns, in his major speeches against Senators Walter George and Millard Tydings. This rhetorical strategy would have made FDR seem less malicious and vindictive, and could have constrained George and especially Tydings to address the real issue—their loyalty as Democrats to the New Deal. Although FDR addressed jurisdictional matters when accusing George to his face in his own state of Georgia, the president and his advisers were not sensitive enough to the separation of powers doctrine. If any one factor could be said to account for FDR's failure in the purge, it may be, as Gravlee suggests, the fact that voters did not condone Roosevelt's federal intervention at the state level; indeed, George and Tydings tellingly turned that stasis against the president.

In treating the exchange between the plebian and the patrician, Bernard Duffy offers a revision of the encounter between President Harry S. Truman and General Douglas MacArthur in 1951. Contrary to a previous study of Truman's speech, Duffy argues that the documents Truman's secretary gave the press supported the president's legalistic reasons for firing the would-be Caesar. Since Truman's ethos was already low with many Americans over his handling of the Korean War, Duffy reasons that HST was rhetorically astute to allude obliquely to MacArthur's firing at the end of his speech. A frontal assault on MacArthur's policy, and especially his character, could have enraged the general's many supporters and made Truman seem petty. Duffy thinks HST's defense for his policy of avoiding a World War III in Korea placed MacArthur in an untenable position — to which MacArthur emotionally replied, "In war there is no substitute for victory." As for MacArthur's apologia, Duffy notes the roles high drama and an Olympian style and delivery played in MacArthur's moving the Congress and the people.

Elected as neither president nor vice-president, Gerald R. Ford, the thirty-eighth president of the United States, began his incumbency on the defensive. Bernard Brock explores how Ford encountered Richard Nixon's legacy on two important matters. A preemptive apology worked once and failed once. Brock believes that Ford effectively used certain criteria that enhanced his policy and character in dealing with the divisive issue of amnesty for Vietnam war draft dodgers. He argues that Ford then violated key tenets of his own apologetic doctrine in announcing Richard Nixon's pardon. He also revises how Ford might have transferred the relative success of his encounter with the amnesty issue to the pardon question.

Resisting the temptation to treat the Iran-Contra affair as another Watergate, Ray Heisey reads the rhetorical controversy *in situ*. Recognizing similarities when they exist, such as the nexus between policy and character in accusations and defenses, that multiple charges motivated numerous apologies, and that Reagan's performances produced new incriminations, he is nevertheless more interested in removing the Teflon from the "Great Communicator's" rhetoric. Heisey holds that Reagan created an argumentative synthesis that fused policy, character, and competency in ongoing *apologiae*. These satisfied enough of his critics enough of the time to allow Reagan to sustain his institutional presidency. With regard to his rhetorical presidency, Heisey believes that eight apologies, more concerned with image than substance, have enabled Reagan to withstand phase one of what is surely the accusation-apology set of the decade. Moreover, Heisey explicates how Reagan cleverly argued definition to co-opt one accusation.

Two studies focus on what occurred when the media not only reported the news but made the news by assuming the role of accuser. In the case of the Columbia Broadcasting System versus Mobil Oil Corporation, George Dionisopoulos and Steven Vibbert detail how CBS initiated an accusation against Mobil, only to witness, as others observed in their studies, an apology heavily freighted with accusations, so much so, in fact, that CBS offered a counter apology to Mobil's offensive defense. Stressing the concept of corporate accountability, they explicate how that issue was the epicenter of the debate between the two businesses. Moreover, they suggest, as Lessl concludes from his study of Bryan and Darrow, that corporations proclaim, like their human counterparts, their motives for the commonweal while portraying their adversaries as being against the commonwealth.

Richard Jensen presents a study of Geraldine Ferraro's responses to two Goliaths in the United States—the media and the Roman Catholic church. Unlike the biblical David, Ferraro was not victorious. Aside from the intrinsic merit of how the first woman vice-presidential candidate spoke under relentless fire, the study unfolds the formidable power that accrues to those parties that can act as prosecuting attorney, judge, and jury. The media scored Ferraro for a number of reasons, her being Italian and a woman figured prominently, and the Catholic church attacked her doctrinal positions. Jensen shows that Ferraro quoted some of Senator John Kennedy's speech at Houston, but there was a paradoxical twist: Kennedy was attacked by Protestants for being Catholic whereas Ferraro was attacked by Catholics for not being Catholic enough on the issue of abortion.

Given the nature of the speech sets, the rhetorical situations in which the exchanges occurred, the adroitness or inappropriateness with which the accusers or apologists communicated, some contributors were able to make some valuable additions to the theory.

First, as often as not, an encounter is not limited to a single accusation and a single apology. Some writers note that several speeches may comprise a speech set and they caution the critic not to overlook this possibility. Smith argues that accusations against President Nixon evolved from arena to arena as Nixon's apologies, as ongoing responses to these charges, produced additional reasons for new specifications against him. Friedenberg shows similar evolutionary tendencies in the Elie Wiesel-Ronald Reagan encounters. Likewise, the charges against Senator Nixon in 1952 unfolded during several days, and, although the "Checkers" speech was his crucial and justly famous apologia, Nixon had coalesced much of his defense in prior statements and speeches. With regard to instances in which a set is characterized by multiple persuasions in only one part of it, several cases illustrate the point. Haapanen traces Khrushchev's two accusatory speeches that motivated Eisenhower's response; Prime Minister Stanley Baldwin actually delivered three accusations against King Edward VIII, who delivered a speech in his royal behalf; and David Henry holds that Senator John Kennedy's famous speech at Houston, Texas, in 1960 was built upon themes of apologia that were developed from earlier exchanges on the Catholic issue. In addition to detailing Kennedy's grace, wit, and intelligence in surmounting powerful Protestant accusations against his Catholicism, Henry also demonstrates another major critical finding that follows.

Second, Henry and several writers, working independently of one another, conclude that the time-worn military aphorism, the best defense is a good offense, makes manifest sense in apologetic discourse. According to Henry, a substantial part of Kennedy's success at Houston, and in his earlier exchanges on the Catholic issue, was a function of his rhetorical strategy to merge accusation with apologia. JFK redefined the issue in terms of religious tolerance and separation of church and state, and then skillfully portrayed his accusers as violators of Article VI of the Constitution that forbade a religious test for officeholders. Burgchardt contends that Senator La Follette defended his attacks aimed at the Wilson administration by accusing his critics of denying his right of free speech in wartime. Huxman and Linkugel observe that General Johnson defended the Roosevelt administration against its detractors by firing a barrage against the kingfish and the radio priest. In turn, Long and Coughlin, ostensibly apologists, countered with accusatory fusillades of their own. In defense of his fund, Nixon changed the tone of his language and the temper of his delivery to a distinctly aggressive stance in the later part of his address.

Third, an inversion of the military dictum can be observed in some accusations. That is, the best offense is a strong defense. Huxman and Linkugel affirm the point when they explicate how General Johnson was at pains in the early parts of his accusation to defend his status and ethos before attacking Long and Coughlin's policies and characters. Henry explains how Senator Kennedy's detractors sanctimoniously proclaimed their religious impartiality before they insidiously attacked the Catholic church's policies and Kennedy's character in a guilt-by-association fashion. Presenting a case against Edward VIII, Baldwin subtly characterized his role in the affair as passive when it was in fact active, and framed his ethos as a loyal supporter of the monarchy while he was easing Edward off his throne.

Fourth, a finding of considerable worth to apologists is that generally speaking, a defender should not dignify the charges by authenticating them. Burgchardt shows that one of the strengths of La Follette's apologia was his refusal to give the accusations against him probative value by refuting them headlong. Holloway notes Oppenheimer unwisely incorporated Nichols' web of accusations, which were woven tightly, into his defense and that mistake was costly; moreover, Holloway revises how Oppenheimer could have functioned more persuasively in the encounter. In their study of the senator and the priest, Huxman and Linkugel argue that Long delivered a stronger defense because he dismissed Johnson's charges, but Coughlin's response was weaker because he enacted the very role the general scored. However, Senator Nixon's defense in 1952 stands as an exception to the rule. A strength of his defense of the fund was his validating the charges. Since the accusations were weakly drawn and missed the crux of the ethical issue, Nixon wisely delivered an apologia to straw issues. In a similar vein, Smith and Heisey, in their respective studies of the Watergate and Iran-Contra cases, conclude that defendants should not interject the criteria for new accusations in their defenses. Unwisely, both Nixon and Reagan did.

In his "March of the Flag" speech, September 16, 1898, Albert Jeremiah Beveridge told his fellow senators, with regard to the silver issue, that "The American people are tired of talking about money — they want to make it." Although others have written about rhetorical theories, the contributors to this book actually apply a construct in a systematic fashion to significant twentieth-century rhetorical exchanges. If the book makes one overarching caveat about rhetorical criticism, it is that however helpful generic theories are in explaining communication behavior, they cannot circumscribe our creative capacity to use speech, in all its unpredictable permutations and combinations, for good and evil.

NOTES

[1]See George Kennedy, *The Art of Persuasion in Greece* (Princeton: Princeton University Press, 1963), p. 86; Aristotle, *Rhetoric*, translated by W. Rhys Roberts (New York: The Modern Library, 1954), 1358b10, 1358b16, 1368b1; Isocrates, *Helen* (Cambridge: Loeb Classical Library, 1945), III, 15; *The Institutio Oratoria of Quintillan*, translated by H.E. Butler (Cambridge: Harvard University Press, 1963), I, Book III ii, 2: Henry George Liddell and Robert Scott, compilers, *A Greek-English Lexicon* (Oxford: Clarendon Press, 1968), pp. 207-8, 926-27: Halford Ross Ryan, "*Kategoria* and *Apologia*: On Their Rhetorical Criticism as a Speech Set," *Quarterly Journal of Speech* 68 (1982): 254-61.

Oratorical Encounters

Apology as Attack: La Follette vs. Robinson on Freedom of Speech

Carl R. Burgchardt

Senator Robert M. La Follette was one of the most controversial politicians of his era. From the 1890s to the end of his life, he was frequently at odds with establishment figures and policies. Never was La Follette more controversial, however, than during the period of his opposition to Woodrow Wilson's wartime program. La Follette earned the wrath of Wilson and a significant part of the public for his opposition to the war, to conscription, to financing measures, and especially to censorship. According to Thomas Ryley, "More than any of the other objectors to war, he remained a symbol of opposition to the conflict and to Wilsonian policies for prosecuting it. In many people's eyes during 1917 and 1918, he was the most hated man in America, for he did not give up on his thesis that America had no business in the war and had been led into it by lies and trickery."[1]

Interestingly, during this period of intense vilification, La Follette delivered one of the finest speeches of his career. On October 6, 1917, he defended himself in the Senate against charges of disloyalty and sedition. This oration is a classic argument for free speech during time of war, and it can be appreciated by itself; however, the complexities and brilliance of La Follette's address can only be fully plumbed by analyzing it as part of a speech set. For on the same day that La Follette presented his case, Senator Joseph T. Robinson of Arkansas, a combative and fiercely partisan defender of Wilson and the Democratic party, launched a savage attack on La Follette's actions and character. His October 6 speech is noteworthy because of its virulence and because it summarized the basic premises and reasoning of La Follette's opponents. Since accusatory and apologetic addresses inform each other in vital ways, the purpose of this essay is to analyze the interaction between the La Follette and Robinson speeches.[2]

La Follette's loyalty had been questioned long before the October 6 debate. His leadership in organizing the Armed Ship bill filibuster caused Wilson to name him as part of "A little group of willful men, representing no opinion but their own. . . ." When La Follette opposed American entry into the war, Senator John Sharp Williams labeled him "pro-German, pretty nearly pro-Goth, and pro-Vandal." The press denounced him in editorials and political cartoons. Once the war started, La Follette opposed military conscription, the Espionage Act, and Wilson's proposed war financing measures. In addition, La Follette introduced a War Aims resolution on August 11, 1917, that called for the United States to "declare definitely" its strategic goals, to condemn the continuation of the war for the purposes of territorial annexation, and to demand that the Allies restate their peace terms immediately. These positions provoked a steady drumbeat of criticism from the press and public officials.[3]

In September of 1917, however, an event took place that eclipsed the earlier controversies. La Follette accepted an invitation to address the Nonpartisan League convention in St. Paul, Minnesota, on September 20. Most of the St. Paul speech contained a tribute to the Nonpartisan League and the Granger Movement, and a discussion of war taxation. However, in response to a question from the audience, La Follette digressed on the causes of the war. He claimed that America had "suffered grievances . . . at the hands of Germany," but not sufficient provocation for war: "I say this, that the *COMPARATIVELY* small privilege, of the right of an American citizen to ride on *A MUNITION LOADED SHIP FLYING A FOREIGN FLAG*, is too small to involve this government in *THE LOSS OF MILLIONS AND MILLIONS OF LIVES!!*" He insisted that Wilson knew the *Lusitania* carried munitions but did nothing to prevent Americans from boarding the ship. The audience cheered these remarks. Then, La Follette briefly defended the right of free speech during wartime. At the close of the speech, he was given a standing ovation, and La Follette counted the evening as a great success.[4]

The next day La Follette was shocked to discover that the St. Paul speech had created a storm of controversy. The Associated Press (AP) story from St. Paul claimed that he had said "We had *no* grievance against Germany" [italics added]. In addition, the AP claimed the tenor of the meeting was disloyal and that La Follette argued the sinking of the *Lusitania* was justified. These errors occurred despite the existence of three stenographic reports of the address. Throughout the United States, speakers and editors characterized La Follette's speech as treasonous. According to David Thelen, after the St. Paul speech La Follette "became the main focus of official and vigilante campaigns to suppress antiwar spokesmen." A number of organizations sent resolutions to Congress calling for La Follette's expulsion. The most influential of these was the Minnesota Public Safety Commission, which formally presented its expulsion petition to the Senate on September 29, 1917.[5]

The Senate scheduled La Follette to make a major address on October 6, 1917. Most observers believed that he would defend himself against charges of disloyalty that arose primarily because of the St. Paul speech. As the day approached, several of La Follette's opponents prepared to attack him, and they manipulated the schedule so that La Follette would have no opportunity to refute them. The public, sensing the likelihood of an impassioned personal defense, packed the galleries on the morning of October 6. In addition, most of the senators were present. La Follette "appeared composed" as he entered the Senate and took his place. He obtained the floor, as had been prearranged, through a question of personal privilege. He stood nearly motionless at his desk and read the speech from manuscript in an unemotional, even detached, way. When he finished the speech, there was from the galleries a spontaneous outburst of applause that had to be silenced.[6]

After La Follette concluded, three senators replied: Frank Kellogg of Minnesota, Joseph Robinson of Arkansas, and Albert Fall of New Mexico. Robinson's speech was the most thorough and memorable of the three. Although it was probably unintentional, Robinson's speech also synthesized the scattered attacks on La Follette that had been filtering in for seven months. Robinson began his speech standing at his desk near the front of the floor, across the aisle from where La Follette sat. He began calmly, but as the speech progressed, he became more agitated and abusive. The virulence of Robinson's attack shocked the floor and galleries into complete silence. A United Press correspondent described Robinson's speech as "the most unrestrained language that ever has been heard in the Senate." In marked contrast, La Follette sat quietly at his desk, making notes for a possible rebuttal. Finally, La Follette turned in his chair so that he could face Robinson directly. Robinson moved toward him, shaking his fist, while La Follette regarded him with disdain. At the climax of the speech, Robinson violated the Senate custom of never addressing a colleague directly. He jabbed a finger at La Follette and shouted: "I want to know where you stand."[7]

La Follette was unable to obtain the floor before adjournment to refute his attackers. However, Senator Fall did permit him to make a brief statement. La Follette announced that he had come prepared to substantiate all of the claims he made in the St. Paul speech, and he desired to answer the charges just made against him. He stated that he would "have to avail myself of some other means of communicating the facts to the public." La Follette probably never suspected that the October 6 address would be his last public speech to answer charges of disloyalty. Although he was motivated to defend himself against the accusations of Robinson and others, he was constrained from doing so by nonrhetorical means.[8]

LA FOLLETTE'S APOLOGIA

In La Follette's speech, there are three interrelated persuasive purposes. In a sense, there are three separate speeches, superimposed in layers. Each layer needs to be peeled off to unlock the persuasive secrets of the work as a whole. The three layers are: (1) policy advocacy, (2) counterattack, and (3) apology.[9]

The top layer proposed a legislative agenda for the Senate. From a structural perspective, this function was the most obvious one. Ironically, La Follette's ostensible purpose for delivering the speech was the one that violated audience expectations most directly. The audience expected a personal defense from La Follette, but on the surface, at least, he did not offer an apology.

La Follette argued that there were two connected problems in society. First, he claimed that there was an organized campaign on the part of business and government to persecute citizens who criticized the war. Second, he maintained that Wilson's administration tried to intimidate Congress into mindlessly supporting the president's war program, which led to unacceptable human and monetary costs. He proposed two policies for the government: citizens should be free to discuss the war in all of its aspects; and Congress should declare the purposes and objects of the war. These policies were supported with copious testimony, historical authority, and legal commentary and precedent, particularly as it applied to the Constitution. At the end of the speech, La Follette refuted possible objections to his proposals and suggested benefits that would accrue from them.

The second layer of La Follette's speech was a counterattack on the characters and actions of his accusers. Early in the speech, La Follette characterized the charges made against opponents of the war, including himself, as "malicious falsehood" and "libel and character assassination." He did not dignify any of the charges by repeating them; he merely portrayed them as unfair, untrue, and reckless. In addition, he argued that the "war party" and "the war-mad press and war extremists" had impure motives. The expulsion petitions and charges of treason were an attempt to punish him for a lifetime of political opposition to concentrated wealth, special privilege, and corporate control of society. The real issue, therefore, had nothing to do with La Follette's loyalty to his country. Moreover, said La Follette, his chief opponents in the war controversy were those who would profit politically or economically from an expanded, protracted war. He also attacked Wilson directly: "The President's leadership" was responsible for the "awful death toll" and the "fearful tax burden." In short, Wilson's actions meant the United States must "*bear the brunt* of the war."

The third, and deepest, layer of the speech was La Follette's defense of past actions. Early on, he established the fact that this speech would go beyond the St. Paul controversy; it would concern the condemnation of all those who opposed the war. Here La Follette used a defensive strategy that B. L. Ware and Wil Linkugel have called transcendence.[10] "If I alone had been made the victim of these attacks," he insisted, "I should not take one moment of the Senate's time for their consideration." But that was emphatically not the case, so he intended to defend the rights of all citizens to speak freely during wartime. Throughout the remainder of the speech, La Follette stated his own opinions and complaints on behalf of citizens. Such a strategy removed the focus of the debate from the specifics of the St. Paul debacle to the larger issue of constitutional rights. Not only did this tactic raise La Follette to a more defensible vantage, but it built his *ethos* (see Glossary) by demonstrating concern for others. It also placed him in the familiar posture of a crusader for the people--morally superior, and on the attack.

At the same time La Follette executed the strategy of transcendence, he implicitly defended himself along the lines suggested by the classical stasis system. He conceded the stasis of fact. He made no effort to deny that he had harshly criticized the government and Wilson's war program. The major thrust of La Follette's personal defense occurred at the level of definition. He argued implicitly that his activity could not be reasonably defined as disloyal. On the contrary, La Follette defined his actions as responsible, positive, and loyal in the truest sense. He contended that "it was the right --the constitutional right--and the patriotic duty of American citizens . . . to discuss the issues of the war." Thus, La Follette defined critical free speech as not treasonous, but actually a duty of conscientious citizens. By implication, those who did not think and speak critically about the war were irresponsible and disloyal to the principles of democracy.[11]

In terms of Congress's right to establish war aims, La Follette maintained it was "an evasion of a solemn duty on the part of the Congress not to exercise that power at this critical time in the Nation's affairs." Congressional control of the war was essential to the functioning of democracy: "on this momentous question there can be no evasion, no shirking of duty of the Congress, without subverting our form of government." Again, La Follette defined his own activity in a positive light and the activities of his critics in a negative light.

Although most of the apologetic layer took place on the stasis of definition, La Follette implicitly addressed the stasis of quality. Indirectly, he claimed that his intentions were laudable when he criticized the government: "It is the suppressed emotion of the masses that breeds revolution. If the American people are to carry on this great war, if public opinion is to be enlightened and intelligent, there must be free discussion." Free speech would aid the efficient conduct of the war; it would maintain the national will to fight. In addition, he argued that his proposed policies would reduce

Germany's motive to fight. La Follette's intentions, then, were patriotic.[12]

The remarkable thing about La Follette's speech is that its three persuasive functions existed so harmoniously together and that each layer stood so well on its own as an organized, rational message. The deliberative layer created the impression that La Follette would not be deterred from his legislative agenda by his critics. It drew attention away from the St. Paul incident by forcing his attackers to refute policy arguments. As part of the policy advocacy, he argued that there were significant problems in society that needed to be solved. This indicted Woodrow Wilson's administration and other members of the "war party" and the "war-mad press." So, the deliberative layer did some of the work of the counterattack layer by discrediting his opponents.

The second layer attacked the actions and characters of La Follette's tormentors. Primarily, it attempted to destroy the credibility of the charges made against him. Further, the second layer forced his opponents to spend time answering the attacks; and potentially, it put them on the defensive. The counterattacks also served a warning that he would not be verbally assaulted with impunity; he was capable of inflicting pain on his opponents, as well.

In the deepest layer, the actual apology, he created definitions that exonerated his past actions. But, each of these definitions, when applied to the actions of his opponents, implicitly functioned as attacks. Thus, the reverse sides of the definitional stasis supported the attacks made in the second layer of the speech. Therefore, La Follette skillfully combined policy advocacy, counterattack, and apology in the same, seamless address.

ROBINSON'S ATTACK

Robinson's speech can be approached in roughly the same way as La Follette's--with three layers. However, the layers in Robinson's speech do not exist congruously in quite the same way that they do in La Follette's. Nonetheless, Robinson's accusation can be considered profitably from the perspectives of (1) a negative, deliberative rebuttal, (2) attacks on La Follette's character, and (3) attacks on La Follette's past actions according to the ancient stasis system.

The obvious structure of Robinson's speech was devoted to refuting La Follette--not just the statements made on October 6, but a whole range of positions since March of 1917. The rebuttal function was Robinson's pretext for delivering the more damaging attacks on character and action. Much of the speech challenged La Follette's public statements about the causes of World War I. Robinson emphatically denied the statement that "the United States went to war solely and principally on the demand of citizens for the right to ride on munition-laden vessels." In general,

Robinson's view of the causes of the war paralleled Woodrow Wilson's war declaration of April 2, 1917. In addition, Robinson denied La Follette's charge that the government had violated the rights of innocent citizens in the name of national security, and he attacked La Follette's War Aims resolution as unfair to the Allies. He also attempted to refute the point that the *Lusitania* carried munitions and that Wilson knew about it but failed to prevent Americans from traveling on the ship.

The second layer of Robinson's speech was an attack on La Follette's character. First, he questioned La Follette's judgment: "Some Senators seem to think that there is a paramount obligation to exercise the speaking power, but there come times when men of judgment remain silent." He also indicted La Follette for being inconsistent. La Follette wanted freedom of speech for himself, argued Robinson, yet he was unwilling to let his critics exercise the same freedom. Further, Robinson all but directly accused La Follette of being a coward. In his most odious attack, he said: "A man who will not fight when his flag is repeatedly fired upon . . . will not fight even if an enemy invaded his home and ravished his daughter in his presence." In another area, Robinson repeatedly claimed that La Follette stated false-hoods, and he implied La Follette did this deliberately. Moreover, in different places he charged La Follette with being careless, ignorant, indifferent, stupid, and foolish. Finally, Robinson attacked La Follette for being arrogant.

Perhaps the most insidious character attacks came when Robinson attempted to identify La Follette with the enemy. He did not explicitly accuse La Follette of helping Germany, but he linked La Follette's name with hated German symbols in an attempt to taint him through verbal proximity. He associated La Follette's name with the "Kaiser," "the crown prince," "Hindenberg," "Ludendorf," and "the Bundesrath." For example, at one point Robinson claimed that Germany would have dominated the United States "if American ships had stayed in port as the Kaiser expressly said and the Senator from Wisconsin impliedly says." In a related tactic, Robinson characterized Germany as lawless, destructive, and "the epitome of barbarism." What kind of person could defend such a nation? Robinson said that he could not comprehend "a Senator who can find it in his heart" to rationalize German actions. Indeed, he implied that La Follette was mentally and morally deficient: "I have no argument that can appeal to any mind which for a moment justifies such cowardly brutality. I will not waste any time in appealing for sympathy to one whose conscience can approve of such outrage." Robinson insinuated throughout the speech that La Follette was immoral and cruel, like the Germans.

The third layer of Robinson's speech revolved around the classical stasis model. The first stasis, fact, was developed in a clear but unsystematic manner. Robinson documented a number of occasions when La Follette had condemned Wilson and the government: the Armed Ship bill filibuster, his speech opposing entry into the war, the War Aims resolution, and the October 6 speech. Robinson did not spend much time on this stasis because all of the events were a matter of public record, and La Follette never denied that he had harshly criticized Wilson's administration.

The next stasis, definition, was the most fully developed. He defined La Follette's actions as disloyal from a number of perspectives. Although he did not outline his criteria for loyalty systematically, one can reconstruct his reasoning by reading between the lines. The first definition stated that La Follette did not exhibit the signs of a patriot; therefore, he must be disloyal. Robinson relied heavily on the patriotic symbols of the flag, the president, and the army in making his emotional appeals. Suspiciously, La Follette did not praise these patriotic symbols in his discourse. Robinson also used a conventional definition of disloyalty: actions that aided and supported the enemy were treasonous. Throughout the speech, Robinson implied or stated that La Follette's actions aided Germany. For example, Robinson said, it is "unfortunate for the Senator from Wisconsin that he has lent himself, his great talents and his services, to the promulgation of the ideas, theories, and desires of the Kaiser."

A less conventional definition proposed that majority opinion in a democracy determined what was loyal. Robinson criticized La Follette because he took "a position that is questioned by a great many of his fellow citizens as disloyal." A related definition stated that loyal people supported the government without question during time of war. According to Robinson, the loyal majority knew "that our Government is now at war, and they are willing to uphold the flag without regard to the merits of our cause. . . ." Yet another related definition claimed that opponents of Wilson and the Democrats were disloyal. Since Wilson's programs were patriotic, anyone who tried to block such legislation was, by definition, unpatriotic. Robinson characterized Wilson's opponents as "slackers," "traitors," and "spies." Because La Follette was clearly an opponent, he belonged in at least one of those categories.

Robinson also devoted some attention to the stasis of quality. He attempted to prove that La Follette's actions were not only disloyal in effect, but also in intent. Stated another way, La Follette's intentions were not laudable, and there were no mitigating circumstances to justify his actions. After insinuating that Germany paid La Follette to oppose Wilson, Robinson claimed that La Follette's ultimate desire was to destroy the United States: "If the Senator from Wisconsin had his will, if the Kaiser had his will, liberty would become a memory, honor a tradition, and tyranny the ruling power throughout this world." Thus, La Follette committed his treason willfully and maliciously, fully conscious of the damage he was doing to his country.[13]

The three functions of Robinson's speech were mutually reinforcing. In the process of refuting La Follette's policy arguments, Robinson implied that La Follette was ignorant, stupid, or foolish. Thus, the refutation layer supported the character attack. Moreover, the stasis of quality was the nexus for many of the character attacks, because the question of laudable intentions certainly impinged on character traits. Because La Follette was a liar, a coward, and morally deficient, it was much easier to believe that his intentions were not laudable in committing treason. Conversely, character flaws were revealed through proving wrongful actions. A person who committed treason very likely had a bad character. Therefore, La Follette's bad actions proved a bad character; and his bad character called all actions into question, even those that appeared innocent on the surface.

The immediate effects of the two speeches were predictable. Robinson's admirers received his speech well. The *St. Louis Republic* reported that "The intense earnestness of the Arkansas statesman and his masterful oratory held the crowded galleries spellbound, while Democrats and Republicans alike on the floor nodded approval of his sentiments." Similarly, La Follette's sympathizers loved his address. It was particularly celebrated by Eugene Debs, who called the address a "classic." In the nation's heartland, many agreed with La Follette — perhaps a majority. But because of the paranoid social climate in the United States, few voiced their support publicly.[14]

As a result of the outcry over the St. Paul speech, and particularly because of the flood of expulsion petitions, the Senate opened an investigation into La Follette's loyalty. From the beginning, most of the committee members wanted to bury the issue, and they delayed active consideration for fourteen months. The majority was uneasy about the La Follette case because of the disturbing precedent it would set to expel a senator for "expressing unorthodox sentiments." By the time the Senate voted on the expulsion resolution, the war had ended, which cooled the patriotic fervor that had burned during the conflict and lessened the animosity toward La Follette. In addition, on May 24, 1918, the Associated Press retracted its original story concerning the St. Paul speech and issued an apology. This event was widely publicized, and major newspapers wrote sympathetic editorials. Finally, the 1918 election put La Follette in a pivotal political position, which motivated Republicans to keep him in his seat. In January of 1919, the Senate defeated the expulsion resolution 50-21. In 1923 the Senate acknowledged the frivolous nature of the disloyalty charges when it voted to reimburse La Follette five thousand dollars to cover his legal expenses.

Even though La Follette was technically vindicated in the Senate after the war was over, in many respects, his political opponents achieved their objectives. The furor over the St. Paul speech and the ensuing loyalty investigation occupied La Follette's attention almost exclusively for over a year; and, as a consequence, his effectiveness as an antiwar spokesman was severely curtailed. Moreover, La Follette found it to be nearly impossible to obtain an effective, national forum for his defense. He received no invitations to speak outside the Senate, and his congressional addresses had to be moderated during the loyalty investigations. He had only the Senate floor, his own, limited-circulation magazine, and a few, local, sympathetic newspapers to make his case to the nation. These minor sources were drowned out by a flood of critical commentary across the country. Thus, La Follette had to fight a pervasive, negative climate of opinion more than an easily defined opponent who could be fought directly.

La Follette's October 6 speech and his other rhetorical efforts were not immediately effective in restoring his reputation. But, over a longer period, he was exonerated. The single misquotation, "We had no grievance against Germany," seemed to trigger most of the denunciations. When the Associated Press apologized, it seemingly discredited all of the charges against him. La Follette's vindication, however, must also be attributed to the rhetorical choices he made on October 6. Since La Follette identified himself so strongly with freedom of speech, it was difficult to damage him without also undermining the Constitution. La Follette successfully forced his accusers into an extreme position with which few were comfortable. During the fever of the war, people were driven to extreme positions, but in the guilty aftermath, the majority realized the wisdom of La Follette's arguments. Indeed, it was the way in which the public record of La Follette's position interacted with subsequent political and social events that won him exculpation. The public's eventual revulsion toward the war, symbolized by its rejection of Wilson's League of Nations appeals in 1919, placed La Follette's actions in a new light. In addition, many admired La Follette's courage, conviction, and consistency; few doubted his sincerity save his most bitter detractors.

To a large extent, La Follette addressed a future audience in his October 6 speech. Where persuasion was not immediately feasible, he opted for placing his arguments in the public record. He was content to submit his case to the judgment of the future. On the freedom of speech issue, history judged him kindly. Particularly in the post-Vietnam era, historical commentators have admired La Follette's opposition to World War I and his steadfast support of basic constitutional rights.[15]

A final reason for La Follette's acquittal was the behavior of his opponents. Critics such as Robinson indicted themselves through their speeches and actions. Robinson violated Senate decorum and shocked many with abusive rhetoric. His discourse flaunted the values of decency and fair play, and his inflamed, irrational rhetoric stood in sharp contrast to La Follette's calm demeanor and measured discourse. Moreover, Robinson discredited himself through the use of highly exaggerated or patently false statements. He said, for example, "I can not find language within the rules of the Senate to appropriately characterize the sentiments uttered" by La Follette on October 6. To a fair observer, however, there was nothing extreme or disloyal about La Follette's speech. When Robinson called his adversary's October 6 speech treasonous, it was difficult to take Robinson's other charges seriously. In sum, Robinson's speech is remembered chiefly today for being one of the most intemperate in the history of the Senate, while La Follette's address is regarded as a classic argument for free speech and representative government.

CONCLUSION

The theory for analyzing speech sets provides insight into an important oratorical encounter and into the methods and world views of La Follette and Robinson. One of the advantages of the classical stasis framework is that it allows a critic to impose order on discourse that is ambiguous, disorganized, or complex. The critic can take each explicit and implicit assertion and assess if it addresses the argumentative approaches of fact, definition, quality, or jurisdiction. The procedure was particularly helpful in divining Robinson's premises, claims, and reasoning, which were immersed in a sea of ambiguities and digressions. The method also worked well in sorting out the three persuasive functions in La Follette's address, which demonstrated that defense can be disguised, either consciously or unconsciously, by complementary speech purposes.

The rhetorical and political motives of the two speakers were clearly different. Of course, despite appearances, one of La Follette's primary motives was to defend himself against charges of disloyalty. He also wanted to create a more enlightened political atmosphere and possibly to build support for a presidential bid based on antiwar and anti-Wilson sentiments. Moreover, he intended to bring public pressure to bear on senators who did not support free speech for citizens and his War Aims resolution.

Robinson, on the other hand, was trying to silence La Follette through threats and intimidation, if not force him out of the Senate altogether. He wanted to bolster public support for a fairly unpopular war and to deter others from attacking the president. Also, he probably intended to enhance his own position as chief Wilson loyalist during the war. He undoubtedly had the sincere, patriotic motivation of wanting to help his nation defeat Germany.

As a partial reflection of differing motives, La Follette and Robinson used contrasting rhetorical methods. La Follette's speech was well organized, subdued, philosophical, and eloquent. When La Follette defined his actions in a positive way, he supported his arguments with clear reasoning and abundant evidence. Robinson's speech, by contrast, was disorganized, intemperate, mundane, and sometimes contradictory. He relied predominately on innuendo, enthymemes, and induction to attack his opponent. Except for the climax of the speech, Robinson made few direct accusations. Instead, he usually phrased an accusation conditionally or hypothetically: "If I entertained the sentiments which the Senator from Wisconsin has expressed in this presence this morning, I would not wait for the United States Senate to pass upon the question of my loyalty or disloyalty; I would seek the companionship of those whom my discussion and my sentiments are calculated to support."

On the basis of stasis analysis, one can draw certain conclusions concerning the competing world views of La Follette and Robinson. At the bottom of their schism were different concepts of duty. La Follette argued it was the solemn duty of citizens or legislators to discuss critically government programs. Robinson, on the other hand, argued that the United States had a fundamental duty to protect the physical well being of its citizens, and this duty was more important than freedom of speech: "We have some duty, my fellow Senators, besides the duty of talking." The government, he believed, would violate its duty if it permitted sedition or treason. As a corollary, the two senators also had different concepts of liberty. La Follette was most concerned with preserving basic civil liberties at home, while Robinson thought it was more important to preserve the liberty of American citizens to travel the high seas and to remain free from the threat of foreign invasion.[16]

This speech set proved to be interesting because there were many areas in which the normal, expected situation was turned on its head. La Follette gave the first speech in this exchange, even though he was the apologist. The ostensible form of his speech was deliberative, and he appeared to be on the offensive, although the most important persuasive task was forensic and defensive. Conversely, the ostensible form of Robinson's address was deliberative and defensive, while its major persuasive thrust was forensic and offensive. The primary audience for La Follette and Robinson was the same: the United States Senate, which would act ultimately on the expulsion petition. In this case, the Senate was functioning as a judicial body as well as a deliberative one. The fact that the Senate fulfilled both functions simultaneously explains, in part, why the La Follette and Robinson speeches were so complex.

The theory is supported well by this case study. However, my research suggests several minor amendments to it. First, Ryan argued that, generally, either character or action perspectives would predominate in attack or defense. He also observed that "the critic may find in accusations and apologies elements of *both policy and character* in a speech." In La Follette's speech, his personal defense was solidly anchored in actions. However, he combined this defense with a strong counterattack based in character, and he also advanced a deliberative case. Each of these functions reinforced the others in important ways. In Robinson's address, character and action attacks were remarkably intertwined, and at the same time, these perspectives bolstered the function of refutation. I agree with Ryan that a character argument must be based on actions, but it is also true that action arguments imply character traits. On the basis of this study, I conclude that many arguments simultaneously address action and character, and they may also support complementary persuasive functions.[17]

Second, although it is undoubtedly true that a speech of accusation usually precedes a speech of defense, this case study points out an apparent exception to the rule. In fact, Robinson and La Follette did not engage each other directly as much as they appealed in parallel for favorable judgments from the Senate, national public opinion, and their local constituencies. It is a fact that La Follette's speech was a defense and Robinson's an attack, and they did clash on the stases of definition and quality, but both speeches were responding to prior events and exigencies. La Follette did not react to a negative image created by Robinson, but rather to a prior "mosaic" of accusatory messages from many sources. Robinson's reading of the accusatory mosaic stimulated and encouraged him to attack his opponent as well as the wrongful actions La Follette allegedly committed.[18]

Finally, Ryan ended his theoretical essay by quoting Quintilian: "accusation necessarily precedes defense. You might as well assert that the sword was invented for the purpose of self-defense and not for aggression." Yet, as the title of this essay indicates, La Follette defended himself largely through the methods of attack. He wielded the rhetorical sword to apologize, and Robinson crouched behind a verbal shield to accuse. In short, La Follette's speech suggests that, in contemporary rhetorical practice, the best defense is sometimes a good offense.

NOTES

[1]Thomas W. Ryley, *A Little Group of Willful Men* (Port Washington: Kennikat Press, 1975), p. 174.

[2]Nevin Emil Neal, "A Biography of Joseph T. Robinson," (Ph.D. Diss., University of Oklahoma, 1958), pp. 152, 464, 466-69; *La Follette*, edited by Robert S. Maxwell (Englewood Cliffs, N.J.: Prentice-Hall, 1969), p. 116.

[3]Ryley, *A Little Group of Willful Men*, pp. 3, 132-33, 164-65; John Sharp Williams, *Congressional Record*, April 4, 1917, p. 235; Belle Case La Follette and Fola La Follette, *Robert M. La Follette*, 2 vols. (New York: Macmillan, 1953), I, 665-67, II, 756-57; H.C. Peterson and Gilbert C. Fite,

Opponents of War, 1917-1918 (Madison: University of Wisconsin Press, 1957), pp. 5-7, 67; David P. Thelen, *Robert M. La Follette and the Insurgent Spirit* (Boston: Little, Brown, 1976), pp. 133-34.

[4]La Follette and La Follette, *Robert M. La Follette*, II, 762-69; Peterson and Fite, *Opponents of War*, pp. 67-69; Robert M. La Follette, "St. Paul Speech," La Follette Papers, Library of Congress, pp. 14, 16, 30; Carl R. Burgchardt, "The Will, the People, and the Law: A Rhetorical Biography of Robert M. La Follette, Sr." (Ph.D. Diss., University of Wisconsin-Madison, 1982), pp. 306-7.

[5]La Follette and La Follette, *Robert M. La Follette*, II, 769-70, 776-77, 780-81; Thelen, *Robert M. La Follette and the Insurgent Spirit*, p. 141; Peterson and Fite, *Opponents of War*, pp. 69-70.

[6]La Follette and La Follette, *Robert M. La Follette*, II, 783-88; Thelen, *Robert M. La Follette and the Insurgent Spirit*, pp. 141-42.

[7]Frank Kellogg, *Congressional Record*, October 6, 1917, pp. 7886-88; Joseph T. Robinson, *Congressional Record*, October 6, 1917, pp. 7888-93; Albert Fall, *Congressional Record*, October 6, 1917, pp. 7893-95; Thelen, *Robert M. La Follette and the Insurgent Spirit*, p. 142; La Follette and La Follette, *Robert M. La Follette*, II, 789-90; Neal, "A Biography of Joseph T. Robinson," pp. 154-55.

[8]La Follette and La Follette, *Robert M. La Follette*, II, 791; Robert M. La Follette, *Congressional Record*, October 6, 1917, p. 7895.

[9]I use the term "policy" in a different sense than the way Ryan used it in his theoretical essay. I define "policy" here as a proposed legislative program.

[10]B.L. Ware and Wil Linkugel, "They Spoke in Defense of Themselves: On the Generic Criticism of Apologia," *Quarterly Journal of Speech* 59 (1973): 280.

[11]Outside of the Senate, La Follette did deny that he had said "We had no grievance against Germany." See La Follette and La Follette, *Robert M. La Follette*, II, 772-75; *La Follette's Magazine*, November, 1917, p. 6.

[12]La Follette, *Congressional Record*, pp. 7878-86, 7895.

[13]Robinson, *Congressional Record*, pp. 7888-93.

[14]The *St. Louis Republic*, October 7, 1917, quoted in Neal, "A Biography of Joseph T. Robinson," p. 155; La Follette and La Follette, *Robert M. La Follette*, II, 791; Thelen, *Robert M. La Follette and the Insurgent Spirit*, p. 143.

[15]Ryley, *A Little Group of Willful Men*, pp. 174-75; Peterson and Fite, *Opponents of War*, pp. 71-72; La Follette and La Follette, *Robert M. La Follette*, II, 795-816, 874-86, 910-11, 927-31; Fred Greenbaum, *Robert Marion La Follette* (Boston: Twayne, 1975), pp. 159-73; Thelen, *Robert M. La Follette and the Insurgent Spirit*, pp. 125-154.

[16]Robinson, *Congressional Record*, pp. 7888-90, 7892-93.

[17]Halford Ross Ryan, "*Kategoria* and *Apologia*: On Their Rhetorical Criticism as a Speech Set," *Quarterly Journal of Speech* 68 (1982): 257. For a discussion of how La Follette combined action and character attacks, see Carl R. Burgchardt, "Discovering Rhetorical Imprints: La Follette, 'Iago,' and the Melodramatic Scenario," *Quarterly Journal of Speech* 71 (1985): 450.

[18]According to Samuel L. Becker, a "mosaic" consists of "various message sets" that are "overlayed to form [a] large and complex communication environment. . . ." See "Rhetorical Studies for the Contemporary World," in *The Prospect of Rhetoric*, edited by Lloyd F. Bitzer and Edwin Black (Englewood Cliffs: Prentice-Hall, 1971), p. 33.

INFORMATION SOURCES ON THE SPEECH SET

Robinson's Accusation

The authoritative text of Robinson's address appears in the *Congressional Record*, October 6, 1917, pp. 7888-93.

La Follette's Apology

The authentic version of La Follette's speech is recorded in the *Congressional Record*, October 6, 1917, pp. 7878-86, 7895.

Selected Bibliography

Burgchardt, Carl R. "Discovering Rhetorical Imprints: La Follette, 'Iago,' and the Melodramatic Scenario." *Quarterly Journal of Speech* 71 (1985): 441-56.

"The Will, the People, and the Law: A Rhetorical Biography of Robert M. La Follette, Sr." Ph. D. Diss. University of Wisconsin-Madison, 1982.

Greenbaum, Fred. *Robert Marion La Follette*. Boston: Twayne, 1975.

La Follette, Belle Case, and Fola La Follette. *Robert M. La Follette*. 2 vols. New York: Macmillan, 1953.

Neal, Nevin Emil. "A Biography of Joseph T. Robinson." Ph. D. Diss. University of Oklahoma, 1958.

Peterson, H. C. and Gilbert C. Fite. *Opponents of War, 1917-1918*. Madison: University of Wisconsin Press, 1957.

Ryley, Thomas W. *A Little Group of Willful Men*. Port Washington: Kennikat Press, 1975.

Thelen, David P. *Robert M. La Follette and the Insurgent Spirit*. Boston: Little, Brown, 1976.

The Scopes Trial: "Darrow vs. Bryan" vs. "Bryan vs. Darrow"

Thomas M. Lessl

The concept of the speech set offers the critic a systemic understanding of public discourse, an understanding that focuses the critic's attention not only upon the rhetorical texts of concern, but also upon one or more additional messages that are their progenitors. From this perspective apologies are by definition tied to some other message(s) of accusation already extant within a common persuasive field.

Reflecting on a speech set, it immediately becomes clear that accusation and apology can be thought of in two ways--as types of utterances but also as types of roles played in a rhetorical situation. As roles, these pairings are manifested at differing levels of formality. The formality of a speaking situation will determine the rigidity or flexibility of accusatory and apologetic roles. Thus, as accusatory discourse, the charges against Martin Luther set forth in Pope Leo X's bulls *Exsurge Domine* and *Decet Romanum* were highly formal and adhered closely to their purposes of calling Luther into account for his doctrines. Those who enter into a discursive exchange within the role definitions set out in a court of law must at least ostensibly play those parts that have been set out for them. But in the informal speech set, the roles of accuser and apologist are defined by situational aspects and are easily reversed.

Yet even in judicial contexts, where the roles of accuser and apologist are formally set out, one still finds certain elements that do not conform to the formally mandated roles. Thus, there was much in Martin Luther's defense at the Diet of Worms that cannot be regarded as apologetic. Because the doctrines he defended at the Diet were opposed to orthodox teaching, Luther was in effect raising accusations against the Roman church that it ultimately, though not immediately, would have to address. In the case of the Scopes trial, the judicial protocol, with its usual construction of rhetorical roles, was superseded by the immensity of the issue that was there deliberated. Indeed, if judicial procedure had been strictly followed the trial could not have lasted more than a few hours.

Clearly, it is meaningful to talk about accusation and apology as paired sets of utterances, but it is equally clear that there is more than one way in which the observer, and indeed participants, can interpret such groupings of rhetorical acts. Both sides in any sort of dispute will often simultaneously claim that they are merely defending their position, while their opponents are the ones making all the accusations. This was certainly true in the Scopes trial. The opponents in this somewhat circus-like moment in American judicial history each behaved in a manner an outsider would regard as accusatory, while simultaneously maintaining that they came to Dayton, Tennessee, on an apologetic mission--to halt some injustice being perpetrated by the other. If the critic, as an outside observer of such an exchange, regards one set of utterances as accusatory and another set as apologetic, he or she is making an important critical determination likely to influence immensely the reader's understanding of the rhetorical event. This essay will demonstrate that *kategoria* and *apologia* may designate both classes of utterances and symbolically constructed roles that, at least in certain circumstances, are subject to reversal. The role definitions one gives to a rhetorical exchange will ultimately determine whether the individual utterances are judged apologetic or accusatory.

The roles of accusation and apology are only firmly established by formality. When one disregards form, it becomes clear that these are reversible rhetorical postures. These interpretations are crucial to those involved in the exchange, for with the roles of accuser and apologist go certain relational implications that potentially contribute to or diminish the *ethos* of a speaker. For those involved, the outcome of a rhetorical interchange hinges on the ability of the combatants to define the audience's perceptions of their postures in a manner favorable to their own interests. In the Scopes affair, each side entered the case determined that its own speech should be viewed as apologetic. The rhetorical behavior displayed by each side seems to indicate the desire of each to be perceived by the public as a victim of the other's wrongdoing. Thus, both sides wished that the observing public would define the sequence of events at Dayton so that the other would be cast as the accuser and they the apologist. Darrow and Bryan both hoped to rally political and popular sympathy around their respective causes. Neither party to this affair wished to be perceived as the aggressor. Thus, both actors in this dramatic trial attempted to help the observing public view these combative interchanges so that he would appear an innocent defender of the faith, rather than a vindictive or even malicious inquisitor.

The Scopes trial, July 10-21, 1925, came about as a consequence of the opportunism of some citizens of Dayton, Tennessee, and the desire of the American Civil Liberties Union (ACLU) to put the state's new "monkey law" to the test. John Thomas Scopes, a retiring young substitute teacher, whose education was actually in physics rather than biology, volunteered to be arrested and brought to trial for teaching evolution. Eager to draw, as one resident would proclaim, "a lot of big fellows" into Dayton for the fight, William Jennings Bryan was immediately solicited by the prosecution. With Bryan's head thus ready for the ax, Clarence Darrow, for the first time in a career in which he had never actively sought a client, found himself soliciting to work without pay as Scope's attorney. Clearly the two most familiar principals in this episode, Darrow and Bryan, came as representatives of two respectively different worlds. Bryan, through his odd blend of populism and fundamental Christianity, spoke for rural Americans as an exponent of the agrarian values, traditions, and beliefs that had long been threatened by the gradual advancement of industrialism. Darrow, a Chicagoan, lived willfully submerged in the gray urban wastelands Bryan had come to despise. He stood for modernism, not only as an ideologue, but also as one of the first prominent rhetoricians to throw off the spacious religiosity of nineteenth-century oratory in favor of a secularized speech that ran much closer to the ground.

As speech sets, the rhetorical transactions that unfolded at Dayton were addressed only intermittently to policy issues. The principals, Darrow and Bryan, were equally as concerned with defending their respective ways of life as with the immediate legality of Tennessee's anti-evolution law. Darrow had a reputation for using court cases as platforms for expressing his views on larger political and philosophical questions, endangering often by doing so the well-being of his clients.[1] At Dayton, Darrow found an opportune moment. Here the whole nation and many outside the United States would be watching as he, with his cold sarcastic talons of rational skepticism, tore open the outward flesh of fundamentalist Christianity and exposed to the world the bigotry and ignorance he believed lay beneath. The real issues that prompted the ACLU to put up its offer to fund any test case of Tennessee's anti-evolution law were lost when it was decided that Clarence Darrow would be chief counsel for the defense. The ACLU committee that selected the defense team, which was comprised not only of Darrow, but also two very bright New York Lawyers, Dudley Field Malone and Arthur Garfield Hays as well as John R. Neal, a very competent local attorney, knew that Darrow's reputation as a radical and agnostic would distract attention from the issues it wished to draw out in this trial.[2] Darrow was chosen only at the insistence of Scopes himself, and over the protests of Felix Frankfurter, a future U.S. Supreme Court justice, who wanted a conservative attorney with more traditional religious orientations. In almost every respect, Clarence Darrow represented what anti-evolutionists claimed about the influence of Darwinism. Darrow not only was a fervent believer in Darwinism, he had also achieved notoriety by applying a social version of the same in arguing those criminal cases that had by this time made his name a household word. Darrow's was not an authentic version of social

Darwinism; it was something more cautious than that, a crudely determinis-
tic interpretation of human misconduct that ultimately removed all
responsibility for criminal behavior from the individual to the environment.
In Darrow's hands the trial became something different than it likely would
have been in the hands of any other attorney.

William Jennings Bryan, who had not practiced law in over twenty-five
years, was equally an odd choice to head the prosecution. Although it is difficult to imagine how the prosecution might have avoided its inevitable
humiliation, Bryan, acting in the trial more as a figurehead of the fundamentalist movement than as an attorney, had primed himself supremely for the
bitter inquisition he was to suffer at Darrow's hands. His presence at the
trial was a consequence both of his fundamentalist religion and his populist
political thinking. Bryan rationalized that anti-evolutionary statutes, such
as Tennessee's Butler Act, were just because they were regulatory laws and
symbolic decrees that voiced the authoritative directives of the popular will.
Bryan had in fact made it quite well known that he was against the inclusion
of penalties in any of the anti-evolution laws of concern.[3] Bryan did not
come to the trial to punish John Scopes. Like Darrow, he came to put his
cause, that of religion, in the limelight, defending it against the accusations
of Darrow and the whole modern world that looked on.

The Scopes trial was not a simple court case but a platform on which the
foremost representatives of two prominent ideologies could fight their
rhetorical battles. At this level, the accusatory and apologetic roles were
not concretely set out. Consequently, as a speech set, the rhetorical events
that occurred in Dayton, Tennessee, in July of 1925 can be perceived in a
number of ways depending on the eyes through which one chooses to view
the interactive sequence. The critic can explicate the event from the
perspective of either of the participants, or from the perspective of an outsider looking in on the event. The relativity of the participants' perspectives
is evidenced in the critical texts. These artifacts reveal an understanding of
how the conflict was understood by those embroiled within it.

DARROW vs. BRYAN

The most obvious but also the least useful way to treat the set is as a judicial transaction. As a trial, this episode was formally cast with Clarence
Darrow as the apologetic spokesman of the American Civil Liberties
Union, defending John Thomas Scopes against the accusation that he had
violated the state's anti- evolution act. However, in order to best understand
the meaning of this trial, the critic might regard its judicial aspects as super-
ficial. On the surface, it might seem that since Clarence Darrow came into
the trial as the counsel for the accused Scopes, his would be an apologetic
rhetoric. The defense team did in fact endeavor to defend Scopes, but they

did so mostly by making accusations concerning the propriety of monkey laws. Darrow's defense was largely an attack against the statute, the "foolish, mischievous, and wicked act" Scopes had violated, and the climate of opinion harkening "back into the sixteenth century" that had brought it into existence. Darrow and Malone chose to say little directly in defense of Scopes, perhaps because formally he had violated the law; rather they turned against his accusers, publicly belittling the brand of fundamental Christianity, the "narrow, ignorant, bigoted shrew of religion" that William Jennings Bryan represented. But while saying much that was accusatory, Darrow and his flock claimed that their's was an apologetic role. By declaring the statute "as brazen and as bold an attempt to destroy learning as was ever made in the Middle Ages," an indignity different only from its medieval precursors in that the state had not provided "that they shall be burned at the stake," Darrow suggested that his and his defendant's roles were analogous to those of the suffering martyr or righteous heretic before the inquisition.[4]

The same depiction of the trial was offered by the other defense attorneys, as well as by Darrow's sarcastic friend H. L. Mencken, who covered most of the trial as a reporter. With their lacerating cynicism, Mencken's writings about the trial offered a most brutal attack against the character of the "yokels" and "yaps" who supported Bryan's prosecution. But in rendering judgment on the affair as a whole, Mencken seemed to view his friends' efforts as a defensive response to what he called an "inquisition." Similarly, Arthur Garfield Hays, one of the team of lawyers who worked on the Scopes defense, would later in his biographical account of these judicial deliberations allude to such persecutions as the burning of Giordano Bruno and Galileo's indictment before the inquisition as forerunners of the Scopes trial.[5]

The above disclosures were all public utterances reflecting the perceived role Darrow and his assistants wished the observing public to give them. Darrow's private letters, however, reveal his real accusatory intentions. In a letter to H. L Mencken, who missed the last day of the trial and the cross-examination of Mr. Bryan, Darrow proclaimed "I made up my mind to show the country what an ignoramus he [Bryan] was and I succeeded."[6] Although there is ample evidence that Darrow came into the trial on the attack, he endeavored at every public juncture to make it appear that the scientific community, represented by educators such as John Scopes, was in a defensive posture, a victim of the most heinous brand of authoritarian bigotry.

BRYAN vs. DARROW

The accusatory intentions that Bryan brought with him to the Scopes trial can be seen in his perception of events on the eve of his being offered the job of chief prosecutor in the case: "We cannot afford to have a system of education that destroys the religious faith of our children. . . . There are about 5,000 scientists, and probably half of them are atheists, in the United States. Are we going to let them run our schools? We are not."[7] Much like the arguments contemporary fundamentalists raise against secular humanists, Bryan's charge was that a minority of modernist scientists were foisting atheism upon an unwilling majority.

Although a fundamentalist in every sense, Bryan had only recently become outspoken against Darwinism. The main reason for this change in attitude seems to have been a growing conviction, resulting from his many campus speaking engagements, that Darwinism was directly tied to a loss of faith among college students. Bryan's growing convictions about the sinister influence of Darwinism were bolstered by his reading of literature proclaiming not only that Darwinism was untenable, but that it was also at the root of numerous modern plagues: it had made possible the Nietzschean rule of force that lead to militant German nationalism, and it now threatened to erode the bases of American morality as well. When the Scopes case was announced, Bryan threw himself at it. He was, after all, the very personification of that brand of rural piety the people of Tennessee were trying to protect. In this regard, Bryan did not come to the trial chiefly as an accuser. Although he came to decry Darwinism, Bryan clearly regarded this activity as requisite to his defense of the faith. Bryan came to accuse evolutionary science of impiety, but only, so he thought, in order that these accusations would vindicate the Christian religion. For the constituent religious population that Bryan represented, the evolutionists were the accusers. It was they who were making a fraud out of the Christian faith. Just as much as Darrow and his colleagues, the prosecutors in this case regarded themselves as victims of a powerful accusatory tribunal.

The prosecution came to Dayton to accuse the scientific community and modernists in general of what Bryan conceived of as a great democratic impiety--that of imposing the will of a small minority upon the majority of Christians. Bryan had been attacking evolutionists in his speeches for several years. Like these speeches, most of what Bryan said during the course of the trial was, on the face of it, accusatory. At the same time, Bryan portrayed his role in the trial as apologetic. Seemingly assured of his own historic importance, Bryan proclaimed in 1923 that in his campaigns against those who teach evolution he was "trying to save the Christian Church from those who are trying to destroy her faith!"[8] Seeming to attribute unwarranted grandeur to his role, Bryan, on the eve of the trial, cast himself as savior of the church: "The contest between evolution and Christianity is a duel to the death. If evolution wins in Dayton, Christianity goes--not suddenly, of course, but gradually--for the two cannot stand together."[9]

Yet despite Bryan's claims that he was saving the church from the onslaughts of evolutionism, to a large degree his defenses amounted to a series of charges accusing evolutionists of all sorts of misrepresentation and impiety. Bryan's only lengthy speech of the trial began on an apologetic note by responding to the charges of bigotry and ignorance that had been previously raised by the defense. But after these issues were settled, Bryan turned against evolutionary scientists, charging that "they would undermine the faith of these little children in that God who stands back of everything and whose promise we have that we shall live with Him forever by and by. They shut God out of the world." And then in the best remembered portion of Bryan's argument, he attempted to appropriate the reasoning used by Darrow himself in his defense of Loeb and Leopold in 1924. Bryan charged that evolution was the "doctrine that gives us Nietzsche, the only great authority who tried to carry this [evolution] to its logical conclusion."[10] In his defense of Loeb and Leopold, Darrow had claimed that the great German's influence had inspired Leopold to commit murder. Bryan extended the rudiments of this borrowed argument by charging that the introduction of evolutionary theory in American education would lead to a brand of destructive nihilism such as was inspired by Nietzsche.

It is quite clear that what to the defense was accusatory rhetoric was regarded by Bryan as defensive. Similarly, those utterances of the prosecution that Bryan took to be an accusatory affront to the Christian religion were to Darrow and his colleagues merely apologetics for evolution and freedom of education. Ultimately, at the close of the trial, Darrow would seem the accuser and Bryan the apologist. This was due in part to Darrow's frustrations with other means of making his point and to Bryan's remarkable willingness to act as Darrow's victim in cross-examination. As a whole, the Scopes trial may be fairly regarded as an ongoing transactive barrage of accusations and apologies emanating mutually from both sides. This is especially clear in a number of statements uttered by each in those climactic moments of the trial during which Darrow had Bryan on the witness stand. Here each of these rivals struggled to make himself appear the apologist:

BRYAN: The purpose is to cast ridicule on everybody who believes in the Bible, and I am perfectly willing that the world shall know that these gentlemen have no other purpose than ridiculing every Christian who believes in the Bible.

DARROW: We have the purpose of preventing bigots and ignoramuses from controlling the education of the United States and you know it, that is all.

BRYAN: Your Honor, I think I can shorten this testimony. The only purpose Mr. Darrow has is to slur at the Bible, but I will answer his question. I will answer it all at once, and I have no objection in the world, I want the world to know that this man, who does not believe in a God, is trying to use a court in Tennessee--

DARROW: I object to that.

BRYAN: [continuing] to slur at it, and while it will require time, I am willing to take it.

DARROW: I object to your statement. I am examining you on your fool ideas that no intelligent Christian on earth believes.[11]

Viewed as a speech set, this rhetorical head-butting that went on before Judge J. T. Raulston of the Eighteenth Judicial Criminal Court of Tennessee can be viewed as a struggle between two parties both striving to establish alternate understandings of their rhetorical roles. The defense, under Darrow's leadership, tried to depict Scopes and the scientific community he represented at the trial as victims of religious backwardness and bigotry. Similarly, although the prosecution was formally committed to strive for Scope's conviction, it tried to depict itself in the role of defender of a persecuted religious faith. The offensive portions of each side's rhetoric during the trial were devoted to bolstering a depiction of the other as aggressor and archfiend.

CONCLUSION

In considering the possible interpretations of a sequence of utterances, the critic can explicate how the participants made sense of the interchange by defining in the texts those evidences of the participants' understandings of the accusatory and apologetic roles. But because these role designations are subject to the relativity of individual perceptions, the critic must also strive to understand the rhetorical meanings of these deliberate orderings.

At Dayton, Darrow regarded himself as a liberal fighting against political aggressors he believed were using fundamentalist religion as a cover for bigotry and backwardness. In court, Darrow assuredly acted the accuser, trying at every turn to ridicule Bryan's antediluvian beliefs, but his own depictions of the ongoing dialogue showed the extent to which he wished to be regarded as apologist. Bryan similarly tried to heap scorn upon evolution as a vain hypothesis perpetrated against the faith of our fathers. At the same time, he, like Darrow, cast himself in the trial as an apologist, as a noble prophet and defender of the faith. Both sides in this controversy seemed bent not so much on winning in court, but on shaping the perceived sequencing of the speech set so that its own side would appear the victim of the other's aggression.

The critic might predict that in the midst of public controversy, the speaker who appears the apologist has a notable rhetorical advantage over the one who appears to be the accuser. Accusation will likely be perceived as an act of aggression, a willful act suggestive of maleficence. Indeed, such a predisposition is built into our judicial system where the accuser is burdened with the obligation of proof. A preference for the apologetic role is also reflected in our Judeo-Christian religions that caution their disciples to avoid accusation at all costs but encourage them always to be prepared to defend the faith. In the same sacred texts, "accuser" is one of the names for Satan. In our culture, accusation can be a dirty business. The apologist, on the other hand, might be viewed in a more favorable light. Self-defense in our culture can be a justification for homicide; it may be an act of aggression, but it is one performed reluctantly for the sake of righteousness. The apologist has the rhetorical advantage, initially at least, of being perceived as an innocent, as the passive target of the other's rage.

These cultural preferences were reflected in the Scopes trial where both sides engaged in accusation while claiming that they were apologists. Clearly, two alternate orderings of the rhetorical sequence are here at work, two ways in which the combative dialogue of this trial can be perceived. Such a view of this event reveals a secondary level, not of content, but of relational meaning that was subtly but competitively negotiated in rhetorical combat.

NOTES

[1] Kevin Tierney, *Darrow: A Biography* (New York: Thomas Y. Crowell, 1979), pp. 206-26.

[2] Arthur and Lila Weinberg, *Clarence Darrow: A Sentimental Rebel* (New York: Putnam's, 1980), p. 319.

[3] Charles Morrow Wilson, *The Commoner: William Jennings Bryan* (Garden City: Doubleday, 1970), p. 417.

[4] See *Bryan and Darrow at Dayton*, edited by Leslie H. Allen (New York: Arthur Lee & Company, 1925), p. 15; *Bryan and Darrow at Dayton*, p. 18; Weinberg, *Clarence Darrow*, p. 328; Darrow through the newspapers had previously tried to lure Bryan into the kind of trap he would later set for him in his cross-examination. *Bryan and Darrow at Dayton*, p. 16.

[5] H. L. Mencken, *Heathen Days 1890-1936* (New York: Alfred A. Knopf, 1943), pp. 214-38; Arthur Garfield Hays, *Let Freedom Ring* (New York: Horace Liveright, 1928), p. 31.

[6] Tierney, *Darrow: A Biography* p. 356.

[7] Ray Ginger, *Six Days or Forever: Tennessee v. John Thomas Scopes* (New York: Oxford University Press, 1958), p. 21.

[8] Ibid., p. 33.

[9] L. Sprague De Camp, *The Great Monkey Trial* (Garden City: Doubleday, 1968), p. 141.

[10] *Bryan and Darrow at Dayton*, pp. 73-76.

[11] *Monkey Trial,* edited by Shelton Norman Grebstein (Boston: Houghton Mifflin, 1960), pp. 164-70.

INFORMATION SOURCES ON THE SPEECH SET

Clarence Darrow and William Jennings Bryan at the Scopes Trial

The speeches made by Darrow and Bryan during the Scopes trial can be found in *Bryan and Darrow at Dayton*, edited by Leslie H. Allen (New York: Arthur Lee & Company, 1925). Bryan's "Last Statement," which was published posthumously, but which Bryan had hoped to use as his closing remarks in the trial, is also included in this text as are excerpts of other statements made by Bryan and Darrow relevant to the trial.

Selected Bibliography

Darrow, Clarence. *Infidels and Heretics: An Agnostic's Anthology*. Boston: Stratford Company, 1929.

D-Days at Dayton: Reflections on the Scopes Trial. Edited by Jerry R. Tompkins. Baton Rouge: Louisiana State University Press, 1965.

De Camp, L. Sprague. *The Great Monkey Trial*. Garden City: Doubleday, 1968.

Koenig, Louis W. *Bryan: A Political Biography of William Jennings Bryan*. New York: Putnam's, 1971.

Scopes, John T., and James Presley. *Center of the Storm: Memoirs of John T. Scopes*. New York: Holt, Rinehart & Winston, 1967.

Tierney, Kevin. *Darrow: A Biography*. New York: Thomas Y. Crowell, 1979.

Weinberg, Arthur, and Lila Weinberg. *Clarence Darrow: A Sentimen-

tal Rebel. New York: Putnam's, 1980.

Wilson, Charles Morrow. *The Commoner: William Jennings Bryan.* Garden City: Doubleday, 1970.

Accusations and Apologies from a General, a Senator, and a Priest

Susan Schultz Huxman and Wil A. Linkugel

When Franklin D. Roosevelt assumed the presidency on March 4, 1933, in the midst of the Great Depression, he moved quickly to revitalize the nation's economy. No fewer than seventeen pieces of New Deal legislation passed through Congress the first one hundred days. Support for the new president was nearly unanimous. In such troubled times, people preferred any kind of action to inaction. But when the economy turned upward, many reverted to their prior political and economic views. Business, which initially had endorsed the National Industrial Recovery Act, began to chafe under the rules and regulations of the codes the act produced. The political Left grew restless as well, claiming that the president had failed to go far enough in assisting the nation's "have nots." Their disenchantment crested in 1935 when well-intentioned people produced a variety of plans designed to serve the needy. The loudest noise on the Left, however, came from two diverse sources: Senator Huey Long in Louisiana and Father Charles E. Coughlin in Detroit. While both endorsed Roosevelt in 1932, contending that his election was essential to national recovery, by 1935, they had withdrawn their support. Long learned early in a meeting with President Roosevelt that he would have little influence in the new administration. Undaunted, the Louisiana senator henceforth aggressively promoted his plan to "Share the Wealth," a scheme that would scale down large fortunes to no more than three or four million dollars, with the money to be used to guarantee everyone a minimum income of $2500 a year. Father Coughlin espoused a similar panacea for national recovery through his "National Union for Social Justice." The Catholic priest used his weekly radio program to promote "a living annual wage" and nationalization of banking, currency, and natural resources. Long and Coughlin soon attracted a large and devoted following. Like Roosevelt, these two crafty politicians understood all too clearly how to cultivate support rhetorically. With hyperbolic prose cast in religious zeal, Long and Coughlin were able to give their causes a veneer of workability, ingenuity, and good sense.

Onto this scene marched General Hugh S. Johnson, a crusty politico and a longtime Roosevelt supporter. President Roosevelt had chosen him in 1933 to administrate the National Recovery Act (NRA) and had given him the task of inducing businessmen to draw up codes of fair competition. But by 1934, the president had heard so many protests about some of the codes that he trimmed NRA's powers, eased Johnson out of office, and replaced him with Donald Richberg. The general, nevertheless, remained a New Deal proponent and a loyal supporter of the president for a few years thereafter. Like Roosevelt, he became concerned about Long and Coughlin's popularity. When Long, in late February, launched an especially spirited attack on the Roosevelt administration and when Father Coughlin, in a radio sermon, described the first two years of the New Deal as a series of failures and spoke harshly of NRA, General Johnson decided to wage war. He chose for his battle ground a dinner to himself on March 4, 1935, on the occasion of the opening installment of his memoirs by the editors of *Red Book Magazine* at the Waldorf-Astoria Hotel, New York City. In a lengthy speech that *Vital Speeches of the Day* simply titled "Pied Pipers,"[1] Johnson attacked Long and Coughlin in an effort to curb their growing popularity. Within a week, Long and Coughlin had recaptured the nation's attention with speeches of self-defense broadcasted over national radio. Taken together, this set of speeches provides fertile ground for critical analysis.

Speeches of accusation removed from the legal setting have attracted little, if any, scholarly attention. The paucity of single speeches devoted exclusively to accusation explains, in part, the lack of critical attention. It is far more common that the exigence for apologetic discourse is a diffused attack from the media, special interest groups, or political parties, rather than a formal attack from a single individual. The disparate nature of accusations has made critical analysis difficult. Not surprisingly, when critics analyze accusatory discourse, it is often as an ancillary interest to apologetic discourse. As a result, critics have not been inclined to treat attack and defense with equal measure.[2] Yet approaching accusation and defense as a set is necessary for valid evaluations. To borrow from the legal field, just as jurors are not asked to arrive at a verdict based entirely on the evidence presented by the defense, neither should critics judge the success of *apologia* without consulting the *kategoria* or vice versa.

Though removed from the legal setting, the theoretical base most often used to describe accusatory and apologetic discourse is the forensic genre. Such a classification is problematic, however, because attack and defense do not fall neatly within the parameters of forensic rhetoric. Aristotle clearly had the courtroom in mind when he wrote of accusation and defense. At no place in the *Rhetoric* is any other setting mentioned, nor any other judge but a juror. More importantly, the ends of the speech set within the legal setting are justice and injustice, not honor and dishonor.[3]

Attack and defense can also be viewed from the epideictic genre. Aristotle described epideictic address as concerned with "praise or blame, honor or dishonor" and as including the elements of "virtue and vice and the noble and the base." Although he wrote extensively about speeches of praise and little about speeches of blame, one can reasonably assume what Aristotle had in mind. In keeping with the aims of epideictic speaking, accusatory rhetoric is designed to denigrate a person's credibility, or personal legitimacy, and, thereby, dishonor or discredit the individual in the minds of auditors. Yet like the forensic genre, the epideictic genre is not completely hospitable to the nonlegal speech of accusation. The hearer in the case of epideictic rhetoric is a "mere observer," one who contemplates the artistic nature of a speech. Auditors of accusatory discourse certainly function as more than casual observers of the accuser's exhibition or display; they are judges of things past in that they are asked to determine the facticity of the charges against an individual.[4]

The nonlegal speeches of accusation and defense are difficult to place in the Aristotelian generic classification schema as the speech set shares characteristics of both epideictic and forensic speaking. Because the Aristotelian genres are so broad, and fail to discriminate, the critic needs to identify the underlying motives of accusation and defense. A motive view of communication, as Walter Fisher has explained, provides the critic with a perspective on rhetorical situations that interrelates speaker, speech, auditors, time, and place, and encourages the critic to view these elements dynamically. Four motives or kinds of rhetorical situations have been outlined by Fisher: affirmation — giving birth to an image, reaffirmation — revitalizing an image, purification — correcting an image, and subversion — undermining an image.[5] Since subversive rhetoric is "anti-ethos" — an attempt to damage the credibility of some person or idea — it is useful to view subversion as the controlling exigence of accusatory rhetoric.

THE GENERAL'S ATTACK ON THE "PIED PIPERS"

Hugh Johnson made three noteworthy rhetorical choices in his attempt to discredit Huey Long and Charles Coughlin. First, Johnson chose to strengthen his own credibility before weakening the credibility of his foes. Sensitive to audience concerns about the sincerity of his purpose, Johnson recognized that he must convey a message of both pro- and anti-ethos dimensions. Second, Johnson used irony to undermine the images of Long and Coughlin. With this stylistic choice, Johnson's speech further substantiates Fisher's claim that irony may be an archetypal pattern of subversive rhetoric.[6] Third, Johnson's accusations were chiefly against character, almost to the exclusion of policy.

That the accuser can feel pressured to strengthen his or her own ethos in the process of weakening another's credibility is a rhetorical obstacle described at length by Frederick Kauffeld. "The accusation is a source of difficulty for the accuser," Kauffeld notes, "because it is liable to be interpreted as a form of revenge." Accusers "must try to convey that they are treating the accused fairly."[7] The accuser's credibility, especially that of good will, can be crucial to the success of the accusation. In condemning the behavior of another, it is only natural for audiences to think that the speaker's intent is malicious. In certain situations, it would seem that the speaker must be careful to convey the attitude that he or she does not derive any personal satisfaction from the attack and that the attack is needed for the public good. If a speaker fails to do these things, the attempt to undermine another person's credibility in the public arena could, in all likelihood, backfire. The speaker might be accused of harboring bitterness, jealousy, or hatred against the person under attack. Accusers can proceed cautiously aware that, like prosecuting attorneys, they incur a burden of proof to establish beyond a shadow of a doubt the guilt of the accused. But speakers in nonlegal settings can face an additional burden of proof that courtroom attorneys do not: they need to establish beyond a shadow of a doubt their own personal integrity and trustworthiness. In short, removed from the courtroom setting, accusatory rhetors are themselves on trial.

Johnson, undoubtedly, recognized that establishing sincerity and trustworthiness could prove difficult given his recent release from the Roosevelt administration as head of the NRA. Presumably, attacks by an individual whose political career has been thwarted are more telling of a bitter man who is lashing out in frustration. One of Johnson's immediate rhetorical tasks was to dispell the notion that he was angry with the Roosevelt administration and merely venting his anger on two individuals who opposed the NRA. On the other hand, Johnson was in an ideal position to savage Long and Coughlin precisely because he had little to lose politically. No longer in a position that required discretion, Johnson was free to issue a blistering attack.

Johnson displayed rhetorical inventiveness in several ways to prove that lashing out at Long and Coughlin was motivated by genuine concern for the well-being of the country and not malice or bitterness. First, Johnson used structure strategically. To dispell initial doubts about the sincerity of his purpose, Johnson devoted the first part of the speech to a brief history lesson of the gloom and despair that surrounded the country in 1932, and Roosevelt's miraculous ability to pull the country through. Johnson spoke in glowing terms of FDR for a full one-third of his speech. Moreover, the praise for FDR's political feats was couched in religious terminology. The following is exemplary:

[F]ranklin Roosevelt knelt at an alter and prayed. Then he went to the Capitol and registered the vow in Heaven that placed upon his back as heavy a freight of human hopes as ever was borne by any man. Our trust was in him so completely that the general prayer was: 'Provide him with all power that he may save us.' Today, shadows have fallen thwart that faith—and it is my purpose here—with what force God has given me—to smash at two of them.

Johnson's ability to use religious overtones to uphold Roosevelt as a paragon of strong leadership was important for several reasons. First, passages like the one cited above created a stark dichotomy between good—FDR, and evil—"the lunatic fringe" as embodied by Long and Coughlin. Second, the religious seriousness of the speech reflected favorably on Johnson's own persona. By defending Roosevelt, Johnson could be perceived as an apostle of goodness. Third, the religious posturing can be viewed as an attempt to undermine Father Coughlin's authority. If FDR were the Christ persona, the allusion is all too clear in the passage above, then Coughlin, who opposed FDR, could only be a devil figure.

Although Johnson used religious language strategically at the outset to debunk Coughlin's potency, he prefaced the attack by identifying with the Catholic church. In one particularly explicit passage, Johnson stated: "I respect all denominations and all true worshipers. I have the deepest regard for the Catholic Church and the Catholic priesthood. I know something of both their valor and their unvarying patriotism during the war....Throughout my life I have had warm friends in that priesthood." Elsewhere, Johnson lauded Al Smith whom he revered as "a truly great American" because Smith "went from Coast to Coast proudly declaring that the Catholic church and priesthood kept out of politics." These were vital prefatory remarks before condemning a priest. Certainly, Johnson was aware that questioning the integrity of one invested in high office could be perceived as blasphemy if substantial evidence were not presented to the contrary.

Johnson further disproved any malicious intent in attacking Long and Coughlin by identifying with a democratic principle that the American people have faithfully enacted. Johnson cited Woodrow Wilson's rule regarding the state of a democracy in times of peril: "The highest and best form of efficiency is the spontaneous cooperation of a free people." This passage depicted the American people as the supporting cast in FDR's monumental task of turning the country around in its darkest hour. The country's ability to rally around the president, Johnson stated, "was the greatest demonstration of the spontaneous cooperation of a free people that we have ever had. It could not have happened in any other country, in any other time, or under any other leader than the President." By playing upon the patriotic spirit of the American people, Johnson prepared the audience for his indictment of the "lunatic fringe" for "the almost complete destruction of the solidarity in which our people started to pull itself out of this hole."

Johnson was also sensitive to the public's suspicion that the administration might have been using him as its mouthpiece. Therefore, he distanced himself from Roosevelt. "At this point I want to make it very clear that I am speaking for myself alone—a gratuitous volunteer," Johnson stated. "Nobody in the Administration has been consulted about this speech. . . .It may interest you to know that without a single exception, they advised against it. 'If you want to hang yourself—go to it.'" By separating himself from the will of the administration, Johnson was able to portray himself as a courageous patriot who deserved admiration, not suspicion. Johnson's next line substantiates this observation: "Nothing did more to convince me that this speech had to be made. If demagogy has reached the point where a man may risk his public standing by attacking it, it is time for somebody to get up on his hind legs and howl."

Perhaps Johnson's most significant strategy to convince the audience that his motive for attacking the lunatic fringe was not self-serving can be found in his expressed reluctance and dissatisfaction at having to give the speech at all. Before Johnson launched his most stinging indictment of Long and Coughlin, he remarked:

This brings me to a part of this speech that I do not relish making. I like Huey Long. He is one of the most plausible Punchinellos in this or any other country. He is an able little devil and I can't help but gleefully admire his cast-iron cheek and his rough and tumble readiness to take on all comers. . . .For Father Coughlin, I have even a closer sentiment. I agree with much that he says. I think he has done more to interest the average man in politics than anybody.

Johnson added sadly that "their warm messages make it very hard for me to say what I know must be said." As with his attempt to differentiate himself from the will of the administration, Johnson would have his audience admire the unpleasant, but noble, task of exposing two threats to the New Deal.

Johnson further grew in stature as a well-intentioned rhetor when he issued some well-worn pathetic appeals. "I am poor myself," Johnson claimed, "but it just happens that I don't owe anybody anything—that I never get anything from anybody without paying for it—that I am on my own—and that I can rest on my record for saying just what I think whenever I feel that it ought to be said and for taking all that's coming to me for saying it." This passage, while passing for vintage apologia, further substantiates the claim that, in this instance, accusatory discourse is both pro- and anti-ethos rhetoric.

The final and most intriguing strategy that Johnson used to establish good will and trustworthiness was a clever justification for the abusive quality of his indictment against Long and Coughlin. Initially, one is struck by what appears to be a glaring inconsistency in Johnson's rhetorical posture. On the one hand, Johnson claimed that he regretted having to condemn Coughlin and Long for their misguided causes. Yet, on the other hand, he used the most inflammatory language to condemn their behavior. One of Johnson's analogies is illustrative:

> Between the team of Huey and the priest, we have the whole bag of crazy or crafty tricks possessed by any Mad Mullah or dancing dervish who ever incited a tribe or people through illusion to its doom — Peter the Hermit, Napoleon Bonaparte, Sitting Bull, William Hohenzollern, the Mahdi of the Soudan, Hitler, Lenin, Trotsky and the Leatherwood God — here they are — all boiled down to two with the radio and the news reels to make them effective.

If Johnson truly regretted having to criticize Long and Coughlin, why were his attacks so vindictive? Johnson himself provided the answer: "It is not what these men say that is dangerous. It is the devilish ingenuity of their way of saying it." Nobody was challenging these men in language anybody could understand, he added. Johnson became that challenger by adopting the powerfully persuasive techniques of the demagogues themselves. In short, what appears on first reading as impropriety of style is, in the final analysis, entirely consistent with Johnson's thesis that "these men are dangerous not for what they say, but for their devilish ingenuity of their way of saying it." Johnson's enactment of "the devilishness of demagogy" proved its persuasive power, but it also conveyed Johnson's cleverness, if not his maliciousness. Johnson's style was abrasive, exaggerated, unfair, and maudlin; but so were the demagogic appeals of Coughlin and Long's. Moreover, if one approved and zealously applauded Johnson's smashing of the lunatic fringe, it would become proof that the "easy magic" of the demagogue was highly persuasive — and in the wrong hands extremely dangerous. The speech was chock full of demagogic devices. Hyperbolic alliterative passages, "there comes burring over the air the dripping brogue of the Irish-Canadian priest... musical, blatant bunk from the very rostrum of religion"; guilt by association, "while I do not for a moment compare Father Coughlin with Talleyrand"; false analogy, "Hitler couldn't hold a candle to Huey in the art of the old Barnum ballyhoo — a new sucker every second!"; and mixed metaphor, "I view as traitors to our common cause all those who... try to break the elbow of our pilot in this Sea of Shoals," are prime examples of Johnson's mock demagoguery.

Johnson's enactment of demagogy captured the dual purposes of the nature of his attack: it was both pro- and anti-ethos rhetoric. The abusive attack seriously eroded the popular image of both Long and Coughlin. The justification for the nature of the attack secured a favorable image of the accuser. In addition, Johnson's ability to communicate the message that demagogy was dangerous, while expressing that message demagogically, confirms Fisher's idea that irony may be a recurring stylistic component of subversive rhetoric.

Having established his own credibility, Johnson proceeded to subvert the ethos of Long and Coughlin. He constructed competing images of each: the one appealing and the other threatening. He first portrayed Huey Long as a "buffoon" figure. He referred to him as an "able little devil," a "plausible little Punchinello," and "the sweet prince of bombast" who was Father Coughlin's little "playmate." To complete the image, the general poked fun at Long's "cane-break drawl" and humorously parodied the Louisiana senator's speech: "Ahm not against de Constitution. Ahm fo' de Constitution. Ahm not against p'ivate p'op'ety. Ahm fo' p'ivate p'op'ety...." This image of Huey Long seemed to add up to harmless lunacy, a buffoon who made a business of amusing others by tricks, gestures, and humorous speech. Johnson's depiction of the priest's seemingly harmless appeal was short but pointed. He attributed Coughlin's ability to enchant thousands and mold them into followers to the "melodious burring" and "dripping brogue" of his radio voice.

Johnson juxtaposed the images of the soothing priest and the animated senator with the image of the Pied Piper. Beyond the senator's twang and the good padre's brogue, underneath the priestly garb, one found "dangerous demagogues" of the "lunatic fringe." Both possessed a "devilish ingenuity," and preached "not construction but destruction – not reform but revolution – not peace but a sword." Like the Pied Piper, they claimed to rid the nation of its "rats" but, in reality, they intended to lead its people astray. Johnson warned that "the most dangerous revolutionary in the world is the sincere one – the more sincere the more dangerous." It might be easy to chuckle over Long's antics, it might be convenient to consider him a misguided lunatic, but one must never forget the message of the Pied Piper: "Two Pied Pipers have come to Hamelin Town, – and you will recall what the Pied Piper was – a magician who, by tooting on a penny whistle, could step into the leadership of rats – or charm innocent children from the safety of their homes." The Pied Piper of the fairytale, in great measure, was dangerous because no one took him seriously. "You can laugh at Father Coughlin," Johnson warned, "you can snort at Huey Long – but this country was never under a greater menace."

In the final analysis, these deceptively appealing images of Long and Coughlin mandated Johnson's speech of accusation. Johnson, no doubt, reasoned that if everyone readily perceived them as villains, their potential for harm would be small; but given their Pied Piper-like charm, it was essential that someone smash their reputations and expose their villainy.

Johnson's attack on Father Coughlin was more complex. In addition to the Pied Piper depiction, Coughlin's legitimacy was undermined in two fundamental ways. First, Johnson charged him with "a prostitution of his holy office" for "using the cloak of religion to seek political power." The general's indictment of Coughlin's priestly role was severe: "We can never respect nor revere what appears to be a priest in Holy Orders entering our homes ... and there, in the name of Jesus Christ, demanding that we ditch the President for Huey Long." Father Coughlin, Johnson charged, was using his structural legitimacy for political ends, not for the religious ends for which it was intended.[8] Having stripped the good Father of his religious garb, Johnson proceeded to subvert the priest's patriotic ties to America by emphasizing his Irish-Canadian heritage. In McCarthyesque style, Johnson delivered an ethnocentric indictment of Coughlin: "This political padre ... does not arraign our President and our institutions in the American language without a Canadian accent, and [he] may or may not now be an American citizen." Attacks on one's religious scruples and national loyalties are arguably the most fundamental of subversive techniques as they go to the wellspring of a culture's values.

Johnson used the same strategy for attacking the respective policies of Long and Coughlin as he did in attacking their characters. He first pointed to the strong appeal their policies had to people who felt deprived of their fair share of the nation's wealth. And, on the surface, Johnson admitted that he could understand some of that appeal. Who did not think, for example, that the very rich had too much money, and that the poor should have more? Who did not think that it would be good if we could guarantee everyone a minimum annual income? And surely the slogan: "Every man a king" appealed to people — at least in a story-book manner. But Johnson warned that Long's Share the Wealth plan was dangerous and totally unworkable. How, Johnson asked, was Long going to get the money from the rich? Long's plan left that matter totally in the air. Additionally, Johnson charged that the figures did not add up. There just simply was not enough money to guarantee everybody $2500. The general concluded that Long's plan was totally unworkable and was lacking in political and economic wisdom. Father Coughlin, on the other hand, "wants to make money out of the wind to pay the public debt and all expenses of government," Johnson alleged. He then maintained the religious character of his speech by turning to the Scriptures to suggest that Father Coughlin was engaged in "promise and performance possible only to the Lord God Almighty!"

In a larger sense, Johnson's policy attacks were used to support the anti-ethos nature of the speech. The basic thrust of Johnson's speech was not simply to point out that Long and Coughlin's plans made no sense but to establish that the authors of the plans were lacking in good sense. The Pied Pipers lacked political and economic expertise and were particularly dangerous because they had such widespread appeal. Johnson justified his decision to subordinate policy attacks in order to subvert character with the remark: "It is not what these men say that is dangerous. It is their devilish ingenuity of their way of saying it."

Johnson's ability to strengthen his own ethos while justifying a devastating character attack of two political foes was persuasive. The editor of *Redbook* received hundreds of telegrams that ran about seven favorable to one unfavorable. Editorials from the *New York Times* predicted that the general's speech would release others from the sort of "moral terrorism" set up by Long and Coughlin, and lauded Johnson's initiative in "breaking through censorship which was unofficial and invisible." *New York Times* reporter Arthur Krock claimed that the speech had delighted the capital community and that "the average politician has found himself suddenly emboldened by the general's boldness." The *Washington Post* headlined its editorial section: "Thank you, General!" Glowing reviews went so far as to predict that "the speech will go down in American history along with the most notable utterances of our statesman."[9] Of course, Johnson's speech has not been preserved in the annals of oratory, but such favorable press so alarmed Senator Huey Long and Father Charles Coughlin that each sought to repair his image in the eyes of the American public.

APOLOGIA FROM THE SENATOR

Three days after Johnson's speech, Long took to the airwaves and demonstrated unequivocally that Johnson's harsh attacks had not daunted the Louisiana Kingfish. Twenty-five million people of the radio audience awaited the verbal thrashing that they expected the fiery senator would give his accuser. What they got was not a harangue, but a sermon, not a retreat, but a charge. Long maintained his image of a resilient politician who thrived on confrontation, attention, and media coverage.

The term "purification" is the key to an assessment of speeches of self-defense. When Fisher introduced the rhetorical motive of purification, he associated it with ideological purification. "Where a rhetoric of affirmation seeks to initiate an ideology and a rhetoric of reaffirmation endeavors to revitalize one," he wrote, "a rhetoric of purification is found in situations in which a communicator attempts to refine one."[10] Somewhat surprisingly, Fisher then proceeded to give two examples of the rhetoric of purification that principally concerned purifying an image. Richard Nixon's "Checkers Speech" quite plainly involved the cleansing of his image; whereas John F. Kennedy's "Houston Ministerial Address" involved both personal and ideological purification. Concluding from this, the purification motive outlined by Fisher embraces character and policy defenses. Both Long and Coughlin sought to purify the public's perception of themselves: Long by refining an ideology, Coughlin by cleansing an image.

Long's apologia demonstrated rhetorical inventiveness in several ways.

First, he transcended the specific charges of Johnson's attack by appropriating Johnson's war metaphor and by transforming the attack on character to a defense of policy.[11] Secondly, striving for image purification, Long adopted a rhetorical posture at odds with the comical, unsophisticated, yet dangerous, depiction of himself drawn by Johnson. Thirdly, Long's justificatory posture of self-defense produced vintage Long rhetoric, both substantively and stylistically.

Long confiscated the war metaphor Johnson had used to extol the virtues of President Roosevelt and transformed it to the administration's war on Long. He began: "It has been publicly announced that the White House orders of the Roosevelt administration have declared a war.... Mr. Johnson was apparently selected to make the lead-off speech in this White House charge...."[12] In turning Johnson's attack on Long into a declaration of war by the administration, Long was able to polarize the opposition, which he variously labeled "the Roosevelt administration," "that gang," "these birds," and "the kitchen cabinet." In this way, he could depict the opposition as formidable, cast himself as the little guy, and dismiss Johnson's role as a "gratuitous volunteer" by associating him with the NRA and the administration. Johnson's sincerity, which the general had spent considerable time demonstrating before attacking Long, was quickly and roundly debunked by Long, who alleged that Johnson was not the courageous patriot or loyal apostle that he purported to be; he was rather "the lately lamented, pampered ex-Crown Prince," and "one of those satellites loaned by Wall Street to the government." In a moment of vindication, not only did Long question Johnson's loyalties, but he accused Johnson of bitterness and malice toward the administration:

> The whole thing of Mr. Roosevelt as run under General Johnson became such a national scandal that Roosevelt had to let Johnson slide out as a scapegoat. I am told that the day the general had to go, when they had waited just as long as they would wait on him, he wanted to issue a blistering statement against Mr. Roosevelt, but they finally saddled him off because they didn't know but what Wall Street might want to lend him to some other President in the future, so he left without.

By portraying Johnson as the administration's ex-spokesman, Long was able to depict the general as insincere, bitter, and unimportant in the scheme of things. Long cast himself as a convenient scapegoat for the administration's woes in an attempt to elicit sympathy for being the lone opposition, his close association with Father Coughlin was not mentioned, and to command respect for being considered such a serious threat. He acclaimed: "They think that Huey Long is the cause of all their worry. They go gunning for me, but am I the cause of their misery?" Elsewhere, he told the radio audience that "they are in a rage at Huey Long." Of Roosevelt, Long commented: "He is one man that can't blame any of his troubles on Huey Long." Yet for rhetorical purposes, Long wanted to be considered the scapegoat of the White House.

In order to convince his national audience that he was a man of integrity and good will, Long refused to legitimize Johnson's charges against him by engaging in a rebuttal. In a dignified and uncharacteristic demagogic posture, Long demurred: "It will serve no useful purpose to our distressed people for me to call my opponents more bitter names than they called me. Even were I able, I have not the time to present my side of the argument and match them in profanity." Long elected to change the argumentative grounds; instead of focusing on personal legitimacy, he assumed a justificatory posture that allowed him to dwell on policy.

Specifically, Long accused FDR of not living up to his campaign promises. In a heartfelt passage, he lamented: "But no heart has ever been so saddened, no person's ambition was ever so blighted as was mine when I came to the realization that the President of the United States was not going to undertake what he said he would do, and what I knew to be necessary if the people of America were ever saved from calamity and misery." Long accused Roosevelt of embracing the same policy as had Hoover. In a moment of satire he told the radio audience that "in the kitchen, the same set of old cooks are back there fixing up the vittles and the grub for us that cooked up that mess under Hoover. There never has been any change in the seasoning." The Hoover comparison was particularly effective because Long had gained his reputation in the late 1920s by denouncing Hoover prosperity.[13] Finally, Long poked fun at the crazy alphabet system of the New Deal. The NRA, for instance, was "one of these New Deal schisms and isms," and just one of many "funny alphabetical combinations. So it was with other New Deal legislation, the PWA, WRA, GINS and every other flimsy combination that the country finds its affairs in business where no one can recognize it."

While Long roundly attacked New Deal legislation, he reserved most of his time for defending his own Share the Wealth plan, a plan designed "for the redistribution of wealth and for guaranteeing comfort and convenience to all humanity." He bolstered the worth of his plan by associating it with Roosevelt's political thought at the time of his election, the Bible, and democratic principles. Wanting to take full credit for the plan calling for the redistribution of wealth, Long stated: "I was one of the first men to say publicly, Mr. Roosevelt followed in my track a few months later, and said the same thing, we said that all of our troubles and woes were due to the fact that too few of our people owned too much of our wealth." After explaining that he had been advocating Share the Wealth since 1932, Long claimed that he and others had "convinced Mr. Franklin Delano Roosevelt that it was necessary that he announce and promise to the American people that in the event he were elected President of the United States he would pull down the size of the big man's fortune and guarantee something to every family." More pointedly, Long declared that "both Hoover and Roosevelt swallowed the Huey Long doctrine and never made one single complaint before the election occurred on November 8, 1932." That two presidents saw the rightness and importance of Long's plan allayed doubt about its demagogic overtones. That it had the backing of the Bible and the support of the founding fathers erased serious consideration over whether the plan was the working of a madman or a pied piper. In no uncertain terms, Long stated: "You will find that what I am advocating is the cornerstone on which nearly every religion since the beginning of man has been founded." To conclude the speech, Long reiterated: "What I have here stated to you will be found to be approved by the law of our Divine Maker. You will find it in the Book of Deuteronomy, from the twenty-fifth to the twenty-seventh chapters. You will find it in the writings of King Solomon. You will find it in the teachings of Christ." Why even the founders of the country saw the rightness, if not the righteousness, of Long's plan. "You will find that it was the exact provision of the contract of law of the Pilgrim fathers who landed at Plymouth in 1620," Long remarked. After quoting from the contract of the Pilgrim fathers, Long had presented sufficient evidence to claim: "In other words, these birds who are undertaking to tell you of the bad things I have done and am advocating, they have failed to note that I not only have the Bible back of me, but that this nation was founded by the Pilgrim Fathers, not to do just what I said, but to go and do all the balance, divide up equally every seventh year and cancel out all debts." It seems that Long was keenly aware that his shift from personal defense to defense of his Share the Wealth plan brought with it rhetorical demands for a proposition of policy—he needed to establish ideological credibility as well as personal credibility.

That Long elected to attack New Deal legislation confirms Lawrence Rosenfield's finding that apologia is not limited to statements of defense. That he chose to defend his policy directly and his character indirectly substantiates Ryan's thesis that apologia should be defined broadly as a speech in defense, a speech that defends policy and character. Long's ability to transcend the specific attacks on his character to bolster the credibility of his plan is evidence of a justificatory posture—one of the four postures outlined by B. L. Ware and Wil A. Linkugel that apologists assume. These authors suggested that justificative address "asks not only for understanding but also for approval." This precisely was Long's goal. The justificatory posture assumed by Long revealed the isomorphic relationship between Huey Long and his Share the Wealth plan. Long sought to purify his own image as a trustworthy, moral, sincere, wise, influential, and courageous politician by justifying his plan on biblical, democratic, humanitarian, and bipartisan grounds.   If the Share the Wealth Society was perceived as just and honorable, so was its author. For many years Long had been so closely identified with the issue of redistributing the wealth in this country that by 1934, it had become a personal crusade for him. He even referred to his policy in this speech, and on other occasions, as the "Huey Long doctrine." Paul C. Gaske has observed that one characteristic of demagogic rhetoric is that a single issue dominates and that the "demagogue is a symbolic figure, inextricably weaving himself and his issue so that they become synonomous." Gaske further noted that Long deliberately created the linkage between himself and his plan in an effort to capitalize on the frustrations people had experienced from the depression, hoping ultimately that this would sweep him into the White House.[14]

In adopting a justificatory posture, Long was able to deliver an apology that was not unlike other rhetorical situations. The very nature of a justificatory posture, which emphasizes transcendence and bolstering strategies, allows the apologist to establish the argumentative grounds, and does not confine the apologist to the agenda layed out by the accuser. In keeping with that posture, Long employed several of his well-worn appeals to further emphasize his embodiment of policy. First, he developed a striking similarity between his identification with the common man and Jesus' identification with the poor and destitute, between his vision for a heaven on earth and Jesus' message of life after death. Long was not merely attempting to be perceived as an authority figure, but as a God figure. Those who embraced the Share the Wealth plan deified Long. Long himself gave the impression that he possessed omniscient qualities.[15] In one such passage he said that: "They ordered a war on me because nearly four years ago I told Hoover's crowd, it won't do, and because three years ago I told Roosevelt and his crowd, it won't do. In other words, they are in a rage at Huey Long because I have had to say, I told you so." In sermonesque style, Long grew in stature by using a homespun analogy to illustrate a moral lesson:

> Well, they are like old David Crockett, who went out to hunt a possum. He saw there in the gleam of the moonlight, a possum in the top of the tree, going from limb to limb, so he shot, but he missed. He looked again and he saw the possum. He fired a second time and missed again. Soon he discovered that it was not a possum that he saw at all in the top of that tree; it was a louse in his own eyebrow. I do not make this illustration to do discredit to any of these distinguished gentlemen; I make it to show how often some of us imagine that we see great trouble being done to us by someone at a distance, when in reality all it may be is a fault in our own make-up.

Long's apology was even characterized by messianic overtones. This quality pervaded because Long was able to adopt a confrontational stance, project himself as a scapegoat, and use light-dark imagery to dramatize the agonistic scene. The following is an exemplary passage:

> I cannot deliver that promise to the youth of this land tonight, but I am doing my part. I am standing the blows; I am hearing the charges hurled at me from the four quarters of the country. . . . It is the same blare which I heard when I was undertaking to provide for the sick and the afflicted. When the youth of this land realizes what is meant and what is contemplated, the Billingsgate and the profanity of all of the Farleys and Johnsons in America cannot prevent the light of truth from hurling itself in understandable letters against the dark canopy of the sky.

At the same time, Long portrayed himself as a champion of the common man by using simple, direct language, a commonsense plan, homespun analogies, and by playing the administration's scapegoat. He portrayed himself as an authority figure by spending the better portion of his time carefully and calmly explaining all six planks of the Share the Wealth plan, a plan that, in giving hope to the poor, read like a sermon. Moreover, Long capitalized on his structural legitimacy — his role as a seasoned senator — to bolster his expertise. Throughout the speech Long reminded his listeners of his lengthy tenure and influence in the Senate. "There was one difference between Roosevelt and Hoover," Long quipped, "Hoover could not get the Congress to carry out the schemes he wanted to try because we managed to lick him on a roll call in the United States Senate time after time when he had both the Democratic and Republican leaders trying to put them over." Long's expertise as a lawyer was also noted: "Some people come to me for advice as a lawyer on trying to run their business."

Long's ability to repair his character by adopting a justificatory posture, a stance characterized by defending policy and becoming policy, transformed his apology into vintage Long rhetoric. The Louisiana senator thrived on attention and conflict. Johnson's harangue played into his hands, providing him with a forum for propagating the Huey Long doctrine. As one correspondent of Long's era noted: "Johnson and Roosevelt between them had managed to transform the Kingfisher from a clown into a real political menace." Earle Christenberry, a member of Long's staff, reported that Long's mail had averaged thirty-four thousand pieces a day prior to March 7, 1935, but that two days after the nationally broadcasted reply to Johnson's accusation his mail increased to sixty-nine thousand pieces, slightly more than double.[16] Johnson's accusatory rhetoric had given Long a national platform and the erstwhile Kingfish seized the opportunity to project not only himself but also his Share the Wealth plan into the limelight.

APOLOGIA FROM THE RADIO PRIEST

Not to be upstaged by the flashy Louisianian, the voice from the Shrine of the Little Flower in Royal Oak, Michigan, took to the airwaves six days later. Father Charles E. Coughlin, "the radio priest," was at his best when behind the microphone. Since 1926, Coughlin had used radio to help build the Shrine's outreach. The precursor of television evangelists, Coughlin was one of the first to make effective use of mass media. With charismatic zeal verging on the histrionic, Coughlin charmed multitudes. By 1930, he was the most popular voice on radio, commanding an estimated radio audience of approximately thirty million. An outspoken priest on secular issues, Coughlin's platform included denouncing socialism, corporate greed, prohibition, birth control, pacifism, internationalism, and the New Deal while supporting his own National Union for Social Justice.[17] Of course, it was precisely because Coughlin insisted on wielding his influence as a secular priest, a paradoxical role in the eyes of many, that General Johnson had accused him of "prostituting a holy office."

Father Coughlin's apologia of March 11, 1935, titled simply: "A Reply To General Johnson" by *Vital Speeches of the Day*,[18] would have been more appropriately titled: "An Eye for an Eye" to reflect the curious rhetorical choices Coughlin made. When juxtaposed with Huey Long's defense, its peculiarity is dramatized. Coughlin attempted to repair his character in ways uncharacteristic of a priest. Rather than don his priestly garb and mount his pulpit, Coughlin elected to refute each of Johnson's accusations by proclaiming his right to assume the role of a patriotic American citizen. Such a tactic, presumably, legitimized the scathing attack that was to follow — a message that scarcely resembled a sermon. Specifically, Coughlin's attempt to repair his character was flawed on three counts. First, contrary to Long's choice, Coughlin aimed to purify his character, not his policy. While not a poor choice in itself, the manner in which he attempted to regain credible status was; he concentrated on bolstering his personal legitimacy as a wise, good, and trustworthy citizen at the expense of supporting his structural legitimacy as a priest. Moreover, Coughlin attempted to grow in stature by pointedly denying each of Johnson's charges — a tactic that tended to further validate Johnson's accusations. Second, Coughlin spent a good deal of the speech roundly debunking Johnson. While this may be a questionable tactic for any priest, the method of attack most certainly made it a poor choice for Coughlin. The priest was both vindictive and forgiving, both angry and kind, which created a glaring inconsistency, and hence lack of credibility, in his accusations. Third, Coughlin did not maintain a consistent posture throughout the address, which gave the impression that Coughlin was defensive, uncomfortable, and ill-prepared to answer Johnson.

Coughlin, no doubt, constructed a defense of character speech because the general had reserved his most stinging criticism for undermining Coughlin's character. Johnson's attack on Father Coughlin was more serious than it was on Huey Long's because he scored Coughlin's religious scruples and his patriotic ties. Unlike Long, Coughlin did not perceive a great need to validate his ideological base. Early in the speech, Coughlin observed: "While you were content to vomit your venom upon my person and against my character, the American public is fully cognizant that not once did you dare attack the truths which I teach." Coughlin then quickly bolstered his policy. "I am not important nor are you. But the doctrines which I preach are important," he quipped. This was followed by two brief paragraphs on the aim of the National Union for Social Justice. The priest, however, did not seize this opportunity to transcend Johnson's accusations by expounding upon the importance of his program, as did Long.

Father Coughlin recognized the need to address his structural legitimacy since Johnson had subverted his priestly image. Coughlin justified his public statements on political issues by differentiating between his roles as priest and American citizen. Coughlin opened his speech by proclaiming his right to assume the role of a common citizen. He stated: "While always a priest I address you neither as the spokesman of the Catholic church nor as the representative of its Catholic following. I speak to you as American to American." In arguing this point, Coughlin asked his audience to consider that in times of crisis, a need for cooperation exists among a nation's people that transcends religious lines. "Together have we not worried through the dark years of this depression?" he implored. Moreover, sensitive to Johnson's ethnocentric indictment, Coughlin justified his role as an American citizen by defending his Americanism. "I am as much, if not more, of an American as you are or ever will be," he snapped. More significantly, Coughlin asserted that a calling to the priesthood did not imply a forfeiture of citizenship. He used a series of analogies to support this principle: "Does our concept of Americanism instruct the teacher that his place is always in the classroom? Does it teach the lawyer that his proper place is circumscribed by the walls of his office? Does it tell the barber that his activities are limited to the tools of his trade?" The analogies, however, failed to dispel the traditional belief that those invested in holy office have assumed more than an occupation. Theirs is an elevated role, an entire way of life. Hence, the clergy are held accountable for their actions in ways that other citizens are not. In the public mind, they do not have the luxury of changing roles as they might change hats. Nonetheless, Coughlin hoped to keep his priestly role intact and his holy office unscathed by asserting his right, albeit a questionable one, to assume two separate roles. With this difference established, the priest turned to repairing his character on personal grounds.

One of the ways in which Coughlin elected to defend himself against

Johnson's "vile" accusations was to engage in a vigorous and exhaustive denial of each accusation. The following passage is exemplary: "For a moment I plan to pause to answer the charges and insinuations which General Johnson so intemperately made against my person. First, he said: 'This political padre may or may not be an American citizen'. . . . Secondly, you categorically accuse me of breaking the religious vow of poverty. . . . Thirdly, you have cleverly insinuated that I was a modern Talleyrand. . . . Fourthly, compared to me Judas Iscariot is a piker . . . ." Such a strategy has an inherent weakness. To build one's case around the position of your opponent is to let him be master of the controversy. As Kenneth Burke has adroitly observed: "If someone said, for instance, 'I maintain that art is made of green cheese,' and you devoted your efforts to maintaining that it isn't, your own statements would be restricted by the nature of the question your opponent had forced upon you."[19] In treating Johnson's accusations separately, Coughlin spent too much time in his opponents' court and ran the risk of reinforcing any merit Johnson's charges might have carried with the audience.

Another way in which Coughlin attempted to purify his image was to portray himself as a wise, virtuous, and trustworthy individual. To bolster his expertise, Coughlin described himself as a seasoned social activist. "Where were you in 1930 and 1931 while we were advocating the New Deal. . . . Where were you in 1932 when our same group was advocating the election of Franklin D. Roosevelt. . . . Where were you in 1933 and 34 . . . ?" The repetitive phrase clearly established a contrast between the veteran Coughlin and the novice Johnson in dealing with the economic problems of the decade. To solidify this image, Coughlin reminded his audience: "Who originated the phrase, 'Roosevelt or Ruin?'" As though this were not enough to convince listeners of his competency on economic matters, the priest launched into a detailed account of how money was manufactured. This rather lengthy passage was designed to silence critics such as Johnson who believed that a priest could not understand the complex workings of money.

To complete the refurbished image of himself, Coughlin strengthened his morality and trustworthiness by associating himself with democratic values, by reminding his audience of his large constituency, and by drawing upon his priestly piety. Coughlin argued that although he had been labeled a "revolutionary" for preaching social justice, he was merely following in the tradition of Washington and Jefferson: "They, too, were called revolutionary," and wished only to "go back to the Constitution." His honorable intentions were reinforced, and Johnson's accusations were diffused, when Coughlin declared: "You have spewed your venom not upon me but upon an organization of people whose membership runs into the millions." The priest appeared virtuous, even holy, by associating himself with Christian heroes. Coughlin referred to himself as "Christ's soldier," classified himself indirectly with "the eleven faithful Apostles" and argued that like John the Baptist and the prophet Isaiah he, too, must risk his life to stand against the wrongdoers. Though anxious to be perceived as an American citizen and not a priest at the outset of his apology, by the time he attempted to cleanse a tarnished image, the two roles were inexorably mixed.

That Coughlin recalled his priestly image to repair his personal image was not only a contradiction from an earlier attempt to separate the two, but it created serious problems when the priest engaged in a rather lengthy vindictive attack against the general. Every bit as vicious as Johnson's accusations, Coughlin spewed his own invective against all facets of Johnson's character. As one dimension of Coughlin's accusatory stance, he, like Long, associated Johnson with a larger, more destructive, force. Since Coughlin claimed to have close ties with the Roosevelt administration, Johnson was not connected with the "kitchen cabinet" but with "Wallstreeters" and "international bankers." In creating a conspiracy between Johnson and the other evildoers of Wall Street, the priest created a justificative motive for lambasting Johnson. But unlike Long, Coughlin extended his attack by singling out Johnson for abuse. From the priest's tirade, three competing images of Johnson emerged: a clown, a casualty, and an evildoer. The general was depicted as "a kind chocolate soldier," and "a sweet prince of bombast" who "strutted upon the stage of this depression like a comic opera general." His rhetoric, Coughlin described as "Punch and Judy oratory" and a "cracked gramaphone record sqeaking the message of his master's voice." Johnson's dynamism debunked, Coughlin discredited the general's expertise. He was "the New Deal's greatest casualty," "a genial ghost," "a political corpse whose ghost has returned to haunt us." The priest's post mortem pronouncement was: "Of the dead let us speak kindly." Yet in the same breath, Johnson was declared the evil "Herod," and "a taskmaster of Bernard Manasses [sic] Baruch."[20] Johnson was to be feared for "preaching prostituted slogans" and "confusing people of my own faith." The general was not only devious but "insane" and "desperate" and content to "vomit" and "spew" his "venom" upon the priest. Johnson was at once a comical, antiquated, and evil foe.

Adding to the confusing image of the general that emerged from the vindictive dimension of Coughlin's accusations were words of forgiveness intermixed with the invective. Such statements as: "My friends, I appeal to your charity, to your good judgment, to your sense of social justice to bear no ill against Gen. Johnson. . . . Today he appears before us a figure to be pitied and not condemned" may have worked to reemphasize Coughlin's priestly role and create the impression that the priest was above such verbal sparring. But in light of the verbal thrashing Johnson had just received, such words could only be interpreted as contrived sincerity, sarcasm, or mockery. The contradictions were glaring. Coughlin condemned Johnson for "underslung vocabulary." Yet abusive language abounded in his own speech.

The radio priest, for all his rhetorical expertise, failed to transmit a clear image of himself or his foe. He, at times, absolved himself by denying each charge and differentiating between his role as an American citizen and his role as a priest, roles that in the final analysis could not be separately assumed. At other places, he justified his stance by bolstering his expertise, morality, and trustworthiness. At still other times, he vindicated himself through a feeble attempt at transcending the issue. But attempts at transcending the accusations ultimately failed because they were inconsistent with Coughlin's primary purpose, which was to beat Johnson at his own game. That inconsistency was epitomized in the priest's conclusion: "The fantastic fusillade of false charges which the genial ghost, the kind chocolate soldier and the sweet prince of bombast so engagingly publicized certainly were not potent enough to arouse my wrath. More important things must be accomplished. I dare not be diverted from my course by a red herring, even though it chances to be a dead one." The priest could not resist fighting Johnson with his own underslung vocabulary. Hence the speech does not end in a genuinely transcendent vein, but in a pretentious one. Ironically, Huey Long utilized a transcendent strategy by sermonizing to his audience on the goodness of his Share the Wealth plan, whereas Father Coughlin, who, as a priest, had the structural legitimacy to transcend such petty accusations and preach the goodness of the National Union for Social Justice, failed to utilize this stance with any effectiveness. Coughlin's initial decision to assume the role of an American citizen, and not that of a priest, prevented him from delivering a sermon, and, ultimately, created the contradictory stances and shifting strategies. Commenting on Coughlin's kind of rhetoric, critic Charles Henry Whittier has observed that the radio priest was "both example and warning of the ambiguities inherent in the merging of patriotism with religion, often a source of national strength and civic virtue but a source in perennial danger of distortion and abuse."[21]

CONCLUSION

The Johnson-Long-Coughlin exchange is worthy of critical appraisal because the speakers were heard by millions of radio listeners and, during the first two weeks in March, the speeches received far more newspaper coverage than any other topic. The encounter may have had the dual effect of prompting other critics who had been silenced by fear to speak out against the senator and the priest, as contended by the *New York Times*, and of raising public awareness, thus strengthening the Long and Coughlin movements significantly, as alleged by Alan Brinkley.[22]

Johnson's accusatory pronouncements are examples of rhetorical subversion. Integral to accusatory discourse seems to be a need for speakers to strengthen their own credibility before attacking their foes. In this instance, at least, Johnson built his *ethos* before attacking his opponents' images. Additionally, Johnson's attack on policy was subordinate to a larger attack on personal credibility. This may be true whenever the speaker's goal goes beyond an attempt to defeat a political idea because such a person outreaches Aristotle's deliberative genre and, as Noreen Kruse has observed, "borrows principles from both forensic and epideictic rhetoric."[23] In undermining the ethos of Long and Coughlin, Johnson developed two images of each: the first one, a depiction of harmless and well-intentioned people, mandated the development of the second, that of two sinister pied pipers, because if these two luminaries were not exposed people might not appreciate the danger of their kinds of rhetoric. Long and Coughlin's apologetic responses to Johnson's accusations were examples of rhetorical purification. Long's apologia can be adjudged strategically superior to Coughlin's because the senator used transcendent strategies inventively, diverting attention from the demagogic qualities Johnson alleged he possessed and focusing upon a plan that appealed favorably to the nation's dispossessed. Long's justificatory posture of self-defense allowed him to present himself as a man of integrity and good will. He justified his plan on biblical, democratic, humanitarian, and bipartisan grounds. Father Coughlin, on the other hand, endeavored to refute each of Johnson's accusations and hurl his own invective at the general--a problematic strategy for a Catholic priest. In this case, the accused enacted the image of himself that his accuser depicted.

NOTES

[1]General Hugh S. Johnson, "Pied Pipers," *Vital Speeches of the Day* (March 11, 1935): 354-60.

[2]See Noreen Wales Kruse, "The Scope of Apologetic Discourse: Establishing Generic Parameters," *Southern Speech Communication Journal* 46 (1981): 278-91; and Halford Ross Ryan, "*Kategoria* and *Apologia*: On Their Rhetorical Criticism As A Speech Set," *Quarterly Journal of Speech* 68 (1982): 254-61; and Lawrence W. Rosenfield, "A Case Study In Speech Criticism: The Nixon-Truman Analog," *Speech Monographs* 35 (1968): 435-50.

[3]Aristotle, *Rhetoric*, translated by Lane Cooper (Englewood Cliffs, N.J.: Prentice-Hall, 1932), 1358b. Aristotle wrote that the elements of forensic speaking are accusation and defense and that such speeches are concerned

with past fact. See, for instance, Ryan and Rosenfield who conceptualize accusatory and apologetic discourse as forensic rhetoric.

[4]Ibid., 1366b, 1358b, 1368a,

[5]Walter R. Fisher, "A Motive View of Communication," *Quarterly Journal of Speech* 56 (1970): 132.

[6]Ibid., 138.

[7]Frederick J. Kauffeld, *Accusing, Proposing, and Advising: The Strategic Grounds for Presumption and the Burden of Proof,* (Ph.D. diss. University of Wisconsin, 1986), p. 94.

[8]The term "structural legitimacy" means the legitimacy that adheres to the person from the office he holds. See David Easton, *A System Analysis of Political Life* (New York: John Wiley, 1965) and Jackson Harrell, B. L. Ware, and Wil A. Linkugel, "Failure of Apologia in American Politics: Nixon on Watergate," *Speech Monographs* 42 (1975): 247.

[9]*New York Times*, March 6, 1935, Sec. L, p. 7; Sec. C, p. 18; Arthur Krock, editorial, *New York Times*, March 6, 1935, Sec. C, p. 18; editorial, *Washington Post*, March 6, 1935, p. 8.

[10]Fisher, "A Motive View of Communication," p. 136.

[11]B. L. Ware and Wil A. Linkugel, "They Spoke In Defense of Themselves: On The Generic Criticism of Apologia," *Quarterly Journal of Speech* 59 (1973): 280. These authors identify "transcending" as one of the four factors of verbal self defense. They explain that "transcending strategies . . . psychologically move the audience away from the particulars of the charge at hand in a direction toward some more abstract, general view of [the rhetor's] character."

[12]Huey Long, "Our Blundering Government and Its Spokesman--HughJohnson,"*Vital Speeches of the Day* (March 25, 1935): 391-97.

[13]James MacGregor Burns, *Roosevelt: The Lion and the Fox* (New York: Harcourt, Brown and World, 1956), p. 212.

[14]Rosenfield, "A Case Study in Speech Criticism: The Nixon- Truman Analog," p. 449; Ware and Linkugel, "They Spoke in Defense of Themselves: On The Generic Criticism of Apologia," p. 283; Paul C. Gaske, "Huey

Pierce Long, Jr.," in *American Orators of the Twentieth Century* edited by Bernard K. Duffy and Halford R. Ryan (Westport: Greenwood Press, 1987), p. 294.

[15]Gaske, "Huey Pierce Long, Jr.," p. 295; Charles Kauffman, *A Theory of Demagoguery*, (M. A. thesis, University of Kansas, 1974), p. 142.

[16]Gaske, quoted in "Huey Pierce Long, Jr.," p. 293; Ernest G. Bormann, "A Rhetorical Analysis of the National Radio Broadcasts of Senator Huey P. Long," *Speech Monographs* 24 (1957): 254.

[17]Charles Henry Whittier, "The Reverend Charles E. Coughlin," *American Orators of the Twentieth Century*, pp. 75-76.

[18]Charles Coughlin, "A Reply to General Johnson," *Vital Speeches of the Day* (March 25, 1935): 368-91.

[19]Kenneth Burke, *The Philosophy of Literary Form* (Berkeley: University of California Press, 1973), p. 228.

[20]Bernard Baruch's middle name was not "Manasses," but "Mannes." Coughlin, we surmise, deliberately misprounced his name in order that auditors might conjure up the image of the evil ruler in the Bible with the same name.

[21]Whittier, "The Reverend Charles E. Coughlin," pp. 78-79.

[22]See *New York Times*, March 6, 1935, Sec. C, p. 18; Sec. L, p. 7; and Alan Brinkley, *Voices of Protest, Huey Long, Father Coughlin and The Great Depression* (New York: Vintage Books, 1983), pp. 7, 291.

[23]Noreen Wales Kruse, *The Eide of Apologetic Discourse: An Aristotelian Rhetorical-Poetic Analysis*, (Ph.D. diss. University of Iowa, 1979), p. 4.

INFORMATION SOURCES ON THE SPEECH SET

Hugh S. Johnson's Accusation

Johnson, Hugh S. "Pied Pipers." *Vital Speeches of the Day* 1 (1935): 354-60. See also the *New York Times*, March 5, 1935, p. 10.

Huey Long's Apology

Long, Huey. "Our Blundering Government and Its Spokesman--Hugh Johnson." *Vital Speeches of the Day* 1 (1935): 391-97. See also the *New York Times*, March 8, 1935, p. 16; and the *Congressional Record*, 74th Congress, 1st session (March 12, 1935): 3436-39.

Charles E. Coughlin's Apology

Coughlin, Charles E. "A Reply to General Johnson." *Vital Speeches of the Day* 1 (1935): 368-91. See also the *New York Times*, March 12, 1935, p. 13; and in Charles E. Coughlin, *A Series of Lectures on Social Justice*. Royal Oak, Michigan: The Radio League of the Little Flower, 1935.

Selected Bibliography

Abernathy, Elton. "Huey Long: Oratorical 'Wealth Sharing'" *Southern Speech Communication Journal* 21 (1955): 87-102.

Brinkley, Alan. *Voices of Protest: Huey Long, Father Coughlin, and The Great Depression*. New York: Vintage Books, 1983.

Bormann, Ernest G. "A Rhetorical Analysis of the National Radio Broadcasts of Senator Huey P. Long." *Speech Monographs* 24 (1957): 237-57.

Gaske, Paul C. "The Analysis of Demagogic Discourse: Huey Long's 'Every Man a King' Address." In *American Rhetoric from Roosevelt to Reagan*, edited by Halford Ross Ryan. Prospect Heights, IL.: Waveland Press, 1983.

___. "Huey Pierce Long, Jr." In *American Orators of the Twentieth Century, Critical Studies and Sources*, edited by Bernard K. Duffy and Halford Ross Ryan. Westport: Greenwood Press, 1987.

Kauffman, Charles. *A Theory of Demagoguery*. M. A. thesis, University of Kansas, 1974.

Whittier, Charles Henry. "The Reverend Charles E. Coughlin." In *American Orators of the Twentieth Century, Critical Studies and Sources*, edited by Bernard K. Duffy and Halford R. Ryan. Wesport: Greenwood Press, 1987.

Prime Minister Stanley Baldwin vs. King Edward VIII

Halford R. Ryan

The Hollywood-like pathos of a king who sacrificed his throne for the woman he loved is a romance well known on both sides of the Atlantic. What is not so well understood is the nature of the spoken word that accounted for King Edward's forced departure. This rhetorical transaction is a study in the persuasive ability of Prime Minister Stanley Baldwin to prepare Parliament and British public opinion for the abdication of their monarch in 1936.

Baldwin's accusation is an illustrative example of how an accuser can manipulate a rhetorical situation to suit his persuasive purpose. Baldwin made two informal or preliminary accusations to get public opinion behind him before he actually delivered his formal and final accusation; thus, he practically guaranteed his success. Concomitantly, the prime minister did not allow Edward to deliver an apology at the propitious moment, but rather forced Edward to deliver his defense only after the abdication was a *fait accompli*, thus minimizing any efficacy Edward's apology might have had with the nation and Parliament.

Stanley Baldwin disliked the king's dalliance with Mrs. Wallis Simpson and he was against the king's proposed marriage to her; consequently, he eventually created a rhetorical situation wherein he asked "Parliament to accept a position which had resulted from a development in which he, almost unaided, had played a leading part."[1] Baldwin had sincerely attempted to persuade the king not to marry Mrs. Simpson, but when Edward remained intractable, Baldwin became eager for the king to abdicate.

On Tuesday, December 1, 1936, Bishop Blunt of Bradford delivered before a Diocesan Conference a mild allusion to the king's apparent disregard for Christian morals and virtues. Although Baldwin had nothing to do with Blunt's address, Geoffrey Dawson of *The Times* inferred that the Bishop's speech was sanctioned by the Government, and that it was therefore meant to signal the press to prepare the country for abdication. Heretofore most Britons were unaware of the crisis, inasmuch as both

Baldwin and the press had been reluctant to reveal the factual implications of the King's proposed marriage. As a result of the Bishop's address and the mistaken belief by the press that the address was sanctioned by Baldwin, on Thursday, December 3, 1936, "Fleet Street lifted the ban which had weighed it down perhaps too long."[2]

THE PRIME MINISTER'S ACCUSATIONS

On Thursday, December 3, Baldwin capitalized on these developments. He moved the rhetorical situation toward the propitious moment — the Greeks called it *kairos* (see Glossary) — by responding to a prearranged Clement Attlee question concerning the possibility of a morganatic marriage (in which Wallis would become Queen but none of their children could ever become monarch). Edward had requested that the Cabinet consider his morganatic compromise. The Cabinet considered then refused it. In his first preliminary accusation, Baldwin used Edward's morganatic marriage proposal to indict Edward's policy and character. Implicit in Edward's morganatic proposal was the obvious inference that he would go to any length, even to exclude his children from the throne, to have Mrs. Simpson as his wife. Baldwin employed this inference to indict the king's character, while declaring that such a marriage would be unorthodox and unconstitutional and that the King's morganatic marriage proposal therefore was impossible:

> In view of widely circulated suggestions as to certain possibilities in the event of the King's marriage, I think it is advisable to make a statement. Suggestions have appeared in certain organs of the Press yesterday, and again to-day, that if the King decided to marry, his wife need not become Queen. These ideas are without foundation. There is no such thing as what is called morganatic marriage known to our law. . . .His Majesty's Government are not prepared to introduce such legislation. . . .I have felt it right to make this statement before the House adjourns to-day, in order to remove a widespread misunderstanding. At this moment I have no other statement to make.[3]

Baldwin used his first accusation to coalesce a bewildered public opinion behind him by demonstrating to the nation and Parliament that the king's policy was unacceptable. Lewis Broad, writing about the abdication twenty-five years later, recognized the efficacy of the Prime Minister's strategy: "Baldwin had timed his statement to produce the maximum effect against the King." Concomitantly, Baldwin barred Edward from addressing his people. Edward had wanted to defend himself after Baldwin's accusation because he believed he could win the people to him by addressing them in a FDR-style fireside chat. Baldwin and the Cabinet refused to give him permission to deliver an apology when it perhaps could have purified the image that Baldwin had affirmed against Edward. The Cabinet rightly reasoned that the king could not expect them "to sanction an appeal over their heads to the people." Edward dropped the matter and even granted, in retrospect, that he could not have rallied behind him all of England and the Dominions.[4]

Over the weekend, public opinion swung behind Baldwin. His persuasive strategy had apparently worked. The proof came on Monday, December 7: "Members of Parliament returned to their place a Westminster fortified by weekend contact with their constituents. They had left for their constituencies uncertain about public opinion. They had returned, particularly from the Midlands and the North, with doubts resolved."[5] Another sign of Baldwin's success was that MPs shouted down Winston Churchill when he tried on Monday to speak against Baldwin's management of the abdication crisis. On Monday, Baldwin also delivered his second preliminary accusation in order to move the rhetorical situation toward the *kairos*. He stressed the stasis of definition to demonstrate that the King would decide his fate. This strategy neatly covered Baldwin's tracks by differentiating his public passive role in the crisis from the king's active role. In reality, the roles were reversed. Although Baldwin had forced the issue over the king's marriage, he skillfully implied that the whole affair was Edward's responsibility, indicating in his accusation that it was the king who must act and only then could he, Baldwin, react:

> In considering this whole matter it has always been, and remains, the earnest desire of the Government to afford his Majesty the fullest opportunity of weighing a decision which invoves so directly his own feature happiness and the interests of his subjects....The subject [of the King's marriage] had therefore been for some time in the King's mind, and as soon as His Majesty has arrived at a conclusion as the course he desires to take, he will no doubt communicate it to his Governments in this country and the Dominions. It will then be for those Governments to decide what advice, if any, they would feel it their duty to tender to him in the light of his conclusion.[6]

These preliminary accusations placed the king exactly where the prime minister wanted him. Baldwin had first turned the fact of the morganatic marriage proposal back on Edward by affirming a new definition of his character and then had defined the marriage-or-throne issue solely as the King's choice. Baldwin had engineered the propitious moment and he delivered his formal accusation against the king on Thursday, December 10, 1936.

The exigence that Baldwin would change through accusatory discourse was Edward's insistence on marrying Mrs. Simpson. Edward either would be king without Wallis Simpson as his wife or he would not be king at all. The audience with the legal power to accept or reject Baldwin's abdication bill was Parliament, although the prime minister was not unmindful of British public opinion. Baldwin faced two interesting constraints. First, he had to present an accusation that would portray a paradoxical image: it must be strong enough to warrant Edward's abdication but weak enough not to destroy the nation's faith in the institution of the monarchy. Second, Baldwin had to exculpate himself of any responsibility in forcing the king off his throne.

Accordingly, Baldwin stressed the stasis of fact for the marriage proposal and alluded to the stasis of definition for the King's character. This strategy focused the mediating audience's attention on Edward the man (and not on the monarchy) and also placed the onus of the crisis on Edward (and not on Baldwin). In an extended classical *narratio* (see Glossary), the prime minister sketched his dealings with his king. In their first meeting, on October 20, at Baldwin's request, the prime minister had deftly alluded to Mrs. Simpson's upcoming divorce and to factual problems it would cause the king. Then Baldwin inserted a subtle attack on the nature of the king's policy, reminding Edward then and the audience now of Edward's marriage policy: "The importance of its [the Crown's] integrity is, beyond all question, far greater than it ever has been." He wanted the audience to doubt Edward's motives in desiring Mrs. Simpson over the crown. The narration of the October meeting continued with interesting details until Baldwin administered the *coup de grace*, squarely placing the marriage proposal, with its attendant character implications, on Edward's shoulders and portraying himself as the innocent bystander: "He said, 'I am going to marry Mrs. Simpson, and I am prepared to go.' I said, 'Sir, that is most grievous news, and it is impossible for me to make any comment on it to-day.'" Lest the audience miss the point, Baldwin reiterated that same theme later in his speech:

> When we had finished that conversation, I pointed out that the possible alternatives had been narrowed, and that it really had brought him into the position that he would be placed in a grievous situation between two conflicting loyalties in his own heart--either complete abandonment of the project on which his heart was set, and remaining King, or doing as he intimated to me that he was prepared to do, in the talk which I have reported, going, and later on contracting that marriage, if it were possible.

Even later in his speech, Baldwin was at pains to demonstrate that the crisis was all the king's responsibility: "He told me his intentions, and he has never wavered from them. I want the house to understand that. . . .My efforts during these last days have been directed. . . .in trying to help him make the choice which he has not made."[7]

The speech was a success. Even Baldwin's political foe, Lord Beaverbrook, understood its efficacy: "It was the picture of a loyal, honest and humble English gentleman who had striven to serve his King and had suffered much in his strivings. He let it be inferred that the difficulties were created by the King and the King alone." Broad concluded that Baldwin had accomplished his two-pronged goal of saving the monarchy and himself:

> The abdication speech was an example of the perfection of Baldwin's rhetoric. It was a report on events that have gone to the making of history, although it cannot pass for history. Rather was it an adaptation of the facts designed to produce an effect on those who heard and on those who, later, were to read, to induce universal acceptance of the King's abdication with the minimum disturbance in the body politic, and to extinguish controversy and to preserve the Crown from the damaging consequences of public conflict.

Robert Sencourt observed that "As the tributes came in from the Empire he [Baldwin] basked in a radiance of gratitude and praise. He deserved it."[8] Baldwin had persuaded the audience within the constraints of the rhetorical situation which he had created. By stressing the stasis of the fact of the king's marriage proposal and only alluding to the stasis of definition for the king's character, he persuaded his audience to accept the abdication bill without damaging the integrity of the monarchy.

KING EDWARD VIII's APOLOGIA

As one will recall, Baldwin and the Cabinet had not allowed Edward to deliver an apology at the propitious moment. From a technical standpoint, then, one might opine that when Edward delivered his speech, it was not an apologia, since there was no audience that could mediate change. Edward was merely the Duke of Windsor and his brother was already King George VI. On the other hand, Robert Smith believed Edward's speech was an apologia, and Edward believed he was delivering an apologia: "Some in the Government looked coldly upon the idea of my supplying an epilogue to a drama upon which the curtain had already descended. And even my mother tried to dissuade me. But I was determined to speak. I did not propose to leave Great Britain like a fugitive in the night." Edward sought to purify through apologetic discourse Baldwin's impugned image against his policy and character. The motivation for Edward's response was self-actualization, which would "show a tendency to live according to his own standards, rather than society's."[9] The King's motives demonstrated he wanted to live according to his own desires by choosing his wife over Britain's demands on him as its dutiful monarch.

Edward admitted the stasis of fact, and he chose to organize the language of his apology around the stasis of definition. His posture was explanatory because he assumed "that if the audience understands his motives, actions, beliefs, or whatever, they will be unable to condemn him." Thus he told his audience, "I want you to understand that in making up my mind I did not forget the Country or the Empire, which, as Prince of Wales and lately as King, I have for 25 years tried to serve." He explained to his worldwide radio audience that he could not "carry the heavy burden of responsibility and to discharge my duties as King, as I would wish to do, without the help and support of the woman I love."[10]

When Edward's and Baldwin's speeches are compared, one can perceive why Edward's apology was not successful. Having admitted the stasis of fact and having declined to discuss the stasis of quality for his policy and character, Edward could only argue the stasis of definition in order to persuade his audience. He was unable to do that because, in the British value system, the monarch has a duty to the nation which transcends wants and desires of ordinary human beings: "The hard fact is, of course, that moral standards expected of men in high places were sterner then than today, and Mr. Baldwin judged the British temper better than did his sovereign." No amount of argument on the definition of his policy and character could effectively purify them. Even though Edward said it "would in the end be best for all" for him to abdicate, his subjects did not accept his placing personal desires above duty. As Christopher Hibbert said, "once the King had gone, few sincerely regretted his departure." Broad noted there "was no general approbation" for Edward's reference to the woman he loved. Sencourt noted that "the general feeling was that it was better he should go." British reaction was predominantly unfavorable. Frances Donaldson noted "the speed at which the British forgot the ex-King," and she supplied a representative response from a loyal subject: "We loved him. We would have drawn our swords for him. And then, by God, *didn't he let us down*!!"[11] The King's explanatory posture on the stasis of definition failed to propitiate or to mitigate his countrymen's condemnation of his policy and character.

CONCLUSION

Stanley Baldwin did not deliver a "one-shot" speech to Parliament on December 10, 1936. Rather, he created that favorable rhetorical situation by moving and molding public opinion with his two preliminary accusations so that when he delivered his formal *kategoria* at the *kairos* his success was assured. Baldwin's winning rhetorical strategy was revealed by a close examination of what classical stases he argued and why. By focusing on the fact of the morganatic marriage proposal and merely alluding to the concomitant negative definition of the king's character, the prime minister persuaded Parliament and the nation that Edward should go without damaging the monarchy itself.

Baldwin's withholding from Edward the advantage of the king's delivering an apologia at the *kairos* severely weakened Edward's opportunity to present his case. Edward's apologia was thereby limited to arguing the stasis of definition. His explanation of his self-actualized motive did not persuade his British audience to condone or exculpate his selfish policy and character.

NOTES

[1]J. Lincoln White, *The Abdication of Edward VIII* (London: George Routledge and Sons, 1937), p. 89.

[2]Hector Bolitho, *King Edward VIII: An Intimate Biography* (New York: Literary Guild of America, 1937), p. 292.

[3]White, *The Abdication of Edward VIII*, pp. 51-52.

[4]Lewis Broad, *The Abdication: Twenty-Five Years After* (London: Frederick Muller, 1961), pp. 121, 118; Duke of Windsor, *A King's Story* (New York: Putnam's, 1947), p. 384.

[5]Broad, *The Abdication*, p. 139.

[6]"Cabinet and the King," *The Times,* December 8, 1936, p. 7.

[7]"Mr. Baldwin's Speech," *The Times,* December 11, 1936, pp. 7-8.

[8]Lord Beaverbrook, *The Abdication of King Edward VIII*, edited by A. J. P. Taylor (New York: Atheneum, 1966), p. 85; Broad, *The Abdication*, p. 149; Robert Sencourt, *The Reign of Edward VIII* (London: Anthony Gibs and Philips, 1962), pp. 141-42.

[9]Robert W. Smith, "Rhetoric in Crisis: The Abdication Address of Edward VIII," *Speech Monographs* 30 (1963): 337; Duke of Windsor, *A King's Story*, p. 407; Noreen W. Kruse, "Motivational Factors in Non-Denial Apologia," *Central States Speech Journal* 28 (1977): 15.

[10]B. L. Ware and Wil A. Linkugel, "They Spoke in Defense of Themselves: On the Generic Criticism of Apologia," *Quarterly Journal of Speech* 59 (1973): 282; White, *The Abdication of Edward VIII*, p. 151.

[11]J. Byran III and Charles B. V. Murphy, *The Windsor Story* (New York: William Morrow, 1979), p. 316; Christopher Hibbert, *Edward the Uncrowned King* (New York: St. Martin's Press, 1972), p. 139; Broad, *The*

Abdication, p. 168; Sencourt, *The Reign of Edward VIII*, p. 206; Frances Donaldson, *Edward VIII* (Philadelphia: J. B. Lippincott, 1974), p. 319. Italics in original.

INFORMATION SOURCES ON THE SPEECH SET

Prime Minister Baldwin's Accusations

Trained newspaper stenographers took down MP's speeches delivered in Parliament because voice recordings were forbidden; therefore, *The Times* contains authoritative texts of Baldwin's accusations.

For the first speech delivered on Thursday, December 3, 1936, see "Mr. Baldwin's Statement," *The Times*, December 4, 1936, p. 8.

For the second accusation delivered on Monday, December 7, 1936, see "Cabinet and the King," *The Times*, December 8, 1936, p. 7.

For the final speech delivered on Thursday, December 10, 1936, see "Mr. Baldwin's Speech," *The Times*, December 11, 1936, pp. 7-8.

King Edward VIII's Apology

The authentic text of Edward's apologia, which was broadcast worldwide, December 11, 1936, from Windsor Castle, is contained in Robert W. Smith, "Rhetoric in Crisis: The Abdication Address of Edward VIII," *Speech Monographs* 30 (1963): 338-39.
A voice recording of Edward's apology is available: "Edward VIII," *Great British Speeches*, Vol. Four 1867-1940, Caedmon Cassette, CDL 52065 (2c).

Selected Bibliography

Bolitho, Hector. *King Edward VIII: An Intimate Biography*. New York: Literary Guild of America, 1937.

Broad, Lewis. *The Abdication: Twenty-Five Years After*. London: Frederick Muller, 1961.

Bryan, J., III, and Murphy, Charles G. V. *The Windson Story*. New York: William Morrow, 1979.

Ching, James C. "Stanley Baldwin's Speech on the Abdication of Edward VIII." *Quarterly Journal of Speech* 42 (1956): 163-69.

Donaldson, Frances. *Edward VIII*. Philadelphia: J. B. Lippincott, 1974.

Duke of Windsor. *A King's Story*. New York: Putnam's, 1947.

Hibbert, Christopher. *Edward the Uncrowned King*. New York: St. Martin's Press, 1972.

Lord Beaverbrook. *The Abdication of King Edward VIII*. Edited by A. J. P. Taylor. New York: Atheneum, 1966.

Ryan, Halford Ross. "Baldwin vs. Edward VIII: A Case Study in *Kategoria* and *Apologia*." *Southern Speech Communication Journal* 49 (1984): 125-34.

Sencourt, Robert. *The Reign of Edward VIII*. London: Anthony Gibs and Philips, 1962.

Smith, Robert W. "Rhetoric in Crisis: The Abdication Address of Edward VIII." *Speech Monographs* 30 (1963): 335-39.

White, J. Lincoln. *The Abdication of Edward VIII*. London: George Routledge and Sons, 1937.

President Franklin D. Roosevelt and the "Purge"

G. Jack Gravlee

After his overwhelming 1936 reelection landslide, Franklin D. Roosevelt faced a series of setbacks in the 1937 Congress with his "Court-packing" plan the most notable victim. Then, in 1938, he attempted to defeat in Democratic primaries selected members of Congress from his own party who had opposed New Deal legislation. The president unconvincingly protested that his actions, quickly labeled a "purge" by the press, were neither vindictive nor related to the Supreme Court issue. Pundits speculated that the Roosevelt magic had vanished, along with a considerable amount of Democratic common sense, and that his political fortunes were beyond recovery.

Although never Roosevelt's word, the "purge" metaphor summoned images of massacres of former compatriots by Fascist and Communist dictators. The term attained a life of its own, was employed widely in the national press, seemingly licensed opponents of all persuasions to use comparable hyperbole, and probably became FDR's greatest obstacle by accelerating emotions considerably beyond his control. The president was branded a "dictator" and a "carpetbagger"; his visit was called a federal invasion, a declaration of war, an "intimidation and terrorism"; his goal was to promote "yes men," "rubber stamps," "Charlie McCarthys"; his actions could cancel states' rights, constitutional rights, civil and religious liberties due to "monocracy," and foster "one-man rule," "The C.I.O., John L. Lewis, and the Communists."[1]

The primary campaigns of 1938 did not conveniently provide a single speech of accusation followed by a single speech of defense. Electioneering never behaves in so orderly a fashion. In the summer, Roosevelt embarked on a western speaking tour that seemed to signal his serious involvement in Democratic primaries, only to be followed by a leisurely holiday of cruising and fishing off the Galapagos Islands before returning for more campaigning in the South. The period was unlike any previous FDR campaign. He vacillated between dedication and indifference, between intensity and relaxation, between "purging" and ignoring. Confusion still prevails as to why he visited some areas and not others, why he castigated some Congressmen and not others. This study will concentrate on three individuals who were Roosevelt targets in 1938: Senator Walter F. George of Georgia, Representative John J. O'Connor of New York, and Senator Millard E. Tydings of Maryland.

THE PRESIDENT'S ACCUSATIONS

With the primaries some two months away, Roosevelt's Fireside Chat, June 24, 1938, without reference to any candidates, established an accusation of policy premised on definition and jurisdiction. He described "two schools of thought, generally classified as liberal and conservative." The liberal school recognized that new conditions called for new remedies that could be developed under "our present form of government." The conservative school, dependent solely on the private sector, would guarantee a return to the governmental inaction of the 1920s. FDR hoped that the voter would ask the policy question: "To which of these general schools of thought does the candidate belong?" He added an accusation of character premised on definition and quality. He defined the true liberal as a believer in "democratic, representative government" as opposed to the "wild man" who embraces "Communism" that is as dangerous "as Fascism itself." He was concerned about candidates who would ignore substantive issues in favor of the "misuse of my own name," "personal attack," "appeals to prejudice," suppression of "individual liberty," all under the "pretense of patriotism." He warned the populace against "yes, but" reactionaries who articulated general support for progressive policies but who consistently opposed specific progressive measures.

Roosevelt's language was deceptive concerning future action. He seemed to say that he would not participate in Democratic primaries. But, the key words in this disclaimer were "as President." For he apparently reserved the right to speak as the leader of the Democratic Party in defense of the 1936 Democratic platform and in situations where "clear-cut" issues surfaced between competing Democratic candidates. This subtle distinction likely eluded radio listeners at the time and could have provoked ill feeling when followed by his direct involvement in selected primaries.[2]

Roosevelt hosted two press conferences and presented four speeches that denounced directly, or by implication, the three Congressmen:

Senator George:	August 10,	speech at Warm Springs, Georgia
	August 11,	speech at Barnesville, Georgia
Rep. O'Connor:	August 16,	press conference at Washington, D.C.
	August 23,	press conference at Hyde Park, New York

Senator Tydings: August 15, speech at Washington, D.C.
                          August 16, press conference at Washington, D.C.
                          September 5, speech at Denton, Maryland

Roosevelt's opposition to Walter George, delivered in the senator's home state, left no doubt as to who was supported and who was opposed. At a luncheon of the Warm Springs Foundation for victims of infantile paralysis, August 10, the president addressed an audience primarily of children with few residents of Georgia in attendance. It was a short, ceremonial, nonpolitical greeting to the patients until he recognized "a gentleman who I hope will be the next senator from this state, Lawrence Camp," federal district attorney from Atlanta. The president's casual endorsement of Camp was his first open attempt to oust a sitting Democratic senator.

The following day FDR was in Barnesville, ostensibly for the purpose of dedicating a rural electrification project. It was the most dramatic moment of the 1938 campaign. It perhaps will remain unique in American political and rhetorical history. The president of the United States traveled to a tiny rural hamlet to read out of the party the senior senator from Georgia, seated on the same platform, who had served the state for sixteen years. Ralph McGill, of the *Atlanta Constitution*, called it the "greatest and most thrilling political spectacle in Georgia's history." The president's accusatory discourse introduced an issue of policy premised on the stasis of fact: The South is the "nation's No. 1 economic problem." His source, a recently released sixty-page National Emergency Council report, written by "distinguished" and "broadminded" Southerners, detailed the region's difficulties in fifteen different categories. Inasmuch as these monumental problems required federal action, he contended that the South must send liberal legislators to Washington to enact solutions. Then his accusation shifted to one of character premised on the stases of fact and quality. "My old friend," Walter George, was not a liberal, did not "speak the same language" as the current administration, and did not deserve votes merely because he was Georgia's senior senator. The question should be one of quality. Was he willing to stand up and fight for those broad objectives of his party and, "in his heart," did he believe in those objectives? Offering no specific elaboration, the president condemned the senator's legislative record. Anticipating the "carpetbagger" challenge, Roosevelt recalled that, with his second home in Warm Springs, he was an "adopted son" and Georgia was his "other state." Although unsuccessful in curtailing future objections, he introduced the jurisdictional stasis in defense of his own character.[3]

The Barnesville address was the most vigorous in content and delivery of all the purge speeches. Roosevelt referred to senator George three times by name, once as the senior senator, and a number of additional times as "my friend." His recommendation on behalf of George's opponent included the name of Lawrence Camp only twice near the conclusion of the speech even though the district attorney probably was not well known to many voters.[4] Perhaps the accusation, geared more to George's destruction than Camp's elevation, was too blunt and negative for a liberal program that supposedly espoused humane values. Even so, the president and the senator had a mutual respect that did not seem to prevail with other purge targets. Roosevelt had taken George seriously, had called him "a gentleman and a scholar," and had asked publicly for his continued personal friendship.

Roosevelt's opposition to Representative John O'Connor, from New York's sixteenth congressional district in Manhattan, assumed an entirely different strategy. He delivered no speeches against O'Connor, but communicated his resistance in sketchy and fragmented remarks during two separate press conferences. His accusation attacked O'Connor's anti-New Deal actions and his character with emphasis on the stases of fact and quality. On August 16, in response to a question concerning the congressman, he read an editorial that characterized O'Connor as "one of the most effective obstructionists in the lower house" who "labors to tear down New Deal strength" and to "pickle New Deal legislation." On August 23, again in response to a question, he condemned O'Connor's simultaneous entry into both the Democrat and Republican primaries as a matter of morality in destroying the original intent of the electoral system.[5] Thus, he dispatched the New Yorker in two short excerpts with only a single favorable mention of his opponent, James Fay.

Roosevelt's tactics with O'Connor differed considerably from those used against George. Even though from different congressional districts, the president and the representative both were New Yorkers which neutralized any response about outside intrusion into state politics. FDR made no speeches and embarked on no trips into New York for the expressed purpose of unseating O'Connor. Unlike speeches, press conferences were neither broadcast nor published verbatim in the newspapers. Accordingly, the president's words and actions, reported secondhand if at all, did not appear to be unfair or heavy-handed. Those voters in the sixteenth district who were familiar with the accusation would have found it simple, brief, and unadorned. In addition, O'Connor's well-known opponent, who came close to defeating him in a previous election, perhaps did not need overt presidential assistance.

In the third "purge" effort, the president's opposition to Senator Millard Tydings of Maryland included two speeches and one press conference. The initial address, commemorating the third anniversary of the Social Security Act and broadcast nationally, August 15, seemed to be unrelated to the Maryland senatorial race. But Roosevelt undoubtedly implied a negative reference to Senator Tydings by praising his primary opponent, Congressman David J. Lewis, "as one of the American pioneers in the cause of Social Security." Earlier in the speech, he developed an accusation of policy based on the stasis of fact by exploring some history of protective legislation. He contended that, since the nineteenth century, the rich never hesitated turning to government for financial assistance and should not now resent the poor doing likewise. Therefore, the Congress needed motivated people of the liberal persuasion who must help the underprivileged "lay the foundation stones" for a better life just as government had assisted business and industry in previous generations. In a positive, optimistic address, the president was able to establish a type of action-oriented policy for the future that would not favor conservative legislators who opposed such programs.[6]

In his August 16 press conference, Roosevelt reversed tactics by delivering a stinging accusation directly against the quality of Senator Tydings' character: "Tydings tells the voters he supports the 'bone and sinew' of the New Deal. He wants to run with the Roosevelt prestige and the money of his conservative Republican friends both on his side." He accused the senator of lying about his attachment to the New Deal, exploiting the advantage of being a Democrat, and taking money under false pretenses.[7]

The nationally broadcast address at Denton, Maryland, September 5, shared all of the political dangers so evident in the earlier Barnesville speech. By now the purge was a reality and no longer a rumor. Enough unfavorable publicity was generated in the month since his Georgia visit to suggest that the Maryland appearance could erode his national popularity. So, which persona would be used--the New Deal philosopher of August 15 aloof from the fray, or the campaign debater of August 16 attacking aggressively? The Denton audience, mindful of his previous Georgia visit and probably expecting the latter approach, likely found the president considerably milder than anticipated. FDR renewed the points contained in the June 24 Fireside Chat, inserted appropriate local adaptation, added praise for Congressman Lewis, and omitted any mention of the absent Senator Tydings.

Roosevelt's accusation was once more premised on the stasis of definition for policy. It reviewed the differences between a conservative and a liberal, a "Mr. A" and a "Mr. B," by utilizing the basic ideas of June 24. This personification inevitably led to an accusation of character that originally was based on definition but quickly changed to quality considerations. "Mr. A" admitted that problems existed that should be remedied, but "found fault with and opposed, openly or secretly, almost every suggestion" from the "liberal school of thought." On the other hand, "Mr. B" cooperated "with his Government" in devising remedies, such as laws for workmen's compensation, parcel post, and unemployment insurance. These acts were specified because "Representative Lewis of Maryland" was a "Mr. B" who had played significant roles in their passage. Although Senator Tydings' name was not mentioned, he obviously was a "Mr. A," not only a conservative but even one of the "reactionaries" who was exploiting "prejudice and class feeling" that led to "political hysteria."[8] In this latter reference, FDR probably alluded to the Tydings' advertisements that were getting a play in the national press and will be mentioned later.

SENATOR GEORGE'S APOLOGIA

Senator Walter George's celebrated response to the purge was delivered over a statewide radio network from Waycross, Georgia, August 15, four days after the president's Barnesville address. Properly surmising that the contest was between himself and Roosevelt, the senator never mentioned his two primary opponents. Likewise, his apologia was a selective response to the president. He did not pursue the accusation of policy, premised on the National Emergency Council report, characterizing the South as the "nation's No. 1 economic problem." Perhaps he was unfamiliar with the report; maybe he felt politically vulnerable in conceding that the South had any problems; or, possibly he feared a New Deal trap to lure him into offering solutions.

The senator introduced an apologia of policy based on the stasis of fact. He admitted voting against specific measures supported by the administration, such as those involving the Supreme Court, governmental reorganization, and antilynching. He opposed Court reform because he wanted separation of the executive and the judiciary branches of government; he opposed reorganization because he wanted to retain the Civil Service Commission; he opposed the antilynching bill because it included the compensation of victims, was the only major crime "on a steady decline," and, after all, "we love the negro." Therefore, his stated policy was one of independence from presidential domination and in accord with his constituents' desires. Among these three measures, only reorganization was mentioned by Roosevelt during the campaign which made the senator's speech appear to be more specific in this respect than the president's. Of course FDR could not mention the Court-packing topic inasmuch as it supposedly had nothing to do with his 1938 actions.

The bulk of George's apologia was an explication of character divided into three general areas. He emphasized stases of fact and quality as a supporter of selected New Deal legislation, praised the president for his past achievements, and concentrated blame on a specific collection of individuals and groups. He declared his dedication to the liberal philosophy several times, and pointed to his support for the Social Security Act, the Railway Retirement Act, "farm reforms, banking reforms, currency reforms," and all "relief measures" to assist the unemployed. He refuted the president's attack, an indictment without a "bill of particulars," on his party loyalty and legislative record.   He countered the jurisdictional stasis by emotionally tracing his roots to a South Georgia tenant farm family, concluding, "I am Georgia bred and born; a full-time Georgian, my friends."

Because the Roosevelt staff dealt in "misinformation," he wanted "to acquit" the president, whom he held in "highest personal esteem," of any nefarious activities. Apparently George checked the latest Gallup Poll, saw the president's 72 percent rating in Georgia and 67 percent rating in the South, and chose not to challenge him directly. He blamed "Tom Corcoran and Bennie Cohen, two New York Wall Street lawyers"; Dr. C. H. Foreman, "the interracial representative" in the Interior Department; Marvin McIntyre, presidential adviser and appointments secretary; James Ford, the Communist party's "negro nominee" for vice president; Labor's Non-Partisan League led by E. L. Oliver; the "Communist group" of John L. Lewis; sit-down strikers; and, all "who bring to our shores foreign and alien methods." Most of these individuals and groups likely were unfamiliar to the audience, but their mention suggested generous quantities of white supremacy, anti-Semitism, nationalism, sectionalism, and anti-unionism.[9]

CONGRESSMAN O'CONNOR'S APOLOGIA

Representative John O'Connor, brother of Basil O'Connor who was the president's former law partner, delivered his CBS radio response from New York City two days after Roosevelt's August 16 press conference attack. The congressman's apologia, a rambling diatribe of anger and frustration, was confined to the virtues of his own character and the wickedness of his opponents. His opening attempted to impeach the source of the editorial that the president embraced in his condemnation. Without naming the *New York Post*, he condemned the "viciously untrue" and "insulting" editorial in a newspaper "long since regarded as communistic." For documentation, he cited the *Congressional Record* of 1937 and 1938. But, of course, the *Record* was no better evidence for guilt or innocence on such a serious charge in the 1930s than it is today. Significantly, O'Connor's colleagues in both Houses, such as Representatives Samuel Dickstein and Edward Curley from his own state and Senator Sherman Minton of Indiana, continued to cite editorials from the *New York Post* and insert them in the *Record* as expert opinion on a variety of topics. Hence, O'Connor's communistic charge was reckless assertion with the *Congressional Record* citation as an illusion of proof. This was the era of the rabid Dies Committee, the publicity starved collection of Congressmen headed by Representative Martin Dies of Texas, who embarked on a "public orgy of Red-baiting." Reactionaries and a good number of conservatives often used communism as a broadside swipe against the New Deal.[10]

From the stasis of the preceding alleged fact, O'Connor moved to that of quality in considering presidential character. Roosevelt's "un-American" intent was to tolerate "only yes-men" in his zeal to "abolish" or render "impotent" the legislature, which would provide "an escalator to a dictatorship." O'Connor saw a "demagogic" challenge to the Bill of Rights manifested in FDR's governmental reorganization bill and the court-packing attempt to control the judiciary. He cited his longevity in office, being elected to eight terms since 1923, as evidence of his independence from Roosevelt as well as freedom from all presidential "coattails."[11]

O'Connor lashed out against the president, presidential sources, past legislation, and future proposals that may resemble past legislation. Considerably less temperate and less selective than the George apologia, it was a negative message that imparted angry despair. The congressman made no attempt to address policy considerations. The mere citation of his chronological endurance in office was an inadequate remedy for the omnibus calamity cataloged in the discourse. Also absent was any effort to effect a rapprochement with the president or the liberal wing of the Democratic Party.

SENATOR TYDINGS' APOLOGIA

Millard Tydings did not await Roosevelt's Labor Day address in Denton before responding to the accusatory statements of mid-August. His half-hour NBC radio presentation of August 21 was carried over all network stations in Maryland and one in Washington, D.C. Unlike the George speech, Tydings gave considerable attention to his primary opponent, David J. Lewis, called him by name twenty-five times, and lectured Lewis directly in some of his closing comments. Like the O'Connor speech, the Maryland senator's apologia did not address policy. It was a categorical defense of his character and an attack on the character of his opponent. It was evident who and what the senator opposed, but there was no clue concerning whether he recognized any current problems, or, if so, whether he had any serious remedies for solving them. This omission is curious in view of the president's recognition over national radio of Congressman Lewis a week earlier as a crucial contributor to the popular Social Security Act. It could be anticipated that the senator, therefore, would itemize some of his own achievements deserving equal recognition.

The overall Tydings' strategy was three-fold. First, he contended that evil forces in Washington were shamelessly interfering unconstitutionally in state elections. Second, he characterized Lewis as a hapless pawn who, unable to stand alone, was coaxed into opposing the senator by those evil exploiters who promised him high-powered, outside assistance. Third, he declared that calamity would result and the Republic would be endangered if the federal intrusion was successful. Tydings did not waste time with niceties. His tripartite strategy was a simple, predictable, unadorned pounding of his opponent's perceived weaknesses.

First, the evil forces in Washington assertion suggested questions of jurisdiction and quality. The senator recalled the "dark days of the Reconstruction era" when a national government employed "fixed bayonets" and "the lash of retribution" against "impoverished people" of the "old South." He cultivated the siege mentality of the Lost Cause before declaring that this same "fear" of "intimidation" and "outside interference" is a reality "today." He conjured up images of the Civil War and its aftermath that made it seem that federal troops would be invading the "Free State" of Maryland at any moment and marking everyone's ballot for them.

Second, Tydings turned his attention to David Lewis, from Maryland's sixth congressional district, who had announced that he would be a candidate for reelection to the House of Representatives several months previously. At that time, he seemingly had no thought of entering the Senate race. Then, the president and his advisers decided to "destroy the political lives" of anyone who differed with the administration. So, David Lewis was called to the White House, had a talk with the president, returned to Maryland, withdrew his candidacy for the sixth congressional district, and became a candidate for the Senate. He permitted himself "to be used as the instrument of persons who do not live in Maryland; who cannot vote in Maryland; who pay no taxes in Maryland; who have no homes in Maryland," but who now "dictate and select the representative that Maryland shall send to the Senate." Tydings charged that, if elected, Mr. Lewis' vote would not reflect the views of the people, or even of himself, but would be the "personal property of the president of the United States." This weak "rubber stamp" required the assistance of a presidential "invasion" of the state during a party primary. How could he expect to serve "a great sovereign State like Maryland" if he were ever elected to the Senate? But matters probably would get worse. The people must brace themselves against a government prepared to "terrorize thousands of citizens" with the threat of job loss as well as the "elimination" of "Federal officers" who supported Senator Tydings.

Third, if the president and Lewis succeeded, calamity would result. If "we surrender" our "sovereign authority," we will destroy "tradition" and "weaken other states." Then, the Supreme Court issue will be revived and the executive will control both the legislature and the judiciary. Hence, a successful purge will destroy the Constitution and bring about a dictatorship. Not limiting his arguments to the spoken word, Tydings placed lengthy advertisements in newspapers throughout the state that called upon the citizens to defend the state against "Federal invasion." These ads quoted portions of Articles Four, Seven, and Eight of "your Constitution" that now is threatened by the "Federal Administration supported by the C.I.O., John L. Lewis and the Communists."

Senator Tydings was heavy-handed in elevating himself as the last hope for Maryland, other states, the Constitution, the separation of powers, and the suppression of a dictatorship. There was time for neither modesty nor subtlety. The life of the Republic was at stake. His apologia, limited to the quality and jurisdictional stases of character, was directed toward the administration and his primary opponent. They were the culprits and he was the martyr. Unlike Senator George, Tydings did not appear the least intimidated by FDR's popularity rating and made no overtures that suggested future reconciliation. Allan Michie and Frank Ryhlick contended that "Mi-Lord Tydings," sardonic and condescending, opposed liberal reform in order to protect the lucrative, robber-baron accounts of his corporate law firm. Roosevelt and Tydings shared a deep-seated dislike for one another that probably was both political and personal. The bitterness of this relationship was evident in the senator's rancorous address as well as in his shocking advertisements.[12]

CONCLUSION

Several nonrhetorical factors were influential. First, Roosevelt's effort appeared to be a better gamble in 1938 than it does today. New Dealers Claude Pepper of Florida and Lister Hill of Alabama won early victories, followed by Alben Barkley in Kentucky and Hattie Caraway in Arkansas. These results, coupled with the president's popularity, offered tangible encouragement. If the purge were not tried, there would be little hope of defeating conservatives and reactionaries; if it were tried and failed, the objectionable characters would not be increased in number. Second, the president was listening more to the White House "elimination committee" that urged overt purges--Harry Hopkins, Harold Ickes, Tom Corcoran, Marvin McIntyre, Ben Cohen, James Roosevelt--and less to the veterans of past campaigns, such as Jim Farley and Jack Garner, who generally opposed his involvement in state politics. Third, the vagaries of local circumstances posed problems. Georgia and Maryland votes were tabulated on a county unit rule system that gave disproportionate power to rural areas where conservatives dominated; liberal voters were more prevalent in cities; Georgia was divided by North-South rivalry, Maryland by East-West, Manhattan by the haves and the have-nots; the most avid New Deal supporters, which included the poor, the unemployed, the aged, and the racial minorities, often were disenfranchised by registration laws, poll taxes, and literacy tests; some candidates could enter multiple party primaries; and some voters could vote in primaries other than those of their party affiliation.[13]

The two senators won comfortably in Georgia and Maryland; the congressman lost in New York. Does this mean that the purge failed with the former and succeeded with the latter? Not necessarily, but analyses of accusation and apology as a speech set in each primary offers additional rhetorical insights. Certainly the distinction between policy and character proved to be valuable. Roosevelt's general accusation in June, followed by the Georgia and Maryland efforts, launched important policy debates on liberal-conservative philosophies, the report of the National Emergency Council, and the history and effect of progressive legislation. These afforded strong bases upon which to build speeches that moved from information, emphasizing stases of fact and definition, toward recommendations for specific action. Unfortunately, after introducing those policy topics, the president omitted specific recommendations and moved to character considerations. He would have been better advised to concentrate more on policy and much less, if at all, on character in the longer speeches.

The White House appeared to be insensitive to the image and substance of the doctrine of federal and state separation of powers. Jurisdictional issues, never handled effectively in the accusation, offered heavy advantages to the purge targets. Alleged federal usurpation of power was the major focus of Tydings' speech and was readily apparent in those of George and O'Connor. Those visits to Georgia and Maryland further incited jurisdictional challenges that the president should have been working to defuse. FDR's accusation against George would have been excessive from any location, but he flaunted his power in going to Georgia to deliver it. The press conference, used exclusively to oppose Congressman O'Connor, provided a less incendiary method of communication. The president was dealing with supposedly spontaneous questions in a democratic setting; he did not "invade" a legislator's diocese; and his remarks were not treated with the fanfare of a major address. Perhaps the press conference offered the best medium for an accusation of character, with the presidential speech reserved for an accusation of policy.

Senator George's apology was the only one that addressed policy. He made an effort to reestablish his liberal record by evoking the stasis of fact. It was sound strategy, made many presidential assertions pale in comparison, and provided a foundation to move into the defense of character. In contrast, Tydings and O'Connor delivered tirades that lacked substance. Policy contentions, in both accusation and apology, remained debatable and adjustable through further exchanges. These advantages are reflected to a limited degree in FDR's condemnation and George's response. On the other hand, character attacks not only foreclosed further substantive considerations, but usually were irreversible.

NOTES

[1] *New York Times*, August-September 1938, *passim*.

[2] Audiotape, FDR 169, *F.D.R. Speaks* (Ann Arbor: Xerox University Microfilms, 1974).

[3] *Atlanta Constitution*, August 11, 1938, pp. 1, 5; August 12, 1938, pp. 1, 8, 10, 11; *New York Times*, August 13, 1938, pp. 1, 3-6; Franklin D. Roosevelt, *The Public Paper and Addresses of Franklin D. Roosevelt,* Samuel I. Rosenman, compiler, 1938 volume (New York: Macmillan, 1941), pp. 363-71. According to the Archivist, Franklin D. Roosevelt Library, no sound recording of the president's Barnesville speech exists.

[4] *New York Times*, August 12, 1938, p. 4.

[5] Franklin D. Roosevelt, *Complete Presidential Press Conferences of Franklin D. Roosevelt* (New York: Da Capo Press, 1972), XII, 24-26, 38.

[6] Audiotape, FDR 175, *F.D.R. Speaks*.

[7] Roosevelt, *Press Conferences*, XII, 26.

[8] Audiotape, FDR 177, *F.D.R. Speaks*.

[9] *Atlanta Constitution*, August 16, 1938, pp. 1, 6, 7; August 14, 1938, p. 9; August 17, 1938, pp. 1, 3; August 10, 1938, pp. 1, 3.

[10] *Congressional Record*, Appendix, 75th Congress, 3rd Session, Vol. 83, Part 10, pp. 1836, 1856, 1924, 2646; Joseph Alsop and Robert Kintner, "The Capital Parade," *Atlanta Constitution*, August 22, 1938, p. 4.

[11] *New York Times*, August 12, 1938, p. 1; August 19, 1938, pp. 1, 5.

[12] *Baltimore Sun*, August 22, 1938, pp. 1, 4; August 31, 1938, p. 2; *New York Times*, August 22, 1938, p. 2; August 31, 1938, p. 7; Allan A. Michie and Frank Ryhlick, *Dixie Demagogues* (New York: Vanguard Press, 1939), pp. 165-71.

[13] *New York Times*, August 14, 1938, p. IV-1; James A. Farley, *Jim Farley's Story: The Roosevelt Years* (New York: McGraw-Hill, 1948), pp. 120-50; Basil Rauch, *The History of the New Deal 1933-1938* (New York: Capricorn Books, 1944), pp. 318-25.

INFORMATION SOURCES ON THE SPEECH SET

President Roosevelt's Accusations

For the Fireside Chat, delivered on June 24, 1938, see audiotape, FDR 169, *F.D.R. Speaks* (Ann Arbor: Xerox University Microfilms, 1974).

For the speech in Warm Springs, Georgia, August 10, 1938, see *Atlanta Constitution*, August 11, 1938, p. 5.

For the speech in Barnesville, Georgia, August 11, 1938, see *Atlanta Constitution*, August 12, 1938, p. 8.

For the radio address from Washington, D.C., August 15, 1938, see audiotape, FDR 175, *F.D.R. Speaks* (Ann Arbor: Xerox University Microfilms, 1974).

For the press conference in Washington, D.C., August 16, 1938, see Franklin D. Roosevelt, *Complete Presidential Press Conferences of Franklin D. Roosevelt* (New York: Da Capo Press, 1972), XII, 23-30.

For the press conference in Hyde Park, New York, August 23, 1938, see Franklin D. Roosevelt, *Complete Presidential Press Conferences of Franklin D. Roosevelt* (New York: Da Capo Press, 1972), XII, 34-44.

For the speech in Denton, Maryland, September 5, 1938, see audiotape, FDR 177, *F.D.R. Speaks* (Ann Arbor: Xerox University Microfilms, 1974).

Senator George's Apology

For the text of George's apology, which was broadcast statewide, see *Atlanta Constitution*, August 16, 1938, p. 6.

Congressman O'Connor's Apology

For the text of O'Connor's apology, which was broadcast nationally, see *New York Times*, August 19, 1938, pp. 1, 5.

Senator Tydings' Apology

For the text of Tydings' apology, which was broadcast statewide and in Washington, D.C., see *Baltimore Sun*, August 22, 1938, pp. 1, 4.

Selected Bibliography

Alexander, Holmes. "Millard E. Tydings: The Man from Maryland." In *The American Politician,* edited by J. T. Salter. Chapel Hill: University of North Carolina Press, 1938.

Burns, James MacGregor. *Roosevelt: The Lion and the Fox.* New York: Harcourt, Brace, 1956.

Farley, James A. *Jim Farley's Story: The Roosevelt Years.* New York: McGraw-Hill, 1948.

Frisch, Morton J. *Franklin D. Roosevelt: The Contributions of the New Deal to American Political Thought and Practice.* Boston: Twayne, 1975.

Grant, Philip A. "Maryland Press Reaction to the Roosevelt-Tydings Confrontation." *Maryland Historical Magazine* 68 (1973): 422-37.

Leuchtenburg, William E. *Franklin D. Roosevelt and the New Deal 1932-1940.* New York: Harper & Row, 1963.

Lippman, Theo. *The Squire of Warm Springs: F.D.R. in Georgia 1924-1945.* Chicago: Playboy Press, 1977.

Mellichamp, Josephine. *Senators from Georgia.* Huntsville, Alabama: Strode Publishers, 1976.

Michie, Allan A., and Frank Ryhlick. *Dixie Demagogues.* New York: Vanguard Press, 1939.

Phillips, Cabell. *From the Crash to the Blitz 1929-1939.* New York: Macmillan, 1966.

Polenberg, Richard. "The Decline of the New Deal, 1937-1940." In *The New Deal: The National Level,* edited by John Braeman, et al. Columbus: Ohio State University Press, 1975. Volume I.

___. "Franklin Roosevelt and the Purge of John O'Connor: The Impact of Urban Change on Political Parties." *New York History* 49 (1968): 306-26.

Price, Charles M., and Joseph Boskin, "The Roosevelt 'Purge': A Reappraisal." *Journal of Politics* 28 (1966): 660-70.

Rauch, Basil. *The History of the New Deal 1933-1938.* New York: Capricorn Books, 1944.

Roosevelt, Franklin D. *The Public Papers and Addresses of Franklin D. Roosevelt.* Samuel I. Rosenman, compiler. New York: Macmillan, 1941.

1938 Volume.

Rosenman, Samuel I. *Working with Roosevelt*. New York: Da Capo Press, 1972.

Schlonick, Myron I. "The President and the Senator: Franklin Roosevelt's Attempted 'Purge' of Maryland's Millard Tydings in 1938." M.A. thesis, University of Maryland, 1962.

Shannon, J. B. "Presidential Politics in the South: 1938, I." *Journal of Politics* 1 (1939): 146-70.

___. "Presidential Politics in the South--1938, II." *Journal of Politics* 1 (1939): 278-300.

Stokes, Thomas L. *Chip Off My Shoulder*. Princeton: Princeton University Press, 1940.

Thomas, David Nolan. "Roosevelt versus George: The Presidential Purge Campaign of 1938." M.A. thesis, University of North Carolina, 1953.

Tindall, George Brown. *The Emergence of the New South 1913-1945*. Baton Rouge: Louisiana State University, 1967.

Wolfskill, George, and John A. Hudson. *All But the People: Franklin D. Roosevelt and His Critics 1933-39*. New York: Macmillan, 1969.

Zeigler, Luther Harmon. "Senator Walter George's 1938 Campaign." *Georgia Historical Quarterly* 43 (1959): 333-52.

President Harry S. Truman and General Douglas MacArthur: A Study of Rhetorical Confrontation

Bernard K. Duffy

Few personal controversies in American history have been more heated or as well publicized as the one sparked by Harry Truman's dismissal of Douglas MacArthur. Truman's radio speech announcing the dismissal and MacArthur's vaunted "Don't Scuttle the Pacific" speech, delivered to a joint session of Congress and broadcast over both radio and television, represent, according to Halford Ryan, a speech set, comprising an accusation and an apology. Of the two speeches, Truman's has already received recent critical attention. In his essay analyzing Truman's speech, Ryan argued that the president committed a serious error in rhetorical judgment when he chose to devote most of the speech to a defense of the administration's foreign policy rather than to delineating the reasons why he dismissed MacArthur.[1] This essay lays the historical groundwork for understanding the speech set, takes issue with Ryan's position that Truman in his radio speech should have justified MacArthur's dismissal on the basis of his insubordination, and presents an analysis of why MacArthur's speech was so successful in the short term, while Truman's position has been more persuasive in the long term.

Ryan's belief that Truman's speech suffered from a failure of focus is shared by D. Clayton James and other historians who reason that the public wanted Truman to explain his action. Ryan postulated that Truman should have used a speech prepared by his staff that dealt with the decision to relieve MacArthur on the basis of MacArthur's unwillingness to accept Truman's authority as commander in chief. Rather, Truman accepted Secretary of State Dean Acheson's counsel and justified MacArthur's dismissal in light of the administration's foreign policy. Specifically, Truman said he had relieved MacArthur because the general did not agree with the administration's goal of achieving peace in the Far East and of reducing the risks of global war.[2]

To follow Ryan's reasoning, Truman's speech was ineffective as an accusation because it did not justify the dismissal in the terms that political commentators and historians have been most willing to accept. In part Truman's speech was itself an apologia which responded to the critics of the administration's foreign policy, including notably the Taft Republicans, and MacArthur himself. Truman's speech rationalized the administration's foreign policy and only rather circuitously suggested why MacArthur was dismissed. As Ryan indicated, direct allegations of MacArthur's insubordination or affirmations of the president's constitutional authority over the military were obtrusively absent in Truman's speech.

If Truman had wanted to develop a case against MacArthur on the grounds of his insubordination to the commander in chief and his unconstitutional intervention in the domain of politics and foreign policy, he had ample evidence at his disposal. In August 1950 MacArthur sent a message to the Veterans of Foreign Wars (VFW) in which he argued for the strategic importance of Formosa. Truman, who had decided not to defend Formosa from Chinese attack nor use the island to house American military bases, was enraged that MacArthur contradicted that position, and seriously considered replacing him. The issue was one of great political sensitivity, since right-wing Republicans saw Formosa as a last bastion of democracy against the Peoples Republic of China. The Republicans blamed the Democratic Party for the loss of China to the Communists and some, like Joseph McCarthy, suggested that there were Communists in government who had helped engineer the Democratic sell-out to communism. So obsessive was this view that on the day MacArthur's dismissal was announced Senator William Jenner declared: "Our only choice is to impeach President Truman and find out who is the secret invisible government which has so cleverly led our country down the road to destruction."[3]

After his fateful advance to the Yalu and the resultant entrance of the Chinese into the war, MacArthur gave interviews to the press and issued statements concerning the unsuccessful offensive. In an interview with *U.S. News and World Report*, he spoke of restrictions placed upon him against entering Chinese territory as "an enormous handicap, without precedent in military history." Acheson reported that MacArthur similarly defended his inability to win a decisive victory in Korea in interviews for United Press, International News Service, and others. These interviews so angered Truman that he later commented that he should have fired MacArthur at that time. Instead he issued an order on December 6 that forbade military commanders and foreign diplomats from giving interviews with the press without prior clearance from the Defense Department.[4]

It was an order MacArthur would violate. Acheson recalled with pique: "Openly defying the President's order of December 6 to military commanders forbidding unauthorized statements to the press, [on March 15] he gave one to Hugh Baillie, President of United Press." A little more than a week later MacArthur committed an even more unpardonable sin. As the administration began a peace initiative, MacArthur issued what he later defensively termed a "military appraisal" of the Korean problem. His appraisal was, in fact, an ultimatum to the Chinese to surrender. It spoke of the Chinese inability to win the war by sheer numbers and implied that if the war were extended to China, her "imminent military collapse" would be in the offing. Acheson correctly assessed it "a major act of sabotage." "Very little," *Newsweek* reported, "has been left for the President to say except to agree with MacArthur."[5]

Spanier observed that MacArthur's statement was a perfect means of insuring the tenacity of the Chinese; agreeing to peace terms in the wake of MacArthur's ultimatum would have made it appear that China had lost the war. Furthermore, there is no doubt that MacArthur wanted the war extended into China, since he felt that the only way to save the Far East from communism was to emasculate China. There is also evidence to suggest that MacArthur felt he was helping to torpedo an alleged secret plan by the administration to appease the Chinese by giving them Formosa and recognition in the United Nations.[6]

Truman, according to Acheson, "in a state of mind that combined disbelief with controlled fury," sent a message to MacArthur that apprised him of the fact that he had violated the December 6 directive against making political statements to the press. Although Truman was apparently already persuaded that MacArthur could not be allowed to continue along this path of insubordination, the climax waited for one more act. Responding to a letter from Republican Minority Leader Joseph Martin of Massachusetts, MacArthur echoed the view of Martin and other Asia-firsters that "Asia is where the Communist conspirators have elected to make their play for global conquest and that we have joined the issue thus raised on the battlefield; that here we fight Europe's war with arms while the diplomatic [*sic*] there still fight it with words." Not only did MacArthur challenge the administration's policy of not diverting its military power from Europe to Asia, he also challenged the idea of a politically limited war and agreed with Martin's desire to unleash Chiang's troops onto the Chinese Mainland. Acheson regarded the letter, which Martin gave to the press and read on the House floor, as "an open declaration of war on the Administration's policy." After the Joint Chiefs of Staff (JCS), Acheson, and others of Truman's advisers unanimously decided to relieve MacArthur, the president revealed that this had been his decision after MacArthur's March 24 ultimatum to the Chinese.[7]

THE PRESIDENT'S ACCUSATIONS

Although Truman arranged to have the secretary of the army, who was in Korea, deliver the decision to MacArthur, the news of his dismissal leaked and the message was transmitted through normal channels. The leak also required that the administration call a press conference on the morning of April 11 to announce the decision.[8] That evening he presented his "Far Eastern Policy" speech on the radio.

The evidence to support Truman's accusation is obviously substantial. In view of the evidence Truman could have presented in his radio speech, why did he choose to deal with the question of MacArthur's dismissal obliquely by buttressing the administration's foreign policy rather than stating bluntly that MacArthur had been dismissed for repeated acts of insubordination, the tactic Ryan believes would have been more effective? In the first place, it is important to realize that Truman wanted to make sure he had dramatic evidence of MacArthur's insubordination before he fired him. That, in fact, is why he did not relieve MacArthur after MacArthur's ultimatum to the Chinese. "I wanted, if possible an even . . . better example of his insubordination, and I wanted it to be one that . . . everybody would recognize for exactly what it was, and I knew that, MacArthur being the kind of man he was, I wouldn't have to wait, and I didn't. He wrote the letter to Joe Martin."[9] In short, Truman believed that MacArthur's letter to Martin was so obvious a reason for dismissing him that any objective observer would concede that it was the right decision.

Joseph Short, Truman's press secretary, presented the evidence at a news conference held at 1:00 a.m. on April 11. The documents included the president's written statement pertaining to the dismissal, the order relieving MacArthur, and "background documents," essentially the physical evidence supporting MacArthur's relief—such things as MacArthur's ultimatum to the Chinese, the president's order to clear any statements with the JCS, and MacArthur's letter to Joseph Martin. According to Truman, "As far as I was concerned, these papers stated the case." In his public statement the president did exactly what Ryan thought would have been strategically most effective in his speech later that evening. He predicated MacArthur's relief on his constitutional insubordination to the commander in chief: "Full and vigorous debate on matters of national policy is a vital element in the constitutional system of our free democracy. It is fundamental, however, that military commanders must be governed by the policies and directives issued to them in the manner provided by our laws and Constitution. In time of crisis, the consideration is particularly compelling."[10] Thus, Truman presented both the reasoning for his decision and the supporting evidence. For those who wanted to listen, Truman's legal case against MacArthur was both clearly expressed and fully substantiated.

Initially, Truman relied upon the press to report his case to the public. The newspapers were divided in their view of the dismissal. On one hand was the opinion expressed by the editor of the *Washington Post*: "There is no room in our society for indispensable men or for ungovernable generals, no provision in our Constitution for the President to play second fiddle. Civil supremacy had to be reasserted, and it was wisest to reassert civil supremacy unmistakably." On the other hand was the frank pronouncement of the *Chicago Tribune*: "President Truman must be impeached and convicted. His hasty and vindictive removal of General MacArthur is the culmination of a series of acts which have shown that he is unfit, morally and mentally, for his high office." MacArthur had friends among the press including Hugh Baillie, head of United Press, and Roy Howard, head of Scripps-Howard, to whom he frequently gave private interviews. These relationships led Drew Pearson to comment that "his press treatment is of a nature unequalled by few other public figures — certainly not by Harry Truman."[11]

That some of the nation's newspapers accepted the reasons for MacArthur's dismissal suggests that the April 11 press conference, together with Truman's written announcement, the supporting documents, and Truman's speech, had been partially effective. It is foolish to think that such a bastion of Republican isolationism as the *Chicago Tribune* would have reacted to the dismissal in any other way than to denounce Truman, no matter what the president had said. But the reasons why Truman dismissed MacArthur were received, reported, commented on, and, in fact, accepted by enough newspapers to suggest that Truman did not make a grievous error in not presenting his entire case in his radio speech.

There were compelling reasons why Truman should not have presented his entire case against MacArthur in the radio speech and why he should have dealt with the question of the administration's foreign policy instead. MacArthur was a hero of no small proportion. For the president personally to indict MacArthur as a prosecutor might plead the case against a criminal would have seemed callous and insensitive, particularly when in some quarters Truman's action was already regarded as a personal assault upon MacArthur. Truman could easily have aroused greater sympathy for MacArthur and additional resentment for the man who fired him. In any event, as Truman said, the documents Short gave the press "stated the case." It is a time-honored political principle that if the reputation of a political rival is to be impugned, it is often best to have someone else say it, or to say it in writing.

The argument Truman used in his speech to justify MacArthur's dismissal, if not the one that has persuaded most historians that the president acted correctly, was, nevertheless, a potentially potent one within the historical context. Truman argued that MacArthur did not accept the administration's policy of attempting to avoid an all-out confrontation with China and the Soviet Union. Any reasonably well-informed listener realized Truman was alluding to MacArthur's highly publicized disagreements with the administration's policy of limiting the conflict in the light of global

political objectives. In his speech Truman opposed the very proposals Mac-
Arthur had made: "But you may ask why can't we bomb Manchuria and
China itself? Why don't we assist the Chinese Nationalist troops to land on
the mainland of China?" Simplifying the issues for rhetorical purposes,
Truman justified MacArthur's dismissal on the grounds that MacArthur was
for war and the administration was for peace. There were those who
believed that the tack Truman took in his speech was politically astute. For
example, the *Christian Century* concluded: "President Truman showed his
keen sense of the political factors which, given time, are effective with the
general electorate when, in his radio speech . . . he rested his whole case for
MacArthur's dismissal on the general's demand to push the fighting beyond
Korea into China. Do the Republicans want to fight a presidential campaign a year and a half from now on *that* issue?"[12]

Although the fact that MacArthur had taken a political position against
the president was well known to virtually everyone, a great many people not
only preferred the general's politics to the president's but defended
MacArthur's right to speak out against him. That Truman was MacArthur's
superior mattered little to those who questioned the "little man" from
Missouri's right to occupy the highest office in the land, to make decisions
about the nation's destiny, or to fire a military leader of the first water.
During the last year of World War II MacArthur was exceeded in popularity
only by General Eisenhower in polls to determine whom the nation most
admired. "Seldom," observed *Time*, "had a more unpopular man fired a
more popular one." Upon realizing he had to fire MacArthur, Truman, obviously sensitive to the rhetorical challenge that lay ahead, is said to have
quipped, "Well I guess I have to relieve God."[13]

The public outrage to MacArthur's dismissal was, according to William
Manchester, "a profound simultaneous experience" unequalled until the
public mourning following John F. Kennedy's assassination.[14] The
Republicans had made MacArthur the symbol of the struggle against what
they and many others viewed as an indecisive foreign policy. In both the
long- and short-term, gaining support for the foreign policy was more important than indicting MacArthur for his insubordination. Firing one of its
most influential critics highlighted and exacerbated the ongoing dispute,
and invited, if not required, the administration to reply to its critics and
defend its foreign policy. Restating that Truman had a right to fire Mac-
Arthur for his insubordination might have helped set the record straight
beyond Truman's written statement and the raw evidence Joseph Short
provided. Whether it would have satisfied MacArthur's many admirers is
quite another question. It certainly would not have made the Republicans
call off the hounds or changed the opinions of those Americans who blamed
Truman for the agonizing stalemate in a war unlike any other in American
history.

Despite the fact that Truman did not make MacArthur's insubordination the major issue in his "Far Eastern Policy" speech, there were those in the press who felt that the rhetorical strategy of the administration was to justify the dismissal precisely on that basis. Indeed, David Lawrence, editor of *U.S. News and World Report*, spoke of "an unmoral and weak-kneed Administration [that] preaches defeatism even as it seeks by innuendo and smears, to persuade the American people that the whole episode is just a disobedience of 'orders.'" Lawrence maintained that this argument was simply a dodge. In arguing that Truman should have emphasized MacArthur's insubordination in his speech, Ryan quoted Howard K. Smith's report of the British response, that if Truman "sticks doggedly to the point — do his opponents favor altering the basis of American government from Republicanism to Bonapartism — . . . no honest American can do anything but admit that Mr. Truman's decision was right." But the British stood to lose a great deal if the United States broadened the war in Asia and naturally wanted the issue of the general's dismissal resolved on the basis of Truman's authority as president, rather than upon the issue of whose foreign policy, Truman's or MacArthur's, was correct. Truman, on the other hand, realized that politically he could not duck the issue of his foreign policy, because, as Smith goes on to say, "Americans, like citizens of other nations, are not all honest."[15]

Within a climate of opinion colored by emotionalism and by the Republican's desire to exploit the dismissal, Truman found it difficult to receive a fair hearing. He tried to meet political fire with fire by using an argument from consequence. He argued that MacArthur's policies, if put into effect, would have led the United States to an all-out war. Compared with the focused legalistic argument Ryan believed would have helped persuade the American public, the more diffuse and dramatic one Truman chose for his speech was aimed to achieve three interrelated persuasive goals: to support the doctrine of containment to which the administration was committed, to discredit MacArthur's and the Republicans' foreign policy position, and to justify the dismissal. There is no question that the speech was ineffective with the majority of the American people, but not necessarily because Truman chose the wrong argument. The legalistic argument Truman presented in his written statement and which was discussed in the national press was also rejected by many people. The mood of the nation made it difficult for the public to look at the matter objectively. These were not normal times as the spectre of McCarthyism with its allegations of a Democratic sell-out to communism revealed. The prevailing hysteria, and the irrationality it produced, were effectively captured by a political cartoon of the period in which an irate legislator, clutching a newspaper reporting MacArthur's dismissal, blurts out: "Who does Truman think he is — President?"[16]

DOUGLAS MACARTHUR'S APOLOGIA

The morning after MacArthur's dismissal was announced a contingent of Republican congressmen led by Taft met in Joseph Martin's office to plan strategy. Although their first thought was of impeaching the president, once they remembered that impeachment would be impossible in a Democratic-controlled Congress, the brainstorming session took another turn. Someone hit upon the idea of telephoning MacArthur to ask him if he would address a joint session of Congress. General Courtney Whitney, MacArthur's aide, answered the call and gave the Republicans the response they wanted--MacArthur would address the body. The Democrats tried hard to block the invitation, but they discovered that this would be impossible since there were temporarily more Republican than Democratic Senators in the Capital. Learning of the futility of further opposition, Truman issued a statement expressing his pleasure at the Senate's invitation to MacArthur. Despite the intense reaction to the general's dismissal at home, MacArthur seemed not to comprehend that he had become a focus of great controversy, and, in fact, feared the rejection of the people.[17]

MacArthur spent the flight from Japan to Hawaii and from there to San Francisco working on his congressional speech. He did not write the entire speech *de novo*, but used elements from material he had written in the past, including the message to the V.F.W. that had so infuriated Truman, and his speech accepting the Japanese surrender on the *U.S.S. Missouri*. MacArthur wrote the speech not so much to justify his acts of criticizing the president, but rather to defend his views of what should be done to win the war in Korea. Indeed, MacArthur presented the same criticisms of the administration's policy that had led Truman to dismiss him. MacArthur's speech, like Truman's, was deliberative, rather than epideictic, although the less than subtle allusions to MacArthur's many accomplishments might lead one to conclude that his speech was also one of self-praise.[18]

The content of MacArthur's speech was a skillful mix of a highly subjective exposition of the "military situation in the Far East," and an argument for the military strategy in Korea he supported. In his introduction, MacArthur attempted to establish a purely patriotic basis of his remarks, holding that the "issues are fundamental and reach quite beyond the realm of partisan consideration."[19] In the first portion of the speech MacArthur argued the principle that the Far East was essential to U.S. security. Employing the hyperbole for which his rhetoric was noted, he claimed that "the whole epicenter of world affairs rotates back toward the area [Asia] whence it started." Implicitly criticizing the Truman administration's policy of refusing to divert military resources from Europe, MacArthur argued that a weakening of any portion of the U.S. chain of defenses along the islands of

the Western Pacific would court disaster. If, for example, Formosa fell to
the Communists, "Such an eventuality would at once threaten the freedom
of the Philippines and the loss of Japan, and might well force our western
frontier back to the coasts of California, Oregon and Washington." Mac-
Arthur, like many others during the cold war, saw the Communist threat as
monolithic. According to MacArthur, the People's Republic of China was
"allied with Soviet Russia" and "aggressively imperialistic with a lust for ex-
pansion."

He also argued that the democratic nations of the Far East were worth
defending. With more than a hint of self-congratulation the proconsul of
Japan praised the new Japanese society he was largely responsible for creating. He spoke of the corruptly governed Philippines, as "a Christian nation"
with unlimited "capacity for high moral leadership in Asia," and of the dic-
tatorially ruled Formosa as possessing a "just and enlightened
administration." MacArthur made the protection of the noncommunistic
states of the Far East appear to be a moral imperative. This was the sort of
rhetoric that delighted the Asia-firsters and infuriated the nation's
European Allies and the Truman administration.

If these were the reasons to take a strong stand in the Far East, why had
the United States failed to win a decisive victory in Korea? Certainly not
through any failure of MacArthur's leadership. Indeed, MacArthur had led
his troops along the road of victory. The answer was as simple as it was
redeeming of MacArthur's strategic prowess. First, the Chinese had inter-
vened with "numerically superior ground forces." Secondly, the president
had been unwilling to commit the military resources necessary to win the
war: "I called for reinforcements, but was informed that reinforcements
were not available." MacArthur did not say that it was his decision to cross
the Yalu River that brought China into the war, and he blamed the president for not allowing him to respond to Chinese entrance with force.
MacArthur outlined the program for victory the president was unwilling to
accept: an intensified economic blockade and Naval blockade against
China, air reconnaissance of China and Manchuria, the bombing of enemy
bases, and the use of Chiang Kai-Shek's forces. But this was a somewhat
sanitized version of MacArthur's plans. He also wanted to sow a field of
nuclear wastes in the demilitarized zone and to unleash Chiang's army upon
Mainland China. The effect would likely be an all-out confrontation with
China and, although MacArthur doubted it, perhaps a war with the Soviet
Union as well. Undoubtedly responding to the president's charge that
MacArthur's program would lead to a widened war, MacArthur said he
resented being called a warmonger and documented his devotion to peace
by quoting from the speech he had delivered on the occasion of the Japanese
surrender.[20]

MacArthur claimed that his views were military ones and "were shared by practically every military leader concerned with the Korean campaign, including our own Joint Chiefs of Staff." A week before his speech, however, the *Washington Post* reported that "top military men at the Pentagon—almost to a man—disagree with MacArthur's Asia-first and widen-the-Korean-war views and honestly support the Government's approved foreign policy." On the day of the speech the JCS said they had agreed with the president's decision to relieve MacArthur, and four days after the speech the *New York Times* revealed that documentary evidence showed the JCS did not wholly agree even with MacArthur's military assessment.[21] The Hearings on the Military Situation in the Far East would prove further that the views of the JCS were quite different from MacArthur's. MacArthur made it appear that the president had been unwilling to accept the advice of the entire military hierarchy, clinging doggedly to a foreign policy that precluded winning the war. The stalemate was the president's fault, not his. It was the president's war—MacArthur said he had not been "consulted before the decision to intervene," though he agreed with its military objective. But the war needed to be fought on a military basis, as MacArthur made plain in this central enthymeme: "But once war is forced upon us, there is no other alternative than to apply every available means to bring it to a swift end. War's very object is victory—not prolonged indecision. In war there is no substitute for victory." According to MacArthur, this was not only his view; it was shared even by the common soldier: "'Why,' my soldiers asked of me, 'surrender military advantages to an enemy in the field?' I could not answer." The alternative was appeasement, and appeasement would lead the enemy to capitalize upon situations of weakness.

Having explained logically, if incompletely, why the war had devolved to a stalemate, MacArthur concluded the speech with a series of pathetic appeals whose effect was cumulative. MacArthur could draw upon a great fund for such appeals, for few matters evoke such strong emotions as the suffering and heroism of war. He spoke of the courage of the Koreans, whose last words to him were "Don't scuttle the Pacific." He lauded the heroism of "your fighting sons in Korea," adding that "It was my constant effort to preserve them and end this savage conflict honorably." And finally, from the barracks ballad that seemed so appropriate in his last days as a soldier, he quoted the now famous line, "Old soldiers never die; they just fade away," and applied it to his present circumstances: "And like the old soldier of that ballad, I now close my military career and just fade away—an old soldier who tried to do his duty as God gave him the light to see that duty." In this, his celebrated peroration, reportedly delivered with tears in his eyes, MacArthur managed both to appeal to the audience's pity and to assert his humility and blamelessness.[22]

Although MacArthur supported through argumentation the program he had urged upon the president, only obliquely did he justify criticizing the administration's foreign policy. His sole defense was that he had expressed military, not partisan political, opinions. But MacArthur, like Truman, did not fully comprehend the nature and consequences of a limited war. During the Korean War, the nation witnessed the end of an age in modern warfare and the beginning of a new one. MacArthur, himself deceived about the nature of the new warfare, could plead his case to an audience that had also not adjusted to the new verities of politically limited conflict. Truman wanted the war limited but unrealistically raised public hopes by talking of winning. As the *New Republic* observed, "[T]he Administration has chosen a wholly unreal course. It is committing the US to a concept of total victory through limited war."[23] MacArthur engaged in no such equivocation. His thesis was univocal, direct, and easily grasped, and thus fulfilled precisely the prescriptions for effective propaganda. This was not a humiliated general explaining himself; it was a man who believed he was right and the president was wrong, and whom the Democrats had placed on center stage to enact his role with supreme confidence and panache. Thus MacArthur evaded the very issue that Ryan says would have been Truman's best argument: that in firing MacArthur, Truman had exercised appropriately his constitutional authority after the general had exceeded his. It was fortunate for MacArthur that a great many people were as willing to blame the president for the Korean stalemate as he was and that the constitutional issue was not one that seemed to concern most people at the time.

The success of MacArthur's speech was owed in part to his distinctive use of the language, which one critic aptly described as rococo. Although perhaps not grandiloquent by the standards of nineteenth-century encomiasts, MacArthur's diction echoed that of the previous century. Portions of the speech are distinctly elevated. MacArthur's hyperboles were frequently in evidence. A benign example is his expansive praise of Congress: "This forum of legislative debate represents human liberty in the purest form yet devised." A naive and deceptive one is his characterization of the Philippines "as a mighty bulwark of Christianity in the Far East." MacArthur also allowed his talent for artful expression to obfuscate his meaning, such as a particularly opaque passage he quoted from his speech on the *U.S.S. Missouri*: "The problem basically is theological and involves a spiritual recrudescence and improvement of human character that will synchronize with our almost matchless advances in science, art, literature, and all material and cultural developments of the past 2,000 years."[24]

MacArthur's delivery, although open to criticism on a variety of scores, was, compared with that of most political speeches, quite extraordinary. Like Franklin Roosevelt, MacArthur was said to be particularly persuasive in one-on-one encounters. Listening to his vocal tone one might think he was speaking not to a thousand people, let alone to thirty million seated before their televisions or radios, but to a few individuals, for although his delivery was grave and by no means intimate, neither was it bombastic. MacArthur's evocative delivery was well suited to the electronic media, which, while reaching the masses, addresses them as individuals.

Descriptions of MacArthur's delivery often showed a preoccupation with his distinctive voice, which was variously described as "warm," "deep," "resonant," "vibrant," "sonorous," at times "soft," and at other times "harsh." *Time* magazine characterized MacArthur's delivery well: "The resonant voice sometimes rasped, sometimes sank almost to a whisper, but never rose from a low confident pitch." Others commented that the delivery was effectively "unhurried and rhythmic." MacArthur's voice conveyed a confidence and determination that made what he said sound like a recitation of distilled truth rather than like partisan pleading. In his speech to the joint session of Congress, he invoked what a journalist had previously described as MacArthur's "Olympian" attitude.[25]

MacArthur played the audience with the grace and virtuosity of a Paganini playing the violin. He sensed the passions each line would excite. He knew how to pause to let the message take effect on the audience or to wait for the applause with which he was interrupted more than fifty times. MacArthur used his expressive voice to convey great pathos, and he projected his character as effectively as a stage actor. The *New York Times* spoke of the speech as "a masterpiece of restrained emotion delivered with all the skill and oratorical power of an Anthony burying Caesar."[26] At times, when expressing particularly poignant sentiments, MacArthur took a cue from the tragedians and lowered his voice instead of raising it. A good example is his quiet rueful delivery of the second portion of the following passage: "'Why,' my soldiers asked of me, 'surrender military advantages to an enemy in the field?' I could not answer." At other times, MacArthur spoke sternly, such as when he expressed the aphorism, "In war there is no substitute for victory." MacArthur also brilliantly underscored vocally the serpentine menace of communism: "Like a cobra, any new enemy will more likely strike whenever it feels that the relativity in military . . . potential is in its favor." MacArthur's delivery took every advantage of the dramatic possibilities of his evocative rhetoric. And, indeed, without the support of his delivery and dramatic persona, the printed speech, despite the purple-passioned prose, pales by comparison.

This is not to say that MacArthur's dramatic delivery met with universal approval. Not everyone agreed with *Time*'s exuberant assessment that: "Douglas MacArthur spoke with a native eloquence that the nation had not heard in years without bombast or gesture." Some thought him a ham. To A. Craig Baird, MacArthur's delivery suggested the excesses of the Asian style, but to the untrained ears of many politicians, journalists, and the majority of the public, MacArthur's delivery gave evidence of a great man's restraint, dignity, and conviction in a time of personal and national turmoil. Although some journalists commented upon MacArthur's physical presence, his voice was probably more important to the effect MacArthur had upon the secondary audience. In 1951 more people owned radios than televisions.[27]

Few events suggest so convincingly the perceptiveness of Kenneth Burke's dramatistic view of persuasion. MacArthur's critics could try to dismiss it as mere histrionics, but it was impossible to persuade the audience that what they heard was any less real, passionate, evocative, or moving because it was also powerful drama. The fact that it was good drama, keyed perfectly to an occasion that stirred intense and complicated emotions, made it persuasive. As Quincy Howe wryly observed, "By a coincidence, rare in the history of drama, the man who acted the part of the old soldier happened himself to be an old soldier whose experiences precisely resembled the experiences of the old soldier whose part he was enacting."[28] MacArthur was consubstantial with the MacArthur he portrayed. An accomplishment virtually unprecedented in theatrical performance, though painfully sought in so-called "method acting," MacArthur managed with no formal training, but with the considerable advantage of a long-running performance.

The objective content of MacArthur's speech was subordinate in the drama to MacArthur himself. What MacArthur said merely supported the audience's perception of him as the great hero, who though sullied by a much disliked president, retained his noble bearing and his commitment to the nation. The emotions that MacArthur's speech called forth intensified the affective responses of the audience toward him.

Dramatically, MacArthur could not have had a better foil than Truman--one the gallant man of arms, who claimed not to have any political ambitions, the other the common man, the haberdasher from Missouri, who by chance and democratic election was also the president and commander in chief. It was a classic case in which the competition between a social and organizational hierarchy produced a double irony. In a situation not unique to a democratic society, MacArthur was born and bred to the purple, but Truman, the bourgeois politician, was president and MacArthur's superior. Yet a large percentage of the public, caring nothing for who was elected to lead, forsook the Constitution and embraced MacArthur as their hero, while holding the president in its contempt. "They cheered," said *Time* in its cover story, "a man of chin-out affirmations, who seemed a welcome contrast to men of indecision and negation."[29] Upon the president were projected the frustrations of the war, while MacArthur, the aristocrat, became the champion of the common man who simply wanted the United States to do what it had in every other conflict of arms--win.

As the president's speech was little more than an argument that could as well have been read as heard, MacArthur's speech and MacArthur as a public persona were animated in an auditory and visual drama that was less cerebral than emotional and moving. It was a deeply involving drama, for about the Truman-MacArthur controversy anyone could have an opinion and feel dead certain he was right. Here was not merely a speech or a speaker but a national event—the homecoming of one of the nation's greatest heroes, marred and emotionally supercharged by an unexpected turn of fate, MacArthur's dramatic dismissal. Like the Scopes Trial, it was a better play with better dialogue than could possibly be written about the same circumstances. It was also a play within a play. The larger play revolved around the rabid anticommunism McCarthy was promoting, the administration's attempt to perfect (compulsively, Burke would say) George Kennan's containment policy and the stepchild of that policy—a tragic war that could not be won. At the same time, Republicans sought desperately to profit from the losing struggle and the anti-Communist hysteria by deposing once and for all the Democrat's two-decade reign of power. These were the dramatic forces that gave the drama its undercurrents and made it an experience that both the Iowa farmhand and the Park Avenue sophisticate could appreciate. The play in which MacArthur and Truman were central characters had reached its denouement because of MacArthur's tragic flaw, his hubris, manifest in an inherent incapacity to take orders he believed would prevent him from winning on the battlefield.

It was a pageant no less than that occasioned by the triumphal return of a Roman Caesar. Dramatistically, Dewey Short was right when he exclaimed: "We heard God speak here today, God in the flesh, the voice of God!"[30] Short simply expressed what many in their moments of complete absorption in the drama fully believed they saw—not a man, or even a general, but someone larger than life, someone who had not merely made history but who in his own lifetime had become history, the consummate dramatic persona. MacArthur was the archetype of the great general whom fate had dealt an undeserved blow, but who, with uncommon nobility, had risen above enmity and bitterness to deliver a message that might save the nation. In their passionate response to MacArthur's speech the audience identified with what they perceived was a moment of transcendent importance. MacArthur skillfully shaped his speech to exploit the audience's frustrations with the Korean War and their strong identification with him, while ignoring the narrow legal issue of his Constitutional right to oppose the Truman administration.

CONCLUSION

The immediate response to MacArthur's address has seldom been matched in the history of American politics. The *New York Times* reported that "When the general had finished, some in the House chamber broke into tears. Spectators cried 'God Bless MacArthur.'" According to a Gallup poll administered after the speech, 54 percent of those surveyed agreed with MacArthur's proposals. The sample group also voted six to one in favor of defending Formosa against a Chinese invasion. Not everyone was moved by the speech, of course, least of all Harry Truman, who upon reading an advance copy had declared: "It was nothing but a bunch of damn bullshit."[31]

MacArthur launched an extensive speaking tour which was, after the speech to Congress, rather anticlimactic. The speeches criticized the administration's foreign policy and may ultimately have detracted from MacArthur's public image. Even his reputation as an orator suffered when, in presenting the 1952 Republican keynote address, the banal content of his speech and his flawed delivery bored the delegates.

History, as Ryan has pointed out, has shown MacArthur to have been wrong and Truman right, although not everyone will agree with that assessment. MacArthur delivered a speech that momentarily thrilled the masses, and although remembered for its high drama, it was not a speech that set a better course for the nation or, for that matter, permanently vindicated MacArthur of the charge that he had defied the commander in chief. It did undoubtedly advance the political objectives of the Republicans and indirectly help the cause of anti-Communist crusaders like McCarthy. Despite MacArthur's statement to the contrary, his speech was decidedly partisan and personal. Truman, on the other hand, presented a speech that is little remembered, although in the end, Truman's position and not MacArthur's has been judged correct.

That MacArthur's speech moved his audience is not as important as the fact that his rhetoric, though clothed as objective advice was, upon closer examination, more intent upon preserving the speaker's reputation and upon damaging the reputation of the man who had fired him. MacArthur's speech amounted to flattery. By and large it told the audience what they were willing to accept: that the war needed to be won militarily rather than diplomatically, and that he was a patriotic and brilliant military strategist while the president was too soft on communism to see the war to a successful conclusion. In the same vein, Truman's accusation of MacArthur, a distinctly unsuccessful one when measured by the standard of its immediate effects, carefully avoided humiliating MacArthur, and clearly delineated a rationale for pursuing a limited war. Of the two speeches the president's was the more restrained, although many commentators attributed this quality to MacArthur's address. In reality MacArthur's speech was full of emotional fireworks and melodrama, and the president's, though sensationalistically invoking the spectre of a third world war, nevertheless appealed more to the audience's intellect than to their passions. Truman, unlike MacArthur, seemed more concerned with defending a policy and a principle, than with defending himself. Applying a standard of judgment Richard Weaver borrowed from Plato, the rhetorical encounter might be summarized simply: Where the president's speech failed to move, MacArthur's speech succeeded brilliantly in moving the audience but for the wrong reasons and in the wrong direction.

NOTES

[1]Halford Ross Ryan, "Harry S Truman: A Misdirected Defense for MacArthur's Dismissal," in *American Rhetoric From Roosevelt to Reagan*, edited by Halford Ross Ryan (Prospect Heights, Ill.: Waveland Press, 1983), p. 93ff.

[2]Clayton James, *Triumph and Disaster, 1954-1964*, Vol. III of *The Years of MacArthur* (Boston: Houghton Mifflin, 1985), p. 602; Ryan, "A Misdirected Defense," pp. 97-99; Harry S Truman, "Far Eastern Policy," in *American Rhetoric from Roosevelt to Reagan*, p. 90.

[3]John W. Spanier, *The Truman-MacArthur Controversy and the Korean War* (1959; rpt. New York: W. W. Norton, 1965), pp. 55-60; James, *Triumph and Disaster*, 462-63; "A President, a General, a Showdown," *Newsweek*, April 23, 1951, p. 23.

[4]"MacArthur's Own Story," *U.S. News & World Report*, December 8, 1950, pp. 16-22; Dean Acheson, *The Korean War* (New York: W. W. Norton, 1971), p. 76; "A President, a General, a Showdown," p. 22.

[5]Acheson, *The Korean War*, p. 101; Spanier, *The Truman-MacArthur Controversy*, p. 200-201; "How the General Scooped the President," *Newsweek*, April 2, 1951, p. 29.

[6]Spanier, *The Truman-MacArthur Controversy*, pp. 201-202; Courtney Whitney, *MacArthur: His Rendezvous with Destiny* (New York: Alfred A. Knopf, 1956), pp. 467-69.

[7]Acheson, *The Korean War*, p. 102; Harry S Truman, *Years of Trial and Hope*, Vol. II of *Memoirs by Harry S Truman* (Garden City, N.Y.: Doubleday, 1956), pp. 443-44, 448; Russell Buhite, ed., *The Far East*, Vol. IV of *The Dynamics of World Power*, edited by Arthur M. Schlesinger (New York: Chelsea House Publishers, 1973), pp. 400-401; Acheson, *The Korean War*, p. 103.

[8]Truman, *Years of Trial and Hope*, pp. 448-49.

[9]Merle Miller, *Plain Speaking: An Oral Biography of Harry S Truman* (New York: Berkley Publishing, 1973), pp. 302-303.

[10]Truman, *Years of Trial and Hope*, pp. 448-49.

[11]Editorial, "The President Acts," *Washington Post*, April 12, 1951, Sec. A, p. 10, col. 2; quoted in "U.S. Press Almost Equally Divided, Pro and Con," *Washington Post*, April 15, 1951, Sec. A, p. 4, col. 1; Drew Pearson, "Truman, MacArthur Rivalry Cited," *Washington Post*, April 10, 1951, Sec. B, p. 13, col. 5.

[12]Truman, "Far Eastern Policy," p. 89; unsigned editorial, "MacArthur," *Christian Century*, April 25, 1951, pp. 511-12.

[13]William Manchester, *American Caesar* (Boston: Little, Brown, 1978), pp. 466, 648; "The Little Man Who Dared," *Time*, April 23, 1951, p. 24; Hanson W. Baldwin, "The Magic of MacArthur," *New York Times*, April 23, 1951, p. 6, col. 4.

[14]Manchester, *American Caesar*, p. 648.

[15]David Lawrence, "A Salute to Courage," *U.S. News and World Report*, April 27, 1951, p. 76; Howard K. Smith, "Thou Art Soldier Only," *Nation*, April 21, 1951, pp. 363-64.

[16]Burck, cartoon, *Time*, April 23, 1951, p. 25.

[17]Manchester, *American Caesar*, p. 647; "A President, a General, a Showdown," pp. 23-24.

[18]Manchester, *American Caesar*, p. 655; James, *Triumph and Disaster*, p. 611; Stephen Robb, "Fifty Years of Farewell: Douglas MacArthur's Commemorative and Deliberative Speaking" (Ph.D. diss., Indiana University, 1967), pp. 203-204.

[19]Douglas MacArthur, [speech to] "Joint Meeting of the Two Houses of the U.S. Congress," in U.S. Cong. Senate, *Representative Speeches of Douglas MacArthur*, 88th Cong., 2nd Sess. Doc. no. 95 (Washington, D.C.: GPO, 1964), p. 14.

[20]Whitney, *McArthur: His Rendezvous with Destiny*, p. 461; *Military*

Situation in the Far East: Hearings Before the Committee on Armed Services and the Committee on Foreign Relations, United States Senate, 82nd Cong., 1st Sess. (Washington, D.C.: GPO, 1951), p. 9.

[21]John C. Norris, "Leaders at Pentagon Disagree with MacArthur's Asia Views," *Washington Post*, April 12, 1951, p. 1; Willard Sheldon, "MacArthur Joins the G.O.P.," *Nation*, April 28, 1951, p. 390; Hanson W. Baldwin, "The Magic of MacArthur," *New York Times*, April 23, 1951, p. 6, col. 3.

[22]"After Week of Tribute," *New York Times*, April 22, 1951, Sec. E, p. 1, col. 3.

[23]"Is MacArthur Winning?" *New Republic*, May 21, 1951, p. 5. For a discussion of Truman's "rhetorical vision" see Ray E. McKerrow, "Truman and Korea: Rhetoric in the Pursuit of Victory," *Central States Speech Communication Journal* 28 (1977): 1-12.

[24]MacArthur also quoted himself, though without mentioning it, in his 1962 speech at the U.S. Military Academy, which uses large sections of a speech to the veterans of the Rainbow Division he delivered twenty-seven years earlier.

[25]"The Old Soldier," *Time*, April 30, 1951, p. 21; Manchester, *American Caesar*, p. 454.

[26] Hanson W. Baldwin, "The Magic of MacArthur," p. 6.

[27]"The Old Soldier," p. 21; Frederick Haberman, ed., "General MacArthur's Speech: A Symposium of Critical Comment," *Quarterly Journal of Speech* 37 (1951): 331; "After Week of Tribute," p. 3.

[28]Haberman, "General MacArthur's Speech," p. 327.

[29]"The Old Soldier," p. 24.

[30]Manchester, *American Caesar*, p. 661.

[31]"After Week of Tribute," p. 1; "The Old Soldier," p. 26; Merle Miller, *Plain Speaking: An Oral Biography of Harry S Truman* (New York: Berkley Publishing, 1973), p. 311.

INFORMATION SOURCES ON THE SPEECH SET

President Truman's Accusations

The president's radio speech is contained in Halford Ross Ryan, ed., *American Rhetoric from Roosevelt to Reagan* (Prospect Heights, Ill.: Waveland Press, 1983), pp. 86-91. A voice recording is available from the Harry S Truman Library, Independence, Missouri, Sr 71-35.

General MacArthur's Apology

The text of MacArthur's apology was published in the *Congressional Record*, although I have used the copy contained in a collection of MacArthur's speeches: U.S. Cong. Senate. *Representative Speeches of Douglas MacArthur*, 88th Cong., 2nd Sess. Doc. no. 95. Washington, D.C.: GPO, 1964, p. 14. A video recording is available: *Great Speeches*. Vol. 1. Alliance Video for Great Speeches Inc. 1985. A voice recording is also available: Great American Speeches. Vol. 4, 1950-1963. Caedmon, TC 2035, n.d.

Selected Bibliography

Acheson, Dean. *The Korean War*. New York: W. W. Norton, 1971.

Beall, Paul R. "Viper-Crusher Turns Dragon-Slayer." *Quarterly Journal of Speech* 38 (1952): 51-56.

Donovan, Robert J. *Tumultuous Years: The Presidency of Harry S Truman, 1949-1953*. New York: W. W. Norton, 1982.

Duffy, Bernard K., "Douglas MacArthur." In *American Orators of the Twentieth Century: Critical Studies and Sources*, edited by Bernard K. Duffy and Halford R. Ryan. Westport: Greenwood Press, 1987.

Haberman, Frederick, ed. "General MacArthur's Speech: A Symposium of Critical Comment." *Quarterly Journal of Speech* 37 (1951): 321-31.

Higgins, Trumbull. *Korea and the Fall of MacArthur: A Précis in Limited War*. New York: Oxford University Press, 1960.

James, D. Clayton. *The Years of MacArthur*. 3 vols. Boston: Houghton Mifflin, 1970-1985.

McCoy, Donald R. *The Presidency of Harry S Truman*. Lawrence:

University Press of Kansas, 1984.

McKerrow, Ray. "Truman and Korea: Rhetoric in Pursuit of Victory." *Central States Speech Journal* 28 (1977): 1-12.

MacArthur, Douglas. *Reminiscences*. New York: McGraw-Hill, 1964.

Manchester, William. *American Caesar*. Boston: Little, Brown, 1978.

Miller, Merle. *Plain Speaking: An Oral Biography of Harry S Truman*. Garden City, N.Y.: Doubleday, 1956.

Phillips, William S. *Douglas MacArthur: A Modern Knight-Errant*. (Revised M.A. thesis) Philadelphia: Dorrance, 1978.

Robb, Stephen. "Fifty Years of Farewell: Douglas MacArthur's Commemorative and Deliberative Speaking." Ph.D. diss., Indiana University, 1967.

Rovere, Richard H., and Schlesinger, Arthur M., Jr. *The MacArthur Controversy*. New York: Noonday, 1951.

Ryan, Halford Ross, "Harry S Truman: A Misdirected Defense for MacArthur's Dismissal." *Presidential Studies Quarterly* 11 (1981): 576-82.

___"Harry S Truman." In *American Orators of the Twentieth Century*, edited by Bernard K. Duffy and Halford R. Ryan. Westport: Greenwood Press, 1987.

Spanier, John W. *The Truman-MacArthur Controversy*. New York: W. W. Norton, 1959.

Truman, Harry S. *Years of Trial and Hope*. Vol. II of *Memoirs of Harry S Truman*. Garden City, N.Y.: Doubleday, 1956.

Whitney, Courtney. *MacArthur: His Rendezvous with Destiny*. New York: Alfred A. Knopf, 1956.

Senator Richard M. Nixon's Apology for "The Fund"

Halford R. Ryan

Senator Richard Nixon's "My Side of the Story" speech, delivered on national radio and television on September 23, 1952, was to apologetic discourse as Franklin D. Roosevelt's First Inaugural Address was to inaugural oratory, as FDR's 1944 Teamsters' Union or "Fala" speech was to campaign speaking, and as Harry S Truman's 1948 acceptance address was to convention oratory. All of these speeches were delivered during difficult situations, all were highly publicized persuasions, and all were pivotal addresses in their respective orator's career. Yet, one characteristic seems to sully Nixon's speech from those addresses. The "Checker's" speech, which nomenclature was a pejorative attempt by the speech's critics to demean it and Nixon, has come to symbolize the nadir of political communication in the 1952 presidential campaign and to reaffirm Plato's charge that rhetoric can make truth appear untruth and untruth the truth. Indeed, Nixon later complained that his speech "was labeled as the 'Checkers speech,' as though the mention of my dog was the only thing that saved my career."[1]

Nixon's complaint has merit. The fund speech contained the artful application of a number of persuasive devices—the mentioning of Checkers was only a minor one of them—that have not been explicated heretofore. Moreover, when the speech is treated *in situ* as a response to a series of charges, Nixon's address can be evaluated in terms of the rhetorical techniques he used to meet the crisis.

"THE FUND": CHARGES AGAINST NIXON'S POLICY AND CHARACTER

The speech set began innocently enough. The story has been told in a number of places how some disgruntled contributors complained about Nixon's fund, how these complaints reached columnist Peter Edson, and how Edson interviewed, at Nixon's invitation, Dana Smith, the fund's trustee. Smith was remarkably candid in his conversations with Edson, who passed his findings to Leo Katcher of the *New York Post*. However, in open-ly cooperating with Edson, Smith inadvertently supplied the core materials for the accusation that ensued. Edson was on a fishing expedition, and the theory of the speech set would suggest that when one is under attack, one should not divulge gratuitous information that could be used later against oneself. Indeed, Stewart Alsop noted that Nixon and his people should have sensed the potential danger in the fund story.[2]

Based on Edson's findings, Leo Katcher composed the first accusation against Nixon. The irony of the *New York Post*'s *kategoria* on Thursday, September 18, 1952, was that Katcher's story was based on Smith's information. First, the fund was a fact by Smith's admission. Katcher characterized the fund with the now-famous charge: "Secret Rich Men's Trust Fund Keeps Nixon In Style Far Beyond His Salary." To support the definition of an elevated life-style, Katcher used testimony from an anonymous donor: "A contributor to the fund, a state official in California, said the appeal to him was based on the fact that Nixon needed a larger home, as befitted a Senator, and that the Nixon's could not even afford a maid"; moreover, he quoted two damaging admissions from Smith: "Dick didn't have enough money to do the kind of job he wanted to do and that we wanted him to do" and "his expenses for such items as entertainment and living expenses would neces-sarily be greater than before."[3] Although this evidence did not prove Nixon lived beyond his means, one could easily infer, if one did not read the ar-ticle too closely or critically, that Nixon probably did live in an elevated style. Although the fund was not public knowledge, neither was it exactly a secret — Nixon and Smith's candor about it was not an instance of "stonewalling," to use a term from the Watergate era. But the gray area in which the fund was solicited and dispersed was conducive to Katcher's defining it as "secret" even if the fund were not exactly what the headline trumpeted. In all, the accusation employed enough sensational language, offered enough apparent evidence, and invited enough inferences to raise a doubt about Nixon's policy and character.

However, not all newspapers perceived a *prima facie* case against the senator. Republican newspapers tended to downplay the story or to bury it, and the *Los Angeles Times* did not print it until Saturday. United Press International relayed the *New York Post*'s story immediately, but Associated Press (AP) did not at first feature the story. The *New York Post*, piqued that Republican papers and the AP did not give its scoop its just due, credited the other news media for disseminating the fund story: "We think radio and newscasts helped a lot; many radio and television commentators seemed far less inhibited than the newspapers."[4] Ironically, the medium that was significantly involved in transmitting the accusation was also the means by which Nixon appealed to the mass audience in order to save his political career.

The second accusation, based on the *New York Post* story, was made by Democratic National Chairman Stephen A. Mitchell on Thursday, September 18. He charged that Nixon had accepted "donations from wealthy California business men to supplement his salary as a Senator," and Mitchell defined that policy as morally wrong: "By no standards of public morals or of private morals can such conduct be condoned or explained away." Although a partisan attack, Mitchell's accusation was more focused and less flamboyant than the *New York Post*'s banner headline, and hence more probative. What has not been emphasized about Mitchell's accusation, however, is the fact that Eisenhower was attacked for his handling of the Nixon affair. Here was an attempt to get at Eisenhower through Nixon. Mitchell juxtaposed the general's "making a great show of indignation over corruption in demagogic speeches" with the loaded question would Eisenhower "gag and swallow" the revelation about the fund or would "he state clearly and firmly that he would not run" with Nixon.[5] Mitchell cleverly hoisted the general on the horns of a dilemma: silence would condemn Ike, but Ike's requesting Nixon's resignation would come back to roost on Eisenhower and his campaign because he was associated with Nixon, and guilt by association was a powerful tool of indictment in the McCarthy era.

On Friday, September 19, Mitchell added another accusation. Again, the strategy was to attack Nixon and through him, Eisenhower. Mitchell wisely narrowed the charge by defining the fund as "a subsidy from persons with an interest in Federal legislation." He called on the senator to resign and then outflanked the general: "It is time for General Eisenhower to cast away either his principles or his running mate." Ike cleverly steered clear of this whirlpool that threatened to suck him into its vortex. The general supported Nixon just enough by noncommittal statements of the wait-to-see variety in order to keep him afloat but not so much that he could not jettison his running mate if it came to that. The onus was on Nixon to clear himself with the general's encouragement but not with his help.

In an obvious attempt to try to preempt a defense from Nixon, Mitchell framed his final accusation specifically and damningly. Hopefully, Nixon would not oblige by: "1. Telling the public exactly what persons gave him these gifts, and how much he got from each person. 2. Telling the people what he spent his money on. . . ." Mitchell then adroitly allowed that that information would enable the public to decide if Nixon failed to file proper tax returns or broke a federal law. His parting shot was a clever instance of *petitio principii*, or begging the question: "if he makes the full facts available to the public, voters can at least judge how serious is the Senator's wrongdoing."[6]

Such a strategy had its rhetorical strengths and weaknesses. On the one hand, Mitchell probably reasoned that Nixon could not or would not reveal the facts, so Nixon's silence would condemn him and taint Eisenhower. On the other hand, if Nixon did give the facts, that disclosure would certify the charge of wrongdoing, would embarrass the contributors, and would probably raise new questions that could fuel fresh accusations. Either choice would be a risky rhetorical route to defend.

Yet, there was a flaw in Mitchell's strategy of accusation. By stressing the policy aspects of the fund, Mitchell inadvertently invited Nixon to defend the fund on Mitchell's criteria: who gave what and how much and how it was spent. If Nixon could do that, Mitchell probably calculated he would not or could not, then Nixon would apparently answer the accusation satisfactorily. By not stressing the ethical qualities of the fund with reference to Nixon's character, Mitchell accidentally diverted attention away from the critical issues: the propriety of the fund's very existence and its relationship to Nixon's habits as a public servant. Mitchell missed the opportunity to make a critical linkage. The fact of the fund superceded policy considerations and went to the crux of the issue — was it an honorable habit to have the fund in the first place? But the real issues were clouded in the *New York Post*'s story and in Mitchell's two accusations, and therefore Nixon was not obliged to clarify them in his apologia.

The Mitchell-Nixon analog is an example of how the theory of the speech set can help identify the pertinent issues from the sham ones. Since Mitchell's *kategoria* focused on factual matters, Nixon wisely accepted the accusation because he may have perceived that it skirted the real issues. In short, the Democratic national chairman actually facilitated Nixon's apologetic strategy of defending the policy's ancillary points (who gave what, how much, etc.) rather than forcing the senator to address the difficult two central issues of the fund's propriety and his habit of maintaining it.

Moreover, an examination of the motive-response relationships in the speech set is instructive. To Mitchell's first charge, Nixon merely released a statement that the fund was not secret and had not been used to defray his Senate expenses, but he did not identify the supporters who gave the money. That answer motivated Mitchell to demand in a second charge on the nineteenth that Nixon name donors and donations. Accordingly, Nixon released the names and figures for the fund that had grown from $16,000 to $18,235 with seventy-six contributors. The *New York Herald Tribune* opined that its "names read almost like a blue book of metropolitan Los Angeles business, professional and social leaders — prominent manufacturers, lawyers, and oil men." As a historical footnote, Nixon also made public a complete and detailed accounting of the fund by category and expenditure.[7]

In a purely technical sense, Nixon answered most of the charge — who gave what--and albeit a little late, how the money was spent. Mitchell issued no more accusations. In fact, the *New York Herald Tribune*, which was the Eisenhower-Nixon ticket's most influential supporter on the East coast, admitted that "On the basis of the revealed facts, Senator Nixon's personal honesty should not be impeached.   We share with General Eisenhower a conviction of the Senator's integrity," but the paper perceptively noted "Yet to receive it [the fund] at all, especially when the source of the support was not publicly affirmed, is to have put the Senator in an ambiguous position."[8]

The newspaper assumed a strange posture. In one breath, it affirmed Nixon's honesty and integrity, but in a second breath, it held that he was in an ambiguous position and therefore called for his resignation with Eisenhower to decide whether to accept it. This was a blow to Nixon. The cloudiness of the accusation-apology speech set can account for some of the paper's lingering doubts about the propriety of the fund because Mitchell's accusation inadvertently allowed Nixon to obfuscate the real issues. But part of the paper's concern was to assure that its candidate, Eisenhower, would not be brought down by Nixon who was expendable.

Why, then, did Nixon deliver a televised speech to clear himself? Ironically, Richard Nixon, the accused, had helped create an era of suspicion and mudslinging against peoples' policies and characters that culminated in the 1952 campaign. This was evident in his campaign in 1946 for Jerry Voorhis' seat in the House of Representatives, in the 1950 campaign against Helen Gahagan Douglas for the U.S. Senate, and in the battle to put Alger Hiss behind bars. These ephemeral attacks, which Senator Joseph McCarthy perfected, were difficult to refute. When the accused cut off an attack, another charge, Medusa-like, spawned anew and drew nourishment from the old one. Nixon evidently understood the political climate he helped to produce, and his rhetorical choices were limited. He could not deny his policy, the fund existed. His only available strategy was to make the fund acceptable by redefining it in a favorable light. The newspapers, even the ones who had supported him and Eisenhower before the fund story broke, would not do his work for him and were in fact calling for his resignation. Eisenhower, who was teetering on the brink of disaster, would not lend Nixon a hand lest he be pulled down should Nixon fall, nor could he prematurely jettison Nixon — what if he were innocent? These events seemed to warrant a response from Nixon. Many jittery Republicans hoped for and advised a resignation speech, but Dick decided to deliver instead a defense.

The senator's decision to deliver a nationally televised apology may have been motivated in part by his apologetic successes before smaller live audiences. His first oratorical response to Mitchell's charge was at Marysville, California, on September 19. Countering that the accusation was a Communist smear tactic, Nixon told the crowd he had actually saved taxpayer's money by not charging the government for excess amounts, that he did not take "fat legal fees on the side," and that he did not have his wife on the payroll, but that Senator John Sparkman, Governor Adlai Stevenson's vice-presidential running mate, did have his wife on the payroll. The crowd applauded.[9]

Nixon did a dress rehearsal of his fund apology speech at Portland, Oregon, on Saturday night, September 20. In that address, he recited again about Pat, about Sparkman, and about how he saved taxpayer's money. Of special interest is how he turned to his advantage the *New York Post*'s and Mitchell's accusations. In a remarkable preview of his famous fund speech, Nixon framed their accusations: "he didn't return it on his income tax, he hid this thing, didn't let the people know about it, it was illegal, it was unmoral, it was unethical"; he also asked two rhetorical questions that later appeared in the fund speech: "Do you think that when a Senator makes a purely political speech in his own state that the taxpayers ought to pay the bill . . .? Do you think, for example, that when I make political broadcasts taxpayers should pay the bill . . .?"; and he phrased a question in his inimitable style: "And now, you say, well, now, look Senator, why all this hullabaloo . . .?" The Portland speech was well received.[10]

The point is that Ralph De Toledano and Lawrence Rosenfield realized that portions of Nixon's fund speech were tried out successfully on smaller live audiences,[11] but neither critic indicated the relationship these rhetorical appeals had to the fund speech's final success, which will be discussed fully in the next section.

Neither has any rhetorical critic detected the logical fallacy Nixon committed in his two early apologies and again in his final defense. The fallacy was this. According to Nixon, he "was saving you money rather than charging the expenses of my office, which were in excess of the amounts which were allowed by the taxpayers, and allowed under the law." How could Nixon "save" taxpayer's money when he had already spent his legal allowance? In case the math is confusing, Glen Lipscomb, the executive secretary of Nixon's Washington headquarters, told a reporter that "It is a private fund to be used to cover expenses of running Nixon's office that are not covered by his government allowance."[12] In other words, Nixon used the fund to pay for additional expenses that exceeded his allotment and not, as he skillfully implied, to "save" the taxpayer's money he could not legally spend anyway. Since Mitchell attacked Nixon by arguing *petitio principii*, then so could Nixon defend with that device. Nixon assumed the propriety of the fund without justifying its necessity. He only replied in kind.

"MY SIDE OF THE STORY"

Fifty-five million Americans watched Richard Nixon's *tour de force* on their newly acquired television sets, while an untold number tuned to their radios. This speech was the first personalized political crisis to be mediated by television, and Fawn Brodie observed that it gave "Nixon a sense of the power of television, and of his special talent in using it." The immediate success of the speech was phenomenal. Movie mogul Darryl Zanuck telephoned Nixon that his effort was the "most tremendous performance I have ever seen." Americans sent about two million telegrams and wrote almost three million letters to voice their positive reception of Nixon's drama, and he claimed in *Six Crises* that more than enough small contributions came in to his office to cover the $75,000 cost of the broadcast. After some *real politik* maneuvering by General Eisenhower, as he stalled for time to test the political winds and to await the decision of the Republican National-al Committee, whose technical decision it was to make whether Nixon should resign, he finally asked Nixon to meet him in Wheeling, West Virginia, in order to mend their political fences. The intricate details of the entire historical episode have been explicated elsewhere, and they are not a concern here. Rather, the purpose is to explain how the speech, which was described by Gary Allen as "one of the most effective political speeches ever delivered,"[13] worked as well as it did. For what has never been explained fully nor adequately by the speech's critics was why the speech was so successful.

To be sure, Henry McGuckin examined the address and found that Nixon successfully employed a number of appeals that were designed to tap the audience's adherence to the "American value system" that Edward Steele and Charles Redding found inherent in American culture in the 1950s. For instance, Nixon appealed to Puritan morality by offering the audience proof of his hard work as a congressman and senator, and tapped patriotism when he demonstrated his ability to catch the alleged Communist spy, Alger Hiss. As thorough and compelling as McGuckin's analysis was, it is only a partial explanation of the speech's efficacy. Lawrence Rosenfield investigated the fund speech and succeeded among its critics in providing the best explanation to date.[14]

Yet, Nixon's speech may be reexamined. In his apologia, Nixon used several rhetorical techniques that John Mason Brown called "high school oratory . . . devices"; however, neither Brown nor other critics have identified these devices.[15] Moreover, no one has described how Nixon fashioned his delivery in order to present himself and his message in a compelling manner. Previous critics' failures to treat the senator's speech techniques and delivery are telling. In conjunction with his language, Nixon's *actio* [see Glossary] was a significant factor in the overall success of the speech. The symbolism of a man under attack, who defended himself in a personal and direct fashion before such an intimate medium as television, was an image to which Americans reacted. Nixon was an archetype for televised political apology. Having no previous roles by which to assess the genre, the American people reacted to the visceral cues of his language and to the visual cues of his sincerity. Since Nixon gave careful attention to his delivery, it would behoove his critics to do the same.

In *Six Crises*, Nixon realized that he must accomplish three goals. First, he had to explain and defend the fund. Second, he wanted to ward off future attacks so that these would "fall on deaf ears." Since he had chosen the route Mitchell probably thought he would not select, Nixon wanted to assure that his apologia would spike any new accusations. Third, he wanted to launch a political counterattack in order to give the audience reasons to vote for his ticket. In his later memoirs, he stated that he divided the speech into four parts: the facts about the fund, an attack against Stevenson, praise for Eisenhower, and a request for action. Rosenfield determined that the speech had three sections: a denial of unethical conduct in maintaining the fund, a revelation of his financial history, and a counterattack on Sparkman and Stevenson.[16] Although these versions differ slightly, they all distill to certain objectives that Nixon obtained by using several rhetorical techniques. He employed the Classical organizational pattern to defend the fund and to counterattack the Democrats, and *tu quoque*, *argumentum ad personam*, *petitio principii*, affirmation by denial, turning the tables, and inoculation to attain his other objectives.

The Classical pattern was originally invented by Korax, a Greek from the fifth century B.C., as an effective organizational strategy for courtroom oratory.[17] Rosenfield noted that "the appropriate argumentative strategy was clearly forensic" for Nixon's speech, but he did not identify Nixon's using the Classical pattern.[18] In the *exordium* or introduction, the orator introduces himself and the speech in such a manner as to make the audience receptive to both; a *narratio* presents favorably the events under consideration; the *confirmatio* gives the arguments that support the speaker's stand; the *refutatio* offers a refutation against the opposition; and the *epilogus*, or conclusion, appeals to the audience for support. The rhetorical device of *tu quoque*, translated as "you also," is a retort that charges one's opponents with doing or saying the same thing as oneself. Nixon used this diversionary tactic to deflect attention from himself to his opponents. *Argumentum ad personam* is directed toward the person or character assassination. *Petitio principii* is begging the question. Affirmation by denial, one of Nixon's knacks, is a technique whereby the orator covertly affirms a point by overtly denying such intention. Turning the tables is a device by which the speaker takes a point made by the opponent and turns it back to harm the opponent. The concept of rhetorical inoculation is borrowed from the medical metaphor. As a physician gives a patient an inoculation to ward off a disease, so may an orator administer the audience a dose of a carefully constructed message to fend off future harmful communications from the opposition.

Senator Nixon set the tone of his apologia in the *exordium*.[19] He subtly indicated that his speech would be an offensive defense. Admitting that he addressed the audience because his honesty and integrity had been attacked, he noted the usual political ploy was to ignore or deny such charges "without giving details." Nixon countercharged that "we've had enough of that in the United States, particularly with the present Administration in Washington, D.C." This *tu quoque* reminded the audience that the Democrats were not pristine.

Nixon went quickly to the *narratio* where he endeavored to portray Mitchell's charges against himself in a favorable light. Not content with a legal definition of the fund, he asked "was it morally wrong?" He then answered his question by stating Mitchell's criteria that would justify the fund. This was a brilliant rhetorical maneuver because Nixon wisely controlled the narrow context in which he would exculpate himself. In response to the *New York Post* story and Mitchell's accusations, Nixon asserted that the $18,000 had not gone for his personal use, was not secretly given or handled, and that no contributor got any special political favors. But he rightly realized that his protestations, given without evidentiary support, from a man whose very credibility was under attack, would not suffice; therefore, he moved to the *confirmatio*, which comprised almost half of his address. The importance of the *narratio* was to give an appearance of answering the charges in order to make the audience receptive to him and his message. The strategy of the *confirmatio* was to reiterate his defense by developing in more detail the arguments for his side of the story.

Within the *confirmatio* section, Nixon marshalled his main arguments by using the method of residues. The method is actually a rhetorical application of the disjunctive syllogism: either A, B, or C; not A, not B, therefore C. By discrediting in turn each allegation against himself, he systematically narrowed the audience's perceptions to the desired residue: his fund was not legally nor morally wrong. In conjunction with the method, Nixon used the rhetorical question, phrased in the manner he had tried out at Portland, Oregon. Each disjunct addressed the queries that might weigh against him in the minds of his listeners. For instance, he began the *confirmatio* with the first interrogatory disjunct: "But then some of you will say and rightly, 'Well, what did you use the fund for, Senator? Why did you have to have it?'" He justified the fund with an enlarged series of rhetorical questions, which he used in a truncated fashion at Marysville and Portland: should taxpayers pay for the cost of printing and mailing political speeches? the costs of political trips? the costs of political broadcasts? Of course, as Nixon knew, any taxpayer would answer "no." He let his audience infer why would a senator who did not use taxpayer's dollars for political expenses use a fund for personal benefit? Nixon raised a doubt.

The second disjunct continued in this vein to discredit the charges while concomitantly enhancing Nixon's financial habits as a public servant. Senator Nixon pointedly phrased the next disjunct: "But then the question arises, you say, 'Well, how do you pay for these and how can you do it legally?'" He answered this question with yet another disjunctive application.

(1) One could be a rich man, but Nixon was not. (2) Or one could put one's wife on the payroll, but Nixon did not have Pat on the payroll; however, he reminded his national audience that Sparkman had his wife on the payroll for the past ten years. To cover this frontal attack on his opponent's practice and character that was inappropriate while ostensibly defending himself, Nixon used affirmation by denial: "Now let me say this. That's his business and I'm not critical of him for doing that. You will have to pass judgment on that particular point." He affirmed his criticism of Sparkman and invited the audience to pass judgment on him by denying such an intent. (3) Or one could continue to practice law, as he said at Marysville, but Nixon did not do that because he realized an inherent conflict of interest that other politicians chose to ignore. (4) Or one could have a fund. The clear impression one had about Nixon at the end of this disjunct was that since he had not used any of the questionable practices others in his position had used, then surely the senator was not the kind of person who would misuse the fund. Moreover, one could easily infer, and perhaps that was exactly what Nixon hoped his audience would do, that the fund was moral: it allowed Nixon to communicate his political messages about K_1C_2, the chemical formula that came to satirize the issues in the 1952 campaign: Korea, Communism and Corruption, to the electorate without directly or indirectly charging those costs to the taxpayers.

Mindful that the audience might still harbor doubts about the fund, Nixon moved to the third disjunct: "Let me say, incidentally, that some of you may say, 'Well, that's all right, Senator; that's your explanation, but have you got any proof?'" The evidence he offered his audience was an audit by Price, Waterhouse & Co., and a legal opinion by Gibson, Dunn & Crutcher. In a nutshell, the opinion stated that Nixon "did not violate any Federal or state law" in the operation of the fund nor did funds paid directly to Nixon for reimbursement of expenses "constitute income . . . either reportable or taxable as income under applicable tax laws." These findings were never challenged, and they cleared the air about the legality of the fund. Not wanting to sacrifice what he had just accomplished, Nixon inoculated at the end of this disjunct to ward off future attacks: "and let me say that I recognize that some will continue to smear regardless of what the truth may be."

With the audit and legal opinion in his favor, Nixon might have ended the argument section. But in what could be termed an exercise in overkill, he proceeded to his last disjunct: "Well, maybe you were able, Senator, to fake this thing. How can we believe what you say? After all, is there a possibility that you may have feathered your own nest?" In this disjunct, Nixon disclosed himself: his war record, how Pat had worked for the government, how they had all their savings in U.S. government bonds, how much their houses cost and how much they owed on them, how much they inherited, how much they owed in personal debt, *ad nauseam*. But two appeals warrant detailed attention. First, Nixon allowed that Pat did not own a mink coat, but that she did have a "respectable Republican cloth coat." The allusion is perhaps lost today but it was meaningful in 1952: a wife of a high figure in the Truman administration was allegedly given a mink coat as a political gift. Nixon effectively turned that table on his opponents. Second, Nixon called on Checkers to perform his tricks. The senator remembered the great success President Franklin D. Roosevelt had in his Teamsters' Union Address, September 23, 1944 — delivered exactly eight years before Nixon's speech — in deflecting charges that he had sent a destroyer back to pick up his dog Fala, whose "Scotch soul was furious" at such charges. In *Six Crises*, Nixon wrote: "I decided to mention my own dog Checkers. Using the same ploy as FDR would irritate my opponents and delight my friends, I thought." In his memoirs, Nixon recorded that he was aware of the technique of turning the tables with Checkers because it would "infuriate my critics if I could turn this particular table on them." Brown believed the Checkers ploy "was the climaxing emotional appeal made by Richard Nixon."[20] What is not generally understood about the Checkers appeal was its efficacy as a rhetorical application of *reductio ad absurdum*. Therein, an orator runs an argument to an absurd conclusion, thereby suggesting that the initial assumption was absurd. Nixon's closing statement of the disjunct clearly implied the absurdity of the charge against the fund by comparing it to the straw issue that Nixon should be compelled to return the dog: "regardless of what they say about it, we're gonna keep it."

Before treating the nature of Nixon's *refutatio*, it is important to note several things about his *confirmatio*. In order to be logically sound, the method of residues must assay all of the disjuncts that reasonably apply to the issue at hand. Nixon defended the fund on three disjuncts: not for personal use, not secretly given or handled, and no special favors given. Barnet Baskerville believed that "Nixon's setting up his three criteria by which to test the morality of his actions was a commendably forthright approach." Actually, the criteria were Mitchell's and the *New York Post*'s. His use of the method of residues gave the desired appearance of answering the accusations, but he did not address the critical issues. Granted, he did prove the fund was not for his personal income, and by letting the newspapers print donor's names and contributions, he adequately answered the secrecy issue, although he might have treated the topic more forthrightly in his speech. However, the senator did not offer any evidence, except for two unsubstantiated assertions, that he had never given political favors to contributors. "This matter of influence, therefore, being central," according to Baskerville, "deserved more attention than it received." Neither did he address the propriety of the fund, except to argue he needed it to "save" money that he had already spent. Therefore, the residue that the fund was moral, even given that he proved it was legal, cannot stand. Rosenfield realized there were merits in Nixon's organizational structure, but rightly complained: "Given such overpowering lead-ins there is little room for an auditor's imagination to function. His mind remains riveted as the argument unfolds. Viewed as a performance-in-time, the inferences are pre-determined by the transitions, and the discourse stubbornly resists efforts by an auditor to participate independently in the communicative act." William Miller clearly understood the efficacy of Nixon's strategy: "Another debating device that can be learned from Mr. Nixon is that it is better to deal with an irrelevancy on which one can make an effective performance than with a relevant point on which one may be less compelling." But as a rhetorical technique to persuade people who do not listen nor read too closely, the method allowed Nixon to give the impression that the charges were fully answered. It may be that if Mitchell had stressed the propriety of the fund and not the "facts," Nixon would have been constrained to address that question in his apologia.[21]

Nevertheless, Senator Nixon certainly gave his audience the assured impression that he had answered all of the accusations against him when he moved to the *refutatio*. In it, he left his defensive position and developed a posture of overt attack against his opponents. Having cleared himself, he counterattacked with *tu quoque* to shift the audience's attention to Stevenson, Sparkman, and the Truman administration. The *refutatio* comprised about one-fifth of his speech and it reeked of the offal that characterized oratory in the 1952 campaign. All of these character assassinations on the Democratic triumvirate were applications of *argumentum ad personam*, pejoratively known as "If you have no case, then abuse your opponent."

Nixon began the *refutatio* in an aggressive manner. He turned the tables on the chairman of the Democratic National Committee who made the ill-advised comment that if one could not afford to be in the Senate, one ought not run for it. Nixon handily capitalized on that gaffe by suggesting that that idea probably did not reflect the thinking of the Democratic party and certainly not that of the Republican party. Nixon then turned on Stevenson with another affirmation by denial: "I believe that it's fine that a man like Governor Stevenson who inherited a fortune from his father can run for President," but Nixon thought it was essential that men of modest means could also run for the office. Nixon next launched a major *tu quoque* attack against Sparkman and Stevenson. The senator charged that the governor had a fund, but again used affirmation by denial to malign Stevenson: "I don't condemn Mr. Stevenson for what he did. But until the facts are in there is a doubt that will be raised." Also, Sparkman had his wife on the payroll, but "I don't condemn him for that." With their feet to the fire, Nixon fanned the flames by placing Sparkman and Stevenson on the horns of a dilemma. He commanded them to come before the American people and tell about their finances, as he had done, "And if they don't it will be an admission that they have something to hide." If they confessed, they would confirm their guilt; if they did not confess, their silence would convict them.[22] In either case, Nixon would win because his *tu quoque* would have been substantiated and it would divert attention to them. Here, again, Nixon effectively turned the dilemma in which Mitchell had tried to place him. Moreover, one should note that Nixon asked Stevenson to "Give the names of people that have contributed to that fund." As he had been embarrassed on the defensive, so would Nixon, now on the offensive, embarrass Stevenson.

Having attacked his opponents, Nixon tried to assure that those attacks would not be redirected at him. He immediately used inoculation effectively: "Now, let me say this: I know that this is not the last of the smears. In spite of my explanation tonight other smears will be made; others have been made in the past. And the purpose of the smears, I know, is this — to silence me, to make me let up." The people who smeared him were, of course, the leftist media people. So, Nixon counterattacked them. He argued a subtle and convincing inference: the same people who were attacking him now were the same people who attacked him in his handling of the Alger Hiss case; since they were wrong in the Hiss case, Nixon let his audience infer they were wrong now. This treatment also used the rhetorical technique of victimage and scapegoat. Nixon portrayed himself as a victim of media attacks. By blaming the fund crisis on the media as scapegoat, he focused the audience's attention not on the fund but on the media that victimized him.

Richard Nixon then weighed in against what was left standing on the political landscape, the Truman administration. He accused it of having lost six hundred million people to the Communists and 117,000 casualties in the Korean War. Having smitten the "K" of the political formula, Nixon raked the muck on "C":

> Take the problems of corruption. You've read about the mess in Washington. Mr. Stevenson can't clean it up because he was picked by the man, Truman, under whose Administration the mess was made. You wouldn't trust a man who made the mess to clean it up — that's Truman. And by the same token you can't trust the man who was picked by the man that made the mess to clean it up — and that's Stevenson.

As for the second "C," Nixon inveighed against the Communists. In what has to be the funniest line in the speech, Nixon attacked Stevenson as unfit for the presidency because he called the Alger Hiss case a "red herring": "He's [Stevenson] accused us that have attempted to expose the Communists of looking for Communists in the Bureau of Fisheries and Wildlife — I say that a man who says that isn't qualified to be President of the United States." While it cannot be determined if Nixon, or the

American people, understood the ironic humor in Stevenson's comment, it is plainly evident that one should look for red herrings in the Bureau of Fisheries and Wildlife.

The last ploy Nixon used in the *refutatio* section has been overlooked by critics, but it, too, served an emotional function and it may be more pathetic than the Checkers appeal. Nixon read a letter from a nineteen-year-old woman whose husband was with the Marines in Korea and had not seen his two-month-old son. Living on $85 a month, she sent Nixon a check for $10, but Nixon assured his audience he would never cash it. This letter served several salutary functions. It tapped the anti-Korean sentiment against Truman's handling of the war, thus bolstering Nixon's political persona. It served as an analogy for the other contributors to the fund: the audience could easily infer that as this well-meaning young woman had contributed to Nixon's campaign with the best of intentions, so had earlier contributors to Nixon's fund. And it suggested that as this young American had faith in Nixon, so should the rest of the American people. But Baskerville observed that even the letter had a flaw because it was "represented as an expression of confidence written *after* the fund disclosure, but which Nixon had actually received and used much earlier in his campaign [italics in original]."[23]

The *refutatio* section was as remarkable as was the *confirmatio*. The aggressive posture of attack, the character assassination of Sparkman and Stevenson, the hatchet attack on the Truman administration, the blatant appeals on K_1C_2, and the victimage and scapegoating on the media, all combined to direct attention from Nixon to his opponents. Except for the attack on the Stevenson fund, Nixon had rehearsed these themes in rear platform appearances on his whistle-stop speaking tour in California and at Portland. In terms of *kairos* [*see* Glossary], the disclosure that Governor Stevenson had a slush fund was propitious. The accusation appeared on Tuesday, September 23, and Nixon wisely worked this late-breaking story into his address. The remarkable paradox about Nixon's speech was that that kind of scrappy campaign oratory found its way into a televised apologia. Yet, that was why the Classical pattern was so useful. Since Myles Martel found that attack and defense were common strategies in presidential campaigns, the amenability of the Classical pattern to the rhetorical situation in 1952 is readily apparent. It allowed Nixon to present his defensive arguments in the *confirmatio* and then to attack his opponents in the *refutatio*. The pattern does not guarantee success, but in the hands of a skilled orator such as Senator Richard Nixon, it proved persuasive.[24]

In the *epilogus*, Nixon phrased the last question on peoples' minds: "And, now, finally, I know that you wonder whether or not I am going to stay on the Republican ticket or resign." Asserting that he did not believe he should quit because he was not a quitter (this is an example of *petitio principii*), and neither was Pat a quitter (he misrepresented for the Irish vote that Pat Ryan was born on St. Patrick's Day when she was actually born the day before), he acknowledged the decision was not his to make but was the Republican National Committee's. In an appeal over Eisenhower's head, which Wills believed was Nixon's way of nettling the General for his ambivalent attitude toward the Senator during the crisis,[25] Nixon asked for specific action by the audience: "And I am going to ask you to help them decide. Wire and write the Republican National Committee whether you think I should stay on or whether I should get off. And whatever their decision is, I will abide by it." This direct appeal channelled listeners' belief in his apologia into direct salutary support for the speaker.

Richard Nixon's delivery for this speech was extraordinarily effective. Harry S Truman might have believed Nixon was "a shifty-eyed goddamn liar," but there was none of that on September 23, 1952. Nixon's eye-contact was outstanding. He credited his experiences as a debater for Whittier College in preparing him to address audiences without notes.[26] He relied sparingly on his speech draft while he was seated at a desk through the *confirmatio* section. The only exception was when he picked up his manuscript to detail his personal finances. But even then, his looking at his notes reinforced the image of accuracy and honesty in the figures, and when he had finished with that part of the speech, he laid down his notes. When he arose from the desk in order to step out in front of the camera during the *refutatio*, he used no notes at all. His direct eye-contact with the home viewers' eyes as they watched their TV sets enhanced Nixon's credibility. He lifted from his desk the legal opinion and audit, and he also showed the letter and check from the young woman. Like the evangelist who holds aloft the Bible or Senator Joseph McCarthy who waived empty laundry lists that supposedly contained names of Communists in the State Department, Nixon's proffering these documents reinforced the legitimacy of his claims.

Nixon's gestures appeared slightly wooden, but they successfully emphasized and reinforced his language. His usual hand gesture was a clenched fist that chopped the air to punctuate his points. When discussing the problem of corruption in government, he implored his audience with open palms not to trust Stevenson or Truman. During the *refutatio*, he assumed a combative posture toward the camera that suited the temper of his language. He matched the assertiveness of his word choice by thrusting forward his head and body and by gesturing vigorously. Little wonder that Bruce Mazlish thought "the Checkers speech was, in fact, a highly aggressive defense."[27] However, in the conclusion of his speech, Nixon wisely placed his hands behind his back, to assume a more meek and modest image, as he asked (rather than commanded) his audience to wire and write the Republican National Committee.

Although McGuckin found emotional stress in Nixon's voice and demeanor, Brown noted that his manner showed "no strain, his voice no tension."[28] In fact, Nixon's voice was superbly modulated. When he admitted that he was not a rich man, he allowed his voice to trail off in a semiembarrassed fashion so that the audience would identify with him. He increased his loudness and punctuated each word when he told his audience they had "never paid one dime for expenses" so they would not miss the point. And his voice oozed with righteous indignation when he asserted he would not return Checkers. Withall, he superbly executed the delivery of his speech.

Lastly, Nixon's diction reinforced the way in which he delivered his apologia. He communicated with homey words such as "folks" and "you know," verbal fillers such as "well" and "now," personal pronouns such as "I," "you," and "we," and vocal contractions such as "get 'em" and "gonna." These words suggested a guileless stylist, a speaker without pretensions to affectations — as juxtaposed to Stevenson who was caricatured for his erudite word choice in his speeches. In short, whereas Stevenson professed to "talk sense to the American people," Nixon did.

CONCLUSION

"For all their victories and acclaim," wrote William Miller, "the champions in the art of persuasion, from the days of the sophists to our own, have been under a bit of shadow. After the applause has died down and a more reflective mood has set in, one is never sure just where conviction ended and sheer artistry began."[29]

Nixon's "My Side of the Story" was like a pointillist painting. Impressionists were more concerned with technique and representation than with reality. Like his apologia, their pictures were optimally viewed from some distance where they presented their best appearance. In reception to his address, a gallery of newspapers took that point of view. The *New York Herald Tribune* editorialized that "Senator Nixon acquitted himself admirably" but was more interested in defending General Eisenhower's handling of the whole episode. The *Kansas City Star* thought the facts and truth "had been given — most frankly, most dramatically and with rare courage"; the *Detroit Free Press* saw on "TV a personality of deep sincerity"; and the *New Orleans Times-Picayune* noted that Nixon "may have taken his own ticket off the defensive."[30]

Some newspapers were apparently persuaded by the artistry of Nixon's rhetorical techniques. The *Chicago Tribune* commented upon his turning the tables: "Nixon has turned adversity to advantage for his party." The *New York Times*, *New York World-Telegram*, *San Francisco Examiner*, *Washington Evening Star*, *Chicago Daily News*, and *Pittsburgh Press* noted, in one way or another, how Governor Stevenson was now under obligation to respond about his fund as Nixon had, and how the Democrats were now on the defensive as a result of the senator's major *tu quoque* attacks. That the newspapers did not respond to his usage of the Classical pattern may be expected. In truth, Nixon's artistry with it was an exemplar of the ability for which Lysias, an ancient Greek logographer or speech writer, was noted — "the art of concealing the art." However, with regard to inoculation, the *Los Angeles Herald Express* sensed its efficacy: "Who will sneer at this report to the country by one who loves his country. Watch, mark them."[31]

However, some editorials examined the canvass closely by looking at the points rather than the picture. Of course, the *New York Post* thought it was a "soap opera." But on the question of the propriety of the fund, some were not beguiled by Nixon's utilization of the method of residues. The *New York Times* regretted "the lack of recognition by Sen. Nixon that he had made any sort of mistake in accepting these funds in the first place"; the *Washington Post* posited the central issue "whether any such private fund can be squared with our American ideals of representative government"; the *Philadelphia Bulletin* perceived the issue precisely: "If there were a flaw in Sen. Nixon's presentation last night, it lay in his representation that the motive for the use of private funds in his behalf was consideration of the taxpayers," and noted that although he gave a certificate of legality from a law firm, "He could present no documents on ethics . . . ."; the *Baltimore Evening Sun* observed that "Nixon . . . did not deal in any way with the underlying problem of propriety"; the *Miami Daily News* asked Nixon to admit that he had made a mistake or "Lacking that, Nixon will continue to appear morally insensitive"; and the *Newark Star-Ledger* noted "He did not, however, explain the weakness of his judgment."[32]

Of *kategoria* and *apologia*, Quintilian wrote: "accusation necessarily precedes defence. You might as well assert that the sword was invented for the purpose of self-defence and not for aggression."[33] The sword that Leo Katcher wielded in his *New York Post* story and that Stephen Mitchell honed in his two accusations was used to attack directly Nixon and indirectly Eisenhower. These men and the media commentators, in addition to many Republicans, not to mention the Democrats on whom the sword was turned, probably miscalculated Richard Nixon's mastery over the chosen weapons. Of his ability to use with finesse persuasive rhetorical techniques and delivery skills, a line from his "My Side of the Story" speech says it succinctly: "Well, they just don't know who they're dealing with."

NOTES

[1]Richard M. Nixon, *Six Crises* (New York: Pyramid Books, 1968), p. 134.

[2]See Nixon, *Six Crises*, pp. 77-79; Fawn Brodie, *Richard Nixon: The Shaping of His Character* (New York: W.W. Norton, 1981), pp. 273-75; and

Stewart Alsop, *Nixon and Rockefeller* (Garden City: Doubleday, 1960), p. 60.

[3]"Secret Rich Men's Trust Fund Keeps Nixon In Style Far Beyond His Salary," *New York Post*, September 18, 1952, pp. 3, 26.

[4]Editorial, *New York Post*, September 22, 1952, p. 25.

[5]"Mitchell's Statement,"*New York Herald Tribune*, September 19, 1952, p. 11.

[6]"Mitchell Urges Nixon to Name Fund Donators," *New York Herald Tribune*, September 20, 1952, p. 6.

[7]"Nixon's Fund Itemized; 76 Gave $18,235," *New York Herald Tribune*, September 21, 1952, p. 1; "Nixon Confirms $16,000 Fund to Help with Senate Expenses," *New York Herald Tribune*, September 19, 1952, p. 1; and "How Fund Was Dispersed," *New York Herald Tribune*, September 24, 1952, p. 1.

[8]Editorial, "The General's Decision," *New York Herald Tribune*, September 24, 1952, p. 8.

[9]"Nixon Phones to Assistants of Eisenhower," *New York Herald Tribune*, September 20, 1952, p. 7.

[10]"Nixon Talk on Political Fund," *New York Herald Tribune*, September 20, 1952, p. 4.

[11]See Ralph De Toledano, *One Man Alone: Richard Nixon* (New York: Funk and Wagnalls, 1969), p. 145, and L. W. Rosenfield, "A Case Study in Speech Criticism: The Nixon-Truman Analog," *Speech Monographs* 25 (1968): 442.

[12]"Nixon Phones to Assistants of Eisenhower," p. 7; "Mitchell's Statement," p. 11.

[13]Brodie, *Richard Nixon*, p. 289; quoted in De Toledano, *Richard Nixon*, p. 151; Nixon, *Six Crises*, p. 127; Gary Wills, *Nixon Agonistes: The Crisis of the Self-Made Man* (Boston: Houghton Mifflfin Co., 1970), pp. 97-99, 107-12; and Gary Allen, *Richard Nixon: The Man Behind the Mask* (Boston: Western Islands, 1971), p. 160.

[14]See Henry E. McGuckin, Jr., "A Values Analysis of Richard Nixon's 1952 Campaign-Fund Speech," *Southern Speech Communication Journal* 33 (1968):   259-69;   Edward D. Steele and W. Charles Redding, "The American Value System: Premises for Persuasion," *Western Speech* 26 (1962):   83-91; and Rosenfield, "A Case Study," pp. 435-50.

[15]John Mason Brown, *Through These Men* (New York: Harper and Brothers, 1956), p. 102.

[16]Nixon, *Six Crises*, p. 108; Richard Nixon, *RN, The Memoirs of Richard Nixon* (New York: Grosset and Dunlap, 1978), p. 104; Rosenfield, "A Case Study," p. 436.

[17]See Kathleen Freeman, *The Murder of Herodes* (New York: W. W. Norton, 1963), p. 32, and George Kennedy, *The Art of Persuasion in Greece* (Princeton: Princeton University Press, 1963), p. 61.

[18]Rosenfield, "A Case Study," p. 438.

[19]For the text of Senator Nixon's speech, see *American Rhetoric from Roosevelt to Reagan: A Collection of Speeches and Critical Essays*, edited by Halford Ross Ryan (Prospect Heights, IL: Waveland Press, 1983), pp. 114-23, or *Vital Speeches of the Day*, October 15, 1952, pp. 11-15.

[20]Nixon, *Six Crises*, p. 109; Nixon, *Memoirs*, p. 99; Brown, *Through These Men*, p. 102.

[21]Barnet Baskerville, "The Vice-Presidentail Candidates," in Frederick W. Haberman, ed., "The Election of 1952: A Symposium," *Quarterly Journal of Speech* 38 (1952): 407-8; Rosenfield, "A Case Study," p. 445; William Lee Miller, "The Debating Career of Richard M. Nixon," *The Reporter*, April 19, 1956, p. 13.

[22]This rhetorical technique haunted President Nixon in the battle over the release of the Watergate tapes.

[23]Baskerville, "The Vice-Presidential Candidates," p. 408.

[24]See "Subsidy for Illinois Aides Charged; Eases 'Sacrifice,' Stevenson Says," *New York Times,* September 23, 1952, p. 1; Myles Martel, *Political Campaign Debates: Images, Strategies, and Tactics* (New York: Longmans, 1983), p. 62.

[25]Wills, *Nixon Agonistes*, p. 109.

[26]Merle Miller, *Plain Speaking: An Oral Biography of Harry S Truman* (New York: Putnam's, 1973), p. 178; Nixon, *Memoirs*, p. 17.

[27]Bruce Mazlish, *In Search of Nixon: A Psychohistorical Inquiry* (New York: Basic Books, 1972), p. 100.

[28]See McGuckin, "A Value Analysis," p. 69, and Brown, *Through these Men*, p. 102.

[29]Miller, "The Debating Career of Richard Nixon," p. 12.

[30]Editorial, "The Air is Cleared," *New York Herald Tribune*, September 25, 1952, p. 22; "Papers Give Opinions on Nixon's Speech," *New York Herald Tribune*, September 25, 1952, p. 16.

[31]Ibid.

[32]Ibid.

[33]*The Institutio Oratoria of Quintilian*, trans. H. E. Butler (Cambridge: Harvard University Press, 1963), I, Book III, ii, 2.

INFORMATION SOURCES ON THE SPEECH SET

The Accusations Against Richard Nixon

For Leo Katcher's accusation, see "Secret Rich Men's Trust Fund Keeps Nixon In Style Far Beyond His Salary," *New York Post*, September 18, 1952, p. 3.

For Stephen Mitchell's accusations, see "Mitchell's Statement," *New York Herald Tribune*, September 19, 1952, p. 11, and "Mitchell Urges Nixon to Name Fund Donators," *New York Herald Tribune*, September 20, 1952, p. 6.

Senator Richard Nixon's Apology

For a text of the speech, see *American Rhetoric from Roosevelt to Reagan: A Collection of Speeches and Critical Essays*, edited by Halford Ross Ryan (Prospect Heights, Ill.: Waveland Press, 1983), pp. 114-23, or *Vital Speeches of the Day*, October 15, 1952, pp. 11-15.

A video recording is available: Richard Nixon, "Checkers" Speech, *Great*

Speeches, Vol. II, Educational Video Group, 1986.

Selected Bibliography

Allen, Gary. *Richard Nixon: The Man Behind the Mask*. Boston: Western Islands, 1971.

Alsop, Stewart. *Nixon and Rockefeller*. Garden City, N.Y.: Doubleday, 1960.

Baskerville, Barnet. "The Vice-Presidential Candidates," in Frederick W. Haberman, ed., "The Election of 1952: A Symposium." *Quarterly Journal of Speech* 38 (1952): 397-414.

Brodie, Fawn. *Richard Nixon: The Shaping of His Character*. New York: W. W. Norton, 1981.

Brown, John Mason. *Through These Men*. New York: Harper and Brothers, 1956.

De Toledano, Ralph. *One Man Alone: Richard Nixon*. New York: Funk and Wagnalls, 1969.

Hart, Roderick P. "Absolutism and Situation: *Prolegomena* to a Rhetorical Biography of Richard M. Nixon." *Communication Monographs* 43 (1976): 204-28.

Mazlish, Bruce. *In Search of Nixon: A Psychohistorical Inquiry*. New York: Basic Books, 1972.

Mazo, Earl. *Richard Nixon: A Political and Personal Portrait*. New York: Harper and Brothers, 1959.

McGuckin, Henry E., Jr. "A Value Analysis of Richard Nixon's 1952 Campaign-Fund Speech." *Southern Speech Communication Journal* 33 (1968): 259-69.

Miller, William Lee. "The Debating Career of Richard M. Nixon." *The Reporter*, April 19, 1952, pp. 11-17.

Nixon, Richard. *RN, The Memoirs of Richard Nixon*. New York: Grosset and Dunlap, 1978.

_____. *Six Crises*. New York: Pyramid Books, 1968.

Rosenfield, L. W. "A Case Study in Speech Criticism: The Nixon-Truman Analog." *Speech Monographs* 25 (1968): 435-50.

Vartebedian, Robert A. "From Checkers to Watergate: Richard Nixon and the Art of Contemporary Apologia." *Speaker and Gavel* 22 (1985): 52-61.

Wills, Gary. *Nixon Agonistes: The Crisis of the Self-Made Man*. Boston: Houghton Mifflin Co., 1970.

In the Matter of
J. Robert Oppenheimer

Rachel L. Holloway

From 1945 until 1954, perhaps no public figure enjoyed greater acclaim than J. Robert Oppenheimer, the father of the atomic bomb. His successful wartime supervision of the Los Alamos laboratory and his numerous advisory posts made Oppenheimer, as Herbert York noted, "by far the most influential nuclear scientist in America during the immediate postwar period."[1] Scientists, politicians, and the general public were shocked when in 1954 President Eisenhower suspended Oppenheimer's security clearance. An inquiry ensued, and Oppenheimer was labeled a security risk. Sumner Pike, a commissioner of the Atomic Energy Commission, felt that the accusations lodged against Oppenheimer masked a deeper issue: "these things are so incredible to me that I almost wonder if there isn't some other motivation behind the apparent one in bringing these charges at this time."[2] Indeed, the Oppenheimer security hearing is best understood as the use of administrative means to achieve political goals. The charges against Oppenheimer's character were motivated by his opponents' desire to destroy his influence in policy matters. Moreover, in the specific rhetorical strategies used by both Oppenheimer and his accusers, the charges against policy and against character were interdependent. The Oppenheimer case, therefore, presents an opportunity to explore the connection between policy and character in *kategoria* and *apologia*. An explanation of the motivations behind the Oppenheimer security hearing provides the background necessary to a theoretical analysis of the issues which arose in the case.

In the years following World War II, prevailing sentiment in the military generally, among elected officials, and in the Atomic Energy Commission itself called for increased nuclear weapons development and buildup. Oppenheimer challenged the predominant policy position with his persuasive advocacy for the control of nuclear weapons. He was instrumental in the first proposals for an International Atomic Energy Agency. After the Soviet Union rejected international control of atomic power, Oppenheimer favored development of limited strategic weapons. Along this line, Oppenheimer's position on the development of the hydrogen bomb was especially frustrating to his opponents.

In October 1949, the general advisory committee (GAC) to the Atomic Energy Commission concluded that the hydrogen bomb did not warrant funding necessary to a crash development program, partly due to technical infeasibility but also on moral grounds. Oppenheimer, as GAC chairman, became the spokesperson for the recommendation. Oppenheimer also openly opposed a weapons development program popular with the Air Force and with certain AEC officials. To some observers, Oppenheimer, in particular, appeared reluctant to secure the United States militarily. Because Oppenheimer wielded great influence politically and publicly, he posed a significant threat to his opposition's policies and program. Their interests required Oppenheimer's removal from public service. Yet, Oppenheimer's popularity and prestige precluded a simple dismissal. A personnel security hearing provided a legitimate means to oust Oppenheimer.[3]

THE ACCUSATIONS AGAINST OPPENHEIMER

On November 7, 1953, William Liscum Borden, former executive director of the Congressional Joint Atomic Energy Committee, mailed a letter to FBI director J. Edgar Hoover that named Oppenheimer as a Soviet agent. In response, the FBI sent a report to the White House, to AEC chairman Lewis Strauss, and to Defense Secretary Charles Wilson. On December 4, 1953, President Eisenhower ordered a "blank wall" placed between Oppenheimer and all classified information. The information in the FBI report was not new. In fact, the information had been reviewed twice and in both cases, in 1943 and in 1947, Oppenheimer had received the highest level security clearance available to atomic scientists. The AEC instituted regular procedures to determine if Oppenheimer was a threat to national security, despite his earlier clearances.[4]

The first procedural step was to inform Oppenheimer of his changed status. Major General Kenneth Nichols, AEC general manager, wrote a letter to Oppenheimer to tell him that his security clearance had been suspended and to instruct him of the steps he must take if he wished to have his case reviewed before a personnel security board.[5] Nichols explained that Executive Order 10450 required the suspension of any individual's employment when "there exists information indicating that his employment may not be clearly consistent with the interests of the national security."[6] Nichols stated that additional investigation into Oppenheimer's "character, associations, and loyalty" raised questions about his employment. The remainder of Nichols' letter listed the "derogatory information" that stood as evidence against Oppenheimer.

Nichols began his specific charges with a lengthy list of Oppenheimer's past associations. The first piece of evidence that Nichols presented was typical of his charges: "It was reported that in 1940 you were listed as a sponsor of the Friends of the Chinese People, an organization which was characterized in 1944 by the House Committee on Un-American Activities as a Communist-front organization." Each charge relied on stases of fact, definition, and quality. First, Nichols asserted that a particular association had occurred, it was a fact. Then, that factual association was defined as Communist. Needless to say, the term "Communist" was highly negative. Implicit within the term "Communist" was a derogatory quality. A Communist association was un-American and therefore unacceptable. Nichols' used this accusational strategy twenty-one times to identify Oppenheimer explicitly with three other Communist organizations and with numerous Communist party members.

Nichols carried the Communist issue further when he pointed to statements made by Oppenheimer that supported a "no hiring policy" for communists at Los Alamos, and then suggested that, despite his statements to the contrary, Oppenheimer indeed had supported employment of communists in classified work. This charge, and several others like it, gave blatant attention to what may be considered inconsistencies, contradictions, or even lies in Oppenheimer's record. Oppenheimer's actions were used as evidence of his flawed character.

Additional negative charges surrounded the Chevalier Incident, perhaps the most damaging evidence to Oppenheimer's integrity. The episode figured significantly not only in Nichols' accusations but also in every other case document. Sometime early in 1943, Oppenheimer's close personal friend, Haakon Chevalier, approached him at a dinner party and told him that George Eltenton, a Berkeley professor, had means to pass technical information to the Soviet Union. Oppenheimer flatly refused to be involved in such transactions. As appropriate as his immediate response was, Oppenheimer failed to report the espionage attempt for eight months. Moreover, when he did finally speak to Army Intelligence officers about the incident, Oppenheimer reported that there had been three approaches rather than one. He also refused to name Chevalier as the intermediary. Oppenheimer maintained this fabricated account of the Chevalier incident during a second interrogation. Finally, in December 1943, Oppenheimer revealed Chevalier as the go-between and admitted that he had lied. He told the officers that there had been only one attempt to gain information. In a 1946 FBI investigation, Oppenheimer again admitted that he had lied in 1943 and that there had been only one approach.

Nichols merely recounted these facts in his accusations and then noted that the Oppenheimers had stayed in touch with the Chevaliers over the intervening years. Apparently, Nichols felt confident that the inquiry itself would explore the implications of these facts because he abruptly turned to an accusation concerning the development of the hydrogen bomb. The history of that accusation is especially noteworthy.

The AEC initiated the proceeding against Oppenheimer. Two AEC attorneys, William Mitchell and Harold Green, actually wrote the letter that was sent under Nichols' authority. Mitchell and Green were given only one specific instruction: Oppenheimer's opposition to hydrogen bomb development was not to be included in the charges. The commissioners feared public backlash if it appeared that Oppenheimer's opinions (or in present terminology, his policies) were on trial. Green, however, wrote a draft that included the hydrogen bomb information. Since the commissioners did not want Oppenheimer's opinions to be challenged, Green constructed the accusation so that it emphasized Oppenheimer's veracity. Interestingly, the H-bomb accusation's final paragraph alluded to Oppenheimer's ability to influence others, the ability which unofficially prompted the accusations against him: "It was further reported that you were instrumental in persuading other outstanding scientists not to work on the hydrogen bomb project and that the opposition to the hydrogen bomb of which you are the most experienced, most powerful, and most effective member, has definitely slowed down its development."[7] This description challenged Oppenheimer's loyalty to and acceptance of administrative decisions. Apparently, because it avoided the commissioners' specific concern, the H-bomb accusation remained in the official letter of charges. As will be shown later in this analysis, the inclusion of the hydrogen bomb charge was critical to the case's outcome.

The H-bomb allegation completed the list of derogatory information. Nichols summarized the twenty-six charges, which focused primarily on Oppenheimer's past policies, so that their implications for Oppenheimer's character were clear: "In view of your access to highly sensitive classified information, and in view of these allegations which, until disproved, raise questions, as to your veracity, conduct, and even your loyalty, the Commission has no other recourse, in the discharge of its obligations to protect the common defense and security, but to suspend your clearance until the matter has been resolved." While "loyalty" was never defined or connected explicitly to any particular charge, an overall reading of Nichols' accusations reveals a subtle undercurrent that at least raised doubt about Oppenheimer's loyalty within his advisory role and to his country in general. Nichols defined Oppenheimer's past actions, and in so doing, implicitly attributed a negative quality to those actions and to Oppenheimer as the corresponding actor. Moreover, the H-bomb evidence subtly interjected the political battles in which Oppenheimer was embroiled without explicitly challenging his right to an opinion. It implicitly invoked a 1950s god-term, "progress," against Oppenheimer. He allegedly had opposed hydrogen bomb development. He had stated that the knowledge of such a weapon, let alone its actual construction, should be avoided. In so many words, Oppenheimer had argued that humankind should halt its growing control of the powerful forces of nature. He argued that, in effect, nuclear "progress" should stop. "Science," another god-term of the 1950s, was intertwined with "progress" in Oppenheimer's opinions. Oppenheimer not only thwarted progress, but he stood in the way of scientific progress. Thus, by including the H-bomb controversy in the letter of charges, Nichols employed two concomitantly powerful terms, "science" and "progress," against Oppenheimer.

Nichols' use of "Communist" and "scientific progress" to degrade Oppenheimer's position was especially effective due to the terms' interactions. Weaver submitted that the strength of terms like "the American Way" rested in the implicit link between "progress" and "American" behavior.[8] To be American meant to be progressive. Conversely, to be against "progress" was to be "un-American." Thus, Oppenheimer was "un-American," not only in his associations, but also because he hindered, if only for a short time, America's destiny of nuclear superiority. Had the H-bomb evidence not been included, the charges against Oppenheimer would have dealt primarily with Oppenheimer's 1930s "left-wing" associations. His advisory decisions and postwar activities never would have entered into the discussion.

In sum, Nichols' strategic accusational choices were compelling. He patterned the case by presenting only negative information. He did not quote the AEC security clearance policy's admonishment to consider both favorable and unfavorable information. Nichols created a list of particulars that were all negative. He established an adversarial atmosphere, even though the proceedings were by definition an "inquiry," not a "trial." Nichols wisely chose the parameters for discussion and highlighted only those rules that eventually led to Oppenheimer's defeat.

OPPENHEIMER'S DEFENSE

Oppenheimer, along with his counsel Lloyd Garrison, responded to Nichols' charges with what Garrison called a "whole man approach" — "We felt there was no way of arriving at a final conclusion about whether this fellow should be entrusted with atomic secrets or not other than the combined judgment of men of the highest integrity and reputation of what they felt about him. This seemed to us much more conclusive than the dredging up of all these incidents from his past which in the extraordinary atmosphere of the time were magnified in importance . . . . a hundred fold."[9]

In accord with the "whole man approach," Oppenheimer replied to the charges with an autobiographical letter that served as the major defense document.[10] Oppenheimer wrote, "I cannot ignore the question you have raised nor accept the suggestion that I am unfit for public service. The items of so-called 'derogatory information' set forth in your letter cannot be fairly understood except in the context of my life and work." Oppenheimer emphasized the stasis of quality, the quality of his actions, and the quality of his character.

Oppenheimer could deny only a very few "facts" as Nichols had defined them. In the abstract, however, denial was possible. Oppenheimer asserted that he was "never a member of the Communist party" and that he "never accepted Communist dogma or theory." But he could not disprove his specific associations with Communists. Because denial was a weak option for Oppenheimer and because the term "Communist" carried, in Oppenheimer's view, vastly different implications in 1954 than it had before 1945, he focused on a redefinition of his pre-World War II associations. In his response to Nichols, Oppenheimer recast his early Communist associations as an innocent search for political identity. He began his redefinition with incredible examples of his political naivete: "I never read a newspaper or a current magazine like *Time* or *Harper's*; I had no radio, no telephone; I learned of the stock market crash in the fall of 1929 only long after the event; the first time I ever voted was in the presidential election of 1936....I had no understanding of the relations of man to his society." Oppenheimer explained that his political interests were awakened by the treatment of his Jewish relatives in Germany and by the effects of the Depression on his students. Yet, he had "no framework of political conviction or experience to give him perspective in these matters." Oppenheimer painted a self-portrait that evinced innocent, if misguided, sympathies. Although his policies perhaps appeared reprehensible in retrospect, Oppenheimer argued that at the time they were originally undertaken, they were noble and innocent. Oppenheimer reassured his judges that as he became aware of the wider, negative ramifications of his activities, he dissociated himself from Communist groups and causes: "By the time that we moved to Los Alamos in early 1943, both as a result of my changed views and of the great pressure of war work, my participation in left-wing circles had ceased and were never to be reestablished." Oppenheimer further supported his "rehabilitation" through a detailed account of his contributions at Los Alamos and as an adviser after the war. His overall strategy was to redefine the facts that he could not deny, and to assert that, in addition to redefining his associations, they had ended and therefore were irrelevant to the question at hand.

Beyond his redefinition strategy, Oppenheimer used the "Communist" issue to bolster his loyalty to security procedures and to the administration. When he discussed a request of transfer for a purported Communist at Los Alamos, Oppenheimer pointed out that "this request, like all others, was subject to the assumption that the usual security requirements would apply; and when I was told that there was objection on security grounds to this transfer, I was much surprised, but of course agreed." Oppenheimer stated that his personal judgment was subordinated to security proceedings. Oppenheimer continued this strategy in his descriptions of the scientific adviser's role.

Oppenheimer sensed that his recognition of a scientist's limited advisory role was important to a defense of his post-World War II actions. He stated that "when I and other scientists were called on for advice, our principal duty was to make our technical experience and judgment available." He noted the limitations of GAC scientists in particular when he wrote the "formulation of policy and the management of the vast atomic energy enterprise were responsibilities vested in the Commission itself. The General Advisory Committee had the role which was fixed for it by statute, to advise the Commission." Later, he again reiterated the scientific adviser's limits: "it was not our function to formulate military requirements." Oppenheimer made his willing subordination most clear in his interpretation of the H-bomb controversy. Not only did he support the GAC's motives in advising against the hydrogen bomb, but he further submitted that he faithfully followed the executive directive that contradicted the GAC's advice:

I think I am correct in asserting that the unanimous opposition we expressed to the crash program was based on the conviction, to which technical considerations as well as others contributed, that because of our over-all situation at that time such a program might weaken rather than strengthen the position of the United States.

This is the full story of my "opposition to the hydrogen bomb".... It is a story which ended once and for all when in January 1950, the president announced his decision to proceed with the program. I never urged anyone not to work on the hydrogen bomb project.... We never again raised the question of the wisdom of the policy which had been settled, but concerned ourselves rather with trying to implement it.

Oppenheimer's denial responded to Nichols' use of the term "loyalty" that encompassed not only allegiance to country but also to the administrative hierarchy as well. Oppenheimer need not have accepted Nichols' definition. As an adviser, he could disagree with military policy. Indeed, Stern reported that Hans Bethe, Albert Einstein, and other leading scientists openly opposed the hydrogen bomb, and noted that Edward Teller, father of the hydrogen bomb, refused to work on projects assigned to him at Los Alamos. None of these scientists were censured. Oppenheimer, on the other hand, accepted Nichols' definition of "loyalty," validated it by his response, and then argued that he fit within it. Oppenheimer's response removed any possibility that he might challenge the implicit political motivations behind the entire case. Haberer argued that Oppenheimer actually aided his accusers as a result: "Oppenheimer's unwillingness to choose a political terrain on which to defend himself abetted the government's unwillingness to examine openly the real ground for attacking him. The public thus never had the opportunity to examine the basic policy questions camouflaged by the deceptive security and loyalty issues. The open decision on his character masked the hidden decision on his policy."[11]

By accepting Nichols' parameters for argument—by situating the dispute around "character," "associations," and "loyalty"—Oppenheimer obliged the dialectical posture created for him by Nichols' position. He unwisely accepted Nichols' terminology and acquiesced to procedural norms. The accused, however, had options other than to respond reactively. As Philip Rief noted at the time, "his response to the rehash of his past in the changed climate of America was, if anything, too appropriate to the pattern of attack." E. U. Condon, another famous scientist, faced security problems similar to Oppenheimer's at the same time. Condon resigned in protest against the government's harassment. Haberer noted that "in contrast to Oppenheimer, Condon fought on his own behalf; in effect, if gestures have any meaning, he acted closely on the assumption that the government needed the scientists rather than the scientists needed the government." Oppenheimer, however, made his mark through government service, and perhaps resignation was inconceivable to him. The government felt that Oppenheimer, in particular, needed the prestige lent by his advisory role. In 1943, one security official noted the "Oppenheimer was deeply concerned with gaining a worldwide reputation as a scientist, and a place in history."[12] Indeed, Oppenheimer argued for his positive value to government in his final paragraphs:

I have had to deal briefly or not at all with instances in which my actions or views were adverse to Soviet or Communist interest, and of actions that testify to my devotion to freedom, or that have contributed to the vitality, influence, and power of the United States.

In preparing this letter, I have reviewed two decades of my life. I have recalled instances where I acted unwisely. What I have hoped was, not that I could wholly avoid error, but that I might learn from it. What I have learned has, I think, made me more fit to serve my country.

Oppenheimer hoped to leave his judges with a positive overall impression. His defense was difficult, however, once he accepted Nichols' framework. He worked to show that he fit Nichols' standards of loyalty. Beyond his assertions, he had little alternative but to attempt subtle redefinitions, a difficult and often unsuccessful strategy.

On April 12, 1954, Oppenheimer faced the personnel security board for the first time. Over the next nineteen days, board members Gordon Gray, Thomas Morgan, and Ward Evans, a board with prestige and status equal to Oppenheimer's, heard testimony that, when compiled, formed a transcript of over nine hundred pages. The transcript's first entries were Nichols' letter of accusation and Oppenheimer's autobiographical reply. The Gray board's decision, delivered on May 27, 1954, resulted from their consideration of Nichols' charges, Oppenheimer's response, supportive testimony, and other government records. The personnel security board voted two to one to deny reinstatement of Oppenheimer's security clearance.

Oppenheimer then requested that the Atomic Energy Commission consider the case. The AEC reviewed the materials of the hearing, and, on June 19, 1954, came to the same conclusion: Oppenheimer was a security risk. Commissioners Strauss, Zuckert, and Campbell wrote the majority decision; Murray concurred but with different reasons.

The decisions to revoke Oppenheimer's security clearance are of special interest rhetorically because, although each group considered identical evidence and although each group arrived at the same conclusion, the three decision statements used three different terminologies to label Oppenheimer a security risk. The presence of a different rationale in each decision document might be expected: defining a "security risk," especially with regard to atomic secrets, was relatively new in 1954. The Oppenheimer case was essentially new and unknown. No precedents for a determination of its complexity existed. Furthermore, the judgmental standards that emerged in the decision statements provide a means for evaluating Oppenheimer's anticipation of and adaptation to his judges.

The Gray board majority opinion is perhaps the most interesting and the most tortured of the documents in the Oppenheimer case.[13] While the board was highly sympathetic to Oppenheimer and held him in great esteem, they felt compelled to decide against his continued service. Indeed, they wrote, "it seemed to us that an alternative recommendation would be possible, if we were allowed to exercise mature practical judgment without the rigid circumscription of regulations and criteria established for us." Ironically, the AEC security criteria stated that "the decision as to security clearance is an overall, commonsense judgment." The more flexible "commonsense judgment" was the standard for which Oppenheimer argued. Unfortunately for Oppenheimer, the Gray board interpreted the guidelines in a different light. Given that the Gray board found all the case's facts to be at least substantially true as Oppenheimer knew they would, their interpretation and application of standards was especially critical to the case's outcome and warrants particular attention.

The Gray board addressed "loyalty" first. They wrote that "if a person is considered a security risk in terms of loyalty, the fact or possibility of active disloyalty is assumed, which would involve conduct giving some sort of aid and comfort to a foreign power." They further equated Communist sympathy with disloyalty. The conclusion with regard to Oppenheimer was foregone accept for the Gray board's position on rehabilitation.

The Gray board held that "the necessary but harsh requirements of security should not deny a man the right to have made a mistake, if its recurrence is so remote a possibility as to permit a comfortable prediction as to sanity and correctness of future conduct." The Gray board stated clearly that Oppenheimer's redefinition of his Communist associations succeeded: "we recognize that 1943 conduct cannot be judged solely in light of 1954 conditions." Only later did Gray and Morgan note that Oppenheimer's current Communist associations (specifically his continued relationship with Chevalier) were unacceptable because they showed a blatant disregard for the security system itself. They wrote, "those who have been associated with the security system during the war years and subsequently and who have been exposed repeatedly to security measures, should not fail to understand the need for their full support of the system." Oppenheimer's early associations might be overlooked but his continued associations, they felt, demonstrated an "arrogance of judgment."

Although the Gray board feared willful disobedience on Oppenheimer's part, they also expressed concern about unintentional security infractions. They argued that "personal weaknesses constitute him a security risk." These weaknesses included a "tendency to yield to pressures of others." The Gray board used a case brought up in the hearing itself to demonstrate Oppenheimer's "tendency to be influenced."

Oppenheimer testified before the House Un-American Activities Committee that his friend, Dr. Bernard Peters, was a former Communist. Peters' teaching position at University of Rochester was threatened as a result. At the urging of Drs. Condon, Peters, and other scientists, Oppenheimer wrote a letter to the Rochester newspaper. The Gray board believed that Oppenheimer's letter repudiated his testimony. Oppenheimer contended that he felt that Peters' politics should have no bearing on his employment and wrote willingly when he was made aware of Peters' plight. In this case, the Gray board did not accept Oppenheimer's definition of the situation.

There was an ironic twist in the Gray board's response on this point. The "tendency toward influence" standard was meant to thwart foreign agents who attempted to gain confidential information from employees. Anyone with security clearance supposedly could withstand any temptation. While the Gray board felt that Oppenheimer might not be able to live up to that standard in the future, they noted that Oppenheimer seemed "to have had a high degree of discretion reflecting unusual ability to keep to himself vital secrets." The Gray board asserted that Oppenheimer was not to be trusted and was trustworthy at the same time. Similar inconsistencies appeared in the Gray board's discussion of the hydrogen bomb charge.

The board stated that the hydrogen bomb matter revealed no disloyalty on Oppenheimer's part but that "whatever the motivation, the security interests of the United States were affected." They believed that Oppenheimer had not been suitably "enthusiastic":

> We must make it clear that we do not question Dr. Oppenheimer's right to the opinions he held with respect to the development of this weapon. They were shared by other competent and devoted individuals, both in and out of Government. We are willing to assume that they were motivated by deep moral conviction. We are concerned, however, that he may have departed his role as scientific adviser to exercise highly persuasive influence in matters in which his convictions were not necessarily a reflection of technical judgment, and also not necessarily related to the protection of the strongest offensive military interests of the country.

Thus the Gray board supported Oppenheimer's right to an opinion but not his right to express that opinion to his superiors or to his colleagues. Gray and Morgan appeared to support Oppenheimer as "loyal" while they simultaneously labeled him a security risk. With tortured logic, they wrote, "we have come to a clear conclusion, which should be reassuring to the people of this country, that he is a loyal citizen."

The AEC majority, Oppenheimer's final set of judges, apparently felt no similar compunction.[14] The AEC was the official body that instigated the proceedings and had to approve the letter of accusations. Given their initial bias, it is not surprising that they too found Oppenheimer a security risk. Nor is it surprising that their rationale was politically strategic.

Like Gray and Morgan, the AEC majority did not label Oppenheimer "disloyal." His public popularity mediated against such a finding, whether the commissioners believed "disloyalty" to be the case or not. They also dropped the H-bomb issue. The ability to justify their position on "character" and "associations" allowed them to accommodate their original concerns about the H-bomb matter. Moreover, the AEC commissioners argued for Oppenheimer's right to a general opinion. They did not echo the Gray board's concern that Oppenheimer had overstepped the bounds of his advisory role. They did not uphold Oppenheimer's right to a technical opinion. Their argument, in the absence of any similar statement by Oppenheimer, suggests that Oppenheimer missed a vulnerable point in Nichols' accusation. First, Oppenheimer easily could have stated that his advisory opinions were simply "advice" and "opinions" to be considered and either accepted or rejected. As noted earlier, he need not have argued that the scientific advisory's role excluded political, military, or moral recommendations. The argument — advanced by Oppenheimer and adopted by Gray and Morgan — only weakened Oppenheimer's case.

Second, Oppenheimer could have adapted the emphasis on American acts to his own advantage. Invocation of freedom of speech, a potentially powerful terminological ally to Oppenheimer, could have been sufficient to defuse the entire H-bomb issue or at least to balance better the poles of opposition. Oppenheimer could have used Nichols' terms against Nichols: to deny a citizen's right to an opinion, whether technical, political, ethical, or otherwise, it itself "un-American."

Beyond the H-bomb charges, the AEC majority merely reiterated Nichols' original charges. The Chevalier incident, among other cases, was used to assert that "the work of Military Intelligence, the Federal Bureau of Investigation, and the Atomic Energy Commission — all at one time or another have felt the effect of his falsehoods, evasions, and misrepresentations." For the AEC majority, this allegation alone warranted Oppenheimer's removal from government service. His associations, however, reinforced their decision.

The AEC majority used an explanation similar to that used by Gray and Morgan to impugn Oppenheimer's "associations": "In respect to the criterion of 'associations,' we find that his associations with persons known to him to be Communists have extended far beyond the tolerable limits of prudence and self-restraint which are to be expected of one holding the high positions that the Government has continuously entrusted to him since 1943."

Like Oppenheimer himself, the AEC majority did not consider past associations alone a matter of concern. It was Oppenheimer's continued and present association with Haakon Chevalier that led to the AEC's negative evaluation of his associations. Oppenheimer stated only that Chevalier was a friend. He submitted to the accusation. Again, Oppenheimer could not deny the truth of his accusers' statements. Given the facts and the standards of judgment, perhaps Oppenheimer's only defense was a direct challenge to the policy issues that motivated the accusations.

The Oppenheimer case received one more negative interpretation. Commissioner Murray departed from the Gray board's and the AEC majority's reasoning and focused on the term "loyalty."[15]

Murray defined "loyalty" first as "a man's love of country," then as a "citizen's cooperation with government," and finally as "a citizen's cooperation with government to thwart Communist infiltration." He developed further standards for government employees. With regard to security, Murray said that "their faithfulness to the lawful government of the United States, that is to say their loyalty, must be judged by the hard standard of their obedience to security regulations." Given Murray's definition, Oppenheimer's fate was set. He had violated security procedures. It was a matter of record. Murray therefore concluded that Oppenheimer was disloyal and therefore a security risk. Against Murray, Oppenheimer literally had no defense.

CONCLUSION

In an evaluation of the strategic rhetorical choices made in the Oppenheimer case, credit first must be given to Nichols for his choice of terms that targeted Oppenheimer's vulnerabilities and called upon the rhetorical forces of the times. "Associations" were especially useful to Nichols' task since Oppenheimer could not deny factual information found in the FBI file. Neither could Oppenheimer deny his improprieties in the Chevalier incident. Although Oppenheimer's redefinition worked to a great degree, in the end his arrogant disobedience and his continued associations were a matter of record. Oppenheimer lost on the stasis of fact: his reinterpretation did not sway his judges from the incontrovertible evidence. When the substance of accusations cannot be denied, a defense becomes that much more difficult to construct.

Despite obvious obstacles, Oppenheimer did not create the strongest possible defense. First, he accepted Nichols' pattern. With that choice, Oppenheimer failed to garner his available, and not insubstantial, rhetorical resources. He gave Nichols' charges credence in his own defense. He did not use his status, his accomplishments, his political knowledge, the documented standards, or even his freedom of speech to his advantage. Second, he interjected terms into the security equation that worked to his detriment. Oppenheimer, more than Nichols, emphasized loyalty to administrative decisions and to the security system. He was vulnerable in both areas and should have avoided a clash on those terms. Whether or not the decision was predetermined, Oppenheimer did little to dissuade his accusers from their chosen path. Even Gray and Morgan, who appeared to have held Oppenheimer in high regard, felt compelled to agree with Nichols' accusations. Oppenheimer did not, and perhaps could not, sufficiently shoulder the burden of rebuttal that he was not a security risk.

The Oppenheimer case exemplifies the importance of terminological choice to the outcome of any dispute and it highlights the rhetorical resources available to governmental agencies interested in justifying an unpopular decision. Clearly, Oppenheimer did little to stand in the way of his accusers. Even if he had chosen a more strategic defense, however, the AEC majority established a strong position through their choice of powerful terms, their use of facts gathered by an indisputable source, the FBI, and their use of those terms and facts in a relatively controlled and legitimate forum--the security hearing. This analysis also demonstrates the yield of government rhetoric. The ability to define terms allowed the AEC to identify the key issues in the dispute and to highlight the standards by which the evidence was to be judged. Nichols concentrated on the negative. His interpretation of documented standards held that certain acts automatically made Oppenheimer a security risk, no matter the positive contributions cited. Oppenheimer's primary assumption contended that positive overall contributions should outweigh minor judgmental errors.   Oppenheimer believed that if a person learned from past mistakes, those errors would make the individual better able to serve. Oppenheimer either did not anticipate or did not adapt to his judges' standards of judgment. Finally, the case demonstrates the intricate connection between policy and character that is often present in a *kategoria/apologia* speech set.   When Oppenheimer's policies were not being used as evidence of his flawed character, his flawed character was an excuse to rid his opponents of his problematic policies. In either case, the connection between policy and character was used to undermine Oppenheimer's position. Together these factors explain why the accusations triumphed over Oppenheimer's defense.

Oppenheimer died on February 18, 1967. At the time of his death, he still was officially a security risk. Although the agency that removed Oppenheimer from government service later gave him its highest honor, his reputation was never cleared. That would have required another security hearing, and Oppenheimer refused to open his life to yet another interpretation.   The personnel security board's findings and the AEC recommendations, which had rewritten Oppenheimer's life, remained intact. The transcript created in 1954 is, to this day, the official record in the matter of J. Robert Oppenheimer.

NOTES

[1]Herbert York, *The Advisors: Oppenheimer, Teller and the Superbomb* (San Francisco: W. H. Freeman, 1976), p. 20.

[2]"The Oppenheimer Hearings," *The Bulletin of the Atomic Scientists* 10 (1954): 234.

[3]For a more thorough explanation of the political issues involved in the Oppenheimer case, see Thomas W. Wilson, Jr., *The Great Weapons Heresy* (Boston: Houghton-Mifflin, 1970).

[4]See Philip M. Stern, *The Oppenheimer Case: Security on Trial* (New York: Harper and Row, 1969), pp. 218-29.

[5]For Nichols' letter of accusations, see United States Atomic Energy Commission, *In the Matter of J. Robert Oppenheimer: Transcript of Hearing Before Personnel Security Board* (Washington, DC: GPO, 1954), pp. 3-6.

[6]"Executive Order 10450," *Federal Register* 18 (1953): 252.

[7]See Nichols' accusations; and see Stern, *The Oppenheimer Case*, p. 226-28.

[8]Richard M. Weaver, *The Ethics of Rhetoric* (Chicago: Henry Regnery, 1953), pp. 213-26.

[9]Peter Goodchild, *J. Robert Oppenheimer: Shatterer of Worlds* (Boston: Houghton-Mifflin, 1981), p. 229.

[10]For Oppenheimer's response to the AEC, see United States Atomic Energy Commission, *In the Matter of J. Robert Oppenheimer: Transcript of Hearing Before Personnel Security Board* (Washington, D.C.: GPO, 1954), pp. 8-20.

[11]See Stern, *The Oppenheimer Case*, p. 371, and Joseph Haberer, *Politics and the Community of Science* (New York: Van Nostrand Reinhold, 1969), p. 247.

[12]Philip Rief, "The Case of Dr. Oppenheimer," *The Twentieth Century* 156 (1954): 222; Haberer, *Politics and the Community of Science*, p. 246; and *In the Matter of J. Robert Oppenheimer: Transcript of Hearing Before Personnel Security Board*, p. 275.

[13]For the Gray board majority opinion, see United States Atomic Energy Commission, *In the Matter of J. Robert Oppenheimer: Texts of Principal Documents and Letters of Personnel Security Board, May 17, 1954, through June 29, 1954* (Washington, D.C.: GPO, 1954), pp. 1-23.

[14]The AEC majority report can be found in *In the Matter of J. Robert Oppenheimer: Texts of Principal Documents*, pp. 51-54.

[15]Commissioner Murray's concurring opinion appears in *In the Matter of J. Robert Oppenheimer: Texts of Principal Documents*, pp. 60-63.

INFORMATION SOURCES ON THE SPEECH SET

Nichols' Accusations

Nichols' letter of charges appeared as "Nichols Presents Charges," *The Bulletin of the Atomic Scientists* 10 (1954): 174-76. Nichols' letter also appeared in the hearing's official transcript. See United States Atomic Energy Commission, *In the Matter of J. Robert Oppenheimer: Transcript of Hearing Before Personnel Security Board.* Washington, D.C.: GPO, 1954, pp. 3-6.

Oppenheimer's Apology

Oppenheimer's letter of defense appeared as "Oppenheimer Replies," *The Bulletin of the Atomic Scientists* 10 (1954): 177-191. Oppenheimer's letter also appeared in the hearing's official transcript. See United States Atomic Energy Commission, *In the Matter of J. Robert Oppenheimer: Transcript of Hearing Before Personnel Security Board.* Washington, D.C.: GPO, 1954, pp. 8-20.

Selected Bibliography

Conscience, Science, and Security: The Case of Dr. J. Robert Oppenheimer. Edited by Cushing Strout. Chicago: Rand McNally, 1963.

Goodchild, Peter. *J. Robert Oppenheimer: Shatterer of Worlds.* Boston: Houghton-Mifflin, 1981.

Haberer, Joseph. *Politics and the Community of Science.* New York: Van Nostrand Reinhold, 1969.

Jungk, Robert. *Brighter than a Thousand Suns.* New York: Harcourt, Brace and Company, 1958.

Lapp, Ralph E. *The New Priesthood: The Scientific Elite and the Uses of Power.* New York: Harper and Row, 1965.

Major, John. *The Oppenheimer Hearing.* New York: Stein and Day, 1971.

Robert Oppenheimer: Letters and Recollections. Edited by Alice Kimball Smith and Charles Weiner. Cambridge: Harvard University Press, 1980.

Stern, Philip M. *The Oppenheimer Case: Security on Trial.* New York: Harper and Row, 1969.

Wilson, Thomas W., Jr. *The Great Weapons Heresy.* Boston: Houghton-Mifflin, 1970.

Nikita S. Khrushchev
vs. Dwight D. Eisenhower

Lawrence W. Haapanen

From 1956 to 1960, the United States carried out a program of aerial reconnaissance over the Soviet Union by means of high- flying U-2 aircraft that,
as far as the American public knew, were conducting weather research
flights for the National Aeronautics and Space Administration (NASA).
The Soviets knew better, but said nothing. President Eisenhower's first
secretary of state, John Foster Dulles, expected the Soviets to remain silent
even if a U-2 were shot down: "If the Soviets ever capture one of these
planes, I'm sure they will never admit it. To do so would make it necessary
for them to admit also that for years we had been carrying on flights over
their territory while they, the Soviets, had been helpless to do anything
about the matter."[1] On May 1, 1960, the Soviets shot down a U-2 near
Sverdlovsk, and captured its CIA pilot, Francis Gary Powers. John Foster
Dulles, it would soon turn out, was wrong.

On the afternoon of May 1, hours after it had become evident to the
CIA that Powers' plane was missing, it was decided by a small group of officials that a previously prepared cover story would be released. This cover
story, issued to the press on May 3, stated that a NASA weather research
plane based at Adana, Turkey, had been reported missing while on a flight
near Lake Van on the Turkish-Soviet border. Meanwhile, word of the missing U-2 was passed to Eisenhower and a few others who had been cognizant
of the top secret overflights. The immediate reaction was a feeling of sympathy for the pilot, rather than apprehension about what the Soviet reaction
might be, for CIA Director Allen Dulles had given assurances that if a U-2
were shot down, "no man would ever be taken alive."[2] Jim Hagerty, the
president's press secretary, was not told of the loss of the U-2 until May 3,
and although he later expressed regret that the government had moved too
fast in putting out a cover story, he defended the story itself "on the grounds
that it was assumed that the pilot had destroyed himself and the plane, leaving the Russians without evidence."[3] In the unlikely event of a Soviet
complaint about the intrusion, the United States could charge that the

Soviets had shot down an unarmed NASA weather research plane. That, at least, was the plan. In the meantime, the Eisenhower administration pressed forward with preparations for the upcoming Paris Summit Conference that would bring the president together on May 16 with Soviet premier Nikita S. Khrushchev, British prime minister Harold Macmillan, and French president Charles de Gaulle.

KHRUSHCHEV'S ACCUSATIONS

Khrushchev had fumed in private over previous American overflights, but the inability of Soviet air defenses to stop the intrusions was too embarrassing to allow a public protest from the Soviet government. Diplomatic protests had been made on two occasions, but Khrushchev had found that "each time the US brushed our protest aside, saying none of the their planes were overflying our territory. We were more infuriated and disgusted each time a violation occurred." Khrushchev now found it possible, in May 1960, to denounce the United States publicly for its aerial spying. The timing was especially propitious, for the Supreme Soviet was about to meet in Moscow, and its opening session would give Khrushchev a highly appreciative audience. When the cover story about a missing weather research plane appeared in the American press, Khrushchev and his colleagues "smiled with pleasure as we anticipated the discomfort which the spies who cooked up this false statement would feel when confronted with the evidence we already had in our pocket." As the interrogations of Powers and the examination of the U-2 wreckage continued, Khrushchev proposed a plan to the leadership of the Supreme Soviet: "I would make a speech . . . and inform the Supreme Soviet that the Americans had violated the sovereignty of our State; I would announce that the plane had been shot down, but--and this was important--I would *not* reveal that the pilot had been captured alive and was in our hands."[4] He cleverly calculated to mislead the U.S. government and cause it to dig itself still deeper into a hole.

Khrushchev probably had little choice in his decision to reveal the ill-fated U-2 overflight. One journalist who covered the Paris Summit Conference and had the opportunity to talk to both Soviet and U.S. sources noted that one member of the Communist Party's top hierarchy, Anastas Mikoyan, "wanted to shove the whole thing under the rug and just send a diplomatic note, but he was overruled."[5] As for Khrushchev, he seems to have been genuinely angered, notwithstanding the fact that U-2s had intruded into Soviet territory regularly for four years. Since his visit to the United States as Eisenhower's guest in 1959, Khrushchev seems to have had a sense of optimism that Soviet-U.S. relations could be improved. For an overflight to occur so close to the Paris Summit Conference struck Khrushchev as a deliberate provocation by the militaristic circles in the United

States, if not necessarily at Eisenhower's orders, and it would be impossible to go to Paris and pretend that nothing had happened.

On May 5, toward the end of his opening address to the Supreme Soviet, Khrushchev surprised the audience with the news that an intruding U.S. aircraft had been shot down by Soviet rockets. His report was part accusation and part boast, the whole effect being to portray the United States as an aggressor that had grown more brazen and had badly underestimated the Soviets' air defenses. In the first fifty-eight sentences of Khrushchev's condemnation of the ill-fated overflight, he used some form of the word "aggression" or "aggressor" twenty-four times in reference to the United States and its actions. At the same time, however, he carefully avoided blaming Eisenhower: "The question arises, who sent this plane that violated the borders of the Soviet Union? Was it sent with the sanction of the Commander-in-Chief of the Armed Forces of the United States of America, who, as everyone knows, is the President, or was this aggressive act committed by the Pentagon militarists without the President's knowledge?"[6] Khrushchev's speech thus gave Eisenhower an out, but there was no hint that the U-2's pilot and much of its equipment had been recovered intact. Those facts would be divulged in the yet undelivered second part of Khrushchev's *kategoria*.

President Eisenhower learned of Khrushchev's speech on the morning of May 5 while participating in a meeting of the National Security Council that, for purposes of a scheduled exercise, was being held at an emergency site outside Washington. After the regular meeting ended, Eisenhower met with a few top aides who had been privy to the U-2 overflights. This group included Allen Dulles; Gordon Gray, special assistant for national security affairs; Secretary of Defense Thomas Gates; Acting Secretary of State C. Douglas Dillon (filling in for Christian Herter, who was attending a NATO foreign ministers' meeting in Turkey); and General Andrew Goodpaster, the president's military secretary. Eisenhower advised against immediately issuing a public statement on the U-2, preferring to wait for Khrushchev's next move. The others present argued that a statement needed to be made without delay to preserve credibility, to which the president assented. The group felt, as Gates later put it, that should the Soviets prove to possess the U-2's pilot or equipment intact, "we should tell the truth at that time."[7] Secretary Dillon was instructed to prepare a press release consistent with the earlier cover story, and the state department was assigned sole responsibility for issuing further statements.

After everyone had returned to Washington later in the morning of May 5, a problem developed when Jim Hagerty announced to the press that both the State Department and NASA would be issuing statements. Whatever the reason for this error, reporters descended on NASA's Washington office, where officials were caught unprepared and hurriedly drafted a statement based on information previously furnished them by the CIA in question-and-answer form. When word of the NASA press release reached the state department, Secretary Dillon and his aides had to discard a draft statement that they had been carefully preparing and quickly draft a release that would, like the NASA release, adhere to the initial cover story.[8] This state department release was issued to the press at 12:45 p.m.; at 1:34 p.m., a message was received at the State Department from Ambassador Thompson in Moscow, stating that a Soviet official had told a foreign diplomat "that they had the pilot."[9] By the time the contents of this message reached Dillon, it was too late to undo the actions taken earlier in the day. Eisenhower went to Gettysburg the following morning for a weekend of relaxation, still keeping his distance in public from the unfolding U-2 crisis, and the government continued to place its reliance on a cover story that was beginning to show considerable wear and tear.

The American response does not seem to have surprised Khrushchev. If anything, he must have been pleased. Now that the Eisenhower administration "talked themselves out and got thoroughly wound up in this unbelievable story," Khrushchev later recalled, "we decided to tell the world what had really happened. The time had come to pin down the Americans and expose their lies."[10] This was the *kairos*, the most propitious moment in the rhetorical situation for a full-scale accusation.

The second part of Khrushchev's *kategoria* formed the main part of his closing speech before the Supreme Soviet on May 7. After a few preliminary remarks about the seven-year plan, he attacked the United States over the U-2 overflight. After recounting the State Department's May 5 press release, he provoked applause and laughter with his announcement, "Comrades, I must tell you a secret. When I was delivering my report to you, I deliberately did not say that the pilot was alive and in good health and that we have parts of the airplane. If we had reported everything at once, the Americans would have made up another version. And now look at how many silly things they have said—Lake Van, scientific research and so on. Now, when they learn the pilot is alive, they will have to think up something else. And they will!"

In this May 7 installment of his *kategoria*, Khrushchev's objective seems to have been primarily that of addressing the stasis of fact. He described the U-2 aircraft, its flight path and destination, the equipment it carried, and so forth, and he also identified the pilot and told something of his background. The impact of this plethora of facts was to offer a detailed indictment of the United States and its actions and underscore Khrushchev's assertion that "no fabricated versions can save the reputation of those who bear responsibility for this treacherous act." The United States had been caught red-handed, and Khrushchev's presentation, replete with photographs purportedly taken by the U-2's cameras, left little room for additional American denials. The facts were clear.

To some extent, Khrushchev also addressed the stasis of definition in his May 7 speech. Especially in view of the upcoming Paris Summit Conference, he saw the U-2 overflight as a provocation meant to "strain the atmosphere and to throw us back from those successes that have been achieved in the relaxation of international tensions." Overall, his purpose was to impugn the policy more than the character of the United States. While the militaristic circles that had sent the U-2 were pictured as immoral bandits, Khrushchev remembered the positive impression Americans had made on him during his 1959 visit, and he avowed, "I still believe that those who met with me want peace and good, friendly relations with the Soviet Union." President Eisenhower was not excluded from this group, for Khrushchev said that he was "quite willing to grant that the President did not know anything about the fact that a plane had been sent into the Soviet Union and had not returned."[11]

If one looks at Khrushchev's May 5 and May 7 speeches as two parts of the same *kategoria*, one might conclude that he put the cart before the horse. He primarily addressed the stasis of definition in the first speech, wherein he stressed the aggressive nature of the overflight, and the stasis of fact in the second speech, wherein he carefully assembled the various facts that proved conclusively the overflight had taken place. This deviation from the more typical order of things was, of course, strategically consistent with Khrushchev's devious design. By holding back the facts, he hoped to ensnare the United States into more lies. The State Department's May 5 press release was Khrushchev's reward for this strategem. Once his *kategoria* was completed on May 7, the stage was set for an *apologia* or defense from Eisenhower.

EISENHOWER'S DEFENSE

Khrushchev's May 7 speech triggered a day of intense discussions in Washington. On the morning of May 7, while Eisenhower golfed in Gettysburg, a meeting of White House, State Department, and CIA officials took place at CIA headquarters. In the afternoon, much the same group (but without Allen Dulles and his CIA aides) met at the state department under the leadership of Secretary of State Christian Herter, who had returned from overseas the previous evening. Assistant Secretary of State Foy Kohler, who was present at the afternoon meeting, later recalled that he was one of the few nontraditionalists present, arguing for an honest statement; a plurality felt that no government, and certainly no head of state, ever publicly admits responsibility for spying. It was this latter position that triumphed, and the new statement that emerged admitted that the U.S. plane missing in Turkey was apparently the same one brought down by the

Soviets but it added a disclaimer by denying any U.S. government authorization for such an overflight. This was accomplished via the following sentence: "As a result of the inquiry ordered by the President, it has been established that insofar as the authorities in Washington are concerned, there was no authorization for any such flight as described by Mr. Khrushchev."[12]

To suggest, as did the May 7 press release, that the United States government had not authorized the May 1 overflight was in keeping with the principle of "plausible deniability," which holds that covert intelligence operations should be conducted in such a way that the responsible government can disavow knowledge of them if they are "blown." In the words of General Goodpaster, plausible deniability "is something of a fiction in many cases but it's a form that they go through in order, I assume, to avoid these things becoming an actual *casus belli*."[13] To deny knowledge of something as serious as the U-2 overflight had the unanticipated side effect, however, of putting Eisenhower in a potentially vulnerable position. He seems to have sensed this on May 7, when the press release was read to him over the telephone for his approval, but he went along with it for the moment.

If one looks for the reasons why the "no authorization" sentence was placed in the May 7 press release, the first clue is in the records of Secretary Herter's telephone calls. At 4:30 p.m. on May 7, while waiting for a call to get through to Eisenhower, Herter talked to Allen Dulles and apparently went over the draft statement with him. Dulles "said there was an inconsistency and the Sec. said this was to get the Pres. off the hook."[14] The inconsistency to which they referred was between the draft statement's assertion that there was a need for surveillance of the Soviet Union, while on the other hand, there was a lack of authorization for the May 1 overflight. President Eisenhower said very little in his memoirs about the May 7 press release, but he did mention that "Mr. Herter felt it important to proceed in such fashion as to afford Khrushchev an 'out' in the event that he desired to minimize the whole affair." It thus appears that the "no authorization" sentence was the work of Secretary Herter. A subsequent book on the U-2 incident asserted that President Eisenhower inserted the "no authorization" sentence into the final draft, but a version of the press release in the Dwight D. Eisenhower Presidential Library, labeled "SECOND DRAFT," is substantially different from the final draft released to the press on May 7, yet also contains the "no authorization" sentence. If it were already present in an earlier draft, then it obviously was not inserted into the final draft by President Eisenhower. The important point is that the president *did* approve the final draft, and it was distributed to the press with the "no authorization" sentence intact. Furthermore, Eisenhower was not "let off the hook" by the release, as he quickly realized.[15]

The impact of the May 7 press release was noted by Vice President

Richard Nixon on May 9 when he cautioned Secretary Herter that "we simply can't leave the President in the posture where he says he doesn't know anything about this; to give this impression would be to imply that war could start without the President's knowledge." Nixon need not have worried; by the time he spoke to Herter, Eisenhower had already decided, apparently on his own, to clear the air by publicly assuming responsibility for the whole program of U-2 overflights over the Soviet Union. He met with Secretary Herter at the White House on Sunday, May 8, and told him to announce that the May 1 overflight had been sent by presidential authority. The State Department did so in a new statement issued on May 9, and two days later, in a press conference on May 11, Eisenhower took full responsibility for the U-2 program and defended it on the grounds of national security.[16]

President Eisenhower's public assumption of responsibility for an act of espionage was unprecedented for a head of state. Many in the United States and overseas saw it as a shocking departure from tradition. Why did he do it? He wrote in his memoirs that he outlined his reasons at a White House meeting on May 9 (actually a meeting of the NSC, the minutes of which are still classified), but he did not specify what they were. John Eisenhower, the president's son and military aide, was at the meeting and recalled that his father said, "We're going to take a beating" over the U-2 incident, "And I'm the one, rightly, who is going to have to take the brunt."[17]

One popular explanation for Eisenhower's decision is that he saw the political consequences that would befall him if he did not avow his prior knowledge and approval of the U-2 overflights. The *New York Times* made reference on May 9 to "the melancholy evidence that our right hand in Washington did not know what our left hand in Turkey or Pakistan was doing," and Walter Lippmann wrote in the *Washington Post* of May 10 that the "no authorization" line in the May 7 press release was "a plea of incompetence" on the part of the Eisenhower administration. Emmet John Hughes, a former speechwriter for Eisenhower, later wrote that the White House was "suddenly aghast at the prospect of predictable Democratic charges of outrageous negligence allowing such 'unauthorized flights' . . . ,"[18] yet Eisenhower gave instructions to admit the truth to Secretary Herter on May 8, before the newpapers had gotten their swipes into print and before the Democrats had voiced their charges. This reduces the likelihood that Eisenhower changed his mind for strictly political reasons — he prided himself on his ability to take considerable heat from his critics and still press on with what he believed to be the best course of action.

If fear of political consequences were not the prime motivation, then what prompted Eisenhower's acceptance of responsibility? It was his personal need for honesty, not just in the sense that one must always be truthful in one's dealings — for that would make any sort of espionage difficult, if not impossible — but honesty in dealing with one's subordinates, in expecting loyalty from them, and showing it to them. If Powers' overflight of the Soviet Union had really been unauthorized, as the State Department's May 7 press release said it was, someone down the chain of command from the president would eventually have to be sacrificed, and it was this prospect that Eisenhower dreaded. Allen Dulles' offer to resign had been rejected on May 5, yet accepting it later was not out of the question if the president had decided to stick with the May 7 "no authorization" position. At the end of May, Eisenhower explained to Gordon Gray that "he simply could not sacrifice a subordinate as many people had wanted him to do." And in August of the same year, he told an old friend, Ellis Slater, that "[t]here is so much discouragement, so much harassment, so much sniping and politics, that top men will not come into government service — hence if errors had been made in the U-2 or other cases, honest mistakes, unavoidable perhaps — he felt that D.E. should assume the responsibility."[19]

On May 9, Secretary Herter made a statement in accordance with the instructions he had received the previous day from Eisenhower. The statement admitted that the United States had for years conducted "extensive aerial surveillance by unarmed civilian aircraft, normally of a peripheral character but on occasion by penetration," and that these missions had been subject to presidential authorization. The statement alluded to the danger of Soviet surprise attack and the rejection by the Soviet government of Eisenhower's "open skies" proposal in 1955, and stated that the U.S. government "would be derelict to its responsibility not only to the American people but to free peoples everywhere if it did not, in the absence of Soviet cooperation, take such measures as are possible unilaterally to lessen and to overcome this danger of surprise attack." The remaining question was how the president would address the issue himself. A press conference was set for May 11, and at the "pre-press conference" on May 10, Jim Hagerty "passed the word that the President didn't need any advice on how to answer questions about the U-2. He wanted to think it through himself tonight and will cut the questions short after the first one."[20]

We know that as Eisenhower prepared himself for the press conference, the subject of the U-2 was uppermost on his mind. On the afternoon of May 10, he told Secretary Herter and General Goodpaster that "[w]ith regard to the plane, he thought that perhaps the best course is to chuckle about it and turn the subject off," but he plainly realized that this would not be possible in a press conference. He arrived the next morning for his press conference with prepared remarks on the subject that had been drafted for the occasion by General Goodpaster.[21]

The defense of the overflights that the president offered in his press conference was prompted by Khrushchev's prior *kategoria*. Eisenhower believed he should place the responsibility for the policy of overflights squarely upon himself. If the responsibility must be assumed publicly, then it followed that the policy must be defended publicly. Given the fact the overflights occurred, Eisenhower on May 11 countered the points made by Khrushchev's *kategoria* by addressing the stasis of definition. Eisenhower defined the policy as a prudent one, defensive rather than aggressive in nature. Specifically, Eisenhower's *apologia* made four important points:

1. There was a need for intelligence-gathering activities. "No one wants another Pearl Harbor," he said without fear of contradiction, and the obsessive secrecy of the Soviet Union had made it necessary for the United States to gather information "in every feasible way."

2. Intelligence-gathering activities must be kept secret, divorced from the "regular, visible agencies of government" and subject to "their own rules and methods of concealment." Hence, the lack of public knowledge of the U-2 overflights, and the earlier disclaimer of them by the government, were defined as necessary precautions and not as evidence of evil intent.

3. The intelligence-gathering activities of the United States had been made all the more vital by the actions of the Soviets, particulary because of their rejection of the "open skies" proposal that, Eisenhower said, would have assured "that no surprise attack was being prepared against anyone." As a result, intelligence-gathering must be considered "a distasteful but vital necessity."

4. With the Paris Summit Conference drawing near, "[W]e must not be distracted from the real issues of the day by what is an accident or a symptom of the world situation today. This incident has been given great propaganda exploitation. The emphasis given to a flight of an unarmed, nonmilitary plane can only reflect a fetish of secrecy."[22]

In his *apologia*, Eisenhower stressed two themes that justified the U-2 overflights: (1) the danger of recurrent conflict made it necessary for the United States to guard against enemy attack, and (2) the difference between the American and Soviet societies (open vs. closed) made it necessary for the United States to use covert means to gather information. The choice of these two themes was appropriate because both were regular themes of the U.S. elite press and could be expected to strike a responsive chord with the American public. In the early 1960s, J. David Singer conducted a content analysis of the *New York Times*, *Department of State Bulletin*, and *Foreign Affairs*, covering the period from May 1, 1957, through April 30, 1960, just one day before the U-2 incident, and found the typical picture of the world to be one of recurrent conflict between opposing belief systems.[23] In his May 11 press conference, Eisenhower appealed to this picture.

One thing Eisenhower did not do was give any hint of apology or regret about the U-2 overflights. This is particulary interesting in light of reservations he had expressed at one time or another about the overflights. In early 1959, he told the NSC that he was "reserved on the request to continue reconnaissance flights on the basis that it is undue provocation. Nothing, he says, would make him request authority to declare war more quickly than violation of our air space by Soviet aircraft." On February 2, 1960, just three months before the U-2 incident, he told his Board of Consultants on Foreign Intelligence Activities that "he has one tremendous asset in a summit meeting, as regards effect in the free world. That is his reputation for honesty. If one of these aircraft were lost when we are engaged in apparently sincere deliberations, it could be put on display in Moscow and ruin the President's effectiveness."[24]   There was no mention of this when Eisenhower spoke on May 11, 1960.

President Eisenhower's *apologia* of redefinition played well with his intended audiences, the American public and the Western allies. Because of his admission of the fact and vigorous defense of the U-2 program, "Allied and neutral nations were impressed and relieved to know that the United States had an effective method of keeping watch over Soviet military preparations, and that was good." Newspaper columnists sniped at the president, and the Democratic opposition in Congress voiced criticisms, but his personal standing with the American public was too high to be damaged seriously. A Gallup poll at the end of May 1960 showed that 58 percent of the public thought that Eisenhower had handled the U-2 affair well, compared to only 29 percent who thought he handled it badly, and his general approval rating actually went up a few percentage points from its level in early April. William White lauded Eisenhower's honesty: "the central point in the whole affair was that the storm in domestic opinion soon passed over, leaving Eisenhower quite unharmed, solely and simply because the American people trusted him."[25]

The effect of Eisenhower's *apologia* was quite different on Khrushchev and the Soviets. To them, he was trying to defend the indefensible. In his memoirs, Khrushchev gave a brief and rather accurate summary of the arguments presented by Eisenhower, and then exclaimed, "Here was the President of the United States, the man who we were supposed to negotiate with at the meeting in Paris, defending outrageous, inadmissible actions!"[26] As far as Khrushchev was concerned, Eisenhower had destroyed completely any opportunity he might have had to avoid being personally tainted by the U-2 incident, and it would be impossible to deal with him at Paris as long as he defended the overflights.

The Paris Summit Conference was an unpleasant postlude to the U-2 incident. Khrushchev demanded at the opening meeting that Eisenhower apologize for the overflight and punish the responsible parties. Eisenhower, angered by Khrushchev's intemperate language and still in no mood to apologize for anything, refused to accede to Khrushchev's demands, although he did announce that as far as he was concerned, the overflights were ended. This was far short of what Khrushchev wanted, and the summit broke up almost as soon as it began. The fears that Eisenhower had expressed on February 2 had come to pass and, as far as improving relations with the Soviets was concerned, his effectiveness had ended.

CONCLUSION

Khrushchev's speeches on May 5 and 7, 1960, constituted an attack on the United States for its policy of sending spy planes over the Soviet Union, and Eisenhower's short speech on May 11, 1960, provided a defense for that policy. Their addresses were a rhetorical speech set; however, this set was not strictly analogous to speech sets in which the two rhetors belong to the same sociopolitical system. Since Khrushchev and Eisenhower were leaders of separate and opposing nations, they were addressing separate audiences with different values. It was not a typical rhetorical set in which two rhetors competed for the loyalties of a common audience. Both Khrushchev and Eisenhower appealed successfully to their respective audiences, but both failed to bring about a result toward which they had both been striving: to allow some improvement in U.S.-Soviet relations. The U-2 overflight produced a crisis that neither rhetor expected or wanted, and each rhetor used language, constrained by his respective national audience, that precluded the compromise each sought.

To the extent that neither rhetor accomplished completely what he set out to do, Khrushchev seemed to have been more successful, since he laid a trap and the United States fell into it. On the other hand, Khrushchev's *kategoria* was in a sense too clever by half. It confused the U.S. government, as he had hoped it would, but the confusion caused tactical mistakes that ultimately made it more difficult for Eisenhower to keep his distance from the whole affair. Once Eisenhower decided to take responsibility for the U-2 overflights, his redefinitional *apologia* effectively eliminated Khrushchev's built-in escape clause, and led directly to the collapse of the Paris Summit Conference, a result neither leader would have wanted in the absence of the U-2 incident.

From the moment the U-2 was shot down near Sverdlovsk on May 1, there was very little that either the United States or the Soviet Union could *do* about what had happened. As a result, what they would *say* became the real issue. Thomas Franck and Edward Weisband, in their study of verbal strategies in U.S.-Soviet relations, pointed out in another context that verbal strategy "requires the same careful planning as any other aspect of strategy for the achievement of national goals. Before an option is chosen, before a verbal strategy is decided upon, its short-, medium-, and long-term effects should be estimated."[27] Both the American and Soviet verbal responses to the U-2 incident lacked this farsightedness, and instead of a carefully planned response on each side, there were verbal moves and countermoves that produced a rhetorical speech set. Perhaps the world was fortunate that the responses were limited to rhetorical acts.

NOTES

[1]Dwight D. Eisenhower, *Waging Peace 1956-1961* (Garden City, N.Y.: Doubleday, 1965), p. 546.

[2]John S. D. Eisenhower, *Strictly Personal* (Garden City, N.Y.: Doubleday, 1974), p. 270.

[3]M. L. Stein, *When Presidents Meet the Press* (New York: Julian Messner, 1969), p. 130.

[4]*Khrushchev Remembers: The Last Testament*, edited by Strobe Talbott (Boston: Little, Brown, 1974), pp. 444-46.

[5]Cyrus Leo Sulzberger, *The Last of the Giants* (New York: Macmillan, 1970), p. 678.

[6]"Khrushchev's Report," *The Current Digest of the Soviet Press*, June 1, 1960, p. 18.

[7]Committee on Foreign Relations, U.S. Senate, *Events Incident to the Summit Conference* (Washington, D.C.: GPO, 1960), p. 132.

[8]Personal communication from C. Douglas Dillon, July 9, 1980.

[9]Committee on Foreign Relations, U.S. Senate, *Report of the Committee on Foreign Relations on Events Relating to the Summit Conference* (Washington, D.C.: GPO, 1960), p. 10.

[10]*Khrushchev Remembers*, p. 446.

[11]"Khrushchev's Closing Speech to Supreme Soviet on U-2," *The Current Digest of the Soviet Press*, June 8, 1960, pp. 4-6.

[12]Foy D. Kohler, *Understanding the Russians: A Citizen's Primer* (New York: Harper & Row, 1970), pp. 326-27; and "Department Statement, May 7," *Department of State Bulletin*, May 23, 1960, p. 818.

[13]*The Eisenhower Presidency: Eleven Intimate Perspectives of Dwight D. Eisenhower*, edited by Kenneth W. Thompson (Lanham: University Press of America, 1984), p. 84.

[14]Telephone Calls, May 7, 1960, Presidential Telephone Calls 1-6/60 (1), Herter Papers, Dwight D. Eisenhower Library. Hereafter given as DDEL.

[15]See Eisenhower, *Waging Peace*, p. 550; David Wise and Thomas B. Ross, *The U-2 Affair* (New York: Bantam Books, 1962), p. 73; and Second Draft, U-2 Incident [Vol. I] (3), Project Clean Up, DDEL.

[16]See Telephone Calls, May 9, 1960, CAH Telephone Calls 3/28/60-6/30/60 (2), Herter Papers, DDEL; and Wise and Ross, *The U-2 Affair*, p. 77.

[17]Eisenhower, *Waging Peace*, p. 551; and Eisenhower, *Strictly Personal*, p. 271.

[18]"Crisis in the Cold War," *New York Times*, May 9, 1960; Walter Lippmann, "The Spy Plane," *Washington Post*, May 10, 1960; and Emmet John Hughes, *The Ordeal of Power: A Political Memoir of the Eisenhower Years* (New York: Atheneum, 1963), p. 301.

[19]Memorandum of Conference with the President, May 31, 1960, 1960 — Meetings with President — Vol. I (3), Records of the White House Office, Office of the Special Assistant for National Security Affairs, Records 1952-61, Special Assistant Series, Presidential Subseries, DDEL; and Ellis D. Slater, *The Ike I Knew* (n.p.: 1980), p. 229.

[20]"Statement by Secretary Herter, May 9," *Department of State Bulletin*, May 23, 1960, p. 816; and George B. Kistiakowsky, *A Scientist at the White House: The Private Diary of President Eisenhower's Special Assistant for Science and Technology* (Cambridge: Harvard University Press, 1976), p. 324.

[21]Memorandum of Conference with the President, May 10, 1960, Staff Notes May 1960 (1), DDE Diary Series, DDEL; and Michael R. Beschloss, *Mayday: Eisenhower, Khrushchev and the U-2 Affair* (New York: Harper & Row, 1986), p. 263.

[22]"The President's News Conference of May 11, 1960," *Public Papers of the Presidents of the United States: Dwight D. Eisenhower 1960-61* (Washington, D.C.: GPO, 1961), pp. 403-404.

[23]J. David Singer, "Soviet and American Foreign Policy Attitudes: Con-

tent Analysis of Elite Articulations," *The Journal of Conflict Resolution* 8 (1964): 451.

[24]Memorandum for Record, February 12, 1959, Intelligence Matters (8), and Memorandum for Record, February 8, 1960, Intelligence Matters (13), White House Office, Office of the Staff Secretary, Subject Series, Alphabetical Subseries, DDEL.

[25]George H. Gallup, *The Gallup Poll: Public Opinion 1935-1971* (New York: Random House, 1972), Vol. 3, pp. 1661, 1672; and William S. White, *The Responsibles* (New York: Harper & Row, 1972), p. 160.

[26]Talbott, *Khrushchev Remembers*, p. 448.

[27]Thomas M. Franck and Edward Weisband, *Word Politics: Verbal Strategy Among the Superpowers* (New York: Oxford University Press, 1972), p. 8.

INFORMATION SOURCES ON THE SPEECH SET

Premier Khrushchev's Accusations

For the first speech delivered on Thursday, May 5, 1960, see "Khrushchev's Report," *The Current Digest of the Soviet Press*, June 1, 1960, pp. 4-19, 44.

For the second speech delivered on Saturday, May 7, 1960, see "Khrushchev's Closing Speech to Supreme Soviet on U-2," *The Current Digest of the Soviet Press*, June 8, 1960, pp. 3-7.

President Eisenhower's Apology

The most authoritative publication of President Eisenhower's May 11, 1960, press conference, which was broadcast on national television, is as Item 143 in the *Public Papers of the Presidents of the United States: Dwight D. Eisenhower 1960-61* (Washington, D.C.: GPO, 1961), pp. 403-15.

Selected Bibliography

Beschloss, Michael R. *Eisenhower, Khrushchev and the U-2 Affair*. New York: Harper & Row, 1986.

Eisenhower, Dwight D. *Waging Peace 1956-1961*. Garden City, N.Y.: Doubleday, 1965.

Eisenhower, John S. D. *Strictly Personal*. Garden City, N.Y.: Doubleday, 1974.

Geelhoed, E. Bruce. "Dwight D. Eisenhower, The Spy Plane, and the Summit: A Quarter-Century Retrospective." *Presidential Studies Quarterly* 17 (1987): 95-106.

Khrushchev Remembers: The Last Testament. Edited by Strobe Talbott. Boston: Little, Brown, 1974.

Powers, Francis Gary. *Operation Overflight: The U-2 Spy Pilot Tells His Story for the First Time*. New York: Holt, Rinehart and Winston, 1970.

Wise, David, and Thomas B. Ross. *The U-2 Affair*. New York: Bantam Books, 1962.

Senator John F. Kennedy Encounters the Religious Question: "I Am Not the Catholic Candidate for President"

David Henry

Three weeks before the May 10, 1960, Democratic presidential primary in West Virginia, Senator John F. Kennedy learned from pollster Lou Harris that a 70 percent-30 percent lead he had held over Senator Hubert Humphrey the previous December had evaporated. Worse, Kennedy trailed Humphrey in the latest polls, 60 percent-40 percent. When Kennedy and his advisers inquired of the West Virginia headquarters what had happened, the response was brief but pointed: "[N]o one in West Virginia knew you were a Catholic in December. Now they know." That knowledge did not portend positively for Kennedy in a state with a 95 percent non-Catholic population, but he countered with a vigorous campaign that resulted in an impressive victory. After the election he concluded optimistically, "the religious issue has been buried here in the hills of West Virginia." His optimisim proved unwarranted.[1]

Although Kennedy, Humphrey, and Vice President Richard Nixon—Kennedy's eventual opponent in the general election—publicly disdained a prominence for religion in the campaign,[2] the question was very much alive after the West Virginia primary. Indeed, Kathleen Jamieson contended that, judged on the weight of anti-Catholic literature distributed against Kennedy and the hours of television and radio time he purchased to respond, Kennedy's religion constituted "the major issue" of the election. His strategy for engaging the issue has long intrigued rhetorical critics, whose attention invariably turns to the candidate's performance in Houston, Texas, on September 12.[3] Kennedy's address that evening to the Greater Houston Ministerial Association and his answers to the questions that followed provide bountiful materials for a critical study in the rhetoric of persuasive encounters.

Halford Ryan and Walter Fisher have concluded that while discourse may serve dual objectives at once, a single purpose or motive will dominate at any one time.[4] Kennedy's rhetoric on religion raises significant questions about this claim, for it is difficult at best to discern a single dominant motive. On one hand, Kennedy's performance at Houston may have been stimulated by a desire to purify the negative image produced by the attacks against him in the campaign, thus fulfilling a definition of *apologia*. On the other hand, however, when viewed in the context of a series of rhetorical transactions throughout the campaign, it may be argued with equal force that Kennedy was on the offensive at Houston, that he used an ostensibly defensive communication setting to question the tolerance and integrity of his inquisitors. A complete appreciation of Kennedy's campaign strategy on the Catholic issue can be gained, therefore, only by expanding the focus beyond a single exchange, and by viewing the candidate's discourse as a brilliant merging of accusatory and apologetic tactics. The approach culminated in Kennedy's redefinition of the issue at Houston from one of the Catholic church's dictatorial nature to one of religious tolerance and reasoned decision making, themes and arguments that had been soundly tested in earlier exchanges.

EVOLUTION OF THE RHETORICAL ACCUSATIONS

Prize-winning historian James MacGregor Burns wrote just prior to the election that the "Catholic Question" had unfolded in three phases. The first emerged from an article in the January 1959 issue of *Look* magazine, in which Kennedy had answered questions about religion and politics. The second consisted in the events of April and May 1960, encompassing the Wisconsin and West Virginia primaries and an address to the American Society of Newspaper Editors. Third was the meeting at Houston, which was "even more dramatic and decisive than the talk to the newspaper editors, although [Kennedy] said almost nothing of importance that was new."[5] Burns' observation reinforces the proposition that an adequate understanding of Kennedy at Houston is contingent on a thorough reconstruction of the rhetorical situation.

Kennedy and his staff knew the religious issue could not be avoided, yet they had little precedent for guidance in developing an appropriate strategy. With Al Smith, the Democrats' nominee in 1928, the only previous Catholic presidential candidate, historical example was thin. Smith had opted for a complete statement of his views in a 1927 issue of *The Atlantic*, and then avoided further discussion of the question. The Kennedy strategy, in contrast, was to engage the problem directly. An early major opportunity for doing so was in response to questions put forth by Fletcher Knebel who interviewed Kennedy in 1958 for an article about the possiblities of a Catholic candidate in 1960. The article appeared the following January, and in it Knebel described Kennedy's theme: "that religion is personal, politics are public, and the twain need never meet and conflict." In three brief paragraphs, Kennedy set forth the foundation for what would become his platform on church-and-state over the next two years. For any officeholder, he observed, "nothing takes precedence over his oath to uphold the Constitution and all its parts—including the First Amendment and the strict separation of church and state." That operating premise guided his positions on specific issues. He was "flatly opposed to appointment of an ambassador to the Vatican;" absolutely against "Federal funds being used for support of parochial or private schools;" and determined that on "such fringe matters as buses, lunches and other services," each "case must be judged on its own merits within the law as interpreted by the courts."[6]

Reaction to Kennedy's statements was curiously mixed. Some protestant leaders, such as the associate director of Protestants and Other Americans United for the Separation of Church and State, termed Kennedy's position "a courageous stand." As one might predict, not all Protestant leaders were so moved. Some attributed his answers to a plot directed from Rome to deceive the public, and urged that the "interests of the nation are safer in the hands of one who does not confess to a foreign, earthly power." And most importantly for the position he was to take over the course of the campaign, criticism came from Catholic quarters. Editors and writers for a wide spectrum of periodicals—including *America*, *Catholic World*, *Catholic Review*, and *Commonweal*—questioned everything from Kennedy's commitment to his oath of office over his church, to his positions on what he had termed fringe matters subject to case-by-case judgment. The *Look* article and its aftermath held a twofold significance. At the immediate level, it helped establish Kennedy's independence from his church on matters of broad philosophy as well as specific issues. For the long term, it portended the rhetorical stance that would emerge as the campaign progressed.

Events bound by and including the primaries in Wisconsin and West Virginia formed a critical juncture for the further testing and development of that stance. By most measures, Kennedy's forces should have viewed the April 5 primary in Wisconsin as a success. Their candidate carried six of ten districts and had won comfortably. But in political contests comfort is in the eye of the beholder, and from the opposition's perspective the view was engaging. Hubert Humphrey had won only four districts, but in the six he had lost, Catholic voter registration dominated. Humphrey therefore interpreted the election results as a victory, and determined to move on to West Virginia with its 95 percent non-Catholic electorate. Kennedy also considered religion to have been influential in Wisconsin, though he attributed that fact primarily to the press' coverage of the election. Consequently, in the midst of the West Virginia campaign, Kennedy visited Washington, D.C., to address the American Society of Newspaper Editors.

Kennedy's speech to the editors on April 21 constituted a formidable development in his communication strategy on the religious question. At first glance, he used the occasion to articulate fully his views on church-and-state. In so doing, he defended his character and the policies he advocated in accordance with the dictates of an *apologia*. He simultaneously moved to the offense, however, charging the press with unduly emphasizing religion in the primaries. The tactic foreshadowed the technique that would serve him well in Houston five months hence.

Kennedy opened with an appeal based on the stasis of fact. "There is no religious *issue*," he declared, "in the sense that any of the major candidates differ on the role of religion in our political life. Every presidential contender, I am certain, is dedicated to the separation of church and state, to the preservation of religious liberty, to an end to religious bigotry, and to the total independence of the officeholder from any form of ecclesiastical dictation." Nor, he continued, "is there any religious *issue* in the sense that any candidate is exploiting his religious affiliation." In particular, "I am not 'trying to be the first Catholic President,' as some have written. I happen to believe I can serve my nation as President — and I also happen to have been born a Catholic." The allusion to what had been written served as a transition to the accusatory phase of the text. The press, he acknowledged, did not create the religious issue, but reporters and editors "will largely determine whether or not it does become dominant — whether it is kept in perspective — whether it is considered objectively — whether needless fears and suspicions are aroused." But had the issue been kept in perspective to date? Not if the Wisconsin primary were exemplary. The candidate had spoken there on farm legislation, foreign policy, defense, civil rights, and several other issues. Though the public seemed genuinely concerned about such issues, Kennedy said, "I rarely found them reported in the press — except when they were occasionally sandwiched in between descriptions of my handshaking, my theme song, family, haircut and, inevitably, my religion." One event captured the press' preoccupation, Kennedy asserted. A map published in the *Milwaukee Journal* the Sunday before the primary accounted for voter strength in each district according to three classes of voters — Democrats, Republicans, and Catholics. He concluded his charge with the observation that he did not believe religion had yet been a decisive issue in any state, and "I do not think it should be made to be. And, recognizing my own responsibilities in that regard, I am hopeful that you will recognize yours also."

Kennedy then raised and answered three questions, each of which would return in the course of the campaign: (1) is the religious issue a legitimate concern in the campaign? (2) can we justify analyzing voters and candidates on a basis of religion? (3) is there a justification for applying a religious test in campaigns for the presidency? With the analysis of each question, Kennedy carefully but surely shifted the grounds of debate from the question of his religion to one of press responsibility. What had begun as a speech of apology had been thoroughly transformed. Thus, when he broached the subject of his own character and behavior, he was on the offensive.

"I am not," he declared, "the Catholic candidate for President. I do not speak for the Catholic Church on issues of public policy — and no one in that Church speaks for me." The proof was in his record. Stands on aid to education, aid to Tito, the Conant nomination, and other issues displeased some Catholic clergymen and organizations, and were approved by others. But the presence or absence of that approval had, and would have, no influence in the making of political decisions. Still, his candidacy had created a controversy and two alternatives had been suggested for its resolution. One course would be to accept the vice-presidency, thus placating the so-called Catholic vote and concurrently avoiding a religious controversy. To accept that course, though, would be to acknowledge that Catholics could rise to the highest levels of power in foreign nations, but that in America one-third of the population is forever barred from the White House. The other alternative was to continue his campaign. Kennedy's beliefs that "the American people are more concerned with a man's views and abilities than with the church to which he belongs," that the "Founding Fathers meant it when they provided in Article VI of the Constitution that there should be no religious test for public office," and that the American people "mean to adhere to those principles today" led him to opt for the latter choice. And in his pursuit of that option, he concluded, the candidate and the press shared responsibility in dealing with the religious issue: it "is my job to face it frankly and fully. And it is your job to face it fairly, in perspective, and in proportion." Accusations about the press worked hand-in-hand with the purification motive in Kennedy's speech to the newspaper editors, reflecting the candidate's emerging tactic for neutralizing the potential liability of his religion. The technique foreshadowed what Lawrence Fuchs termed Kennedy's dual strategy of declaring his independence while putting others on the defensive, an approach put in force in the West Virginia primary.[7]

On May 3, Kennedy and Humphrey met in a televised debate in Charleston, West Virginia. The format entailed five-minute speeches by each candidate, followed by rebuttals of equal length. Questions submitted by readers to the *Charleston Gazette* and presented to the candidates by a newspaper man and a television newscaster comprised the remainder of the session. Two questions pertained to the issue of religion. Couched in broad terms, the first arose slightly over half-way through the encounter: "Vice-President Nixon by inference has said this country has nothing to fear until such time as an individual without religion, an atheist or an agnostic, is a candidate for President. Would you care to comment on this?" Kennedy seized the opportunity to stress his commitment to the Constitution and the guarantees of individual freedoms it afforded. The "Constitution is quite explicit," he began, "and says there shall be no religious test for office in Article VI; and, of course, in the First Amendment, says Congress shall make no laws" abridging religious freedom. If, he continued, "we've started to apply religious tests of one kind or another, then really something important in American life would go out. So, I must say that I believe that people should be free. That's the important thing: to believe as they wish, providing they are loyal Americans and devoted to Constitutional principles." The final clause was crucial, for in it Kennedy moved, as he did in dictating to the newspaper editors their responsibility, from accused to accuser. He was devoted to the religious freedoms the Constitution ensured; by inference, those who opposed him were opponents of that document and its provisions.

The other question on religion followed shortly, and was far more precise. Ned Chilton, assistant to the publisher of the *Gazette*, read it: "Mr. Kennedy, this question has been sent in, name withheld, from Charleston: 'The Roman Catholic Church's position on truth versus error assumes a right to discriminate against Protestants in some countries where Catholics are in the majority. Do you agree with the Church's reported attitude that where Protestants are a minority they shouldn't be permitted equal status?" After noting that he "wholly disagree[d]", "couldn't disagree more," and found the idea "wholly repugnant to our experience," Kennedy moved to what was crystallizing as the foundation of his position on the religious issue. "This country was founded on the principle of separation of church and state," he declared. "This is a view that I hold against any other view, and it's the view that I subscribe to in the Constitution." Kennedy not only pledged himself to the Constitution, but also reasserted its primacy in his thinking, even when it conflicted with the doctrines of his church.

Kennedy was also on the offense and his detractors on the defense in a second dimension of the West Virginia campaign. The Kennedy organization attracted the support of Franklin Delano Roosevelt, Jr., who became a key supporting player in allaying concerns about the candidate's religion. Roosevelt's role was both instrumental and symbolic. As a participant in the campaign, his most prominent capacity was as Kennedy's compatriot in a television commercial constructed as a question session. Roosevelt put to the candidate questions written by Kennedy's staff, and interjected between questions his summaries of the senator's views and what Jamieson termed his blessing on each answer. The questions attended to the issues that had preoccupied Protestant leaders from the campaign's inception: would he abide by the church's wishes on state matters? could he participate fully in non-Catholic ceremonies should his office so require? would Kennedy attempt to influence Catholic countries that persecuted their Protestant minorities? could he ensure that Catholics among his appointees would be as open-minded and fair as he? Roosevelt's endorsement of Kennedy's answers carried enormous symbolic power in

West Virginia, a state in which his father was revered. His approval implied both party and Protestant support and, united with the candidate's own performances in campaign appearances and the debates with Humphrey, it subdued the Catholic question on primary day.[8]

Although Kennedy did not, as he had hoped, "bury the religious issue in the hills of West Virginia," he had developed by spring a potent strategy for addressing it in future encounters. The central tenet that undergirded his discourse was an unquestioned commitment to the separation of church and state, as mandated by the Constitution. Supporting arguments in turn derived their force from Constitutional authority. Of equal importance to the substantive base of Kennedy's rhetoric was the tactic of transforming situations that ostensibly called for defensive discourse to occasions in which he became the accuser. The appearance of two polemics in the fall completed the evolution of the rhetorical accusations Kennedy would ultimately encounter at Houston. On September 8, the *New York Times* published the texts of statements by two prominent Protestant organizations on the question of church-state separation. Protestants and Other Americans United for the Separation of Church and State (P.O.A.U.) counted among its leadership Bishop G. Bromley Oxnam who, with the Reverend Dr. Eugene Carson Blake, had articulated a mainstream Protestant perspective on the controversy in a widely read *Look* magazine article the preceding May.[9] Although the P.O.A.U. statement was viewed as more moderate than that of the National Conference of Citizens for Religious Freedom, attention to it is instructive for within the moderate tone were couched charges and techniques that paralleled and thereby helped to legitimize those of the National Conference. Intoning that the moment for "calm analysis and sober speech about the religious issue in the current political campaign" was at hand, the P.O.A.U. defined itself as the appropriate group for such speech. The organization's credentials stemmed from its status as an educational group with "a permanent aim--the preservation of the American tradition of the separation of church and state." In line with that aim, the organization endorsed no candidate or party; its members included Democrats, Republicans, and independents, and it wanted them all to remain loyal to its purpose regardless of their political preferences in the election. With their credibility thus established, framers of the statement turned to the issue of the religious bigotry and scandal that had permeated the campaign. They found such behavior reprehensible, but moved to argue that when "a candidate belongs to an organization which champions [partial union of church and state], it is not bigotry or prejudice to examine his credentials with the utmost care and frankness, and to ask how far his commitment goes." By attending initially to the group's character and self-appointed charge, P.O.A.U. created an impression of detachment from the fray. Its statement then made Kennedy's character and/or positions on the cited controversies the avowed center of attention, thereby appearing to establish an objective basis for hearing out a candidate on controversial issues. The focus then shifted subtly and swiftly, however, from the candidate and his views on church doctrine to an indictment of the doctrine itself. Thus, although Kennedy was the object of judgment, his fitness for office was to be assessed by scrutiny of Roman Catholic church policy.

The core of the statement specified the church's support of partial church-state union, promotion of public funding for parochial schools, and call for diplomatic representation of the Vatican as critical concerns. "These policies," concluded the writers, "are clearly inconsistent with the American concept of separation of church and state, and, to the extent that any candidate supports or endorses them, he is unfitted for the Presidency of the United States." At the same time, though, to the "extent that he repudiates these policies and demonstrates his independence of clerical control, he is entitled to our praise and encouragement." The structure of the remainder of the statement was dispositionally creative and illustrated the bind in which Kennedy found himself for explaining either his character or his positions on policy. P.O.A.U. praised Kennedy for "declaring frankly that basic government financial support for parochial schools is unconstitutional. We have likewise praised him for his opposition to the appointment of an American Ambassador to the Vatican." But, "[w]e are skeptical about his equivocal words on birth control," and "concerned, too, about his silence in regard to the official [Church] boycott of public schools." The document then abruptly proceeded to a forceful and detailed articulation of objections to Catholic policy. In leading to the brief peroration, the lengthy denunciation of government treatment of Protestants in countries dominated by Catholics was rhetorically well placed. The conclusion returned to the independent, objective tone established at the outset by asserting a desire for P.O.A.U. members to "decide for themselves, on the basis of all of the evidence" what the election of a "Roman Catholic" might mean for church-state relations. The light praise for the Roman Catholic in question, carefully coupled with "concern" and "skepticism," succeeded by inflammatory examples of abusive church policies, hardly ensured independent decisions.

The P.O.A.U. statement reflected what might be expected from accusatory discourse. It addressed matters of policy and character, affirmed the reasonableness of its viewpoints by casting its creators as objective educators, and put Kennedy in the tenuous position of having to account for his own views by defending church policy.[10] Whereas this statement at least intimated that Kennedy had been responsive to some of the group's concerns, the one released by the National Conference of Citizens for Religious Freedom was far less charitable.

The National Conference shared P.O.A.U.'s doubts about the ability of a Catholic to break with the church over policy, but it was equally convinced that no member of the church had the requisite character for ascending to the presidency. In contrast, the Conference counted among its leadership some of the most prominent figures in American religion, including Dr. Norman Vincent Peale, syndicated columnist, best-selling author, and head of Manhattan's Marble Collegiate Church; Dr. Daniel Poling, editor of the *Christian Herald* and unsuccessful Republican candidate for Mayor of Philadelphia in 1951; Dr. Harold Ockenga, pastor of Boston's Park Street Church; and Dr. L. Nelson Bell, editor of *Christianity Today* and father-in-law of the Reverend Billy Graham. The Reverend Donald Gill, a Baptist minister on leave from his post with the National Council of Evangelicals, served as executive coordinator of the conference. At the press conference called to accompany the release of the group's statement, Peale and Ockenga made clear the Conference's doubts about any Catholic's ability to operate independent of the church. It was inconceivable, they maintained, that "a Roman Catholic President would not be under extreme pressure by the hierarchy to accede to its policies with respect to foreign relations." Ockenga argued that Kennedy's alleged insistence on church-state separation was analogous to Nikita Khrushchev's advocacy of world peace during the Soviet Premier's tour of the United States in 1959. Just as the Communist interpretation of world peace differed from that of the free world, so did the Catholic perception of church-state separation deviate from the Protestant view.[11]

The National Conference's statement opened with a glaring credibility differentiation between its membership and the Kennedy-Khrushchev perspective. After alluding to the meeting's representation of thirty-seven Protestant denominations, the document called for tolerance and discretion, disdained hate-mongering and bigotry, and noted that "persons who are of the Roman Catholic faith can be just as honest, patriotic and public spirited as those of any other faith." Nevertheless, the authors continued, the critical question was whether a member of that church could exercise civil responsibilities without ecclesiastical interference. The dilemma posed for the "current Roman Catholic contender" for president stemmed from his specific statements that he "would not be so influenced" versus his church's insistence that "he is duty-bound to admit to its direction. This unresolved conflict leaves doubts in the minds of millions of our citizens." The remainder of the statement exacerbated those doubts and conflicts by defining the nature of the Catholic church's policy and by impugning Kennedy's character.

The first line of argument was that all Catholics were by definition unable to separate church and state. The most severe indictment of church policy was its commitment to church-state union. The "Roman Catholic

Church is a political as well as a religious organization," the statement held, whose hierarchy traditionally "has assumed and exercised temporal power." Not only was such a position anathema to American constitutional doctrine, but the linkage of church and state resulted in oppression where the Catholic church was in the majority. Offenses included the "denial of equal rights to all of other faiths," the extension to Catholics of "privileges not permitted to those of other faiths," and the arrest, imprisonment, and persecution of Protestant ministers and workers in Catholic-controlled nations such as Colombia and Spain. Further, the church made binding on all members "the belief that Protestant faiths are heretical and counterfeit and ... have no right to exist." Consequently, members who held elective office would be forbidden participation in non-Catholic ceremonies, thus precluding fulfillment of the duties of office. "Would not a Roman Catholic President," the Conference asked, "thus be gravely handicapped in offering to the American people and to the world an example of the religious liberty our people cherish?" The alleged inability of Catholics to participate in ceremonies sponsored by other faiths was a veiled reference to a 1947 incident in which Kennedy, then a member of the House of Representatives, had initially accepted Dr. Poling's invitation to participate in a ceremony in Philadelphia and then withdrew. The event would become an issue of dispute at Houston. It is important to note its roots in the Conference's characterization of Catholic doctrine, for it was in part through that doctrine that his detractors impugned Kennedy's character.

In the Conference's statement itself, however, his character was questioned even more directly. The framers saw a discrepancy between Kennedy's actions in the House and his behavior in the Senate. The "record shows," they observed, that one of the bills introduced by Kennedy in the House "had as its purpose federal aid to education which included private and parochial schools." He "also sought to amend the Barden bill in the Eighty-first Congress in such a way as to provide funds for parochial schools." The group acknowledged, on the other hand, that Kennedy was "the only Senator of Roman Catholic faith who voted against the Morse amendment to the Aid-to-Education Act in the Eighty-sixth Congress in 1960." The Conference's primary concern was which inclination would accompany Kennedy to the White House. "We are hopeful," they wrote, "that the newer phase of Senator Kennedy's thinking on the issue will prevail, but we can only measure the new against the old." The statement retreated from its derisive tone toward the candidate in its concluding paragraph, but its accusatory intent was no less evident. The presence of a religious issue in the campaign could not be attributed to any one candidate, the Conference said in returning to its operating assumption, because it "is created by the nature of the Roman Catholic Church which is, in a very real sense, both a church and also a temporal state."

The National Conference's contributions to the *kategoria* were a specific indictment against Kennedy's character, an elaboration of the P.O.A.U.'s challenge of the Catholic church's commitment to church-state separation, and the addition to the charges advanced of the credibility of formidable religious leaders.[12] Although these charges might understandably put most rhetors on the defensive, Kennedy's performance at Houston revealed his rhetorical capacity to reshape his listeners' perceptions concerning the roles of accuser and accused.

KATEGORIA AND *APOLOGIA* MERGE: KENNEDY AT HOUSTON

The audience gathered at Houston, Texas, on September 12 no doubt shared in large measure the suspicions raised about Kennedy's character and the church's power by the Protestant groups' statements. Three hundred members of the Greater Houston Ministerial Association, heavily southern Baptist in representation, and an additional three hundred spectators eagerly awaited the Democratic candidate's appearance, for the format emphasized a lengthy question-and-answer session to follow a relatively brief prepared address. Kennedy's speech and his responses to the questions illuminate his skill in converting a hostile atmosphere rife with potential liabilities to an asset for the remainder of the campaign.

The bulk of the speech functioned as an exercise in *apologia*, for Kennedy attended to the matters of his policy views and personal convictions that arguably needed explanation. Approximately two-thirds of the way into the address, however, he shifted subtly in tone and substance from a defensive to an accusatory posture. In the final phase, he established the tenor for the question session, during which Kennedy often seemed more in control of the flow of discussion than did his interrogators. His strategy allowed him to move the focus from a question of religion and church-state separation to an issue of tolerance. His ability to redefine the debate recast Kennedy from apologist to accuser.

Kennedy's speech has been variously termed his "most persuasive campaign speech," the "centerpiece of the session," and "a firm, honest, eloquent, and probably even decisive address." Kennedy's manner contributed heavily to such praise. His black suit and tie put him in the uniform of his immediate audience, and though one observer recounted the candidate's nervousness, another was more impressed with the senator's control and platform presence than at any point in the campaign. Consensus seems to have fallen to the latter perspective, particularly when considering the speech as a televised address. Jamieson lauded the performance as Kennedy's "most eloquent . . . either as candidate or president," a claim she rooted in David Halberstam's description of the event as the "mastery of a great new skill in televised politics: deliberately allowing

someone else to rig something against you that is, in fact, rigged for you."
Kennedy was calm, in control, and poised. He had heard the questions and
dealt with the issues almost constantly since the campaign's inception. The
ministers asking questions, in contrast, varied from openly hostile to
suspecting naively that they were putting forth the issues for the first time.
As a result, Halberstam wrote, the "Houston audience was, much to its own
surprise, a prop audience." Kennedy controlled the script as well as the set
and props. The re-casting of the religious question to an issue of tolerance
constituted the most important plot change, which was difficult to effect
without offending the unwitting co-players. As Pierre Salinger, Kennedy's
press chief, told the candidate when asked the mood of the audience,
"They're tired of being called bigots." Kennedy rose to the challenge.[13]

Kennedy based the conversion of the issue, from one of religious
doctrine to a matter of tolerance, on appeals to religious liberty and the
"Golden Rule," constitutional guarantees, and the ideals of fair play and
consistency vs. the spectre of religious tests. The appeals addressed matters of character and policy, the stock topics of *apologia*, but what lent them
force was the speech's clever structure. The first four paragraphs comprised
an ingenious exordium that identified the charge. The "so-called religious
issue," he began, "is necessarily and properly the chief topic here tonight."
But, he continued, "I want to emphasize from the outset that I believe we
have far more critical issues in the 1960 campaign: the spread of Communist influence, until it now festers ninety miles off the coast of
Florida — the humiliating treatment of our President and Vice President by
those who no longer respect our power — the hungry children I saw in West
Virginia, the old people who cannot pay their doctor's bills, the families
forced to give up their farms — an America with too many slums, with too
few schools, and too late to the moon and outer space." Praise for his
audience followed. Although these are the real issues, Kennedy said, issues
which "know no religious barrier," they "have been obscured — perhaps
deliberately — in some quarters less responsible than this." Surely he would
now receive a fair hearing, as he "state[d] once again — not what kind of
church I believe in, for that should be important only to me, but what kind
of America I believe in." His phrasing framed the essence of his argument;
religion was established as a private matter while a candidate's vision for
the nation was in the public domain.

The separation of church and state intimated by Kennedy's phrasing carried over to the body of the text. Proofs of his fidelity to church-state
separation as well as the refutation of unfounded charges about his views
and character, were impressed on the listener by dint of the argument's
divisions. The roles of church and state comprised Kennedy's most extensive *apologia* for policy. The purification motive underlay his declaration
at the argument's outset that "I believe in an America where the separation

of church and state is absolute—where no Catholic prelate would tell the President (should he be a Catholic) how to act and no Protestant minister would tell his parishioners for whom to vote." Religion must not be an issue, he argued, for "while this year it may be a Catholic against whom the finger of suspicion is pointed, in other years it has been, and may someday be again, a Jew—or a Quaker—or a Unitarian—or a Baptist." Not only was the immediate audience of Baptists potentially at risk if religious bigotry became a political issue, but the mention of the Quakers formed a subtle but potentially important allusion to his opponent's religion. What, then, should be the role of religion in America? Kennedy offered a vision of "an America where religious intolerance will someday end—where all men and churches are treated equal," and where "Catholics, Protestants, and Jews" alike would join together to promote "the American ideal of brotherhood."

Having established spirituality as the proper sphere of religion, Kennedy turned to civic matters. He averred a commitment to a "President whose views on religion are his own private affair." The chief executive must not "subvert the First Amendment's guarantees of religious liberty," nor should others "work to subvert Article VI of the Constitution by requiring a religious test" for election. The complete separation of religious and political matters mandated a president "whose public acts are responsible to all and obligated to none—who can attend any ceremony, service or dinner his office may appropriately require him to fulfill—and whose fulfillment of his Presidential office is not limited or conditioned by any religious oath, ritual or obligation." At this point in the address, Kennedy had clearly demarcated the boundaries between church and state. Completing his defense of character, he initiated the transition into the speech's accusatory phase. Noting that he had fought in the South Pacific and that his brother had died in Europe, he exploited the words of the National Conference's statement of the previous week. He shifted the burden of proof for character from himself to his detractors: "No one suggested then that we might have a 'divided loyalty,' that we did 'not believe in liberty' or that we belonged to a disloyal group that threatened 'the freedoms for which our forefathers died.'" In an effort to affirm an image of the opposition as intolerant, he separated the immediate listeners from others who might oppose his election on religious grounds. Cognizant of Salinger's advice that the audience was weary of being charged with bigotry, the candidate first declared his opposition to political persecution "by any religious group, Catholic or Protestant, to compel, prohibit or prosecute the free exercise of any other religion." The dictum held for any country, he continued, and "I hope that you and I condemn with equal fervor those nations which deny their Presidency to Protestants and those which deny it to Catholics." Lest the message be insufficiently clear, Kennedy moved from broad principle to the particular case of his candidacy: "I am not the Catholic candidate for

President. . . . I do not speak for my church on public matters — and the church does not speak for me."

In the final third of the address Kennedy was fully on the offensive. He tied independence, a god-term in American political life, to the division between religion and more pressing issues. If "I should lose on the real issues," he told those assembled, "I shall return to my seat in the Senate satisfied that I tried my best and was fairly judged." If, on the other hand, "this election is decided on the basis that 40,000,000 Americans lost their chance of being President on the day they were baptized, then it is the whole nation that will be the loser in the eyes of Catholics and non-Catholics around the world, in the eyes of history, and in the eyes of our own people." Just as he expected voters to exercise independent judgment, he pledged independence from his church and committed himself to the Constitution in a peroration made powerful by a brilliantly conceived concluding tactic. After noting that he would be free to fulfill the pledge of office, one almost identical to that he had taken as a member of Congress for fourteen years, he closed by reciting from the presidential oath of office: "I can, and I quote 'solemnly swear that I will faithfully execute the office of President of the United States and will to the best of my ability preserve, protect and defend the Constitution, so help me God.'" Thus declaring his own independence and fairness, Kennedy shifted the challenge to his listeners to demonstrate tolerance and charity.[14]

Following polite applause, however, the tone of questions from the floor indicated that strong reservations about the candidate's church-state policies remained. As he had been in the West Virginia primary debates in May as well as for the *Look* article the year before, Kennedy was ready. E. E. Westmoreland, president of Houston's South Bay Baptist Church, for example, prefaced his question by observing that he had been told that his colleagues in St. Louis intended to ask the Democrat the same question the following night, so he wanted "you to answer to the Houston crowd before you get to St. Louis." Westmoreland asked Kennedy to send to Cardinal Cushing, "Mr. Kennedy's own hierarchical superior of Boston," an appeal, to be forwarded to the Vatican, that sought official endorsement as church policy the position on church-state separation the senator had laid as the cornerstone of his campaign. Kennedy responded with good humor to Rev. Westmoreland's preface, then turned serious. "[A]s I do not accept the right of any, as I said, ecclesiastical official, to tell me what I shall do in the sphere of my public responsibility as an elected official," he noted, "I do not propose also to ask Cardinal Cushing to ask the Vatican to take some action." The answer stimulated strong applause, but doubts persisted. Another question from the floor asked if other Catholics he appointed to serve in his government would be "free to make such statements as you have been so courageous to make?" Kennedy made it clear that he was confident his statements reflected the viewpoint of potential appointees as well as the great majority of American Catholics. The turning point of the encounter came with Kennedy's response to a quick but pointed follow-up question: "Do you state it with the approval of the Vatican?" Kennedy's anger was visible but controlled as he addressed the now quiet and tense gathering: "I don't have to have approval in that sense." Loud applause signalled support and prevented his completion of the answer. Approval followed again as he concluded the issue for good that evening by saying simply, "It seems to me that I am the one that is running for the office of the Presidency and not Cardinal Cushing and not any one else."

In addition to his ability to separate church and state, the assembled ministers were concerned with how Kennedy might use his office. An exemplary issue was one that had arisen earlier and been handled efficiently. Max Delcke, president of the Gulf Coast Bible College and pastor of the First Church of God in Houston, asked, "If you are elected President, will you use your influence to get the Roman Catholic countries of South America and Spain to stop persecuting Protestant missionaries?" Kennedy did not hesitate before saying, "I would use my influence as President of the United States to permit, to encourage the development of freedom all over the world." The rights of free speech, assembly, and religious practice, he maintained, are rights "I would hope the United States and the President would stand for . . . all around the globe without regard to geography, religion or" — audience applause prevented completion of the answer.

Although Kennedy handled such pure policy questions deftly, issues that blended matters of character and policy continued to concern the audience. An incident from 1947 constituted the primary basis for questioning whether Kennedy's behavior would match his alleged devotion to church-state separation. The *Christian Century* brought attention to the issue in a January editorial. Kennedy had accepted an invitation in 1947 to speak at the dedication of the Chapel of the Four Chaplains in Philadelphia. He later withdrew, claiming that he had been misled. He thought he had been invited as a representative of Congress, but when he learned he had been chosen to speak for the church he declined, for such a role ran counter to the provisions of the Constitution. However, Dr. Daniel Poling, a leader of the National Council and the man who had invited Kennedy, asserted that Kennedy's decision had been dictated by Dennis Cardinal Dougherty of Philadelphia, a charge repeated in the editorial. If "Mr. Kennedy were President," the editors argued, "he would be subject to the same kind of discipline that he acknowledged as Senator."[15]

The event afforded Kennedy an opportunity in the question session to implement the shift from defense to offense that had defined the strategy of the speech. His antagonists ultimately became unwitting allies in the transformation. The first question, asked early, tied the Chapel of the Four

Chaplains to a broader concern for Kennedy's capacity to participate in non-Catholic ceremonies. Kennedy gave a detailed explanation of his side of the 1947 event, then concluded that "my grounds for not going were private." But if the ceremony involved "were a public matter, I would be glad to go as an individual but I could not go as a [church] spokesman." A more skeptical question followed shortly. K. O. White, pastor of Houston's downtown First Baptist Church, read to Kennedy portions of a memorandum from Dr. Poling that disputed Kennedy's earlier explanations and challenged the senator's credibility. Kennedy met the assertion that Poling had invited him as a public servant, not as a Catholic, with a quotation from Poling's own book that described Kennedy as "spokesman for the Catholic Faith." After questioning Poling's memory and hence his credibility, Kennedy aimed for closure by redefining the issue: "This took place in 1947. I had been in politics probably two months and was relatively inexperienced. I should have inquired before getting into the incident." But, he asked, is "this the best that can be done after fourteen years? Is this the only incident that can be charged?" The question impressed the audience, who dropped the matter when Kennedy concluded that though "it was imprudent of me in accepting it, I don't think it shows unfitness for holding public office."

Kennedy completed the transformation from defense to offense with his answer to the final question. With little time remaining, he refocused attention from an inquiry centered on technical church doctrine to his theme of religious tolerance, which he cast as a matter of reason. Since "this fight for religious freedom is basic in the establishment of the American system," he began, "any candidate for the office . . . should submit himself to the questions of any reasonable man." It would be unreasonable, he said, for him to be rejected because of membership in his church, despite his commitment to church-state separation, his avowed devotion to the Constitution, and his record that lent credence to his words. "What I would consider to be reasonable in an exercise of free will and free choice," in contrast, "is to ask the candidate to state his views as broadly as possible, investigate his record to see whether he states what he believes and then to make an independent, rational judgment, as to whether he could be entrusted with this highly important position." The appeal to the listeners as men of reason not only concluded the session, but also embodied Kennedy's strategy of defusing the religious issue by converting the matter to questions of tolerance and justice.[16]

CONCLUSION

Although editorial and public opinion were mixed, Kennedy's speech had immediate and long-term effects on the campaign. An independent group of one hundred religious, education, and political leaders published on the day of the speech a statement on religious liberty. Even though most Protestant periodicals remained either skeptical or hostile, the *Christian Century* officially shifted its stance from opposition to Kennedy to neutrality, and *Christianity in Crisis* became even more sympathetic to the Democrat. A few days after the speech, Norman Vincent Peale announced that he was no longer affiliated with the National Conference of Citizens for Religious Freedom, and denied that he had ever participated in the framing or propagation of the group's statement. In addition to putting his accusers on the defense, the Kennedy campaign continued the offensive begun at Houston. One-, five-, and thirty-minute versions of the session were aired as television commercials in strategically selected markets, and the themes that crystallized on September 12 formed the candidate's stock responses to the religious question in interviews and personal appearances. Thus, when Kennedy identified religious freedom, church-state separation, and faith in the Constitution as the foundation of his views in a television interview on Reformation Sunday, eight days before the election, protestant leaders stifled plans for a nationwide movement against Catholicism.[17]

An analysis of the rhetoric of the Catholic question in 1960 suggests that the critic of the speech set might on occasion be most productive if his or her focus is not limited to the two-discourse format. The two Protestant groups' statements of September 7, for instance, clearly provided the immediate impetus for Kennedy's appearance at Houston. Yet by examining the evolution of the rhetorical situation from early 1959 to September of the following year, far more is revealed about the exchange between Kennedy and the Protestant groups than would otherwise be the case. In reality, Kennedy adapted his rhetoric to the tenets of accusation and apology in an ongoing fashion. His preparation for the *Look* magazine interview, the early Democratic primaries, and the address to the American Society of Newspaper Editors had readied him thoroughly for the final encounter. Having dealt with both the issues that would likely arise and the tactics for establishing the strongest position, he was prepared to transform a heavily problematic situation into a position of strength. Kennedy converted a defense or *apologia* into accusatory discourse. The issue ultimately became not his Catholicism, but the place of religious tolerance, fairness, and charity in American society. Where the motive of purification might have undergirded pure *apologia*, it is evident that Kennedy's discourse as much aimed to affirm an image of his detractors as to dispel negative perceptions of himself. Both motives merged in a blending of *kategoria* and *apologia* in creating appropriate discourse for the rhetorical situation.

NOTES

[1]Theodore H. White, *The Making of The President 1960* (New York:

Pocket Books, 1961), p. 121; "Religion--Campaign '60," *Newsweek*, September 12, 1960, p. 61.

[2]See Felix Belair, Jr., "Religion as Issue Denounced Again By White House," *New York Times*, September 8, 1960, pp. 1, 16; Anthony Lewis, "Nixon Seeks Date to End All Talk of Religion Issue," *New York Times*, September 12, 1960, pp. 1, 19; "Nixon's TV Remarks on Issue of Religion," *New York Times*, September 12, 1960, p. 19.

[3]Representative studies include Kathleen Hall Jamieson, *Packaging the Presidency* (New York and Oxford: Oxford University Press, 1984), pp. 124-36; Harold Barrett, "John F. Kennedy Before the Greater Houston Ministerial Association," *Central States Speech Journal* 15 (1964): 259-66; Hermann G. Stelzner, "John F. Kennedy at Houston, Texas, September 12, 1960," *Rhetoric and Communication*, ed. Jane Blankenship and Hermann G. Stelzner (Urbana: University of Illinois Press, 1976), pp. 223-235.

[4]Halford Ross Ryan, "*Kategoria* and *Apologia*: On Their Rhetorical Criticism as a Speech Set," *Quarterly Journal of Speech* 68 (1982): 257; Walter R. Fisher, "A Motive View of Communication," *Quarterly Journal of Speech* 56 (1970): 136-39.

[5]James MacGregor Burns, "The Religious Issue," *Progressive*, November 1960, pp. 21-22.

[6]Lawrence H. Fuchs, *John F. Kennedy and American Catholicism* (New York: Meredith Press, 1967), pp. 165-69; Fletcher Knebel, "Democratic Forecast: A Catholic in 1960," *Look*, March 3, 1959, p. 17; White, *The Making of the President 1960*, pp. 112-14.

[7]"I Am Not the Catholic Candidate for President," *U.S. News & World Report*, May 2, 1960, pp. 90-92; Fuchs, *John F. Kennedy and American Catholicism*, p. 172.

[8]"Kennedy-Humphrey Television Debate in Charleston, West Virginia," *Speeches for Illustration and Example*, ed. Goodwin F. Berquist (Chicago: Scott, Foresman and Company, 1965), pp. 170-75; Jamieson, *Packaging the Presidency*, pp. 125-26.

[9]Rev. Dr. Eugene Carson and Bishop G. Bromley Oxnam, "A Protestant View of a Catholic for President," *Look*, May 10, 1960, pp. 31-34.

[10]"Protestant Groups' Statements--P.O.A.U.," *New York Times*, Sep-

tember 8, 1960, p. 25.

[11]Courtney Sheldon, "Church-and-State Issues Debated, *Christian Science Monitor*, September 8, 1960, p. 1; Peter Braestrup, "Protestant Unit Wary on Kennedy," *New York Times*, September 8, 1960, pp. 1, 25; and "The Power of Negative Thinking," *Time*, September 19, 1960, p. 2

[12]"Protestant Groups' Statements--National Conference," *New York Times*, September 8, 1960, p. 25.

[13]James L. Golden, "John F. Kennedy and the 'Ghosts'," *Quarterly Journal of Speech* 52 (1966): 351; Jay David, *The Kennedy Reader* (Indianapolis: Bobbs-Merrill, 1967), p. 362; "Test of Religion," *Time*, September 26, 1960, p. 21; Ernest K. Lindley, "As Kennedy Goes," *Newsweek*, September 26, 1960, p. 56; Jamieson, *Packaging the Presidency*, pp. 125-30

[14]John F. Kennedy, "Speech to Greater Houston Ministerial Association," *American Rhetoric from Roosevelt to Reagan*, 2d ed., ed. Halford Ross Ryan (Prospect Heights, Ill.: Waveland Press, 1987), pp. 152-55.

[15]"Why Senator Kennedy Withdrew as Speaker," *Christian Century*, January 27, 1960, p. 93; W. H. Lawrence, "Kennedy Assures Texas Ministers of Independence," *New York Times*, September 13, 1960, pp. 1, 22.

[16]The exchange is drawn from Dean Alwyn Kemper, "John F. Kennedy Before the Greater Houston Ministerial Association, September 12, 1960: The Religious Issue" (Ph.D. diss., Michigan State University, 1969), p. 208.

[17]For assessments of editorial opinion, public reaction, and related facets of the event's impact, see: "Judgments and Prophecies," *Time*, September 26, 1960, p. 22; Lawrence E. Davies, "Religious Issue Debated," *New York Times*, September 14, 1960, pp. 1, 32; Gladwin Hill, "Reaction of Ministers," *New York Times*, September 14, 1960, pp. 1, 32; Stanley Kelley, Jr., "The Presidential Campaign," *The Presidential Election and Transition, 1960-1961*, ed. Paul T. David (Washington, D.C.: The Brookings Institution, 1961), p. 79, note 26; Fuchs, "John F. Kennedy and American Catholicism," pp. 182-84; Jamieson, *Packaging the Presidency*, pp. 133-34.

INFORMATION SOURCES ON THE SPEECH SET

Protestant Groups' Accusations

For texts of the charges made by both Protestants and Other Americans

United for Separation of Church and State and the National Conference of Citizens for Religious Freedom, see *New York Times*, September 8, 1960, p. 25. The National Conference's statement is reprinted in Deane Alwyn Kemper, "John F. Kennedy Before the Greater Houston Ministerial Association, September 12, 1960: The Religious Issue" (Ph.D. diss., Michigan State University, 1969), pp. 215-17.

John F. Kennedy's *Apologia* at Houston

A complete vidoetape of John F. Kennedy's speech to the Greater Houston Ministerial Association and the question-and-answer session that followed is held at the John F. Kennedy Library. Copies of the thirty-minute campaign commercial adapted from the session are also extant, one of which is in the possession of the author.

Printed texts are readily available. Reliable sources include the *New York Times*, September 13, 1960, p. 22; Theodore H. White, *The Making of the President 1960* (New York: Pocket Books, 2d ed, 1961), pp. 468-72; *American Rhetoric from Roosevelt to Reagan*, ed. by Halford Ross Ryan (Prospect Heights, Ill.: Waveland Press, 1987), pp. 152-55; and Jay David, *The Kennedy Reader* (Indianapolis: Bobbs-Merrill, 1967), pp. 363-67.

The question-and-answer session transcript is less widely in print, yet is accessible in the *New York Times*, September 13, 1960, p. 22.

Selected Bibliography

Barrett, Harold. "John F. Kennedy Before the Greater Houston Ministerial Ministerial Association." *Central States Speech Journal* 15 (1964): 259-66.

Fisher, Walter R. "A Motive View of Communication." *Quarterly Journal of Speech* 56 (1970): 131-39.

Fuchs, Lawrence H. *John F. Kennedy and American Catholicism*. New York: Meredith Press, 1967.

Golden, James L. "John F. Kennedy and the 'Ghosts'." *Quarterly Journal of Speech* 52 (1966): 348-57.

Ions, Edmond S. *The Politics of John F. Kennedy*. London: Routledge and Kegan Paul, 1967.

Jamieson, Kathleen Hall. *Packaging the Presidency*. New York and Oxford: Oxford University Press, 1984.

Kelley, Stanley, Jr. "The Presidential Campaign." In *The Presidential Election and Transition*, edited by Paul T. David. Washington, D.C.: The Brookings Institution. 1961.

Kemper, Deane Alwyn. "John F. Kennedy Before the Greater Houston Ministerial Association, September 12, 1960: The Religious Issue." Ph.D. diss., Michigan State University, 1969.

"Kennedy-Humphrey Television Debate in Charleston, West Virginia." In *Speeches for Illustration and Example*, edited by Goodwin F. Berquist. Chicago: Scott, Foresman and Company, 1965.

Kennedy, John F. "I Am Not the Catholic Candidate for President." *U.S. News & World Report*, May 2, 1960, pp. 90-92.

The Kennedy Reader. Edited by Jay David. Indianapolis: Bobbs-Merrill, 1967.

Sorensen, Theodore C. *Kennedy*. New York: Harper & Row, 1965.

The Speeches of Senator John F. Kennedy: The Presidential Campaign of 1960. 87th Congress, 1st Session, Senate Report 1331. Washington, D.C.: GPO, 1961.

Stelzner, Hermann G. "John F. Kennedy at Houston, Texas, September 12, 1960." In *Rhetoric and Communication*, edited by Jane Blankenship and Hermann G. Stelzner. Urbana: University of Illinois Press, 1976.

"Text of Statement by Churchmen and Scholars on Religion and Politics." *New York Times*, September 12, 1960, p. 22.

White, Theodore H. *The Making of the President 1960*. New York: Pocket Books, 1961.

Windt, Theodore Otto, Jr. "John Fitzgerald Kennedy." In *American Orators of the Twentieth Century: Critical Studies and Sources*, edited by Bernard K. Duffy and Halford Ryan. Westport: Greenwood Press, 1987.

Eight Alabama Clergy
vs. Martin Luther King, Jr.

Ronald K. Burke

Protest by blacks in the United States extends as far back as the latter half of the seventeenth century when the slave population in America began to expand. The impulse to resist oppression continued into the twentieth century with the formation of the National Association for the Advancement of Colored People (NAACP) in 1909.

In 1948, the Congress of Racial Equality (CORE) sponsored a "Journey of Reconciliation" in which racially mixed groups defied Jim Crow laws and rode together on buses through several border states. A year later, after continuous hostility from Southern Democrats, the Democratic party adopted a strong civil rights plank. About this time, President Harry S Truman desegregated the United States Army.

In 1954, the Supreme Court ruled in *Brown vs. the Board of Education* that separate but equal schools were unconstitutional. Then, in 1955 Rosa Parks refused to yield her seat on a bus to a white man in Montgomery, Alabama. Mrs. Parks was taken to the police station and fingerprinted. Immediately, a young black minister named Martin Luther King, Jr., organized the Montgomery Improvement Association that successfully boycotted the city's transit system. This bus boycott is considered to be the major turning point for the most sweeping social movement in United States history. From this time to the early 1960s, blacks and whites conducted "sit-ins" at restaurants throughout the South, rode on segregated buses as "Freedom Riders," integrated swimming pools and churches, marched for freedom, and worked to integrate the public schools. With this intensified protest permeating all levels of society in the South, King went to Birmingham — a fortress of racism — to confront segregationists.

On Good Friday, April 12, 1963, the Reverend Martin Luther King, Jr., openly defied an Alabama Supreme Court order forbidding demonstrations by leading a march of fifty or more followers "and some one thousand onlookers" through the streets of Birmingham, Alabama to protest the city's racial policies. Not the least bit intimidated by this symbolic act, a phalanx of police officers and fire fighters led by an outspoken segregationist, Commissioner of Public Safety Eugene "Bull" Connor, "moved swiftly, dispersing and arresting King and about fifty demonstrators."[1] To spur a dramatic breakthrough in the civil rights movement, King selected Birmingham as the location for the protest marches. As historian Lerone Bennett, Jr., noted: "On Wednesday April 3, 1963 Martin Luther King, Jr. stepped from an airliner and announced that he would lead racial demonstrators in the streets of Birmingham until 'Pharaoh lets God's people go.'"[2]

During King's stay in the Birmingham jail cell, there appeared in the newspaper a plea signed by eight leading white churchmen urging protestors to call off their demonstrations. Those eight priests, rabbis, and ministers criticized the marches for being "unwise and untimely."[3] Having the clergy enter the situation proved to be an unexpected boon to the campaign. King, who had a remarkable flair for the dramatic and an imagination peculiar to charismatic leaders, replied with a civil rights classic, "Letter from Birmingham Jail." Melinda Snow remarked that it was "an eloquent expression of the philosophy of the American civil rights movement of the fifties and sixties."[4] Richard Fulkerson reported that it "has already become an American classic," and Haig Bosmajian believed: "We can now place among the lists of great public letters Martin Luther King's 'Letter from the Birmingham Jail,' dated April 16, 1963."[5]

Although a public letter is not a speech, it can serve a rhetorical end. Bosmajian declared that "The public letter, in the tradition of Emile Zola's 1898 letter to the President of the French Republic denouncing the Dreyfus decision and Thomas Mann's 1937 public letter to the Dean of the Philosophical Faculty of the University of Bonn, has long been a means of persuasion used by reformers and politicians, writers, and prisoners." Since King was a person in jail, he was not at liberty to deliver a traditional apologetic speech. Furthermore, Snow believed the letter was sermonic, observing that King, like St. Paul, "shrewdly used his prison cell as an ironic pulpit and the letter as a means to reach his audience."[6] In King's case, the letter was his available means of persuasion.

ACCUSATION BY THE ALABAMA CLERGY

In their letter to King, the eight Alabama clergymen attacked King's policy as well as his character. They wanted to subvert King's policy of confrontation and they aimed to undermine King's character by what Walter Fisher labeled a "subversive rhetoric."[7]

At the beginning of the letter, the clergymen presented three facts appropriate to the rhetorical situation. The first fact reminded the reader that in January of 1963 the clergy had presented "An Appeal for Law and Order and Common Sense." The second fact stated that there has been a "call for honest and open negotiation of racial issues and some citizens have taken to work to various problems." The third fact was that the city has been "confronted by a series of demonstrations by some of our Negro citizens."[8] Upon close examination the so-called facts were accusatory. For example, when reference was given to the fact that they had appealed for law and order, they implied that King's policy would lead to chaos; moreover, they indirectly charged that the activists were not using their common sense. By calling for "honest and open negotiation," they directed the audience's attention to the notion that as men of God they wished to sit down with the dissenters and solve the problem, but King did not. The insinuation was: "We are willing to negotiate, why aren't you?" In noting that the demonstrators were "some of our Negro citizens," the innuendo was that those who were not white were not peaceful. Through the application of the stasis of fact to the statement of accustion, the clergy cleverly positioned themselves as highly principled men of God searching for a way to quell potential social unrest, but the Reverend King was not.

As to the stasis of quality regarding King's policy, the accusers implied that the protestors were irresponsible. They noted that the disruptions "have not contributed to the resolution of our local problem." Quality was again argued when they implied that the wisdom of the leader should be questioned because the demonstrations were "unwise and untimely." In essence, the clerics said that the activists avoided any attempt to take constructive actions to create more desirable conditions in Birmingham.

Not only did the clergy undermine King's policy, but they attacked King's character by alluding to him as an interloper. For instance, in the third paragraph of their letter, they said the demonstrations were "directed and led in part by outsiders." In the next paragraph they charged that outsiders were not needed to settle their local disputes:

We agree rather with certain local leadership which has called for honest and open negotiation on racial issues in our area. And we believe this kind of facing the issues can best be accomplished by citizens of our own metropolitan area, white and Negro, meeting with their knowledge and experience of the local situation. All of us need to face that responsibility and find proper channels for its accomplishment.

By using such phrases as "local leadership," "our area," "Our own metropolitan area," and "local situation," the clerics tried to limit the negotiations to Birmingham residents. They implied that outsiders were not wanted. They let their audience infer that King and his people made it their business to foment the kind of demonstrations that had already occurred in the city, and that perhaps they really sought to gain control of the city. The clerics' strategy corresponded precisely to what Fisher labeled a "subversive rhetoric": "Subversive rhetoric is an anti-ethos rhetoric; that is, it invariably is an attempt to undermine the credibility of some person, idea, or institution. One of its chief modes accords with what is sometimes called

the 'devil theory' of persuasion. The strategy is to make a man, idea, or institution consubstantial with Satanic attributes and intentions."[9]   In brief,
the clergy intimated that members of the protesting group were "consubstantial with Satanic attributes and intentions." The analysis of the letter
showed that the clerics attacked King's policy and character by arguing
definition and quality. There matters stood until King responded to the letter.

MARTIN LUTHER KING, JR.'S, APOLOGIA

As stated earlier, the clergy's public statement created an unexpected
boon to the civil rights campaign. The clerics' accusation gave King the opportunity to deliver a detailed explanation of the movement's *raison d'etre*
in his now famous "Letter from Birmingham Jail." In investigating King's
apologia, B. L. Ware and Wil Linkugel isolated the factors and postures in
verbal defense, and these are helpful in the present study.[10]

In King's letter, three factors were present: denial, bolstering, and
transcendence. Denial is defined as: "the simple disavowal by the speaker
of any participation in, relationship to, or positive sentiment toward
whatever it is that repels the audience."[11] In the letter, King repudiated the
accusation that he was an outsider by offering reasons for being in Birmingham. "I think I should indicate," he asserted, "why I am here in Birmingham,
since you have been influenced by the view which argues against 'outsiders
coming.'"[12] King offered four reasons why he was not an intruder. The first
reason was that "I along with several members of my staff, am here because
I was invited here." Second, he reminded them that "I have basic organizational ties here." The Southern Christian Leadership Conference, based in
Atlanta, Georgia, of which King was president, had affiliations in the South,
and the Alabama Christian Movement for human rights was one of them.
His third and fourth reasons criticized the notion of the "outsider." Hence,
his third reason was that he traveled to places where injustice existed, as the
prophets of the eighth century B.C. did and as Paul did to spread the gospel
of Jesus Christ. Lastly, King replied that there was an interrelatedness of
communities and states.

King effectively denied the charge that he was an outsider on legal and
moral grounds. By definition, he had a legal right to be there because an
organization to which he belonged invited him to Birmingham. Morally, he
had every right to be there. Inasmuch as he believed that all men and women
are brothers and sisters under the skin, he felt compelled to be where persecution occurred. The ministers could not easily ignore King's persuasive
argument. Was it not their duty as ordained clerics to be present where
there were violations of human rights? Was it not difficult for these men
of the cloth to indict one who practices the word of Christ? King also used

bolstering which is defined as "any rhetorical strategy which reinforces the existence of a fact, sentiment, object, or relationship."[13] Bolstering is a form of identification because it reaffirms audience perceptions. For instance, King first used it to express discontent with states below the Mason-Dixon line: "Too long has our beloved Southland been bogged down in a tragic effort to live in monologue rather than dialogue." The phrase "too long" reminded the audience of decades of strained race relations. "Our beloved Southland," moreover, invoked what Kenneth Burke referred to as consubstantiality, that is, "men have common sensations, concepts, images, ideas, attitudes that make them consubstantial."[14] The word "Southland" was meant, therefore, to bring to mind sensations, concepts, and images of the South. King effectively identified with his audience's roots and love of the region. Additionally, the term "bogged down" conveyed the notion of regression and not progress. By invoking the neutral word "Southland," King hoped to establish the idea that blacks and whites should work together enthusiastically to overcome the deteriorating relations. This argument also helped to reinforce the image that King was not an outsider — he was from the South, too.

Moreover, King said the lack of communication between blacks and whites had been a "tragic effort to live in monologue rather than dialogue." He used the word "tragic" in the sense that racial strife could have been avoided, but in place of coexisting, blacks and whites retreated from interacting with one another. By bolstering, King tried to unify the parties by appealing to love of homeland, of "Southland." He appealed to common sense by implying that rather than being divided by monologue they could be united in dialogue.

The final rhetorical strategy King used was transcendence. According to Ware and Linkugel, transcendence strategies "psychologically move the audience away from the particulars of the charge at hand in a direction toward some more abstract general view of his character."[15] King's use of transcendence is illuminating. He wrote that segregationists may have a legitimate concern since activists were breaking the law. But he recognized that there are two kinds of law: just and unjust. He agreed with St. Augustine that "an unjust law is no law at all." He countercharged that the city of Birmingham reflected injustices in its laws in three ways: (1) it required some to obey while others were not required to obey the same law; (2) it was unjust "if it is inflicted on a minority that as a result of being denied the right to vote, had no part in enacting or devising the law"; and, (3) it was unjust when laws were employed "to maintain segregation and to deny citizens the First Amendment privilege of peaceful assembly and protest." After describing the distinction between a just and an unjust law, King defended his policy and character by transcending to a more elevated plane by saying:

> Of course, there is nothing new about this kind of civil disobedience. It was evidenced sublimely in the refusal of Shadrach, Meshach, and Abednego to obey the law of Nebuchadnezzar, on the ground that a higher moral law was at stake. It was practiced superbly by the early Christians who were willing to face hungry lions rather than submit to certain unjust laws of the Roman Empire.

These Biblical examples were well chosen. The clergymen could not deny the applicability of the Biblical times to the present. Moreover, these examples would have persuasive efficacy with the audience because they could easily infer how King responded to the "higher moral law" that liberates and not to the earthly immoral law that subjugates.

The posture King assumed in his *apologia* was explanation. He hoped that "if the audience understands his motives, actions, beliefs, or whatever, they will be unable to condemn him."[16]

King defended the protests by explaining them: "In any nonviolent campaign there are four basic steps: collection of the facts to determine whether injustices exist, negotiation, self-purification, and direct action." He gave a detailed elucidation of each one of the four basic steps. As to "whether injustices exist," King noted that Birmingham had an "ugly record of police brutality," "unjust treatment of Negroes in the courts," and "bombings of Negro homes and churches." When he tried to negotiate, King said the city fathers "consistently refused to engage in good-faith negotiation." For self-purification King said they had workshops on nonviolence and asked themselves a series of questions about entering into violent encounters. Needless to say, the final step of direct action was implemented.

King then replied to the charge that the protests were ill-timed. He explained that "freedom is never voluntarily given by the oppressor, it must be demanded by the oppressed." This notion of timing was significant insofar as *kairos* (see Glossary) was concerned. Having been told that the demonstrations were ill-timed, King replied that he never participated in any direct action that was well-timed. He turned the point back on his accusers: "For years now I have heard the word 'Wait!' It rings in the ear of every Negro with piercing familiarity. This 'Wait' has almost always meant 'Never.' As one of our distinguished jurors once said, 'Justice too long delayed is justice denied.'"

In the next section of the letter King continued to exercise his rhetorical posture of explanation. In perhaps the most moving statement on the deprivation of black people's God-given rights to emerge from the civil rights movement, King showed how a society spawned segregation, lynchings, drownings, police brutality, and intimidated children. He decried widespread poverty amidst an affluent society:

> Perhaps it is easy for those who never felt the stinging darts of segregation to say "Wait." But when you have seen vicious mobs

lynch your mothers and fathers at will and drown your sisters and brothers at whim; when you have seen hate-filled policemen curse, kick and even kill your black brothers and sisters with impunity; when you see the vast majority of your 20 million Negro brothers smothering in an air-tight cage of poverty in the midst of an affluent society. . . .then you will understand why we find it difficult to wait. One passage in particular was notably powerful: "When you suddenly find your tongue twisted as you seek to explain to your six-year-old daughter why she can't go to the public amusement park that has just been advertised on television, and see tears welling up when she is told that Funtown is closed to colored children, and see ominous clouds of inferiority beginning to form in her little mental sky. . . ." King easily assumed an explanatory posture because he had confronted hatred and bigotry most of his life.

CONCLUSION

In this encounter, the eight Alabama clergymen expressed dissatisfaction with the black community's determination to redress their grievances by making an appeal for law and order and calling for negotiations. Further, in an attempt to discredit King, the clergy charged that "outsiders" were leading the demonstrations. The clergy's letter criticized King's course of action and questioned his moral character.

King responded to these criticisms with three of the four factors of verbal self-defense, denial, bolstering, and transcendence. He denied the allegations that he was an outsider by demonstrating that he had ties to the area and that he was invited there. He built on that kind of defense by using language that supported his consubstantiality with his audience by referring to the "Southland" of which he was clearly a member. And in one of the most moving parts of his letter, he appealed to a higher moral law that bound his accusers with him: as clerics, they were all obliged to do God's work.

King was wise to select explanation for his posture of self-defense. The efficacy of explanation was that it allowed him to detail the reasoning behind the civil rights movement and thereby to imply the justification for his policy in Birmingham. Thus, he was able to defend his policy by elucidating his character that informed the policy, and the righteous policy he championed was a positive indication of his moral habits. Although the eight Alabama clergymen's letter is not as famous as King's letter, it must be credited with motivating the Reverend King to compose in the crucible of confrontation an efficacious personal *apologia* that ranks as one of the most eloquent civil rights proclamations of the twentieth century.

NOTES

[1]Lerone Bennett, Jr., *Before the Mayflower: A History of the Negro in America 1619-1964* (Baltimore, Penguin Books, 1966), p. 334.

[2]Ibid., p. 330.

[3]"Public Statement by Eight Alabama Clergymen" is in Charles Muscatine and Marlene Griffith, eds., *The Borzoi College Reader*, 3rd ed. (New York: A. A. Knopf, 1976), pp. 233-34; also reprinted in Melinda Snow, "Martin Luther King's 'Letter from Birmingham Jail' as Pauline Epistle," *Quarterly Journal of Speech* 71 (1985): 321.

[4]Snow, "'Letter from Birmingham Jail' as Pauline Epistle," p. 318.

[5]See Richard P. Fulkerson, "The Public Letter As A Rhetorical Form: Structure, Logic, And Style in King's 'Letter From Birmingham Jail,'" *Quarterly Journal of Speech* 65 (1979): 121, and Haig A. Bosmajian, "Rhetoric of Martin Luther King's Letter From Birmingham Jail," *Midwest Quarterly* 8 (1967): 127.

[6]Snow, "'Letter from Birmingham Jail' as Pauline Epistle," p. 319.

[7]Walter R. Fisher, "A Motive View of Communication," *Quarterly Journal of Speech* 56 (1970): 131-39.

[8]Muscatine and Griffith, "Public Statement by Eight Alabama Clergymen," p. 233-34.

[9]Fisher, "A Motive View of Communication," p. 138.

[10]B.L. Ware and Wil A. Linkugel, "They Spoke in Defense of Themselves: On the Generic Criticism of Apologia," *Quarterly Journal of Speech* 59 (1973): 273-83.

[11]Ibid., p. 274.

[12]I quote from the "Letter" published in *The Christian Century* 80 (1963): 767-73.

[13]Ware and Linkugel, "They Spoke in Defense of Themselves," p. 277.

[14]Kenneth Burke, *A Rhetoric of Motives* (New York: The World

Publishing Co., 1950), p. 545.

[15]Ware and Linkugel, "They Spoke in Defense of Themselves," p. 280.

[16]Ibid., p. 283.

INFORMATION SOURCES ON THE SPEECH SET

Eight Alabama Clergymen's Accusation

The "Public Statement by Eight Alabama Clergymen" first appeared in the Birmingham *Post Herald* on Saturday April 13, 1963. Also the letter is included in Charles Muscatine and Marlene Griffith, eds., *The Borzoi College Reader*, 3rd ed. (New York: A. A. Knopf, 1976), pp. 233-34 and Melinda Snow, "Martin Luther King's 'Letter from Birmingham Jail' As Pauline Epistle," *Quarterly Journal of Speech* 71 (1985): 321.

Martin Luther King, Jr.'s, Apology

King wrote the "Letter" on the margins of the newspaper in which the clergymen's statement appeared while he was in jail. He continued the letter on scraps of writing paper supplied by a friendly black trusty and then concluded on a pad of paper his attorneys gave him. The American Friends Service Committee had 50,000 copies of the letter printed for distribution. Later, after refining, it became a significant chapter in *Why We Can't Wait* (1964). This analysis is based on the copy in *The Christian Century* 80 (1963): 767-73. The letter is included in several college anthologies: Charles Muscatine and Marlene Griffith, eds., *The Borzoi College Reader*, 3rd ed. (New York: A. A. Knopf, 1976); Arthur M. Eastman *et al.*, eds., *The Norton Reader*, 4th ed. (New York: W. W. Norton, 1977); Caroline Shrodes, Harry Finestone, and Michael Shugrue, eds., *The Conscious Reader*, 2nd ed. (New York: Macmillan, 1978); Richard E. Young, Alton L. Becker, and Kenneth L. Pike, *Rhetoric: Discovery and Change* (New York: Harcourt, Brace & World, 1970); Halsey P. Taylor and Victor N. Okada, eds., *The Craft of the Essay* (New York: Harcourt Brace Jovanovich, 1977); and Forrest D. Burt and Cleve Want, eds., *Invention and Design: A Rhetorical Reader* (New York: Random House, 1978). It also appears in Edward P. J. Corbett, *Classical Rhetoric for the Modern Student*, 2nd ed. (New York: Oxford, 1971); Staughton Lynd, ed., *Nonviolence in America: A Documentary History* (Indianapolis: Bobbs-Merrill, 1966); George Ducas and Charles Van Doren, eds., *Great Documents in Black American History* (New York: Praeger, 1970); and Herbert J. Storing, ed., *What Country Have I? Political Writings by Black Americans* (New York: St. Martin's, 1970).

Selected Bibliography

Anatol, Karl W., and John R. Bittner. "Kennedy on King: The Rhetoric of Control." *Today's Speech* 16 (1968): 31-34.

Aptheker, Herbert. *Essays in the History of the American Negro.* New York: International Publishers, 1969.

Bennett, Lerone, Jr. "The King Plan for Freedom." *Ebony* (1956).

___. *What Manner of Man: A Biography of Martin Luther King, Jr., 1929-68.* Chicago: Johnson Publishers Co., 1976.

Bowen, Harry W. "A Reassessment of Speech Delivery." *Today's Speech* 14 (1966): 21-24.

Golden, James L., and Richard D. Rieke. *The Rhetoric of Black Americans.* Columbus, Ohio: Charles E. Merrill, 1971. 247-62.

Keele, Lucy A. M. *A Burkeian Analysis of the Rhetorical Strategies of Martin Luther King.* Ph.D. diss., University of Oregon, 1972.

King, Martin Luther, Jr. *Strength to Love.* New York: Harper & Row, 1963.

___. *Stride Toward Freedom: The Montgomery Story.* New York: Harper & Row, 1958.

___. *Why We Can't Wait.* New York: Mentor Books, 1964.

___. *Where Do We Go From Here: Chaos or Community?* Boston: Beacon Press, 1968.

___. "Interview," *Playboy, January, 1965,* pp. 65-74, 76-78.

___. "Pilgrimage to Nonviolence," *Christian Century,* April 3, 1964, pp. 439-41.

Klein, Mia. "The Other Beauty of Martin Luther King's 'Letter from Birmingham Jail.'" *College Composition and Communication* 32 (1981): 30-7.

Lewis, David Levering. *King: A Biography*. Urbana: University of Illinois Press, 1978.

Lincoln, C. Eric, ed. *Martin Luther King, Jr., A Profile*. New York: Hill & Wang, 1970.

Newson, Lionel, and William Gorden. "A Stormy Rally in Atlanta." *Today's Speech* 11 (1963): 18-21.

Oates, Steven B. *Let the Trumpets Sound*. New York: Harper & Row, 1982.

Smith, Donald H. "In the Beginning at Montgomery." *Southern Speech Communication Journal* 34 (1968): 8-17.

Spillers, Hortense J. "Martin Luther King and the Style of the Black Sermon." *The Black Scholar* 3 (1971): 14-37.

Westin, Alan F., and Barry Mahoney. *The Trial of Martin Luther King*. New York: Crowell, 1974.

Senator Edward M. Kennedy and the Chappaquiddick Tragedy

William L. Benoit

A mass media apologia is a significant form of discourse today.[1] Such a speech is undeniably dramatic. The suspense that arises as Americans anticipate what the apologist will say — not to mention the question of how the apologetic discourse will be received by the audience — inevitably piques interest. The advent of electronic media permits mass audiences to be apprised of alleged indiscretions of a public figure and, fittingly enough, it also provides a mass forum for an apologist to cleanse his or her reputation. One such apology was designed to salvage the political career of Edward M. Kennedy, a U.S. senator and presidential hopeful, from the rumor and suspicions that arose surrounding the death of Mary Jo Kopechne. Americans were shocked and unsure what to think about one of the most prominent senators of the era, a man who was unquestionably a serious contender for the highest office in the land.

THE ACCUSATIONS AGAINST KENNEDY

On July 18, 1969, a party was held at Chappaquiddick Island, near Martha's Vineyard. This cook-out was thrown primarily for six girls who had worked for Bobby Kennedy in 1968, and it was attended by Senator Edward M. Kennedy, several married friends, and Kennedy's chauffeur. Kennedy left to drive Mary Jo Kopechne back to her hotel. At approximately 11:15 p.m., the car went off Dike Bridge, resulting in the death of twenty-eight-year-old Mary Jo Kopechne. Kennedy did not report this accident until the next morning, some eight or nine hours later, after the car had been discovered by others and the body removed from it.

Kennedy remained sequestered at Hyannis Port for days (except for a brief trip to attend Miss Kopechne's funeral) until he left to plead guilty to leaving the scene of an accident, and to deliver his nationally televised apologetic address. Numerous key Kennedy advisers joined him there, including Robert McNamara, Theodore Sorensen, and Judge Robert J. Clark, while others participated by telephone, for example, Arthur Schlesinger and John Kenneth Galbraith. It was widely assumed that they assisted in orchestrating Kennedy's apologetic discourse. Kennedy did not speak to the representatives of the news media during this time. Nor were other members of the Chappaquiddick party, or those visiting the Hyannis Port compound, very open with reporters. In fact, it was reported that offers of $20,000, $25,000, and even $50,000 for the entire story of the party and related events were spurned. Ironically, Kennedy's silence, and resultant dearth of information about the tragedy, invited — if not demanded — the speculation that inevitably arose between the reporting of the accident and Kennedy's apology a week later, speculation that Kennedy was forced to try to quell in his address.

Although there was no *kategoria* in the traditional sense of the term, that is, there was no formal speech of accusation here, the public eye and ear were nevertheless filled with reporting and speculation that undeniably had the same *effect* as a formal speech of accusation. The *Washington Post* reported that before his speech a "bitter whispering campaign" about this incident had "already begun," and the *New York Times* observed that a consequence of the unanswered questions concerning the incident was "a spate of ugly speculation, political and personal."[2]

One of the first accusations leveled at Kennedy occurred when newspapers widely reported the prosecutor's intention to charge him with leaving the scene of an accident. This was followed immediately with questions concerning Kennedy's failure to report the accident promptly. As the *New York Times* put it, "According to the Senator's own account, that was nearly eight hours after the accident."[3] These accusations centered on the stasis of fact, but accusations of quality soon appeared. A major concern that emerged after about three days of investigation was Kennedy's state at the time of the accident. Chief Dominick Arena was interested in whether Kennedy was intoxicated at the time of the accident.[4] The *Washington Post*, in one of the few statements from the parties involved, declared that "Miss [Ester] Newberry was reticent on one point: Had there been drinking at the party?"[5] Although it competed with the Apollo 11 moon walk and President Nixon's decision to travel around the world, this story was in the news every day following the tragedy, whether it was for the initial reporting of the tragedy, the decision to press charges for leaving the scene of the accident, revocation of Kennedy's operator's license, Kennedy's trip to Miss Kopechne's funeral, or concerns about intoxication.

After a few days, the questions became increasingly pointed. Instead of simply reporting the events from Edgartown, the *Chicago Tribune* alluded to "many conflicting versions of what Kennedy did before and after the accident," and wondered in an editorial "whether justice in this case will be administered without respect to wealth or family influence."[6] Similarly, a

Washington Post editorial declared that "the brief statement the Senator has so far made is not good enough. Worse, there are good reasons to doubt that it is even accurate."[7]

The queries raised by this tragedy were myriad. However, the many questions tended to resolve into four overriding and persistent accusations that seemed to have the most serious implications for Senator Kennedy's political career:

1. Was Kennedy responsible for the accident (and therefore for Miss Kopechne's death)?

2. Were Kennedy and Kopechne intoxicated and/or engaged in immoral activities during or prior to the accident?

3. Why did Kennedy fail to report the accident and resulting death to the police immediately?

4. Was Kennedy fit to hold public office?

As a result of these issues, widespread doubt was raised about Kennedy's political future.[8]

No successful politician could have been oblivious to this climate of hostile opinion that mushroomed over the span of time between the accident and his public statement, even amidst the shock and grief he must have felt over this tragedy. Concerned with his current tenure in the Senate, and mindful of his presidential aspirations, Kennedy felt compelled to defend his character and his actions in a nationally televised address.[9]

KENNEDY'S APOLOGETIC DISCOURSE

Kennedy faced a complex apologetic situation. This was true in part because there was no formal *kategoria*. In some ways his task would have been easier if Kennedy faced a simple set of charges, if he had faced a clearly identifiable attacker. In this situation, however, he could not hope to, and perhaps he had reasons not to want to, answer each and every suspicion, rumor, and question. On the other hand, as long as Kennedy addressed the major points of concern, the fact that he did not face a single, well-defined attack provided him with some latitude in defining the "accusation" that he would address. In this case, the ultimate ground of the accusation concerned his actions, the fatal automobile accident, and Kennedy's subsequent inaction, his failure to report it in a timely fashion. Thus, it appeared that his apology would be concerned primarily with a defense of policy; however, Kennedy's action prior to the address completely altered the complexion of this situation.

Kennedy informed his audience near the beginning of his speech that earlier that morning he had entered a plea of guilty to "leaving the scene of an accident."[10] Later in the speech he reported that "I felt morally obligated to plead guilty to the charge of leaving the scene of an accident." While he carefully avoided explicitly accepting responsibility for Miss Kopechne's death, his statement could be construed as an implicit admission of responsibility: he did not attempt to deny that he was driving the car during the accident, or that a fatality had occurred. It is, of course, one thing to admit to leaving the scene of an accident, or even to driving an automobile that was involved in an accident, but quite another thing to admit responsibility for another's death.

It might appear on the face of it that he had no choice but to plead guilty to leaving the scene of an accident. But was it really necessary for him to do so? Jack Olsen revealed that the prosecutor in this case, Walter Steele, was aware that this issue was not as clear as it seemed:

> Massachusetts was a compulsory insurance state, and the intent of the legislation had been to force a driver involved in a two-car collision to make himself known to the other driver and to the police, so the matters of identification and insurance could be worked out. It would be simple for a defense attorney to argue that the law was inappropriate to one-car accidents, and that Senator Kennedy, in his befuddled postaccident state, had not realized that he was legally required to contact the police forthwith.[11]

Nor were the Kennedy forces convinced that he had no choice but to plead guilty to this charge. In a secret meeting between two of the Kennedy lawyers and prosecutor Steele and Police Chief Arena, Judge Robert Clark said "Now, I'm sure I don't have to tell you two gentlemen that there are technical defenses to this charge. There are technical defenses, but there are also considerations that transcend the usual criminal case and we've got to be guided by those considerations."[12] These considerations surely concerned Kennedy's image, and were political in nature. It may well be significant in this connection that Kennedy said in his speech that he felt "morally," not "legally," obligated to plead guilty.

Furthermore, there was an important strategic reason for pleading guilty to the charge of leaving the scene of an accident. First, given the fact that he had left the scene of an accident, and failed to report it for some nine hours, it would have created a very unfavorable impression on public opinion to attempt to use a technical defense to avoid this charge. Furthermore, this action, while never directly admitting culpability for Miss Kopechne's death, took away the argumentative ground from his accusers. There is a preference in discourse for not belaboring the obvious. Barry Schlenker noted that when an apology is seen as sincere by the audience, further condemnation can only be seen as revenge.[13] Therefore, Kennedy's detractors would seem unreasonably vindictive to harp on his responsibility for Miss Kopechne's death. Of course, some of his critics did so, but it is likely that many were discouraged from doing so, and those who did probably were seen in an unfavorable light.

This strategy also shifted the remainder of his apology from a defense of actions to one of character. Kennedy knew that no legal action, such as prosecution for involuntary manslaughter, was seriously contemplated by the authorities. Thus, although an action was the source of the accusations, his initial statement in his apology tended to shift his defense to grounds of character, to Kennedy himself, and to the manner and quality of the act he performed.

Kennedy related his grief and remorse over the tragedy. "This last week," he said, "has been an agonizing one for me and the members of my family, and the grief we feel over the loss of a wonderful friend will remain with us the rest of our lives." Researchers have found that the guilty who appear remorseful and who have suffered are viewed more favorably than those who do not.[14] Thus, Kennedy's response to the first general accusation, a question of fact, was an admission and an apology that displayed his remorse and suffering. Having done this, Kennedy's apology proceeded to relieve him of culpability through the stasis of quality.

On the basis of his guilty plea, he appeared to accept responsibility for the tragedy. Indeed, Kennedy denied that he would attempt to shift the blame: "I do not seek to escape responsibility for my actions by placing the blame either on the physical and emotional trauma brought on by the accident or anyone else." However, this discourse was more complex than it appeared on the surface.

Although Sherry Butler asserted that Kennedy "had no one but himself upon whom he could place blame," David Ling explained how Kennedy described the events of July 19-20 in language that, if accepted, demonstrated that other factors were really responsible for the accident.[15] Kennedy's strategic use of language functioned to mitigate the quality of his act. For instance, Kennedy related the fact that "the car that I was driving on an unlit road went off a narrow bridge which had no guard rails and was built on a left angle to the road." Based on this description, the situation caused the accident, not Kennedy. He appeared to deny this scenic causality while actually, but subtly, affirming it. This had the effect of arguing the quality of the act, by pointing to mitigating circumstances.

In the same vein, Kennedy wondered whether an "awful curse did actually hang over the Kennedys." This accomplished two results. First, for those auditors willing to accept the "awful curse" theory, it reinforced the attempt to shift blame away from himself. How could he be at fault if a sinister curse was really the cause? Second, it secured sympathy from his audience, including those who were unwilling to accept the presence of a "curse," by evoking memories of the violent and unexpected deaths of his brothers.

Kennedy's admission of guilt, for leaving the scene of the accident, and his statement that he would not attempt to shift the blame, functioned to condition the audience to accept his description of events, which subtly shifted the blame away from him. Why should the audience question his statements, or think that he was twisting or slanting the facts, when he had just admitted his guilt? Only if he had denied responsibility would the audience be suspicious of his remarks. Thus, although Kennedy's apology seemed to accept responsibility for Miss Kopechne's death, he never explicitly did so. On the contrary, his description of events shifted the blame away from him.

Early in the speech, Kennedy addressed the second major accusation, that of immorality and intoxication. He simply and directly denied them altogether:

There is no truth, no truth whatsoever, to the widely circulated suspicions of immoral conduct that have been leveled at my behavior and hers regarding that evening. There has never been a private relationship between us of any kind. I know nothing in Mary Jo's conduct, on that or any other occasions — and the same is true of the other girls at the party — that would lend any substance to such ugly speculation about their character. Nor was I driving under the influence of liquor.

He explained that "Only reasons of health prevented my wife from accompanying me," for she was pregnant at the time. He implicitly denied that she, and the other wives, were purposefully excluded from the party for suspicious reasons. Both of these statements denied the rumors about immoral behavior and the first one ruled out intoxication as qualities of the act.

However, his response was considerably more sophisticated than mere denial. He subverted the credibility of his attackers in two different ways in the longer passage. First, he widened the scope of the accusation to include Miss Kopechne and the other five women. This meant that the charges of immorality were not simply aimed at him, but were also aimed at the unfortunate victim of this tragedy as well as the other girls. The accusers may be able to impeach Kennedy's character with impunity, but Kennedy portrayed them as callous to hurl these kinds of accusations at Miss Kopechne and the other women. Second, Kennedy characterized this speculation as "ugly." Thus, he initiated a counterattack on the character of his accusers. Early in his speech, he characterized the accusations as "whispers and innuendo," and he developed this motif throughout his talk. None of these implied appellations, promulgators of "ugly speculation," of "whispers and innuendo," were particularly pleasant. This strategy functioned as a variant of denial, undermining the credibility of his accusers, and thus reduced the likelihood that the audience would accept the accusations of intoxication and immoral behavior.

Kennedy responded to the third accusation — failure to report the accident immediately — in a manner similar to his treatment of the first accusation. He admitted that his failure to report the accident until the next morning was wrong: "I regard as indefensible the fact that I did not report the accident to the police immediately." However, this statement interestingly occured directly after he mentioned his concussion, his exhaustion, and his state of shock. Kennedy described his state after "repeated efforts to save Mary Jo" as one of "utter exhaustion"; he reported that "I was overcome . . . by a jumble of emotions, grief, fear, doubt, exhaustion, panic, confusion, and shock," and his physicians diagnosed him as having "suffered a cerebral concussion as well as shock." If one accepts his version of the events, it accounts for his failure to report promptly the accident to the police. Again, although he asserted that he would not engage in shifting the blame, his description of reality functioned to mitigate the act. This strategy of shifting the blame to his physical and psychological condition argued the stasis of quality by attempting to influence audience perceptions of how the act occurred.[16] Kennedy also mentioned that he told his two friends, Joe Gargan and Paul Markham, "not to alarm Mary Jo's friends that night," thereby suggesting another reason for not reporting the accident until morning.

In his speech, Kennedy also argued the stasis of jurisdiction to deal with the fourth accusation of fitness for office, another subtle aspect of the apology. In effect, Kennedy successfully shifted the controversy from the court of judicial opinion to the court of public opinion by pleading guilty to the charge of leaving the scene of the accident. Specifically, he shifted the controversy to his constituents, who were his most favorable jurors.

This strategy readily accounts for the section of his apology in which he mentioned the names of several past Massachusetts statesmen in an obvious attempt to identify himself with them: "The people of this State — the State which sent John Quincy Adams and Daniel Webster and Charles Sumner and Henry Cabot Lodge and John Kennedy to the United States Senate — are entitled to representation in that body by men who inspire their ultimate confidence." He also flattered his constituents, by observing that "You and I share many memories — some of them have been glorious, some have been very sad. The opportunity to work with you and serve Massachusetts has made my life worthwhile." The mention of sad memories, once again, easily evoked images of his assassinated brothers and earned him a measure of sympathy from his audience. Notice that if his home state, the one most likely to be sympathetic to him, supported him, he could argue later that he had been vindicated without ever submitting the question to a nationwide vote.

CONCLUSION

It would be unrealistic to expect that an incident such as the Kopechne tragedy would not have a negative impact on Kennedy's image, no matter what he did in the speech. He admitted leaving the scene of an accident, in which a young unmarried woman had died, and he failed to report the accident for hours. Still, he managed to minimize his losses considerably. Kennedy's speech was successful in securing the support of the people of Massachusetts. Telegrams and other messages to the senator's office were reportedly running ten to one in his favor. In that state, "Teddy's overall slippage in the polls was only 9 points, from 87 percent in March to a still mighty impressive 78 in August." National polls revealed similar results: 85 percent favorable before the Kopechne tragedy and 74 percent after it.[17] Kennedy's speech managed to maintain, or salvage, his image with about three-fourths of the public.

One critic did not interpret the reaction to this apology as favorable. Basing her conclusion upon the verbal reactions of political commentators and the same polls cited above, Butler asserted that Kennedy's speech "scored strong negative responses." However, she failed to report the figures cited above, 78 percent still favorable in Massachusetts, 74 percent nationwide. She reported that "approval of Kennedy fell, soon after his speech, from 83 percent to 68 percent," but did not reveal that this figure was highly selective, representing only independents. Moreover, she reported that "the percentage of persons extremely favorable to Kennedy declined from 49% before the accident to 34% following Kennedy's reporting of the accident." It seems unreasonable to omit all other favorable responses, which bring the total of all favorable responses to 74 percent, as reported earlier. She indicated that "the college-educated rejected Kennedy's televised explanation by 49% to 30%," another highly selective figure. Finally, the article she took her figures from actually concluded that "In terms of the overall respect in which Kennedy is held, the poll indicated no radical shift as a result of Chappaquiddick."[18]

However, the early, generally favorable, reaction slowly eroded over time. James Burns reported that

The early burst of popular sympathy seemed to fade away during the following weeks. In a Harris Poll immediately after the accident more people than not believed that Kennedy had tried to save Mary Jo, that "nothing immoral" had taken place between the two, that he was not drunk, that he had suffered enough, that he was not displaying qualities that disqualified him for "high public trust"; three months later the vote of confidence was sharply down on all these questions.[19]

Yet, by early 1970, public opinion began another upswing. William Honan reported that the Becker Research Corporation, commissioned by the *Boston Globe*, found approval in Massachusetts initially increased to 84 percent after the speech, fell to 78 percent over the next two months, and then peaked at 87 percent by the spring.[20] This reaction is not altogether surprising, for the strategies present in the speech were in many instances subtly efficacious. After a lapse of several months, what would the typical voter be more likely to remember: that he pled guilty, or that the bridge had been narrow, unlit, and built at an angle to the road? Even the guilty plea may have been remembered after the passage of time not as a plea to the simple charge of leaving the scene of an accident, but as an admission to causing Miss Kopechne's death — something he explicitly avoided stating, but that was clearly implied by his statement. Thus, the immediate reaction was quite favorable, and then after a few weeks the reaction tempered a bit as the audience tended to forget the specifics and subtle strategies of his defense. However, after a period of time, the electorate seemed willing to forgive almost any breach of conduct, as William Holmes Honan pointed out:

> Robert Kennedy, to cite one example, lived down his reputation as a McCarthyite (he actually worked for the late Senator Joseph McCarthy's subcommittee) and later became the darling of the chic radicals for whom McCarthyism was next to satanism. . . . Richard Nixon has survived his reputation as a smear artist, a hatchetman, a Congressman in the pay of Business. . . . Grover Cleveland even went on to be elected to be the 22nd President of the United States after it was revealed that he had fathered an illegitimate son.[21]

Thus, it appears that public opinion initially rose, then declined, and finally rose again over the first several months, a perfectly understandable reaction to this complex and subtle apologetic discourse.

It appears that Kennedy's speech managed to allay the suspicions of many (of course, some extremist opponents would never accept Kennedy's version of the time of day) at the time of the crisis. It left several questions unanswered (e.g., how could he have mistaken a left turn onto a paved road for a right turn onto a dirt road), and raised others, so the reaction was not quite so favorable after a few weeks. It appears that the gradual erosion of memory for details in the audience would at first not favor Kennedy, for his more specific claims and relatively subtle strategies would less likely be remembered than his more dramatic plea of guilty, but over the long run, the public was willing to forgive and/or forget a great deal. His senate seat seems quite safe, his presidential hopes dimmed, but not entirely extinguished. Kennedy's apology thus primarily employed the stases of quality for accusations 1 and 3, fact for accusation 2, and jurisdiction for accusation 4 in a generally successful effort — especially immediately and over the long term — to defend his character in the face of public opinion after Mary Jo Kopechne's tragic death.

NOTES

[1]Examples of rhetorical criticism of mass media apologies include: Sherry Devereaux Butler, "The Apologia, 1971 Genre," *Southern Speech Communication Journal* 36 (1972): 281-90; Ellen Reid Gold, "Political Apologia: The Ritual of Self-Defense," *Communication Monographs* 46 (1978): 306-16; Jackson Harrell, B. L. Ware, and Wil A. Linkugel, "Failure of Apology in American Politics: Nixon on Watergate," *Speech Monographs* 42 (1975): 245-61; Noreen W. Kruse, "Apologia in Team Sport," *Quarterly Journal of Speech* 67 (1981): 270-83; Kruse, "Motivational Factors in Non-Denial Apologia," *Central States Speech Journal* 28 (1977): 13-23; and B. L. Ware and Wil A. Linkugel, "They Spoke in Defense of Themselves: On the Generic Criticism of Apologia," *Quarterly Journal of Speech* 59 (1973): 273-74.

[2]"The Latest Kennedy Tragedy," *Washington Post*, July 24, 1969, p. A18; "Mystery and Tragedy," *New York Times*, July 25, 1969, p. 46.

[3]See "Teddy Escapes, Woman Drowns When Auto Plunges Off Bridge," *Chicago Tribune*, July 20, 1969, p. 1; "Kennedy Survives Fatal Auto Crash, Faces Negligence Count," *Los Angeles Times*, July 20, 1969, p. 1; "Kennedy to Face Charge in Crash for Leaving Scene," *New York Times*, July 21, 1969, p. 19; and "Kennedy Held Blameless by D.A.," *Washington Post*, July 21, 1969, p. A3.

[4]See "Drunk Driving Charge Against Teddy Weighed," *Chicago Tribune*, July 23, 1969, p. 2; "Conduct at Kennedy Party Probed: Question of Drinking Arises," *Los Angeles Times*, July 23, 1969, p. 16; and "Officials in Kennedy Case Rounding Up Statements," *New York Times*, July 24, 1969, p. 16.

[5]"'Nobody's Hiding Anything,' Girl at Party Says," *Washington Post*, July 24, 1969, p. A8.

[6]See "Teddy Gets Hearing to Defend Self in Fatal Auto Accident," and "The Kennedy Episode," *Chicago Tribune*, July 22, 1969, pp. 4, 12.

[7]"Latest Kennedy Tragedy," *Washington Post*, p. A18.

[8]See "Kennedy Career Feared Imperiled," *New York Times*, July 21, 1969, p. 19; "Kennedy May Not Run in '72 — Mansfield," *Los Angeles Times*, July 23, 1969, p. 17; and "Hopes for a Kennedy Explanation Fade into

[9]I do not argue that Kennedy necessarily intended to use each of the strategies I discuss here, or that he expected all of the effects I suggest. I do claim that, for the audience, these strategies probably functioned in the manner suggested here. My criticism is designed to analyze the discourse and its probable effects, not Kennedy's state of mind, his intent, or his motives at the time of composition.

[10]Senator Edward M. Kennedy, "Kennedy's Television Statement to the People of Massachusetts," *New York Times*, July 25, 1969, p. 10.

[11]Jack Olsen, *The Bridge at Chappaquiddick* (New York: Ace Books, 1970), pp. 173-74.

[12]Ibid., p. 191.

[13]Barry R. Schlenker, *Impression Management* (Monterey: Brooks/ Cole, 1980), p. 155.

[14]W. Austin, E. Walster, and M. K. Utne, "Equity and the Law: The Effects of a Harmdoer's 'Suffering in the Act' on Liking and Punishment," in *Advances in Experimental Social Psychology*, edited by L. Berkowitz and E. Walster (New York: Academic Press, 1976).

[15]See Butler, "The Apologia, 1971 Genre," p. 284, and David A. Ling, "A Pentadic Analysis of Senator Edward Kennedy's Address to the People of Massachusetts, July 15, 1969," *Central States Speech Journal* 21 (1970): 81-86.

[16]Ware and Linkugel, "They Spoke in Defense of Themselves," suggested that he employed the strategy of differentiation by distinguishing his normal self from his confused condition following a concussion, shock, and exhaustion (p. 279).

[17]"The Kennedy's: The Disinvited," *Newsweek,* September 29, 1969, p. 38; "Troubled Times for the Democrats," *U.S. News and World Report*, August 11, 1969, p. 21.

[18]Butler, "The Apologia, 1971 Genre," pp. 285-86; "The Disinvited," p. 38; "Public Reaction: Charitable, Skeptical," *Time*, August 8, 1969, p. 17.

[19]James MacGregor Burns, *Edward Kennedy and the Camelot Legacy* (New York: W. W. Norton, 1976), p. 161.

[20]William Holmes Honan, *Ted Kennedy, Profile of a Survivor: Edward M. Kennedy after Bobby, After Chappaquiddick, and After Three Years of Nixon* (New York: Quadrangle Books, 1972), p. 117.

[21]Ibid.

INFORMATION SOURCES ON THE SPEECH SET

Accusations Against Senator Kennedy

As explained, there was no single accusatory speech in this instance; however, Kennedy's televised apology was prompted by the extensive electronic and print media coverage of the accidental death of Mary Jo Kopechne.

Senator Edward M. Kennedy's Apology

The text of Kennedy's apology, which was broadcast nationally, is printed in "Kennedy's Television Statement to the People of Massachusetts," *New York Times*, July 26, 1969, p. 10. It is reprinted in *American Rhetoric from Roosevelt to Reagan*, edited by Halford Ross Ryan, 2nd edition (Prospect Heights, Ill.: Waveland Press, 1987), pp. 200-203.

Selected Bibliography

Burns, James MacGregor. *Edward Kennedy and the Camelot Legacy*. New York: W. W. Norton, 1976.

Butler, Sherry Devereaux. "The Apologia, 1971 Genre." *Southern Speech Communication Journal* 36 (1972): 281-90.

Honan, William Holmes. *Ted Kennedy, Profile of a Survivor: Edward M. Kennedy after Bobby, After Chappaquiddick, and After Three Years of Nixon*. New York: Quadrangle Books, 1972.

Ling, David A. "A Pentadic Analysis of Senator Edward Kennedy's Address to the People of Massachusetts, July 15, 1969." *Central States Speech Journal* 21 (1970): 81-86. Reprinted in *American Rhetoric from Roosevelt to Reagan*, pp. 204-11.

Olsen, Jack. *The Bridge at Chappaquiddick*. New York: Ace Books, 1970.

Tedrow, Thomas L., and Richard L. Tedrow. *Death at Chappaquiddick*. Gretna: Pelican Publishing, 1980.

Willis, Larryann C. *Chappaquiddick Decision*. Portland: Better Books, 1980.

Levin, Murray Burton. *Edward Kennedy: The Myth of Leadership*. Boston: Houghton-Mifflin, 1980.

Rust, Zad. *Teddy Bare, The Last of the Kennedy Clan*. Boston: Western Islands, 1971.

President Richard M. Nixon and the Watergate Scandal

Craig Allen Smith

The rhetorics of accusation and defense revolve around three questions: did a culpable act occur, who was responsible, and how was guilt resolved? Watergate illustrates how these questions are transformed through the on-going dialogue. Watergate was historically important because it contributed to the demise of two presidents, three attorney generals, three top-level presidential aides, and many others. But it is rhetorically significant because it entails virtually all strategies of accusation and defense, it illustrates the danger of redefining the charges, and it highlights the danger of narrowing the critical focus.

THE EVOLVING ACCUSATIONS AND DEFENSE

The Watergate controversy began when five burglars were arrested in Democratic National Committee (DNC) headquarters at the Watergate complex on June 17, 1972. President Richard Nixon recalled getting "disturbing news from [Chief of Staff] Bob Haldeman that the break-in of the Democratic National Committee involved [James McCord] who is on the payroll of the Committee to Re-elect the President [CRP]."[1] But although the president and his aides learned of the break-in almost immediately, they never attempted to legitimize it. Nixon was concerned "more by the stupidity of the DNC bugging attempt than by its illegality" and he hoped no White House people were involved "because it was stupid in the way it was handled; and . . . because I could see no reason whatever for trying to bug the national committee."[2] Haldeman realized that burglars, whether White House or CRP sponsored, were problematic regardless of motive. Attention therefore turned to identifying those responsible.

The *Washington Post* quickly discovered one burglar's CIA connections and McCord's status as CRP's security coordinator. A statement attributed to CRP Director John Mitchell claimed that CRP was simply one of the McCord agency's clients, but the *Post* charged that McCord was a full-time

CRP employee, thereby implicating CRP in the break-in. A second line of complicity emerged when the *Post* reported that two burglars' address books contained the White House telephone number of E. Howard Hunt.

Democratic Party Chairman Lawrence F. O'Brien then announced a million dollar lawsuit because of CRP's "potential involvement" in the break-in and a "clear link to the White House."[3] The DNC suit was a gamble. Evidence of CRP involvement was circumstantial and a court decision vindicating the White House and CRP would have politically damaged the Democrats. But litigation implied proof of CRP complicity, brought the rules of civil procedure (including subpoena power and depositions) to bear on CRP, challenged CRP to reconcile its behavior with its "Law and Order" theme, and created a second judicial arena lest the original criminal prosecution be limited to the burglars.

President Nixon thereupon took two unwise steps. First, he categorically declared that "there was no White House involvement [in the break-in] whatsoever," thereby precluding distinctions among active and passive involvement by present and past employees. Indeed, Nixon himself suspected that White House Special Counsel Charles Colson had authorized the burglary to fulfill a presidential directive. But while denying White House complicity, Nixon shrewdly ignored the allegations against CRP because he knew that McCord, Hunt, G. Gordon Liddy, and others including Mitchell had probably been involved.[4]

Nixon's second and most damaging act occurred in a morning meeting with Haldeman on June 23, 1972. Concerned that CRP money in the burglars' possession could be traced through campaign contributors, Nixon told Haldeman to ask General Vernon Walters of the CIA to warn FBI Director L. Patrick Gray that its investigation would endanger national security by reopening the Bay of Pigs fiasco. As Nixon's memoirs explained, "If the CIA would deflect the FBI from Hunt, they would thereby protect us from the only White House vulnerability involving Watergate that I was worried about exposing—not the break-in, but the political activities Hunt had undertaken for Colson." This was done "deftly" because Nixon "did not want [the CIA] to get the idea that our concern was political—which, of course, it was." Henceforth the president and his associates were engaged in a criminal conspiracy to obstruct justice. The transcript of this conversation later rendered Nixon's resignation unavoidable. Haldeman claimed that Nixon himself initiated the ideas of CIA intervention and financial support for the burglars on June 20th, but his account cannot be verified.[5]

White House strategy clarified during the week between the June 17 break-in and the June 23 involvement of the CIA. Counsel John Dean, the self-proclaimed "lynchpin of the cover-up" conspiracy, explained that the White House sought to contain the Justice Department investigation to the five burglars and their superiors Hunt and Liddy, who would receive hush money. These strategies were intended to minimize the political significance of the break-in, to distance the White House from the controversy, to curtail efforts to investigate anyone beyond the burglars, and to punish only the burglars for the culpable act. "The 'stonewall' strategy functioned from the very first episodes of the cover-up," according to Dean. "It was instinctive, from the very top of the Administration to the bottom . . . developed in small reactions to the flurry of the day's events. There was not time to take stock of the whole case or to plan a careful defense . . . . Instead, we found ourselves trying to hold a line where we could. But the line could not be held."[6]

The defensive postures formulated during June dominated the summer of 1972 as Republicans nominated Nixon and Agnew for "Four More Years" and Democrats nominated George McGovern and Thomas Eagleton, later replaced by Sargent Shriver. With the Vietnam War almost over and the economy healthy, Nixon and Agnew maintained an insurmountable lead and Watergate received scant attention. White House efforts to contain the DNC suit were rewarded when Judge Charles Richey ruled on August 22 that all pretrial depositions would remain sealed until after the election. Whether he had been influenced or not, Judge Richey's decision furthered the White House plan.[7]

But if Watergate were a minor national story it was nevertheless major Washington news. The *Washington Post* assigned local reporters Bob Woodward and Carl Bernstein to the case and, when other news organizations turned their reportorial resources elsewhere, they pursued it. On August 1 they reported that "A $25,000 cashier's check apparently earmarked for President Nixon's re-election campaign was deposited . . . in a bank account of one of the five men arrested in the break-in." Fundraiser Kenneth Dahlberg had not "the vaguest idea" how his check, given to CRP Finance Chair Maurice Stans or CRP Treasurer Hugh Sloan, had found its way into the account from which $5,300 in break-in funds had come. The story implicating Sloan and Stans prompted a General Accounting Office audit that discovered Stans maintained an irregular "campaign security fund" at CRP. The GAO referred eleven possible violations of the new Campaign Finance Act to the Justice Department for investigation.[8]

President Nixon discussed Watergate for the first time since June at an August 29th press conference. Buoyed by his large lead over McGovern, Nixon tempted fate. He argued that "the guilty should be punished" but resisted appointment of a Special Prosecutor since the FBI, the Justice Department, the Government Accounting Office, the Senate Banking and Currency Committee, CRP, and John Dean were already investigating. He failed to mention that the FBI had been influenced by the CIA, that the Justice Department was reporting to the White House, that the Senate Banking and Currency committee was unlikely to get subpoena power, or that CRP was an interested party. Indeed, as Dean later wrote: "I damn near fell off the bed at what I heard next . . . . 'I can say categorically that [Mr. Dean's] investigation indicates that no one in the White House staff, no one in the Administration, presently employed, was involved in this very bizarre incident.' . . . What a reality warp. . . . I had never heard of a 'Dean investigation' much less conducted one. . . ."[9]   In short, he refused to appoint a special prosecutor because of continuing investigations that he knew to be, at best, toothless.

Surprisingly, with the containment defense safely proceeding Nixon transformed the culpable act from the break-in to the "cover-up." "We are doing everything we can to . . . investigate it and not to cover it up" he volunteered, "[since] what really hurts in matters of this sort is not the fact that they occur, because overzealous people in campaigns do things that are wrong. What really hurts is if you try to cover it up."[10] President Nixon unwisely transformed the issue from whether people in the White House and/or CRP broke into DNC headquarters to whether any effort to delay, impede, obstruct, or influence investigations had occurred; henceforth, that act would be considered an even greater offense. Clearly, Nixon's transformation contributed to his eventual predicament.

The federal grand jury indicted the burglars, Hunt, and Liddy, on September 15, 1972, and the Justice Department said that the indictments ended their investigation. The containment strategy was working. But Woodward and Bernstein reported the indictments as an incremental development: "Though the indictment does not touch on the central questions about the purpose or sponsorship of the alleged espionage, it alleges . . . new details."[11]   Their anonymous source, "Deep Throat," and their relentless inquiries had led them to believe that the Watergate break-in was only one in a series of efforts by White House/CRP personnel to maximize illegally and unethically their power. Their accusation transcended the break-in and cover-up and postulated a policy of covert domestic intelligence operations.

Woodward and Bernstein elaborated their CRP allegations during the fall of 1972. They reported that Stans gave $50,000 that paid for the break-in to Magruder and Bart Porter, and that Deputy Director Fred LaRue and Political Coordinator Robert Mardian used single-sheet accounting to handle many otherwise unrecorded funds. The *Post's* bombshell story of September 29 charged that John Mitchell had been one of five persons to control a secret fund used to spy on Democrats — an allegation vehemently denied by the former attorney general and CRP director. On October 4 the *Los Angeles Times* published an exclusive interview in which CRP security guard Arthur Baldwin detailed the DNC break-in and said that his wiretap transcripts were sent to the White House.[12]

President Nixon had said that no one in the White House had been involved in the break-in and, indeed, the unraveling allegations concerned CRP. But that distinction was a fine one: Mitchell had been attorney general, Mardian had been an assistant attorney general, Stans had been commerce secretary, Magruder had worked for Haldeman, and Magruder, Liddy, and Hunt had earlier occupied White House offices. Because of the inbreeding among the administration and CRP the ties were clear enough to undermine Nixon's technical denial. Asked to make a "clean breast about" Watergate at his October 5 press conference the president condemned the break-in as useless, relied solely on the FBI investigation and the indictments, and declined comment on cases still before the courts.[13] He had resisted the opportunity to change course because the plan was holding together and the election was only a month away.

But the allegations continued to broaden. On October 10 the *Post* headlined that "FBI Finds Nixon Aides Sabotaged Democrats" through a "massive campaign of political spying and sabotage conducted on behalf of President Nixon's re-election and directed by officials of the White House and [CRP]." Presidential Press Secretary Ron Ziegler evaded twenty-nine press questions about Presidential Appointment Secretary Dwight Chapin's hiring of Donald Segretti to sabotage opposition campaigns, and CRP dismissed the allegation as "not only fiction but a collection of absurdities" (although it was later substantiated by FBI Director Gray). The *Post* also reported multiple acts of sabotage against the McGovern and Muskie campaign.[14]

On October 12, Chairman Edward Kennedy of the Judiciary Subcommittee of the Senate Committee on Administrative Practices and Procedures ordered a preliminary inquiry into the Watergate charges. The Senate Watergate investigation thus began largely because the *Post* had created doubt about the scope of the criminal indictments and the campaign of political espionage, while the White House avoided the mounting questions.

By election day the *Post* revealed that Nixon's lawyer, Herbert Kalmbach, was the paymaster for the secret cash "spy-fund"; the *New York Times* revealed telephone calls from Segretti to the White House, Chapin, and Hunt; and Woodward and Bernstein reported that CRP Treasurer Hugh Sloan had linked Haldeman to the secret fund before the grand jury.[15] When Sloan denied the story because he had never been asked about Haldeman under oath many Republicans charged that the *Post* was an arm of the McGovern campaign. President Nixon won reelection with 61 percent of the popular vote.

The burglary trial began on January 8, 1973. Prosecutor Earl Silbert charged that Liddy had run amok while doing legitimate political intelligence work for CRP—a scenario that meshed with the White House's containment strategy. The *New York Times* and the *Post* reported that money to buy guilty pleas was passing through Hunt to Barker and the burglars.[16] Four of the burglars subsequently pleaded guilty while Liddy and McCord were found guilty on January 30, 1973.

The containment strategy had apparently succeeded. But Judge Sirica was distressed that "all the facts have not been developed by either side" and Woodward and Bernstein bluntly reported that "The Watergate bugging trial was marked by questions not asked of witnesses, answers not given, witnesses not called to testify, and some lapses of memory by those testifying under oath."[17] Emphasis upon procedural questions and unresolved issues reduced the likelihood that these low-level convictions would redeem the administration by providing psychological closure.

Since neither the judge nor the reporters had uncovered the "whole story," the investigative drama shifted to the U.S. Senate. The Senate would have two arenas in which to investigate Watergate: the Judiciary Committee's confirmation hearings for Acting FBI Director L. Patrick Gray and the Select Committee on Campaign Practices chaired by Senator Sam Ervin (D-N.C.).

Gray's confirmation hearings were pivotal because the president was publicly committed to the thoroughness of the Bureau's secretly deflected Watergate investigation. Gray volunteered FBI reports confirming the Segretti-Chapin-Kalmbach connection. Worse, he testified that Dean had been informed of the Bureau's interview schedule and had even seen their confidential reports. Still worse, Dean had given the contents of Howard Hunt's White House safe to Gray who, on his own initiative, destroyed this evidence. Interest in Dean's testimony understandably increased even as Gray's own prospects dimmed.

Since White House strategists knew that Dean's testimony would both heighten the drama and undercut their containment strategy, President Nixon issued his March 12 statement on "Executive Privilege." He would provide "all necessary and relevant information through informal contacts" but would not permit his staff to respond to subpoenae. He argued that executive department officials could be subpoenaed by congressional committees because their departments were congressionally authorized, but that his staff served only at his pleasure and authorization.[18]

The executive privilege statement was a rhetorical gamble involving three audiences. He needed to assure the public that he had complied with his August 29 promise to cooperate; he needed to convince a hostile Senate that he would fairly and honestly provide "all necessary and relevant" materials; and he needed to persuade the judiciary of the legality of his position. Although Jackson Harrell, B. L. Ware, and Wil Linkugel view this as Nixon's first personal *apologia*, his statement responded to implicit charges of cover-up, not complicity in the break-in.[19] This highlights the seriousness of Nixon's break-in/cover-up transformation of August 29, because a personal *apologia* for the break-in had apparently become unnecessary. It will never be known whether executive privilege would have protected presidential staff from congressional subpoenae because events destroyed the containment strategy.

On March 21, 1973, John Dean told President Nixon that Hunt wanted immediate "hush money" and warned him of a "cancer on the Presidency." Two days later Judge Sirica revealed McCord's charges that defendants had been pressured into silence and perjury. Gray's nomination was withdrawn in early April and Nixon met with Attorney General Richard Kliendienst and his Assistant, Henry Peterson.[20]

While avoidance and containment strategies had contributed to the landslide reelection, they had allowed accusers to establish their case. President Nixon was now compelled to face the public. Harrel, Ware, and Linkugel contended that Nixon's primary error lay in not leading the crusade for political morality. But that choice was made soon after the break-in and facilitated reelection, the Vietnam settlement, and time for the controversy to abate. The "stall" was also important in Nixon's second term. As Raymond Price expressed it, "Even if he were guilty, I wanted him to win the fight, to complete his term of office, to finish the work he had begun." Convinced that the Watergate activities were no different from tactics used by previous administrations, the Nixon staff saw a liberal/Democratic/press conspiracy to undermine their historic contributions.[21]

Nixon's April 17 press release signaled an imminent defensive change. He announced a compromise with the Ervin Committee under which a witness could assert executive privilege in answer to any question while testifying in executive session. This upheld separation of powers and applied only to the Ervin hearings. He also revealed that intensive new inquiries had begun and that "there have been major developments in the case . . . [and] real progress has been made in finding the truth." Reiterating his condemnation of cover-ups Nixon said that "no individual holding . . . a position of major importance . . . should be given immunity from prosecution" (Dean was privately negotiating for just such immunity).[22]

The April 17 statement ended the strategy of avoiding the issue in three ways: Nixon permitted his aides to testify in the Senate, he personally reported unspecifiable developments that suggested a strategic shift, and he acquiesced to televised Senate hearings. But avoidance was still exercised in the briefing hour that minimized evening news coverage, the reiteration of executive privilege, the ambiguous "new developments," and his repeated commitment to truth, cooperation, and prosecution. This statement should therefore be viewed, not as Harrell, Ware, and Linkugel suggest as continuing avoidance, but as a transition from prior statements that tried to minimize public reaction to an otherwise abrupt change in posture.

The White House transcripts contradicted Nixon's claim that televised hearings were "never a central issue" to him. When he asked "How bad is it if we go on television?" Haldeman mistakenly predicted that only Public Broadcasting would carry the hearings gavel to gavel. Even then Nixon worried about coverage of breaking developments. Daniel Schorr noted "incessant, almost obsessive discussions about whether the Senate hearings could be stalled, shunted into executive session, compressed into a single week, or at least kept off prime time."[23]

The April 17 statement radically changed the rhetorical climate. Dean announced that he would implicate others rather than become the scapegoat, Price recommended that Haldeman consider resigning to save Nixon, and Nixon himself told Price, "If you think I should resign just write it into the next draft [of the April 30 address] and I'll do it."[24] Moreover, the press and public were anxious to learn about the president's "major developments." In addition, Gray admitted destroying Hunt's documents, thus undermining the competence and integrity of the FBI. With McCord, Hunt, and Dean ready to talk to the courts, the Senate, and the public via television, Nixon went on television.

Nixon's address of April 30, 1973, explained that he had become aware of new information on March 21, 1973, and had "*personally assumed* the responsibility for coordinating intensive new inquiries . . . [and] *personally ordered* the investigators to get all the facts and *report them to me*" (emphasis added). Those facts caused him to accept the resignations of Haldeman, Ehrlichman, Kliendienst, and Dean, while absolving Haldeman and Ehrlichman "of any implication of personal wrong-doing." Nixon pledged to "do everything in my power to bring the guilty to justice and to purify the political process" and announced Elliot Richardson, "a man of unimpeachable integrity and rigorously high principle" to whom "I have given absolute authority to make all decisions bearing upon the prosecution of the Watergate case," as the new attorney general.[25]

Nixon had abandoned avoidance and appeared on prime-time television to establish publicly his positive leadership. This impression was strengthened by his explicit statements of personal responsibility for both the acts of his subordinates and the conduct of future investigations. Although new information facilitated this strategic shift, Nixon's admission and the resignations undercut confidence in his earlier categorical denials and rendered him either duplicitous or gullible, neither of which boosted his personal legitimacy.

While appearing to claim personal responsibility, Nixon's condemnation of the break-in and his promise to prosecute the guilty really allowed him to blame criminal actions on the convicted conspirators and to let Haldeman, Ehrlichman, and Dean take the blame for the cover-up. Effective victimage required that the audience could attribute all guilt to the sacrificial victims, but Nixon tried to use his waning credibility to absolve Haldeman and Ehrlichman. This absolution of his associates was contradictory because it directly countered Nixon's attempt to end Watergate through victimage. Indeed, his speech drove Dean toward the prosecutors when he saw himself becoming the scapegoat.[26]

But even if guilt had been effectively transferred to the scapegoats, the victimage still would have been only partial because Nixon and Price had misphrased the pledge to investigate. They wanted to pronounce the administration and political system purified, but said that: "I pledge to you tonight from this office that I *will do* everything in my power to insure that the guilty are brought to justice and that such abuses are purged from our political processes in the years to come long after I have left this office" (emphasis added).[27]

The choice of the future tense personally committed Nixon to a crusade against abuse of power, whereas a past tense could have portrayed him as a political savior. Moreover, the President narrowed the grounds for legitimate confrontation with Richardson because attacks on his integrity, principle, or authority would have undermined Nixon's judgment and/or cooperativeness.

The April 30 address therefore brought Nixon personally into the Watergate affair, raised doubts about his early denials, stripped him of his top aides, pledged him to investigate, increased public interest, drove an incriminating witness to the prosecution, and limited the bases for future challenges to the new attorney general. It is difficult to imagine a less productive speech.

During May of 1973 a new presidential staff was assembled, the Ervin Committee hearings opened, and Richardson appointed Special Prosecutor Archibald Cox. The president spoke to the press on May 22, 1973, and outlined a defense of personal absolution. He denied knowledge of, or participation in, the break-in and cover-up including offers of clemency and funds for the defendants, attempts to implicate the CIA, and knowledge of the Fielding burglary. Subsequent evidence seems to confirm that he did not know about the specific burglaries in advance, but that he knew of and even initiated many of the other plans.[28]

Nixon's need to clear *himself* is a direct consequence of his April 30 address, his professed confidence in Gray's now infamous FBI investigation, the August 29 break-in/cover-up transformation, and the discrepancy between executive privilege and the resignations. The press statement reflected both Nixon's conviction that the controversy was spearheaded by the press and Democrats and his hope of stopping the press without escalating his public commitment. But the untenable denials presented verifiable claims for the press, public, prosecutors, and senators.[29]

When the dismissed aides testified before the grand jury and the Ervin Committee they followed different paths: Mitchell justified, Ehrlichmann explained, and Haldeman tried to victimize Dean who cooperated by mortifying himself.[30] This coincidental cafeteria of testimony did nothing to focus the hearings, but it heightened the drama. Everyone agreed that Dean's testimony would be important. As the lynchpin of the cover-up and the president's chief accuser, Dean was both valuable and vulnerable. If he were discredited by the Senate, the public, the press, or the courts, he could be blamed for both Watergate and slander. But his testimony was detached, professional, and open.

Ironically Richard Nixon, who frequently admonished his aides to study the Alger Hiss case, failed to recognize the ironic role reversal in this Senate drama. Nixon was now cast as the respectable Alger Hiss and Dean was his Whittaker Chambers.[31] Through mortification Dean, like Chambers, reserved the right to implicate those who professed innocence. By the end of Dean's testimony in late June, the Ervin hearings had become Dean's word against the president's. Then the dam broke.

On July 16, 1973, presidential aide Alexander Butterfield testified that President Nixon secretly taped his meetings and telephone calls. Ervin and Cox immediately requested the tapes to resolve the Nixon/Dean standoff but Nixon invoked executive privilege. Ordered by Judge Sirica to explain how Cox's intraexecutive demand undermined separation of powers, White House attorneys claimed that presidents are "answerable to the Nation but not the courts." The Ervin committee filed suit in federal court while Cox challenged the president's right to withhold evidence. Gallup reported that approval of the President had dropped 37 points since January to 31 percent.

Daniel Schorr voiced the popular belief that the Ervin committee's investigation opened the door to impeachment and that television "enabled Americans psychologically to cross that threshold." But Michael Robinson has demonstrated that the televised hearings undermined public respect for everyone associated with Watergate—Nixon, the Senate, and the press—while not increasing public perception of Nixon's guilt. In short, the televised hearings left Nixon, the Senate, and the press all vulnerable.[32]

Nixon tried to exploit his accusers' vulnerability in his August 15, 1973, address. After differentiating his nominal responsibility for the actions of others from his Constitutional responsibility to defend the office against "false charges" he countercharged that the hearings had "become increasingly absorbed in an effort to implicate the President personally." He reiterated his confidence in usually reliable investigative sources that had proved unreliable and justified withholding the tapes because confidentiality "is a much more important principle" than cover-up. Still unprepared to denounce his supporters, Nixon blamed the sociopolitical climate of 1972 for fostering understandable, if deplorable, misconduct.   He further charged that urgent matters were being ignored by Congress and he challenged the public to "demand to know why."[33]

This address had some success as an apologia.   Pollsters noted his popularity increased by 8 percent. Although this is typical of most presidential addresses, it nevertheless seemed to turn temporarily the tide.   The attempt to transfer guilt to Congress might have worked at the height of his popularity, but now it could only apply the brakes to his slide.   Moreover, it exacerbated the country's problems by further undermining public confidence in government without creating any positive foundation for his own defense.   Barry Brummet has argued that only mortification could have saved Nixon, but his statements of October 5, April 30, and May 15 had created a situation in which he could not reclaim innocence without admitting incompetence.[34]

The most important element of the August 15 address, however, was President Nixon's position on the tapes.   By asserting "confidentiality" rather than "executive privilege" Nixon forged a protective dilemma. Verification of his denials required the tapes that could not be surrendered on the grounds of confidentiality. But any adjudication of his confidentiality claim could be challenged on the grounds of separation of powers.   The debate moved into the courts during August, September, and October as the White House fought demands for the tapes.

The net effect of the address was to brake Nixon's personal decline at the expense of public confidence in the Congress, while sealing his fate in protection of the tapes on the legally dubious grounds of confidentiality before the only source of legitimate authority untainted by the controversy.   Even as he gained leverage over Congress Nixon shunted the debate into the courts.   Harrell, Ware, and Linkugel regarded this as the end of Nixon's personal apologia which precluded their consideration of the evidentiary role of the tapes, adverse judicial rulings, and the dismissal of the special prosecutor.   Their analysis therefore failed to consider the instrumental rhetorical events set in motion by this address.[35]

Spiro Agnew resigned the vice presidency and pleaded nolo contendere to charges of income tax evasion on October 10 and the president nominated Gerald R. Ford to the vacancy. Replacing the polarizing Agnew with the unifying Ford changed the ramifications of impeachment/resignation.   Nevertheless, Ford delivered a series of Nixon defenses prepared by the president's speechwriters.[36]

On October 12, the day of the Ford nomination, the court ruled that the president must release the tapes. He chose not to appeal to the Supreme Court, either because the speed of the decision indicated that litigation would not cause the public to lose interest or because it raised the specter of losing in the Supreme Court.

The White House decided to prepare transcripts of the tapes to preserve executive privilege but stipulated that Cox could subpoena no further tapes. Cox's insistence prompted his dismissal, along with Richardson's and Assistant Attorney General William Ruckelshaus' resignation in the "Saturday Night Massacre" of October 20, 1973. Characterized as an effort to "avoid Constitutional confrontation," the terminations ignored a relevant question: If the constitutional arguments for confidentiality (August 15) and executive privilege (March 12 and August 15) were sound, why did Nixon not give the Supreme Court an opportunity to uphold them?

Richardson resigned because he "believed the discharge of Cox to be inconsistent with the conditions of his confirmation by the Senate" and therefore juxtaposed his Nixon-created persona of "unimpeachable integrity" and "absolute authority" with Nixon's own declining popularity. The "Massacre" and Nixon's silence about it contradicted his vow of personal responsibility to get the facts, to cooperate with investigators, and to compromise on executive privilege wherever possible. By so strenuously arguing to retain the tapes, Nixon engendered suspicion that he might tamper with or withhold important evidence.[37]

The first impeachment resolution had been introduced on July 31, shortly after the president had refused to release tapes to the Ervin Committee and Cox. But the firing of Special Prosecutor Cox prompted the Democratic leadership of the House to authorize Judiciary Committee consideration of impeachment on October 22, 1973. Had the tapes been released to Cox, serious consideration of impeachment might have been avoided. But the pledge of "cooperation" had become the issue, with Nixon meaning "voluntary cooperation grounded in executive authority" and Congress and the Courts meaning "compliance with the functional necessities of legislative investigation and criminal prosecution."

President Nixon's counteroffensive continued with a televised news conference from Disneyworld in November, significant primarily because of its interaudience pressures: Nixon spoke to the television public and AP editors about his dealings with their reporters and the courts. He distributed copies of prior statements, promised his tax records, and joked with the editors and praised their newspapers. His 1974 State of the Union address attempted to finalize the victimage of Congress begun on August 15th. Nixon declared that "One year of Watergate is enough" and proclaimed that "the time has come . . . for all of us to join together in devoting full energies to these great issues that I have discussed tonight." He pledged cooperation but noted that he would follow the precedent "set by every president from George Washington to Lyndon B. Johnson of never doing anything that weakens the Office of the President" and stated that he had "no intention whatever of walking away from the job."[38] But Nixon's counteroffensive stopped neither the House Judiciary Committee's impeachment discussions nor new Special Prosecutor Leon Jaworski's pursuit of the tapes.

As sentiment for impeachment mounted the Judicary Committee tried to define the criteria of "high crimes and misdemeanors." The interpretations ranged from the hardcore defenders' "clear treason" to "a clear pattern of misconduct" from the most rabid accusers. Majority Counsel John M. Doar's February 21 report argued that many impeachment cases never mentioned criminality and that noncriminal actions could require impeachment from office for "undermining the integrity of the office, disregard of constitutional duties and oath of office, arrogation of power, [and] abuse of the governmental process." He further stipulated that impeachment required a "substantial" record of misconduct rather than separate or isolated incidents. President Nixon predictably denounced Doar's grounds as too broad and argued that criminality was necessary to justify impeachment.[39]

President Nixon's position therefore sufferred a serious setback when, on March 1, he was named an unindicted co-conspirator in charges of obstruction of justice, perjury, bribery, obstruction of a congressional committee, obstruction of a criminal investigation, and involvement in conspiracies to commit each of these crimes.[40] Although a sitting president cannot be indicted, his status suggested that even his own "criminality" standard for impeachment might prove precarious.

Nixon made his last aggressive stand on April 29, 1974. He responded to a Judiciary Committee subpoena for sixty-four tapes with a televised address. He recounted events since the break-in, asserted that "The basic question at issue today is whether the President personally acted improperly in the Watergate matter," and announced that his release of transcripts of forty-two tapes would "once and for all show that what I knew and what I did ... were just as I have described them ... from the beginning." Reiterating his claims of executive privilege and confidentiality and deploring the leaks and rumor associated with the investigation, he asserted that the transcripts contained everything relevant and invited Senate Judiciary Committee Chairman Peter Rodino (D-N.J.) and ranking Republican Edward Hutchinson (R-Mich.) from the Committee to authenticate them. Specifically, he claimed that the transcripts would prove that he first learned of the cover-up on March 21, 1973, that he only considered paying money to Hunt for national security reasons, and that he was always trying "to discover what was right and to do what was right."[41]

Nixon's April 29 address crystallized the issues. As the president climbed further out on the limb he became critically vulnerable to a variety of plausible developments: omissions or inaccuracies in the transcripts, signs of any motives other than what is right, and evidence of any presidential cover-up prior to March 21. Nixon's culmination of twenty-two months of defensive rhetoric thereby set the stage for his own impeachment hearings. He had outlined the key issues, defined the evidentiary standards, and provided the evidence. Indeed, his problems continued as Rodino and Hutchinson found the transcripts incomplete and replaced them with Judiciary Committee transcripts, while Jaworski subpoenaed sixty-four more tapes.

The impeachment defense was devised by James St. Clair — a constitutional lawyer defending a criminal case with his hands tied. Although Price regarded a defense that focused on the nonpayment of hush money to Hunt as "legally sound, politically it proved woefully inadequate — and unfortunately what we were engaged in was a political rather than legal battle." Indeed, the White House exploited the dual legal/political nature of the hearings. Lukas noted that Nixon's "refusal to respond to subpoenas, his public release of edited transcripts, his White House chats with his congressional 'jurors,' his frequent use of television and public speeches to argue his case — all were techniques plainly inappropriate for a defendant in a criminal trial." However, the president demanded of the Committee the secrecy, stringency, and impartiality of a nonpolitical court. In short, the president's counsel approached impeachment legally while the president approached it politically but criticized Committee members who did so.[42]

Handed the central issues, evidentiary standards, the evidence, and a narrow and technical White House defense, the televised Judiciary Committee Hearings resulted in three Articles of Impeachment all derived from Nixon's own defense. Article I charged Nixon with obstruction of justice that evolved from his condemnation of cover-ups, his vows of cooperation, his assumption of personal responsibility, his efforts to absolve his implicated aides, his dismissal of the Prosecutor, and his submission of incomplete and inaccurate evidence. It passed 27-11 on July 27, 1974. Article II, charging that he had abused his constitutional powers by using the IRS, the FBI, the CIA and the "plumbers" to harass citizens, frustrate investigators, and to interfere with executive operations, stemmed from his stonewall defense that drove investigators to pursue all loose threads while offering no justification for suspicious activities. It passed 28-10 on July 29, 1974. And Article III, charging Nixon with willfully denying subpoenae related to Congress's constitutional powers of impeachment, resulting from his tenacious commitment to executive privilege and confidentiality in cases where it did not apply, passed 21-17 on July 30, 1974.The committee had been expected to pass at least one article because of its 21-17 Democratic majority, but Rodino and the White House both doubted that an obviously partisan vote would lead to impeachment. Consequently, Rodino and the Democrats sought to persuade liberal and moderate Republicans such as Cohen, Fish, Railsback, Smith, McClory, and Butler, while the White House stressed partisanship. When warnings of Rodino's partisanship were validated by a news story, the White House overreacted and offended several Republican members of the Committee. Six of the Committee's seventeen Republicans—more than anyone had thought possible—ultimately voted for the first two impeachment articles. Nevertheless, Nixon would be safe until the House voted to impeach and the Senate voted to convict him. House debate was scheduled for August 19 with gavel to gavel television coverage. Speechwriter Raymond Price believed that the battle could be won in the Senate as it and the national audience became decreasingly partisan. But the crushing blow came on July 24 when the Supreme Court ruled in U.S. v. Nixon that "The generalized assertion of privilege must yield to the demonstrated specific need for the evidence in a pending criminal trial." This required Nixon to provide Jaworski with sixty-four additional tapes. The most damaging was a tape of the June 23, 1972, meeting in which Nixon told Haldeman to have the CIA deflect the FBI's investigation. Price, Haldeman, and Attorney J. Fred Buzhardt all acknowledged that this "Smoking pistol" tape provided sufficient evidence to prove both Article I, obstruction of justice, and Article II, abuse of power, while the Court's decision itself undermined Nixon's defense against Article III, subpoena defiance. The transcripts were "at variance" with his statements and undermined his case, and he now argued an even more restricted defense: "that when all the facts were brought to my attention, I insisted on a full investigation . . . and prosecution."[43]

The smoking pistol revelations contradicted Nixon's defense, confirmed most of the charges against him, and embarrassed most of his supporters. As President Nixon saw any hope of winning in the House or Senate evaporate he resigned on August 8, 1974. Richard Katula noted the surprisingly vindictive tone of the resignation speech as Nixon denied his *intent* to cover-up while pointing to a legacy of peace. Noreen Kruse explained this as a move from earlier "survival responses" to a "social response" motivated by the need to "restore or regain affection, status, mastery, prestige or esteem" now that survival was out of the question.[44]

Indeed, Nixon's professed reason for resigning was not remorse but lack of support. Even the resignation speech left America short of redemption. The magnitude of the transgression had grown from a third-rate burglary to a cover-up to a constitutional crisis even as the victims had grown in stature from Washington operatives to CRP officials to White House aides and, ultimately, to a president. But like so many others before him, Nixon avoided the mortification that might have reunited the country. Public discussion therefore turned to the possible indictment and prosecution of Richard Nixon for his role in the conspiracy. Guilt had been purged from the presidency, but not from the electorate that had overwhelmingly endorsed him only twenty-one months before.

Gerald Ford tried for a month to reunify the nation torn by the trauma of Watergate, and on September 8, 1974, issued a blanket pardon for Richard Nixon. Aide Robert Hartmann explained four reasons for Ford's decision: he wanted to sweep the entire mess into the "ashcan of history," he secretly dreaded the likelihood of a Nixon suicide, he sincerely believed that a pardon was morally necessary, and he believed that waiting would only make the necessary pardon more divisive.[45] The political repercussions were disastrous. To extend Richard Ben-Veniste's metaphor, CRP and the entire Nixon White House had spent two years trying to get the Watergate monkey off their backs. Rather than killing the monkey, Nixon resigned to get it out of the White House, only to have Ford adopt it. The Senate investigated the pardon decision and it was the most frequent reason why Americans voted against Gerald Ford in the 1976 election. The American electorate that had so enthusiastically endorsed Richard Nixon in 1972 punished Gerald Ford for the pardon and finally closed the door on Watergate.

CONCLUSIONS

Why, then, did the Watergate scandal unfold as it did? This essay suggests four conclusions which deserve further study. First, accusers who allow defendants to define the charges reduce their own burden of proof. The White House denounced the break-in and categorically denied complicity before being accused. As prosecutors and press investigated, the president charged that cover-up was actually the more heinous crime and vowed to cooperate. When he withheld that cooperation on constitutional grounds he invited judicial intervention. And when forced by the judge to divulge the tapes, his criterion for vindication invited examination of his motives, his memory, and the congruence between his defense and the tapes. With the exception of "high crimes and misdemeanors," Richard Nixon defined his own crisis. Accusers needed only to hold Richard Nixon's feet to the fire that he had so readily fanned. Of course, defining the terms of encounter is half the battle and defendants may define the charge in a way that facilitates exoneration. But accusers who concede the defendant's definition, where reasonable, husband their rhetorical artillery and increase the probability of conviction. Apologists should respond to charges, not make them.

Second, treating accusation and defense in contemporary America requires the recognition of multiple audiences and their spheres of control. Lloyd Bitzer's familiar rhetorical situation proposes a speaker trying to enlist the assistance of an audience capable of positively modifying his exigence through the management of constraints.[46] Watergate defendants faced a rhetorical three-ring circus of audiences with differing constraints and powers. Courts used formal procedures, testimony, and argument from precedent to render formal decisions and sentences. Congress used somewhat less formal procedures to elicit information and to humiliate some defendants. The press followed journalistic and dramatic imperatives to follow the trail of heroes and villains. And the public at large employed heterogeneous and ambiguous standards, garnered from the above three sources of information, to revise their impressions of America's institutions and leaders. President Nixon tried to use all four arenas, not always wisely, to buttress his defense. Woodward and Bernstein, for example, lacked subpoena power and their evidence was inadmissable in court, while the courts were unable to indict a president. A focus upon any one arena ignores the rhetorical climate created by the other three arenas and the arena to which subsequent deadlocks are routed.

Third, televised national hearings can undermine accusers and defendants almost equally with dire consequences for the polity. President Nixon improved his position during the Ervin hearings only relative to Congress and the press. If televised hearings helped America to cross the psychological threshhold toward impeachment, that passage was not an ennobling one. The Republican losses in 1974, the 1976 defeat of Gerald Ford, the "national malaise" that engulfed President Carter, and the antigovernment sentiment of the Reagan Era all affirm the view that there were no winners in Watergate. But when the alternative was vindication of a president who had violated his oath of office by obstructing the judicial process, by abusing the powers of the IRS, CIA, and FBI, and by defying the legal power of subpoena, the conflict was necessary. The national trauma resulted directly from President Nixon's tenacious refusal to admit culpability in the face of conclusive evidence that he had violated his own standards of conduct. John Dean warned Nixon of a cancer growing on the presidency. In a sense, Congress, the courts, and the press used both radiation and the surgery of impeachment to cure that cancer. But the cure wracked the body politic and the recovery has been long and difficult. Potential accusers should recognize that they, as well as their targets, will be soiled by their charges. Accusations should not be used for personal gain, but neither should they be avoided for personal safety. Similarly, defendant public officials should realize that their personal defenses can severely injure the public trust.

Fourth, Watergate suggests that the admission of culpability requires dramatistic redemption through mortification or victimage rather than "healing themes." The break-in's illegality was never questioned. But as perceptions of its significance grew, redemption required increasingly significant victims. By the time the burglars had been convicted the transgression had been expanded by Nixon into the cover-up charge and by the *Post* into domestic intelligence operations. In either event the indicted burglars were insufficient victims and both guilt and suspicion diffused throughout the established order. Watergate entailed no "Failure of Apology," as Harrell, Ware, and Linkugel have concluded. It was a "Failure of Exculpation" as President Nixon himself contributed to the growing sense of culpability while deflecting it toward others: the Democratic Party, the American press, the Senate, the House of Representatives, the CIA, the "hardball" nature of American politics, the sociopolitical climate of 1972, and a truckload of then prominent individuals: Hunt, Liddy, Colson, Magruder, Mitchell, Stans, Dean, Haldeman, Ehrlichman, Cox, Sirica, Woodward and Bernstein, Dan Rather, Daniel Schorr, Daniel Ellsberg, and the White House "enemies list." It is little wonder that public confidence in our societal leadership waned, even as Presidents Nixon and Ford stressed healing and unity. Healing themes may be useful when differences can be construed as guiltless, but Kenneth Burke's thesis that guilt demands punishment is affirmed in Watergate. Even when exculpation works, as for Nixon it did not, the specter of guilt stalks its victims and its appetite grows. America has never seen a political scandal the magnitude of Watergate and with reasonably good fortune we shall not witness an encore. The central rhetorical lesson of Watergate may be that a president should not embark on a course of conduct that he cannot either abandon apologetically or comfortably defend. All parties agreed that the Watergate break-in was an illegal and improper act. Because Nixon accepted nominal responsibility for his subordinates and claimed personal responsibility for the investigation he unnecessarily implicated himself. And because he would neither repent nor blame his loyal subordinates, he facilitated the diffusion of guilt and suspicion throughout the American polity. When he could neither justify his operations nor abandon them he assured that the reputations of countless institutions and individuals would be damaged for his own sake.

NOTES

[1]Richard M. Nixon, *RN: The Memoirs of Richard Nixon* (New York: Grosset and Dunlap, 1978), p. 627.

[2]Ibid., pp. 629, 627; see also H. R. Haldeman with Joseph DiMona, *The Ends of Power* (New York: Dell Publishing, 1978), pp. 27-29.

[3]Carl Bernstein and Bob Woodward, *All the President's Men* (New York: Simon and Schuster, 1974), pp. 20-22, 26-27.

[4]Richard Nixon, "The President's News Conference of June 22, 1972," *Weekly Compilation of Presidential Documents* [hereafter *WCPD*] 8 (1972): 1078-79; see the reconstruction of the unexplained 18 1/2 minute gap in the tape of the June 20 meeting in Haldeman, *The Ends of Power*, pp. 43-44; and Nixon, *RN*, pp. 627, 635.

[5]Haldeman, *The Ends of Power*, pp. 60-62, 50-54; Nixon, *RN*, pp. 641-

42.

[6]John Dean, *Blind Ambition* (New York, Simon and Schuster, 1976), pp. 118, 114, 116-17.

[7]Bernstein and Woodward, *All the President's Men*, p. 50 and Dean, *Blind Ambition*, pp. 132-33, suggest that Judge Richey's decision was not coincidental.

[8]*Washington Post*, August 1, 1972, p. 1; August 27, 1972, p. 1.

[9]Richard Nixon, "The President's News Conference of August 29, 1972," *WCPD* 8 (1972): 1306-12; Dean, *Blind Ambition*, pp. 124-125.

[10]*WCPD* 8 (1972): 1306-12.

[11]*Washington Post*, September 16, 1972, p. 1, and Bernstein and Woodward, *All the President's Men*, p. 72.

[12]Bernstein and Woodward, *All the President's Men*, pp. 107, 114; and *Washington Post*, September 29, 1972, p. 1.

[13]Richard Nixon, "The President's News Conference of October 5," *WCPD* 8 (1972): 1489.

[14]*Washington Post*, October 10, 1972, p. 1; and Bernstein and Woodward, *All the President's Men*, pp. 148-52, 153-57, 302.

[15]Bernstein and Woodward, *All the President's Men*, pp. 166-67, 174, 104.

[16]Ibid., p. 259.

[17]*Washington Post*, January 31, 1973, p. 1.

[18]Richard Nixon, "Executive Privilege," *WCPD* 9 (1973): 253-55, and Raymond Price, *With Nixon* (New York: Viking Press, 1977), pp. 246-49, 220-21.

[19]Jackson Harrell, B. L. Ware, and Wil A. Linkugel, "Failure of Apology in American Politics: Nixon on Watergate," *Speech Monographs* 42 (1975): 253-54.

[20]Price, *With Nixon*, p. 222.

[21]Harrell, Ware, and Linkugel, "A Failure of Apology in American Politics: Nixon on Watergate," p. 255; Price, *With Nixon*, p. 92; Nixon's and Price's memoirs argue that presidential behavior should be judged only relative to the behavior of previous presidents, but that argument never surfaced in their public defenses. See Price, *With Nixon*, pp. 240, 285, and Nixon, *RN*, pp. 628-629.

[22]Richard Nixon, "The Watergate Investigation," *WCPD* 9 (1973): 387.

[23]Daniel Schorr, *Clearing the Air* (Boston: Houghton-Mifflin, 1977), p. 97.

[24]Price, *With Nixon*, pp. 223, 97, and 101.

[25]Richard Nixon, "The Watergate Investigation: Presidential Address to the Nation," *WCPD* 9 (1973): 433-38; cf. Dean, *Blind Ambition*, pp. 226-76.

[26]See Bruce Gronbeck, "The Rhetoric of Political Corruption: Sociolinguistic, Dialectical, and Ceremonial Processes," *Quarterly Journal of Speech* 64 (1978): 156-57; Howard H. Martin, "A Generic Exploration: Staged Withdrawal, the Rhetoric of Resignation," *Central States Speech Journal* 27 (1976): 247-57; and Dean, *Blind Ambition*, pp. 275-76. Price, *With Nixon*, pp. 358 and 103 speculates that Nixon was driven to absolve them because of his personal loyalties and the trauma and tension of the times.

[27]*WCPD*, p. 435.

[28]Richard Nixon, "The Watergate Investigation: Statements by the President," *WCPD* 9 (1973): 693-98. Price told presidential staffers that Nixon thought Richardson had appointed Edward Cox (Nixon's son-in-law) as Special Prosecutor, *With Nixon*, p. 236. Haldeman says that the May 22 statement was initially intended to preempt Dean's testimony while retaining the national security cloak. Apparently Haldeman forgot the details of their June 23, 1972, meeting and could not warn the President (Haldeman, *The Ends of Power*, p. 300).

[29]Harrell, Ware, and Linkugel, "A Failure of Apology in American Politics: Nixon on Watergate," pp. 256-57.

[30]See Richard Crable, "Ethical Codes, Accountability, and Argumentation," *Quarterly Journal of Speech* 64 (1978): 30-31.

[31]Richard M. Nixon, *Six Crises* (New York: Doubleday, 1962), pp. 1-76, esp. pp. 74-76.

[32]Schorr, *Clearing the Air*, p. 99; Michael J. Robinson, "The Impact of the Televised Watergate Hearings," *Journal of Communication* (Spring 1974): 17-30.

[33]Richard M. Nixon, "The Watergate Investigation: The Presidential Address to the Nation," *WCPD* 9 (1973): 984-91.

[34]Barry Brummett, "Presidential Substance: The Address of August 15, 1973," *Western Speech Communication* 39 (1975): 249-59.

[35]These accounts magnify the relative importance of the speech because they minimize or ignore other Watergate rhetoric.

[36]Gerald R. Ford, Vice Presidential Files - Speeches, (Ann Arbor, MI: Gerald R. Ford Library).

[37]Ronald L. Ziegler, "Watergate Special Prosecution Force and Department of Justice," *WCPD* 9 (1973): 1271; Richard Nixon, "Presidential Tapes and Documents," *WCPD* 9 (1973): 1329-1331.

[38]Richard Nixon, "Associated Press Managing Editors Association," *WCPD* 9 (1973): 1345-55; Richard Nixon, "State of the Union," *WCPD* 10 (1974): 121.

[39]Summarized by J. Anthony Lukas, *Nightmare: The Underside of the Nixon Years* (New York: Viking Press, 1976), p. 644; Richard Nixon, "President's News Conference of February 25, 1974," *WCPD* 10 (1974): 250-56.

[40]For a detailed account of the indictments see Leon Jaworski, *The Right and the Power* (Houston: Gulf Publishing, 1976), pp. 176-81.

[41]Richard M. Nixon, "Subpoena of Presidential Tapes and Documents," *WCPD* 10 (1974): 450-58.

[42]Price, *With Nixon*, p. 275; Lukas, *Nightmare*, p. 682.

[43]See Theodore H. White, *Breach of Faith* (New York: Atheneum, 1975), pp. 5-7, 346-48; Lukas, *Nightmare*, pp. 693-96; Price, *With Nixon*, pp. 265, 290; Haldeman, The *Ends of Power*, p. 300; and Richard Nixon, "Release of Additional Transcripts of Presidential Conversations," *WCPD* 10 (1974): 1008-9.

[44]Price, *With Nixon*, (pp. 308-352) ironically explains that the White House staff concealed the resignation to foster the impression that the President would fight impeachment; Richard A. Katula, "The Apology of Richard M. Nixon," *Today's Speech* 23 (1975): 1-6; see Nixon's references to "larger issues" on August 15, 1973, January 20, 1974, and April 29, 1974; his special calendar remarks of April 30, 1973, and Price's comments in *With Nixon* (p. 92); Noreen W. Kruse, "Motivational Factors in Non-Denial Apologia," *Central States Speech Journal* 28 (1977): 14.

[45]Robert L. Hartmann, *Palace Politics: An Inside Account of the Ford Years* (New York: McGraw-Hill, 1980), pp. 268-69.

[46]See especially Lloyd F. Bitzer, "Functional Communication: A Situational Perspective," in *Rhetoric in Transition*, edited by Eugene E. White (University Park: Pennsylvania State University Press, 1980), pp. 21-38.

INFORMATION SOURCES ON THE SPEECH SET

The Accusations

Bernstein, Carl, and Bob Woodward. *All the President's Men*. New York: Simon and Schuster, 1974.

Ben-Veniste, Richard, and George Frampton. *Stonewall: The Real Story of the Watergate Prosecution*. New York: Simon and Schuster, 1977.

Dash, Samuel. *Chief Counsel: Inside the Ervin Committee*. New York: Random House, 1976.

Dean, John. *Blind Ambition*. New York: Simon and Shuster, 1976.

Ervin, Samuel James. *The Whole Truth: The Watergate Conspiracy*. New York: Random House, 1980.

Jaworski, Leon. *The Right and the Power*. Houston: Gulf Publishing, 1976.

Schilling, Joan H. *The Watergate Index: An Index to Watergate Material as Reported in the "Washington Post,"* June 16, 1972- June 30, 1973. Wooster, OH: MicroPhoto Division, Bell and Howell, 1975.

Sirica, John J. *To Set the Record Straight: The Break-in, the Tapes, the Conspirators, the Pardon.* Berkeley, CA: Westworks, 1977.

Thompson, Fred D. *At This Point in Time: The Inside Story of the Senate Watergate Committee.* New York: New York Times Book Co., 1975.

United Press International and The World Alamanac. *The Impeachment Report.* New York: New American Library, 1974.

U.S. Congress, Senate. Select Committee on Presidential Campaign Activities. *The Final Report of the Select Committee on Presidential Campaign Activities.* 93rd Cong., 2nd sess. S. Rept. 93: 981. Washington, D.C.: GPO, 1974.

U.S. Watergate Special Prosection Force. *Final Report.* Washington, D.C.: GPO, 1977.

Washington Post, August 1, 1972, p. 1; August 27, 1972, p. 1; September 16, 1972, p. 1; September 29, 1972, p. 1; October 10, 1972, p. 1.

The Defenses

Ehrlichman, John. *Witness to Power: The Nixon Years.* New York: Simon and Schuster, 1982.

Frost, David. *"I Gave Them a Sword": Behind the Scenes of the Nixon Interviews.* London: Macmillan, 1978.

Haldeman, H. R., with Joseph DiMona. *The Ends of Power.* New York: Dell Publishing, 1978.

Hunt, Howard. *Undercover: Memoirs of an American Secret Agent.* New York: Berkley Publishing, 1974.

Liddy, G. Gordon. *Will: The Autobiography of G. Gordon Liddy.* New York: St. Martin's Press, 1980.

McCord, James. *A Piece of Tape: The Watergate Story Fact and Fiction.*

Rockville, Md.: Washington Media Forum, 1974.

Magruder, Jeb Stuart. *An American Life: One Man's Road to Watergate*. New York: Atheneum, 1974.

[Attorneys for] Nixon, Richard M. "Disclosure of Grand Jury Materials," *WCPD* 10 (1974): 710-13.

_____. "The Supreme Court Case: Briefs Filed by the President's Attorneys," *WCPD* 10 (1974): 657-709.

Nixon, Richard M. *RN: The Memoirs of Richard Nixon*. New York: Grosset and Dunlap, 1978.

_____. "The President's News Conference of June 22, 1972," *WCPD* 8 (1972): 1078-79.

_____. "The President's News Conference of August 29, 1972," *WCPD* 8 (1972): 1306-12.

_____. "The President's News Conference of October 5, 1972," *WCPD* 8 (1972): 1489.

_____. "Executive Privilege," *WCPD* 9 (1973): 253-55.

_____. "The Watergate Investigation," *WCPD* 9 (1973): 387.

_____. "The Watergate Investigation: Presidential Address to the Nation of April 30, 1973," *WCPD* 9 (1973): 433-38.

_____. "The Watergate Investigation: Statements by the President, *WCPD* 9 (1973): 693-98.

_____. "The Watergate Investigation: Presidential Address to the Nation of August 15, 1973," *WCPD* 9 (1973): 984-91.

_____. "Presidential Tapes," *WCPD* 9 (1973): 1329-31.

_____. "Associated Press Managing Editors' Association," *WCPD* 9 (1973): 1345-55.

_____. "State of the Union," *WCPD* 10 (1974): 121.

_____. "The President's News Conference of February 25, 1974," *WCPD* 10 (1974): 250-56.

_____. "Subpoena of Presidential Tapes and Documents," *WCPD* 10 (1974): 450-58.

_____. "Release of Additional Transcripts of Presidential Conversations," *WCPD* 10 (1974): 1008-09.

Nixon, Richard M., and James St. Clair. "Supreme Court Decision," *WCPD* 10 (1974): 829.

Price, Raymond. *With Nixon.* New York: Viking Press, 1977.

Stans, Maurice H. *The Terror of Justice: The Untold Story of Watergate.* Chicago: Regnery Books, 1984.

Ziegler, Ronald L. "Watergate Special Prosecution Force and the Justice Department," *WCPD* 9 (1973): 1271.

Selected Bibliography

Baudhuin, E. Scott. "From Campaign to Watergate: Nixon's Communication Image," *Western Speech* 38 (1974): 182-89.

Brummett, Barry. "Presidential Substance: The Address of August 15, 1973," *Western Speech Communication* 39 (1975): 249-59.

Friedman, Leon, ed. *United States v Nixon: The President Before the Supreme Court.* New York: Chelsea House, 1974.

Garza, Hedda. *The Watergate Investigation Index: Senate Select Committee Hearings and Reports on Presidential Campaign Activities.* Wilmington, Del.: Scholarly Resources, 1982.

_____. *The Watergate Investigation Index: House Judiciary Committee Hearings and Report on Impeachment.* Wilmington, Del.: Scholarly Resources, 1985.

Harrell, Jackson, B. L. Ware, and Wil A. Linkugel. "Failure of Apology in American Politics: Nixon on Watergate," *Speech Monographs* 42 (1975): 245-61.

Katula, Richard. "The Apology of Richard M. Nixon," *Today's Speech* 23 (1975): 1-6.

Lang, Gladys Engel, and Kurt Lang. *The Battle for Public Opinion During Watergate: The President, The Press, and the Polls.* New York: Columbia University Press, 1983.

Lukas, J. Anthony. *Nightmare: The Underside of the Nixon Years.* New York: Viking Press, 1976.

Martin, Howard H. "A Generic Exploration: Staged Withdrawal, the Rhetoric of Resignation." *Central States Speech Journal* 27 (1976): 247-57.

Kruse, Noreen W. "Motivational Factors in Non-Denial Apologia." *Central States Speech Journal* 28 (1977): 13-23.

Muzzio, Douglas. *Watergate Games: Strategies, Choices, Outcomes.* New York: New York University Press, 1982.

Rangell, Leo. *The Mind of Watergate: An Exploration of the Compromise of Integrity.* New York: W. W. Norton, 1980.

Robinson, Michael J. "The Impact of the Televised Watergate Hearings." *Journal of Communication* (1974): 17-30.

Rosenberg, Kenyon C. *Watergate: An Annotated Bibliography* Littleton, Colo.: Libraries Unlimited, 1975.

Schuetz, Janice. "Communicative Competence and the Bargaining of Watergate." *Western Journal of Speech Communication* 41 (1978): 105-15.

Smith, Myron J. *Watergate: An Annotated Bibliography of Sources in English.* Metuchen, N.J.: Scarecrow Press, 1983.

Gerald R. Ford Encounters Richard Nixon's Legacy: On Amnesty and the Pardon

Bernard L. Brock

Gerald R. Ford's encounter with Richard Nixon's legacy presents an interesting study to understand the limitations and possibilities inherent in presidential rhetoric. All politicians must consider the consequences of their political actions. If they do not, they risk facing accusations for which they are unable to respond convincingly. Ford, in his initial encounter, was rhetorically effective in preempting troublesome accusations against his policy; but on the heels of that success as Ford extended the encounter, he needlessly facilitated accusations against his policy that ultimately, some critics suggest, resulted in his losing the presidency in 1976.

On August 9, 1974, immediately following the resignation of Richard Nixon, President Gerald Ford acknowledged the political task before him, "I assume the Presidency under extraordinary circumstances never before experienced by Americans. This is an hour of history that troubles our minds and hurts our hearts." As the first unelected president of the United States, Ford assumed the leadership of a nation divided by its long involvement in Vietnam and demoralized by the Watergate scandal, both legacies from Nixon's administration. Ford realized that his main task was to unite a nation and heal its spirit. He accepted this challenge when he said, "What we need now is a time to heal."[1] Further, in his first address to Congress, Ford set a tone of moderation and unity as he assumed the role of statesman.

Mindful that his words as chief executive would be scrutinized with care to detect his similarities and differences with Nixon, Ford initiated a rhetorical strategy that was designed to separate himself from Nixon's problems and negative qualities but to capitalize on Nixon's positive policies. His tactic was to identify himself and his administration with Nixon's praiseworthy goals and to minimize negative identification that would be used against him as the basis for political accusations. His first opportunity to confront the Nixon legacy and to initiate this healing process was "The President's Address," delivered before a joint session of the Congress on August 12,

1974.[2]

An examination of his address reveals the characteristics that enabled Ford to assume the role of statesman and to start the healing process. Ford opened with the urgency of the nation's business. His first words were, "My fellow Americans, we have a lot of work to do. My former colleagues, you and I have a lot of work to do. Let's get on with it." And he quickly added, "The Nation needs action, not words." Ford was not looking back and was not interested in discussing what had brought the country to its present state. Instead, he intended to lead the country forward.

Ford's next move was to present himself as above politics. He did this by stating that Congress would be his "working partner." He also separated himself from Nixon's superior attitude toward Congress when he said, "As President, within the limits of basic principles, my motto toward the Congress is communication, conciliation, compromise, and cooperation." Ford's qualities were those of a statesman and stood in stark contrast to Nixon's imperial presidency. Ford added that as "working partners" they should solve problems together and that he "intended to listen" because Congress spoke for the people.

Having set the tone for his administration, Ford moved to the most pressing business. "My instinctive judgment," he said, "is that the state of the Union is excellent. But the state of our economy is not so good." He identified inflation and budget deficits as the major problems. However, he warned "against unwarranted cuts in national defense," and he added, "This is not time to change that nonpartisan policy." He extended his role of statesman into economic policy when he requested, "Support your candidates, Congressmen and Senators, Democrats or Republicans, conservatives or liberals, who consistently vote for tough decisions to cut the cost of government, restrain Federal spending, and bring inflation under control."

Having established fighting inflation as his first priority, Ford placed other items on his agenda. Education, health care, and international trade were matters the president and Congress must work on together in a "spirit of cooperation" and "compromise."

Next, Ford introduced foreign policy. This gave him an opportunity to identify with the successes of the Nixon administration, "Over the past 5 1/2 years in Congress and as Vice President, I have fully supported the outstanding foreign policy of President Nixon. This policy I intend to continue." Ford obviously thought it was important to counter any thought that he would be a weak leader, "A strong defense is the surest way to peace. Strength makes detente attainable. Weakness invites war as my generation knows from four very bitter experiences."

Ford, in discussing foreign policy, presented a series of statesman-like pledges directed toward all interested nations. He then closed with a general pledge, "I say to you in words [of John Kennedy] that cannot be improved upon: Let us never negotiate out of fear, but let us never fear to negotiate."

At the end of the address, Ford, again, found it necessary to separate himself from the activities that had become associated with Watergate, "There will be no illegal tappings [tapings], eavesdropping, bugging, or break-ins by my administration. There will be hot pursuit of tough laws to prevent illegal invasion of privacy in both government and private activities."

Ford initiated the process of healing the divisions within the country and uplifting its demoralized spirit, and his initial public acceptance was 71 percent.[3] Ford successfully assumed the role of statesman as "a successful leader in public affairs, ... who in the creation and guidance of public policy displays careful preparation, wisdom, and personal integrity."[4] He did this by (1) stressing the importance of getting on with the nation's business, (2) treating Congress and the American people as important working partners, (3) identifying with the foreign policy accomplishments of the Nixon administration while simultaneously disassociating himself from the activities of Watergate, and (4) pledging to be politically evenhanded and willing to negotiate with others. This successful formula for statesmanship can be used as a standard for evaluating Ford's encounter with Nixon's legacy of Vietnam and Watergate.

PREEMPTING ACCUSATIONS: FORD'S RHETORIC ON AMNESTY

Ten days after Gerald Ford became president, he traveled to Chicago, Illinois, to address the Veterans of Foreign Wars Convention. He took this occasion to attack the Vietnam portion of the Nixon legacy. Without any prior warning, Ford announced his intention to act on "offenses loosely described as desertion and draftdodging."

Ford took a courageous step because throughout the 1960s both the war and opposition to it had escalated until, in 1967, American was torn over a war it did not seem able to win. Opposition became strong enough to force President Johnson into negotiations with the North Vietnamese and from running for reelection. Richard Nixon, who during the campaign had announced a plan for peace, was elected president by a narrow margin. For years, Nixon sustained a strategy of slowly withdrawing American troops to give the impression of reducing American participation while simultaneously escalating the South Vietnamese role as well as the bombing in the North. However, when he was reelected, Nixon was committed to complete withdrawal of American troops. When Ford assumed the presidency, America's role in Vietnam was limited to aid, South Vietnam was quite weak, and the country was divided over what had become the longest war in American history.

Ford opened his speech with a variation on the theme of unity he had sounded in his Congressional address, "let me talk today about some of the work facing veterans — and all Americans — the issues of world peace and national unity." Then he quickly gained the audience's approval by announcing the new administrator of the Veteran's Administration. This was followed with a direct appeal to veterans, "I think it is about time that we should stop thinking of veterans in terms of different wars. . . . I salute the men of many campaigns — of World War I, World War II, Korea, and Vietnam."

Ford led into the amnesty issue by identifying the policy he opposed, "I stated my strong conviction that unconditional, blanket amnesty of anyone who illegally evaded or fled military service is wrong." He then prepared the audience for news they would not like, "Yet, in my first words as President of all the people, I acknowledged a Power, higher than the people, Who commands not only righteousness but love, not only justice but mercy." He also declared his faith in the "American system of justice." With that preparation, he announced that he planned to review the "status of some 50,000 of our countrymen convicted, charged or under investigation, or still sought for violations of the Selective Service Act of the Uniform Code of Military Justice. . . ." and that he wanted "them to come home if they want to *work* their way back." "So I am throwing the weight of my Presidency," Ford went on to say, "into the scales of justice on the side of leniency." He finally appealed for a unified acceptance of his proposal, "I ask all Americans who ever asked for goodness and mercy in their lives, who ever sought forgiveness for their trespasses, to join in rehabilitating all the casualties of the tragic conflict of the past."

Ford tried to convince his shocked audience that he was concerned about the welfare of veterans and especially about the unemployment rate for Vietnam veterans. He pointed out, as a veteran himself, he would work for peace through military preparedness, and he asked their help in dealing with the nation's problems, "Together we are going forward to tackle future problems, including the scourge of inflation which is today our Nation's public enemy number one." He closed by subordinating all individual interests to America, "Let us now work for America, in which all Americans can take an even greater pride. I am proud of America. You are proud of America. We should be proud to be Americans."

Ford chose the VFW as the ground for his first real encounter with the Nixon legacy and took his first step in healing the nation by attempting, through a limited amnesty, to take the issue of Vietnam off the public agenda. Even though the responses from his immediate audience was chilly, Americans generally were pleased by his words and certainly by his intentions. The *Washington Post* said, "President Ford has had the courage to raise it [amnesty] before a veterans convention in the first days of his presidency," and it added, "he dared to venture out into the dangerous middle ground between 'granting oblivion, or a general pardon,' on the one hand, and, on the other, a harsh refusal to do anything about the problems of the Vietnam exiles other than to confront them with the full force of the law." The *Los Angeles Times* strongly supported Ford's position, "Mr. Ford is right, of course. Our intervention in Vietnam came to an end more than a year and a half ago, and the wounds left by the longest and least popular war in American history are healing. But a true reconciliation requires the government to moderate the present alternatives — prison or lifelong exile — for those who would not bear arms." The editorial went further and compared it to "granting a pardon to Mr. Nixon." The *St. Louis Post-Dispatch* placed Ford's action in the context of the American Bar Association's resolutions that "the law should be enforced 'regardless of the position or status of any individual'" and that Vietnam draft resisters should receive immunity "in exchange for two years of service in an organization such as the Peace Corps."[5] Ford's first news conference of August 28, 1974, presented further evidence that his limited amnesty was well received. The press did not ask a single question about the amnesty issue in contrast to six Watergate and Nixon pardon-related questions.[6]

The nation generally accepted and appreciated Ford's first efforts to address the Vietnam portion of the Nixon legacy. But how consistent was the speech with the role of statesman and the standards Ford had established in his congressional address? The first standard stressed getting on with the nation's business. He had indicated that "these young Americans should have a second chance to contribute their fair share to the rebuilding of peace among ourselves and with all nations." He wanted them to help all Americans get back to work. The second standard was to treat Congress and the American people as working partners. This standard was overlooked because the announcement came without any warning or allowing Congress or the people to participate in the process. However, he had recommended working through the legal system, so he was not going completely alone. The third standard was to disassociate himself from Nixon's Watergate activities while identifying with his foreign policy successes. Nixon had strongly opposed amnesty. Ford's middle ground approach, therefore, successfully made him independent of Nixon, except as amnesty was compared to a potential pardon for Nixon. The fourth standard was to be politically evenhanded. The editorials and public acceptance of 71 percent suggest Ford was successful politically. Ford's rhetoric enabled him, just ten days after he assumed office, to confront successfully the divisive issue of Vietnam.

INVITING ACCUSATIONS:
FORD'S RHETORIC ON NIXON'S PARDON

On Sunday, September 8, 1974, one month after assuming office, Ford requested national television coverage for an important announcement. Again, without prior notice, Ford decided to confront the second portion of the Nixon legacy, Watergate, with what he knew would be an unpopular action.[7] Watergate, which had begun as a break-in and bugging, escalated from a caper, to an incident, to a scandal, to a conspiracy, and finally to political warfare. Throughout all these stages, Richard Nixon was unsuccessful in putting it behind him to get on with the nation's business, so it eventually resulted in a divided nation and Nixon's resignation.

Ford started his announcement by communicating the agony he felt, "I have learned in this office that the difficult decisions always come to this desk." He also wanted to prepare his listeners for the unexpected, "I must admit that many of them do not look at all the same as the hypothetical questions that I have answered freely and perhaps too fast on previous occasions." Just ten days earlier in his first news conference, Ford had said in answer to whether he would pardon Richard Nixon, "There have been no charges made, there has been no action by the courts, there has been no action by any jury. And until any legal process has been undertaken, I think it is unwise and untimely for me to make any commitment." However, Ford wanted to make it clear that he was doing what he felt was right, "I have promised to uphold the Constitution, to do what is right as God gives me to see the right, and to do the very best that I can for America."

Ford then went to the heart of his subject, "Richard Nixon, and his loyal wife and family." He acknowledged the seriousness of the situation and attempted to create some sympathy for Nixon, "accusations hang like a sword over our former President's head, threatening his health as he tries to reshape his life." The problem as Ford saw it, was "After years of bitter controversy and divisive national debate, . . . I am compelled to conclude that many months and perhaps more years will have to pass before Richard Nixon could obtain a fair trial by jury. . . ." Ford indicated that he believed in "equal justice for all Americans," but he was afraid Nixon could not receive equal justice. Instead, "he would be cruelly and excessively penalized either in preserving the presumption of his innocence or in obtaining a speedy determination of his guilt in order to repay a legal debt to society." Ford was especially concerned about what would happen during Nixon's extended trial, "Our people would again be polarized in their opinions. And the credibility of our free institutions of Government would again be challenged at home and abroad." Ford added that "it is not the ultimate fate of Richard Nixon that most concerns me. . . . My concern is the immediate future of this great country." Ford then presented his final appeal, "I feel that Richard Nixon and his loved ones have suffered enough and will continue to suffer, no matter what I do, no matter what we, as a great and good Nation, can do together to make his goal of peace come true." He closed by announcing an "absolute pardon unto Richard Nixon for all offenses against the United States. . . ."

Ford subsequently presented related documents to the press — "Granting Pardon to Richard Nixon," "Letter of Agreement Between Former President Nixon and the Administrator for General Services," and "Text of Legal Opinion by the Attorney General." Following Ford's statement and the release of the documents Philip Buchen, counsel to the president, held a news conference. Buchen presented a statement that was followed by intensive questioning.[8] The two issues that were most frequently probed were the disposition of the tapes and other presidential materials and whether there had been an agreement in advance.

Ford's second rhetorical encounter with the Nixon legacy was decidedly not as successful as his first. The pardon of Nixon shocked the nation in contrast to its surprise at the limited amnesty. The country was so preoccupied with Nixon that it did not seem to hear Ford's message of getting on with the nation's business. Newspapers that had supported limited amnesty attacked him. The *St. Louis Post-Dispatch* said, "Mr. Ford's precipitate act of clemency is more than a self inflicted wound on his Administration; it is a lethal stroke against the principle of equality under the law on which the nation's entire system of justice rests." The *Washington Post* focused on Ford's justification, "Because he approached the problems of disposing of the Watergate scandals from the wrong direction, President Ford came out in the wrong place. The issue has never been the personal fate of Richard Nixon. . . ." The *Los Angeles Times* discussed both the justification and the principle involved, "President Ford's reasons for pardoning Richard Nixon were compassionately presented, but we believe Mr. Ford made a serious mistake in granting the pardon now. It is not consistent with the fundamental American principle that sets everyone equally before the law, and that puts no man, not even the President above the law." The *New York Times* pointed to Ford's confusion, "President Ford has sadly confused his responsibilities to the Republic and his understandable sentiments toward one who has inflicted grave damage upon the body politic."

Some editorials did support Ford's action. The *Detroit News*'s was typical: "If anybody doubted that President Gerald Ford could make tough decisions, the new President disposed of that doubt by his controversial — and, in our opinion, correct — decision to pardon Richard Nixon." It went further and echoed his reasoning, "Mr. Ford has acted to shut the book on a chapter of conflict and political passion that paralyzed the ability of his predecessor to conduct the affairs of state and could have impaired his own ability to do so."[9]

With Vietnam, Ford announced the limited amnesty, and it was generally accepted. But with the Nixon pardon, the encounter extended for weeks
through all Ford's news conferences and even into an unprecedented
presidential appearance before the Congressional Subcommittee on
Criminal Justice.

At Ford's news conference on September 16, 1974, most questions dealt
with the Nixon pardon and other Watergate-related issues.[10] In this conference, Ford shifted emphasis in his justification for the pardon away from
Nixon toward the country, "The main concern that I had at the time I made
the decision was to heal the wounds throughout the United States. . . . It
seemed to me that as long as this divisiveness continued. . .the responsible
people in the Government could not give their total attention to the
problems that we had to solve at home and abroad." One reporter tied the
amnesty and pardon issues, "If your intention was to heal the wounds of the
Nation, sir, why did you grant only a conditional amnesty to the Vietnam
war draft evaders while granting a full pardon to President Nixon?" Ford's
response minimized the importance of his justification for both amnesty
and the pardon. He said, "The only connection between those two cases is
the effort that I made in the one to heal the wounds involving the charges
against Mr. Nixon and my honest and conscientious effort to heal the
wounds for those who had deserted military service or dodged the draft.
That is the only connection between the two." Also, Ford, in focusing on
the nature of the specific offenses, demonstrated that he did not completely understand the larger picture and the rhetorical aspects of the encounter.
The questioner implied that he was middle of the road in one instance and
not the other. His response could have defended the pardon as a middle of
the road action by indicating that he had not pardoned all those involved
but only went as far as was necessary to heal the nation. Other questions
made it clear that reporters were concerned that the pardon might prevent
the true Watergate story from ever surfacing, that prior to Nixon's resignation Ford might have agreed to pardon, and that Ford had gone back on his
promise of "openness and candor" with Congress and the American people.

Ford's formal statements and news conferences did not put the pardon
issue to rest, so he was requested to appear before the Congressional Subcommittee on Criminal Justice. He could have refused the invitation, but
that behavior would have suggested he had something to hide and would
have resembled Nixon's Watergate activities. On October 17, 1974, Ford
appeared before the committee. His opening statement stressed the theme
of getting on with the nation's business instead of Nixon's situation, "I
wanted to do all I could to shift our attention from the pursuit of a fallen
President to the pursuit of the urgent needs of a rising nation." During the
questions following his statement, congressmen in various ways attempted
to bring out that Ford's main concern was for Nixon, but he consistently em-

phasized "that the attention of the President, the Congress, and the American people would have been diverted from the problems that we have to solve. That was the principal reason for my granting the pardon."[11]

Ford's pardon of Nixon may not have been popular, but did it conform to the standards of statesmanship he had established? The first standard was getting on with the nation's business. The pardon was such a shock and so unpopular that it became an important issue itself preventing Ford from moving forward. Ford's initial justification focused too much on Nixon rather than the country, so his rhetoric encouraged people to view the pardon from this more narrow perspective. The second standard was treating Congress and the American people as important working partners. This standard was definitely violated. He not only gave no warning of the pardon, but in his first news conference, he misled the press when he suggested that it was inappropriate to act before the legal process had progressed further. Clearly, Ford had not considered Congress or the public as working partners in this decision. Rather, he seemed to be Nixon's partner. The third standard was to identify with Nixon's successful foreign policy and separate himself from Watergate activities. The pardon entangled Ford in Watergate. The most damaging accusation was that Ford had agreed to the pardon prior to Nixon's resignation, but people also were concerned that the truth on Watergate would never be revealed as a result of the pardon. These issues were what forced Ford to testify before the Subcommittee on Criminal Justice. Ford never satisfactorily answered these accusations. They remained doubts during his entire administration and even were important in his loss to Carter in 1976. The fourth standard was to be above politics — to be politically evenhanded. The full pardon, justified from the perspective of Nixon's situation, was interpreted as very politically partisan, especially when contrasted to the limited amnesty given to Vietnam draft evaders. The pardon communicated that the rich and powerful were above the law, while the less-fortunate, even though motivated by their sense of what was right, could not be forgiven and must suffer the consequences of their actions.

CONCLUSION

Ford's period as a statesman was brief. It ended quickly by Nixon's pardon, and his public acceptance plummeted from 71 percent to 49 percent. The role of partisan politician stayed with him throughout the rest of his administration, which was perceived as conservative in economic and foreign policy. Instead of becoming a "working partner" and "problem solver" with Congress, they became adversaries. This resulted in Ford's governing through veto and ultimately in a negative image that prevented his reelection. The rhetorical question worth asking regarding these events is, "Could

Ford have pardoned Nixon and still have maintained his role as statesman?" The standards for statesmanship Ford established in his first address before Congress can serve to construct a different rhetorical justification for the pardon.

By the time Ford appeared before the congressional sub-committee, he had shifted his primary defense from concern over the Nixon family to a national perspective of getting on with the nation's business. He apparently realized his rhetorical mistake and made the necessary adjustment. But, at the outset, Ford should have justified the Nixon pardon in terms of a national perspective as he had justified limited amnesty. He should have gone back to his first address and reminded people of his words, "I have a lot of work to do. Let's get on with it." He needed to document how present and future divisions over Watergate prevented him from acting. James Klumpp and Jeffrey Lukehart, in their analysis of the Ford pardon speech, argued that Ford unsuccessfully attempted to replace a legal process with a moral justification. They indicated that Ford placed the legal and moral in a dialectic order and was unable to gain transcendence into the moral, and they concluded, "His effort quite simply lacked the strategic insight to lead the public to the new framework he envisioned."[12] By focusing on the actions necessary to move the country forward, Ford might have been able to use national interest to gain transcendence above the interest of any individual or group to fulfill this standard of statesmanship. Thus, the legal-moral dichotomy could have been subordinated to expediency for the nation.

Moreover, shifting his perspective from Nixon to the nation might have enabled Ford to include Congress and the American people as working partners. With amnesty, Ford had initially acted on his own, but the final process included others. Unfortunately, Ford completely bypassed Congress and the people and went against their desires. By making the primary issue "getting on with the nation's business," Ford could have eliminated, through the pardon, the obstacle that prevented the partnership from being implemented. The key to achieving this standard was making the pardon the secondary rather than the primary issue. Ford's rhetoric needed to be refocused.

Identifying with Nixon's foreign policy accomplishments while disassociating himself from Watergate activities was a critical test. This had not posed a significant problem with limited amnesty. Ford had an opportunity with the pardon to make the nation's business include foreign policy. It would have been important for Ford to stress how foreign policy was hampered as a result of the national division, and how the pardon would focus unity and action forward, not backward.

To appear politically evenhanded was probably the most important characteristic of the statesman. Shifting the rhetorical emphasis from

Nixon to the nation certainly would have aided in achieving this goal. But another rhetorical change in his pardon probably would have strengthened his position even more. Just two weeks earlier, Ford had confronted the first portion of the Nixon legacy by announcing limited amnesty to Vietnam draft evaders. Ford could have provided not only the same justification of ending division and putting the issue aside for the Nixon pardon, but he could have also announced both actions — limited amnesty and a limited pardon — to the nation in the same address. To justify the pardon as limited, Ford needed to make the pardon conditional on a stronger statement of responsibility from Nixon. With this approach, people could have seen him as above politics. When he was attacked for favoring Nixon and placing him above the law, he could have responded quickly and effectively "not any more than the draft evaders" and "the welfare of the country needs to be placed above any individual or group." Ford's sincere desire "to heal the nation's wounds" and to get "the country revved up and moving" would have been more credible, and he might have been able to maintain the role of statesman. It is impossible to know the impact this change might have had on his later actions and on perceptions of his administration; nevertheless he definitely did not need to facilitate attacks about his entanglement in the Watergate affair.

Ford, who had launched his administration with a fine rhetorical effort, was reasonably successful in his encounter with Nixon's Vietnam legacy, but, in contrast, his encounter with the Watergate legacy weakened him for the remainder of his presidency. Because Ford had sufficient foresight to initiate his role as statesman and apply it to Vietnam, one wonders why he did not extend this role into his encounter with Nixon's Watergate legacy. An examination of Ford's rhetoric as it reflects his pattern of thought will provide an answer. His opening line in the joint address was, "My fellow Americans, we have a lot of work to do. My former colleagues, you and I have a lot of work to do. Let's get on with it." Ford was not an ideologue nor a sophisticated rhetorician, but he did speak and apparently think in personal terms. His plan for amnesty was a personal one, "I want them to come home if they want to *work* their way back." Much of his problem with the pardon was that he made too personal an appeal, ". . . Richard Nixon, and his loyal wife and family. Theirs is an American tragedy in which we all have played a part." His much publicized and soon abandoned WIN (Whip Inflation Now) campaign was designed to fight inflation at the individual rather than governmental level. Clearly, Ford's rhetoric revealed a concern for the individual in personal and moral terms. This was precisely the approach that prevented his being a statesman on the Nixon pardon and caused him to be perceived as a partisan politician. If Ford were primarily concerned with the individual and personal problems rather than the broader national perspective, why did he initially assume the role of statesman? Ford was also an intuitive politician who in this emergency had the instinct to personalize the country and to realize that it needed healing. However, this instinct failed to lead him above the personal to the national interest in his rhetorical encounter with Nixon's Watergate legacy.

NOTES

[1]Ford's perspective toward Nixon's troubles and his own early problems may be found in Gerald R. Ford, *A Time to Heal* (New York: Harper & Row, 1979).

[2]Texts of all of Ford's addresses may be found in *Weekly Compilation of Presidential Documents* [hereafter *WCPD*] 10 (1974).

[3]"Ford Popularity Recovering after Post Pardon Deadline," *Gallup Opinion Index* #113, November 1974, p. 18.

[4]*Dictionary of Political Science*, edited by Joseph Dunner (Totowa, N.J.: Littlefield, Adams & Co., 1970), p. 499.

[5]All reactions to Ford's speech are from *Editorials on File* 5 (September 1-15, 1974): 1094-1108.

[6]"The President's News Conference of August 28, 1974," *WCPD* 10 (1974): 1069-73.

[7]A discussion of the details behind the pardon is provided by Ford's adviser, Robert T. Hartmann, in *Palace Politics: An Inside Account of the Ford Years* (New York: McGraw Hill, 1980); and a critical account is provided by Clark R. Mollenhoff, *The Man Who Pardoned Nixon* (New York: K. S. Giniger Company, 1976).

[8]The related documents and text of Buchen's news conference may be found in *WCPD*, 10 (1974): 1103-1118.

[9]All reactions for Ford's pardon of Nixon are from *Editorials on File* 5 (October 1-15, 1974): 1094-1108.

[10]"The President's News Conference of September 16, 1974," *WCPD*, 10 (1974): 1157-62.

[11]"Pardon For Former President Nixon," *WCPD* 10 (1974): 1301-1316.

[12]James F. Klumpp and Jeffrey K. Lukehart, "The Pardoning of Richard Nixon: A Failure in Motivational Strategy," *Western Journal of Speech Communication* 41 (Spring 1978): 116-23.

INFORMATION SOURCES ON THE SPEECH SET

Ford's Accusation

For Ford's speech to a joint session of Congress on August 12, 1974, see *Public Papers of the Presidents of the United States, Gerald R. Ford, 1974* (Washington, D.C., GPO, 1975), pp. 6-13.

Ford's Apology

In Ford's televised address, September 8, 1974, see *Gerald R. Ford, 1974,* pp. 101-104.

Selected Bibliography

Editorials on File 5 (September 1-15, 1974): 1094-1108; (October 1-15, 1974): 1094-1108.

Ford, Gerald R. *A Time to Heal.* New York: Harper & Row, 1979.

Hartmann, Robert T. *Palace Politics: An Inside Account of the Ford Years.* New York: McGraw Hill, 1980.

Klumpp, James F., and Jeffrey K. Lukehart. "The Pardoning of Richard Nixon: A Failure in Motivational Strategy." *Western Journal of Speech Communication* 41 (Spring 1978): 116-23.

Mollenhoff, Clark R. *The Man Who Pardoned Nixon.* New York: K. S. Giniger Company, 1976.

CBS vs. Mobil Oil:
Charges of Creative Bookkeeping in 1979

George N. Dionisopoulos and Steven L. Vibbert

Americans experienced the depths of the energy crisis in the fall of 1979. The average price per gallon for gasoline had increased from 67 cents in 1978 to over a dollar in less than a year and drivers had to cope with long lines and little gasoline at the neighborhood station. This situation was exacerbated by the fact that most Americans did not believe the energy crisis was real. Polls indicated that a majority of the people thought the oil companies had created the energy crisis in order to boost demand and profits for petroleum products. As *Newsweek* remarked, in the "energy conscious world" of 1979, anything related to enormous oil profits would be a resonant issue.[1]

Third-quarter earnings figures for much of the oil industry were announced on October 24, 1979. Among those companies reporting, Mobil Oil posted a 130.6 percent profit increase compared with the third-quarter figures of 1978.[2] That night, CBS News used these figures as the lead story in its national broadcast. That report seemed to feature Mobil as the main actor in a story about oil industry price gouging, profiteering, and creative bookkeeping. In response to the manner and accuracy of this coverage, Mobil undertook a $275,000 national advertising campaign charging that CBS had prefabricated most of its report. CBS then was forced to offer a response of its own to the charges leveled by Mobil Oil.

The CBS-Mobil Oil speech set is intriguing for a variety of reasons. First, an examination of the exchange offers some interesting insights concerning the nature of accusations and apologies as corporations employ them. Second, in examining the set, it became apparent that the accusation-apology relationship may encompass an accusation, an apologia, and a counterresponse to the apologia. The extension of the original theory, which was concerned only with the *kategoria-apologia* relationship, may better account for the kind of rhetorical behavior that transpires between accuser and accused within the court of public opinion.

When dealing with corporate encounters, the concept of accountability is critical. As Peter French noted, accusations of ethical impropriety imply "that the subject is accountable."[3] Recently, the operating environment of modern corporations has changed to include added dimensions of corporate accountability.

The contemporary corporation exists in an environment in which sociopolitical pressures act as countervailing forces upon organizational decision making. Modern corporations are no longer judged merely by their profits, they must also pay particular attention to the societal demands placed upon them. Whereas companies of several decades ago had to answer only to stockholders, modern corporations are pressured by a politicized society. The situation in which the modern corporation functions has been described by Robert Heath:

> As a by-product of the 1960's civil rights, ecology, and antiwar movements, the activities of our major institutions have been carefully scrutinized and criticized. Due to the penchant of United States citizens to seek an even-more-perfect state, a confluence of interests focuses on the accountability and performance of major institutions.[4]

In other words, there is a widespread recognition that the contemporary organizational environment includes a prominent ethical dimension in which organizations are held accountable.

The politicized operating environment of today's corporation has produced some widely disparate criteria by which to evaluate the ethical status of a company, and concomitantly, a greater corporate awareness of the necessity of being socially and politically oriented. In an effort to help define a standard of ethical business practice, and to illustrate how they are adhering to it, many corporations have made extensive use of advocacy advertising aimed at defending their interests and promoting understanding. That approach, noted Prakash Sethi, is premised on the belief that advocacy advertising can "contribute to a greater understanding on the part of the public of what can be reasonably expected of corporations in meeting society's expectations."[5]

Oil companies, in particular, have made great use of advocacy advertising, and one of the most active has been the Mobil Oil Corporation. Mobil began its corporate advocacy efforts in 1970. During the oil embargo of 1973-1974, the corporation intensified its efforts, running "op-ed" advertisements every Thursday in the *New York Times*. Since that time, Mobil has placed regular advocacy advertisements in several major newspapers across the country, and has developed a biweekly "Observations" column, which appeared in the Sunday Magazine supplements of five hundred newspapers. As Herb Schmertz, Mobil's vice president for public relations, stated, "There's a dialogue out there, and you're either in it or you're not. We've decided we want to be in it." The use of formats such as the "op-ed" ads, and the Sunday "Observations" column, have helped to establish the Mobil persona as a weekly fixture of American life. In 1978, alone, Mobil

spent nearly a quarter of its $21 million public relations budget to place ads in leading papers and magazines to argue for mass transit and a national energy policy, champion higher quality T.V. fare, debunk congressional proposals to break up the oil companies, and to debate vigorously in print with the media wherever coverage of oil industry matters incurred the company's wrath.[6]

The company's wrath was incurred on October 24, 1979.

ACCUSATIONS OF CREATIVE PROFITEERING

On October 24, 1979, Walter Cronkite began the CBS Evening News:

Good evening. Five more oil companies today reported high profit increases for the third-quarter, among them the giant Mobil, whose July-August-September profits were 131% higher than the same quarter last year. SOHIO reported a 191% gain, Sun was up 65%, CITGO up 64% and Marathon up 58%. Ray Brady Reports. [Ray Brady reported]: Mobil, like other international oil companies, says the big profits were not made here, but in foreign markets, which would mean that foreign consumers were the ones getting hit. . . . [Experts say] that this is not necessarily so.[7]

The report that followed detailed how oil company profits generated from American consumers could be turned into "foreign profits" through what Brady labeled "a [simple] matter of bookkeeping." The report explained how oil companies could purchase crude in Saudi Arabia for $18 a barrel and sell this oil at a profit to a succession of their own subsidiaries located outside of the United States. By the time the oil reached a marketing firm in the United States, it would sell for $35 a barrel, but the resulting profits would be recorded as foreign. The closing shot was of Brady delivering the concluding tag-lines of the story, with the Mobil logo in the background.

It is important to note that this broadcast did not make an explicit accusation directed at Mobil. The charge of creative bookkeeping was purported to be an industrywide practice. However, Mobil seemed to be singled out as the main actor in a story of industry price-gouging and profiteering. Cronkite's opening statement included earnings figures from other oil companies, but the profits of "the giant Mobil" were featured clearly. Although not the highest, Mobil's profits were the first figures mentioned and were distinctly separated from the others. Brady's opening statement also highlighted Mobil. In fact, Mobil was the only specific company mentioned by him. Finally, the use of the Mobil logo in the story's closing shot employed television's ability to juxtapose audio and visual messages to create a unique reality for the viewer.

As the theory would predict, the CBS News story began with the stasis of fact, focusing upon whether an action — creative bookkeeping — was done. Although purporting to deal with an industrywide practice, the accusation was worded and presented in a manner that seemed to feature Mobil as the chief villain in this drama.

Indeed, the accusation had struck a sensitive nerve. The industry was aware of public skepticism about their practices, and Mobil was sensitive to the media's reporting on the energy crisis. According to Mobil's Herbert Schmertz, the media coverage of the energy crisis had taken two forms:

> gossip and economics. The former has been sensational — scandal, rumor, accusations — and the latter has been scholarly and considerably less titilating. Scandal and rumor have thrived. They have shock value and are simply more fun to read. They produce heroes and villains and facile answers.[8]

The day after the industry's third-quarter earnings were released, the *Wall Street Journal* observed that television "news viewers this week are seeing a lot of oil footage showing motorists lined up last summer at gasoline stations. That is TV's way of illustrating the news that profits of some major oil companies went skyhigh in the third quarter," and the *Christian Science Monitor* warned that an "emotional" analysis "might tie the long lines of the summer to higher profits."[9]

Thus, in the fall of 1979, Mobil faced a situation where a report of organizational behavior, or at least a report that intimated unscrupulous behavior, "caused people to consider them immoral or unethical."[10] The company believed that CBS's *kategoria* required a calculated response. Perceiving themselves within the courtroom of public opinion, accused of unethical behavior, Mobil offered an apologia.

MOBIL'S RESPONSE: AN APOLOGIA AND AN ATTACK

Mobil was not alone in viewing the televised reports of third-quarter profits as an attack. A spokesperson for the American Petroleum Institute (API), an industry trade organization, told the *Christian Science Monitor* that the API had "received a number of its member companies' complaints about television coverage of third-quarter profits in October and earlier coverage of the U.S. supply situation." It was the API's contention that "the elements of fairness and balanced, accepted journalistic attributes have not been applied by the networks in a number of energy stories."[11]

But Mobil offered the most elaborate defensive response. Part of this apologetic response sought to purify the negative image of Mobil affirmed by the CBS broadcast. But Mobil's response also adopted an accusatory tone toward CBS, thus creating an exigency to which the network would be forced to respond.

Although all three major networks had reported the industry's third-quarter profits, Mobil's response singled-out CBS's coverage "because its report was the most misleading."[12] The campaign to attack the manner and accuracy of CBS's reporting began with a two-page advertisement Mobil placed in the *New York Times*. Eventually, Mobil placed this two-page spread in the *Boston Globe, Washington Post, Washington Star, Boston Herald-American, Atlanta Constitution, Chicago Tribune*, and the *Los Angeles Times*.

The first page was titled, "19 Dull and Unsensational Facts About Our Profits the TV Networks Didn't Tell You — And Won't Allow Us To Tell You."[13] The ad explained that most of Mobil's third-quarter earnings had come from foreign sources. Some of the profit was actually "book profit" on inventories, and resulted in a cash loss because the revalued oil was subject to taxation and would have to be replaced at higher prices. Mobil stated that its U.S. profits had increased only 32 percent over 1978. Next, this ad told readers how Mobil's expenditures for new sources of energy had "greatly exceeded our profits." The ad concluded with a section headed "You Be the Judge." This section complained that "every day the network news departments condense a mass of material into a severely limited format." This format highlighted a "strong emphasis on sensationalism and dramatic confrontations," which lacked "the depth and the careful analysis needed for sound public judgments." Mobil explained how the networks had "refused to sell us air time to present our point of view, even when we offered to buy additional time so that those who differed with us could reply at our expense." The ad closed with Mobil's contention that the worst "casualty in all this has been the public's understanding of important issues." Mobil had been forced to resort to the format of print advertisement, but "ads like this cannot possibly have the impact of network news broadcasts. Television's information blackout is, we suggest, the real 'rip-off' of the American people." The Mobil logo appeared at the bottom of the page.

But it was another advertisement that constituted Mobil's major apologetic response. This ad was both a denial that Mobil engaged in the practices suggested by CBS News and a direct attack on the presentation and accuracy of the report. In large type, the ad bore the headline: "How CBS on October 24, 1979, Prefabricated the News." The primary importance of this advertisement is indicated by the fact that although the target newspapers carried the two-page spread, the "How CBS" response was printed as a one-page ad in the magazines *Broadcasting, Time*, and *Advertising Age*. Mobil was not as much concerned with CBS's reporting of its profits, as it was with CBS's implication that these profits were due to an unscrupulous practice of creative bookkeeping, a distinctly ethical charge. Mobil responded to the broadcast specifically as though it were a charge of unethical behavior.

Mobil argued that the scenario CBS had constructed was not an accurate portrayal of the company. Mobil began by reprinting a transcript of the CBS story as it had appeared on the broadcast of October 24, 1979. Mobil then denied that it had indulged in the type of fiscal practices described in the story: "The thesis developed by CBS news about foreign earnings bore absolutely no relationship to the earnings the viewer was led to believe were under discussion: Namely Mobil's."

The denial was developed further when Mobil asserted it should not be held morally responsible, because it had never engaged in the unethical behavior. The company claimed:

Mobil does not engage in such practices — and after countless investigations of our activities by the U.S. Congress, and after regular and thorough audits by the Internal Revenue Service, nobody has ever suggested we've even tried to do it.

Mobil explained that their "effort to convey useful information to the public . . . didn't stand a chance [because it] didn't fit the scenario CBS had constructed." Mobil counterattacked that "shoddy TV journalism" was angering a public "that would have understood the facts, honesty presented." Indeed, from Mobil's perspective, the CBS story had affected the company's public image: "No wonder — if [the public] think[s], as CBS news suggested, that foreign profits are made by selling Saudi crude from one to another of our own subsidiaries and raising the price steeply with each transaction."

Mobil's response concluded by condemning "this sort of biased and careless presentation of energy news," "shoddy TV journalism," and proclaimed that a clear "injustice was done not only to Mobil and the rest of the oil industry, but to the American public's need to know the facts."

However, Mobil did not go into an elaborate justification for its 131 percent increase in profits. Instead, it used the apologetic form to purify its character by denying that the increase was due to "creative bookkeeping," an unethical practice — ascribed to Mobil by CBS — that would reflect an unethical and unworthy character. But Mobil's response also made specific charges against CBS News and the manner in which the network had prepared and offered its story. In fact, the tone and focus of Mobil's ad accused CBS News — an organization whose public image depends largely upon a reputation for accuracy — of actually prefabricating a story.

In essence, Mobil's "How CBS" ad turned the tables on CBS. The CBS News story had suggested that the semimonopolistic situation enjoyed by Mobil had been employed unethically to produce obscene profits that benefited the company at the expense of the American people. Mobil's response denied that it had engaged in the unethical behavior, and then countered that the semimonopolistic situation enjoyed by CBS was used unethically to prefabricate a story with no basis in fact. Thus, Mobil's apology gave birth to a new image against CBS and acted as a prime mover to push this speech set into its third phase.

CBS'S RESPONSE TO THE RESPONSE

CBS's apology, which constituted the third and final element of the speech set, was not very elaborate. In fact, it consisted of only a brief statement released to the media the day after Mobil's "How CBS" ad was published in the *New York Times*. However, this response is useful in helping one to assess the outcome of the speech set.

Mobil's attack on CBS's coverage of oil industry profits must have struck a note within the broadcast news industry. Even though not mentioned in the Mobil ad, ABC felt a need to respond. The company announced publicly that although it was "not easy for anyone to plow through the thicket of an oil company's accounting," ABC's coverage had been "reasonable and included Mobil's statement that the bulk of profits came from overseas."[14]

In its statement, CBS News maintained that it would "[stand] by its report." The network's spokesperson emphasized that Ray Brady's report "dealt not primarily with Mobil but with the international oil companies' method of reporting their profits." According to CBS, the October 24 story "labeled the opinion of oil company critics as precisely that, and not as the opinion of CBS News." Further, the day of the broadcast CBS had sought unsuccessfully to obtain an on-camera interview with a spokesperson from Mobil. The network's reply ended by proclaiming that CBS would not be intimidated by Mobil. The statement said that CBS News would "continue to report on all sectors of the energy industry, including Mobil, and [would] continue to reflect the views of a wide variety of observers on the question of oil company profits." According to the *New York Times*, the spokesperson declined to go beyond the prepared statement.[15]

CBS sought to purify, through a rhetorical posture of denial, the image of the network Mobil developed in its "How CBS" ad. However, as the final element of the speech set, the network's reply seemed to be grounded solely in a precise, literal interpretation of the report's contents. The concentration on denotative meaning, while ignoring any connotative messages suggested in the broadcast, is not very convincing.

The denial issued by CBS seemed to ignore some important elements of the situation in question. The network's claim that the story did not deal directly with Mobil is true. However, that statement does not appear to address the fact that the story was presented in a way that suggested that Mobil was guilty of ethical transgression, nor was it apparently cognizant that the broadcast came at a time when there was an emotional climate that surrounded energy issues in general, and the oil industry in particular.

Although it is difficult to determine the effects of this rhetorical interaction, there are some findings that can be mentioned. Mobil's "How CBS" ad forced CBS to state publicly that it had not accused Mobil of the unethical practice of creative bookkeeping. Mobil and its supporters could take this as a vindication.

Moreover, this exchange prompted some of the media to turn their focus inward and examine their coverage of the oil industry and the energy crisis. Some of this coverage resulted in stories that were beneficial to Mobil's public image. For example, the *Los Angeles Times* echoed Mobil's claim that during the energy crisis the American public had been "forced to listen to hyperbole," when it "should have been [given] reasoned judgments." The *Christian Science Monitor* warned that an emotional analysis might connect the oil industry's third-quarter profits with the long gas lines of the previous summer. However, a closer inspection would reveal that most of the increase resulted from inventory profits which would have to be replaced at a higher cost. By the end of November, it was assumed that the recent profits of the oil companies were obscene, but that they were not due to the unethical practice of creative bookkeeping.[16]

CONCLUSION

In dealing with the CBS-Mobil exchange, it became apparent that a corrective to the theory was in order. There may be instances, certainly the CBS-Mobil set is one of them, when it is beneficial to conceptualize the speech set as consiting of an accusation, an apology, which may include elements of *apologia* and *kategoria*, and an apology to the apology-turned-accusation. The critic may use this conceptualization to illustrate how the contested issues changed as the speech set progressed; moreover, it may aid the critic to assess the outcome of this form of rhetorical behavior.

Another benefit of this study concerns insights into apologetic discourse offered by corporations. First, this study illustrates the irreducible nature of an organization's social persona. Discourses of accusation and/or defense relating to organizations concern actions or decisions that are attributed not to individuals within the corporation, but to the corporation-as-actor. This is true even though such acts could be seen as the acts of individual human agents within the organization. John Ladd supports such a position and notes that corporate social decisions are performed by an organizational officer as actor, "but owned by the organization as author. For all the consequences of the decisions so made are imputed to the organization and not to the individual decision-maker."[17] As this case study has illustrated, accusations and apologies dealt with the social persona of the organizations involved, not with particular human agents. Thus, from a critical perspective, the social persona of these organizations may be treated within a speech set as the irreducible rhetorical agents.

Second, when acting in the court of public opinion, corporate agents that make accusations against other corporations may portray themselves as acting on behalf of the American people. In the initial accusation examined herein, CBS News phrased its broadcast to imply that Mobil had engaged in an unethical practice that hurt the American public through higher gasoline prices. CBS offered the public the opportunity to identify *with* it as a representative of the moral community, and *against* a clear villain represented by Mobil Oil. Mobil's response denied that it had engaged in unethical actions, and it accused the network of committing an injustice to the American public's need to know the facts. Thus Mobil's message turned the tables by offering the public an opportunity to identify *with* the company as a champion of the moral community, and *against* the clear villain represented by CBS News.

Given the suggestion that recent changes in the operating environment of contemporary organizations include expanded dimensions of corporate ethical accountability, one may reasonably expect that areas of corporate accusatory and apologetic discourse will arise, and that the speech set model offered herein may be used to explicate these rhetorical phenomena.

NOTES

[1]"A Mobil Message Stays Out of Focus," *Newsweek*, February 11, 1980, p. 76.

[2]Anthony J. Parisi, "Mobil Net Up 130.6% in Period," *New York Times*, October 25, 1979, p. D1.

[3]Peter A. French, "The Corporation as Moral Person," *American Philosophical Quarterly* 16 (1979): 211.

[4]Robert L. Heath, "Corporate Advocacy: An Application of Speech Communication Perspectives and Skills—and More," *Communication Education* 29 (1980): 28.

[5]Prakash Sethi, "Corporate Political Activism," *Public Relations Journal* 36 (1980): 28.

[6]Marilyn Much, "Fighting Back With Issue Ads," *Industry Week*, July 21, 1980, p. 45; "Mobil Corp. Wants Fair Publicity," *New Orleans Times-Picayune*, October 21, 1979, p. 30; and "The Corporate Image: PR to the Rescue," *Business Week*, January 22, 1979, p. 50.

[7]"How CBS on October 24, 1979, Prefabricated the News," *Time*, November 12, 1979, pp. 40-41.

[8]Herb Schmertz, "A Difference of Opinion: An Energy Story the Press Hasn't Told," *Fortune*, November 5, 1979, p. 153.

[9]"Mobil Corp. Post Record 130% Rise in 3rd Period Net," *Wall Street Journal*, October 25, 1979, p. 6; Ron Scherer, "TV's View of Oil Profits Draws Bitter Complaints," *Christian Science Monitor*, November 7, 1979, p. 10.

[10]Noreen W. Kruse, "The Scope of Apologetic Discourse: Establishing Generic Parameters," *Southern Speech Communication Journal* 46 (1981): 278-79.

[11] Scherer, "TV's View of Oil Profits Draws Bitter Complaints," p. 10.

[12]Eleanor Blau, "CBS-TV, After Mobil Ad, Sticks by Profits Report," *New York Times*, November 6, 1979, p. C6.

[13]"19 Dull and Unsensational Facts About Our Profits the TV Networks Didn't Tell You — And Won't Allow Us To Tell You," *New York Times*, November 5, 1979, p. B4.

[14]Blau, "CBS-TV," p. C6. "Mobil's Mad," *Broadcasting,* November 12, 1979, p. 80.

[15]See *Broadcasting*, November 12, 1979, p. 80; the statement by CBS was labeled a "reply" by Eleanor Blau in the *New York Times*; Scherer, "TV's View of Oil Profits Draws Bitter Complaints," p. 10.

[16]John F. Lawrence, "We Don't Need Labels to Recognize Advocates," *Los Angeles Times*, November 4, 1979, p. 9; Scherer, "TV's View of Oil Profits Draws Bitter Complaints," p. 10.

[17]John Ladd, "Morality and the Ideal of Rationality in Formal Organizations," *The Monist* 54 (1970): 493-94.

INFORMATION SOURCES ON THE SPEECH SET

CBS's Accusation

The text for the CBS broadcast can be found in the Mobil ad "How CBS on October 24, 1979, Prefabricated the News," *New York Times*, November 5, 1979, p. B5.

Mobil's Response

"19 Dull and Unsensational Facts About Our Profits the TV Networks Didn't Tell You—And Won't Allow Us to Tell You," *New York Times*, November 5, 1979, p. B4.
"How CBS on October 14, 1979, Prefabricated the News," *New York Times*, November 5, 1979, p. B5. The periodical version of this advertisement can be found in *Time*, November 12, 1979, pp. 40-41.

CBS's Response to the Response

The following articles reported on the contents of the CBS statement of November 6, 1979:
Eleanor Blau, "CBS-TV, After Mobil Ad, Sticks by Profits Report," *New York Times*, November 6, 1979, p. C6.
Ron Scherer, "TV's View of Oil Profits Draws Bitter Complaints," *Christian Science Monitor*, November 7, 1979, p. 10.

Selected Bibliography

Crable, Richard E., and Steven L. Vibbert. "Mobil's Epideictic Advocacy: 'Observations' of Prometheus-Bound." *Communication Monographs* 50 (1983): 380-94.

Goodpaster, Kenneth E., and John B. Mathews. "Can a Corporation Have a Conscience?" *Harvard Business Review* (January/February 1980): 132-41.

Lerbinger, Otto. "Corporate-Media Relations." In *Big Business and the Mass Media*, ed. Bernard Rubin. Lexington: D. C. Heath and Company, 1977.

Pennings, Johannes M. "Corporate Social Responsibility: A Must or a Virtue?" *New Catholic World*, November/December 1980, pp. 260-62.

Thompson, Donald B. "Issue Management: New Key to Corporate Survival." *Industry Week*, February 23, 1981, pp. 77, 79-80.

The Media and the Catholic Church vs. Geraldine Ferraro

Richard J. Jensen

Few events in recent history have intrigued the American public as much as the historic vice-presidential nomination of Geraldine Ferraro during the 1984 election. Her nomination and the subsequent relentless attacks on her personal finances by the press dominated the early months of the election. In a dramatic news conference on August 21, 1984, Ferraro confronted members of the press with her apologia. The conference temporarily quieted attacks on Ferraro but within a few days she found herself in a dispute with the Catholic church over the issue of abortion. The press reported that conflict in vivid detail. Although she tried, Ferraro was unable to quiet successfully the debate over abortion.

Although there were speeches given in each of these situations, the main accusation and apologies were played out in daily media reports. The press reported its accusations against Ferraro. Ferraro attempted to respond in interviews, press conferences, and press releases, while at the same time trying to organize and run a political campaign. Likewise, the press carried the Catholic hierarchy's attacks and Ferraro's responses.

It would be easy to say that the American public was the judge in this political debate, but that would be too simple in this case. In reality, the press was both the accuser and the jury. The media had virtual control over the debate: they chose the issues that were discussed, defined the criteria Ferraro had to meet in order to clear her name, and then judged her effectiveness.

In her battle with the Catholic hierarchy, it would be easy to say American Catholics were the audience, but again, that is too simplistic. Because abortion was such a controversial topic during the 1984 election and because of the rise of the religious right in this country, the entire nation was the audience.

The motives of the accuser formed a crucial part of these two debates. Since Watergate and the subsequent resignation of President Nixon, the press has often been charged with being overzealous in its coverage of certain stories. In Ferraro's case there can be little doubt that the press often used questionable tactics in covering the stories.[1]

The 1984 election began in an auspicious manner. An aging but popular Republican president, Ronald Reagan, entered the contest as an overwhelming favorite to be reelected. Reagan's opponent, former vice-president Walter Mondale, was faced with the difficult task of unseating such a popular incumbent.

Because Mondale was so far behind in the polls, he decided to take a risk. The Democrats knew that Reagan was making inroads among blue collar and ethnic voters in the cities so the choice of an Italian Roman Catholic from Queens was seen as a positive one for the Democrats. The addition of Ferraro to the ticket injected much needed interest in the Mondale candidacy. The initial response to Ferraro's nomination was positive, many observers believed Ferraro would improve the Democrats' chances of carrying their states. Although Ferraro was initially skeptical about a female candidate, she later decided that such a choice was reasonable because a woman on the Democratic ticket could make a difference.[2]

Unfortunately, Ferraro's presence on the ticket did not aid in Reagan's defeat. Before the campaign could get started, the press began to question Ferraro's handling of her personal finances. Instead of concentrating on campaign strategy, she had to spend too much time detailing her finances: "I pointed out to the press that my vice-presidential disclosure statement would exceed what any other candidate had ever filed. I kept repeating it. And repeating it. And repeating it."[3]

The 1980s were unique in American religious history—a time when Catholics and fundamentalists agreed on many issues. Catholic and fundamentalist agreement was based on the rise of abortion as an issue, the growing activism of Catholic bishops, and an improved economic status that allowed many Catholics to drift into the Republican party.[4]

Ferraro found herself under attack from Catholic bishops, particularly the Archbishop of New York, John J. O'Connor. Unlike the issue of finances, Ferraro was unable to quell the attacks with an apology, even though she tried on several occasions.

THE PRESS AS ACCUSER

The press covered the immediate euphoria over Ferraro's nomination and detailed its historic significance. There were numerous articles on the "Ferraro Factor" and much interest in the "Housewife from Queens."[5] After reading the early reports, it can be concluded that the press was not comfortable covering her candidacy.

Many of the early stories focused on the problems of a female candidate. For example, during her first campaign trip to the South, Ferraro toured a soybean-and-cotton farm with Mississippi's agriculture commissioner, Jim Buck Ross. The seventy-year-old Ross explained how the state was in the process of developing new crops such as catfish, crayfish, grapes, and blueberries. Ross asked Ferraro if she could bake blueberry muffins. She replied that she was able to and asked if he could. Ross replied: "Down here . . . .the men don't cook." The story received wide coverage in the press. The press also often focused on the problems of a mixed ticket. "Mr. Mondale and Mrs. Ferraro," Maureen Dowd wrote, "are facing questions . . . .of manners, semantics, and body language. . . . The way they handle the campaign will forever change the public perception about men and women in politics, the experts agree."[6] There were numerous articles on how each candidate should act and much speculation on campaign etiquette.

Most of these issues were quickly eclipsed by concern over Ferraro's policies. The press's accusations against Ferraro followed a classical sequence.

The press first questioned Ferraro's use of her maiden name. The press was unwilling to accept Ferraro's explanation that she used the name out of respect to her mother but claimed that she used Ferraro because it was a familiar name to Queens voters. The press then compared her actions to the controversy in the primaries over Gary Hart's name change: "that is what Gary Hartpence said in trying to twist a cool political-advertising decision into evidence of family fealty. A little phoniness goes a long way." The press next scored Ferraro's description of herself as a typical Queens housewife who bought things on sale like other women. One reporter turned her positive image into a negative one: "but most housewives in Queens do not have husbands able to make legal or illegal $110,000 loans before crucial primaries." Although attempting to create the image of a typical housewife, Ferraro also faced the "catch-22 that confronts professional women: she cannot afford to seem strident or severe, nor can she seem weak or gushy. She has to appear strong but not hard, good-looking and well dressed but not frivolous or girlish." The press often labeled her as "spunky" or "feisty" but one whose "spunk can turn to bile." This thin line was a constant problem in the campaign and one the press commented on frequently.[7]

A further and perhaps more dangerous problem was what the press saw as Ferraro's lack of experience, particularly in foreign policy. Members of the press set out to prove the fact of her inexperience by labeling her as a novice. That lack of experience was highlighted in reports of internal organizational problems in the campaign. A typical article concluded: "Mrs. Ferraro, a three-term House member who had no need for a professional staff with national experience, appears to have had more difficulty than usual."[8]

An article in *Newsweek* stated that "Ferraro also predicted that her '84 campaign will turn nasty." That same article contained some initial reports about her congressional financial disclosures and early speculation about her husband's business deals. The press set out to prove that their speculation was fact. On August 7, 1984, the Washington Legal Foundation, "a conservative public interest law firm," charged Ferraro with violating the Ethics in Government Act "by not providing details of her husband's financial activities since her election to Congress." Ferraro called the charges an attempt to embarrass her politically "and said that in the next 10 days she would release a complete account of her business deals and those of her husband: 'I want it to be full; I want it to be complete.'" At the same time, articles began detailing business dealings of her husband, John Zaccaro, by listing violations of codes in buildings he owned and publishing interviews with Zaccaro's tenants—most of whom made negative comments about him.[9]

In the midst of the attack, Ferraro announced that she would release both her and Zaccaro's tax returns. She soon retracted that promise with a statement that her husband would not release his tax forms. Ferraro quoted her husband's reaction: "Gerry, I'm not going to tell you how to run the country, you're not going to tell me how to run my business. . . . You people married to Italian men know what it's like." The reactions to her comments were swift and harsh, and focused on the stasis of quality: "Disclosing tax returns, as originally promised, would not amount to telling Mr. Zaccaro how to run his business. It would tell the nation whether the operation of this family business compacts with the public interest . . . .in trying to wave the matter off, she has taken refuge in unattractive stereotypes of Italian men and their wives."[10]

Ferraro attempted to silence the uproar by explaining that she was not denigrating Italian men but was describing her husband as "a very patient, independent and private person. No one in the world thinks more highly of my husband than I do."[11] She stated that her husband had not been offended by the remark. Ferraro asked the press to wait until her financial information was released before drawing conclusions, but the press continued to print stories that repeated past coverage and speculated on Ferraro/Zaccaro's motives for not providing all the information sought by the press.

FERRARO'S APOLOGIA FOR FINANCES

The dramatic press conference on August 21, 1984 was described by one reporter as "the most critical single political moment an American woman had ever faced and one of the most memorable press conferences of modern times." The reporters at the press conference were described as a "wolfpack" but Ferraro was praised for showing "an astonishing knack for handling journalistic inquisitors. The reporters . . . .were as jumpy and eager as hounds." Even before the press conference, however, some reporters had drawn conclusions. In an editorial William Safire stated that the release of the information "will justify the initial reluctance of John Zaccaro to put his tax returns on the table. I suggest these answers will lead to a great many more questions." Safire was skeptical because Ferraro and Zaccaro "in their sworn public documents have laid a foundation of lies and evasion."[12]

During the conference Ferraro stated: "I probably brought it upon myself by promising more than I could deliver . . . .but I ended up delivering, didn't I." Members of the press agreed: "After two weeks of media coverage, enough to rival any soap opera for intensity and complexity of plot, Geraldine Ferraro's responses during a ninety-minute press conference left the public wondering whether its suspicions of sleaze had been over-aroused." Reporters referred to the press conference as a "Checkers for the 80's," but did see differences between the two events because Nixon "faced only the camera, not 200 reporters, and he had a script."[13]

Ferraro's apology to the press occurred in two stages: during the heat of the campaign she responded daily to the press, then dramatically in the press conference. Months later in her autobiography, *My Story*, she further explained and justified her actions. During both apologies she expressed the pain the accusations caused her and her family: "I knew what I was getting into. . . . I climbed into a boxing ring and I was ready to put on the gloves with any of the guys. But what they did was they took my husband who was standing on the side and pulled him into the ring."[14] At that point she stated that if she could have imagined the pain the campaign would inflict on her family she might have said no to Mondale's offer.

Although she had no proof, Ferraro believed that many of the attacks were based on her gender. She detailed how on many occasions she had to answer condescending questions from reporters as to whether she was strong enough to be commander-in-chief. In her autobiography she detailed a grilling she received on "Nightline" from Ted Koppel. Later Koppel was asked if he and other reporters were harder on Ferraro because she was a woman. "Yes we were," was his reply. She then argued that many of the press attacks were really character attacks on her Italian background. She quoted Ben Bradlee, executive editor of the *Washington Post*, to support her conclusion: "I don't think the press . . . .would have put that kind of energy into it if we'd been talking about somebody named 'Jenkins.'"[15]

Ferraro charged that the press knowingly printed errors that slanted a particular story. She illustrated that charge by pointing to press distortion of a remark she made to a student in Missouri. The student requested advice on whether to register as a Democrat or Republican. She asked the student's views on the nuclear arms race. He replied that he was too busy with homework to think about the issue. She then said that considering his priorities he ought to register as a Republican. The press picked up the story and made the remark seem vicious. Ferraro believed that if the public had known her side, they would have understood that it was a cheap shot.

Ferraro also claimed that the issue of family finances was blown out of proportion because the press did not understand the process she went through in preparing her reports. The first problem occurred because she had such a brief time to prepare records that would satisfy the Mondale campaign staff. She claimed she had only forty-eight hours.

During the press onslaught, Ferraro realized that any simple misstatement would be magnified. In her autobiography she attempted to explain how the mistake over her husband's tax forms occurred. Ferraro's staff drew up a press release that she read quickly, not picking up the statement that her husband would also release copies of his tax returns. She compounded that error when she announced that Zaccaro refused to release his forms: "I knew as soon as I saw the ripple through the press corps that I had made a major mistake. But there was no way to take back the words. Instead I tried to change the subject — and only made it worse" with the comment about Italian men. After that comment she realized that her candidacy "had been struck an almost fatal blow before the campaign had begun. And I had done it to myself."[16]

During the press conference, she relied on the stasis of quality in answering charges by the press. She said that she would answer any question until the reporters were finished. This showed she had nothing to hide. That stasis was further illustrated in her quote that "no other candidate in history had ever gone so public with his or her financial affairs. But at the same time, no other candidate had ever had to undergo such a siege . . . .from the press."[17]

One other problem Ferraro faced was her own candor and feistiness. Television often showed segments of her "tossing off a funny line or bashing Reagan" while ignoring serious remarks. Her major problems in the campaign might have lessened if she had not been so blunt. For example she said on the tax issue she would have done better with less straightforward answers: "I would have tried to figure out a way to answer the question on whether my husband was going to release his taxes — not by telling the truth, I will always tell the truth — but I should have had a circuitous answer that was a nonanswer, which you know politicians and others as well can do."[18]

Although most articles stated that Ferraro's apology was persuasive, some remained unconvinced. A typical statement was printed in the *New York Times* on August 22: "It remained unresolved, however, whether Mrs. Ferraro's financial transactions and disclosures totally complied with the spirit and the letter of the law."[19]

After the press conference, the Ferraro campaign seemed to gain energy. At a convention of teachers, she stated: "Today is the first day of the rest of my campaign. . . . Normally I began a speech by saying I'm delighted to be here. After this week I have to tell you I'm absolutely thrilled."[20]

But the press would not let the issue die. Many articles in the press continued to question why Ferraro did not include Zaccaro's finances in her congressional disclosure statements. The articles admitted that his finances did not have to be included because of a "narrow exemption" in the requirements. The words "narrow exemption" seemed to use the stasis of quality to question her actions. Reporters also added unsupported comments to stories. For example, a writer in *Newsweek* commented on the couple having "remarkably little taxable income from 1974 to 1977." When Ferraro and Zaccaro refused to discuss their finances before 1978 the reporter added, "but judging from their comfortable Forest Hills lifestyle, the most plausible explanation is that they were sheltering their income heavily."[21]

Eventually, even members of the press began to question whether they had been too harsh in their scrutiny. Those who accepted this view stated that Ferraro was attacked for being a woman and an Italian: "If Geraldine Ferraro is stoned without defenders, she will be only the first to fall. The stones will always be there, piled high, ready for the next Italian, the next Catholic, the next woman."[22]

ACCUSATIONS BY CATHOLIC LEADERS

The accusations by Catholic leaders were again based on the stasis of fact. They claimed that a letter Ferraro signed in addition to other members of Congress for Catholics for Free Choice misrepresented the church's position on abortion. The accusations focused not only on past policies but also questioned future policies Ferraro might enact once she became vice-president.

Although Ferraro was a practicing Catholic, the leadership of the church was closer to President Reagan than Ferraro on many issues of morality, especially abortion. Reagan appeared in Catholic churches where he stated: "We are for life and against abortion." At some Catholic churches Reagan heard himself openly praised by Catholic leaders.[23]

At the beginning of the campaign there seemed to have been an informal agreement among Catholic leaders not to speak for or against specific candidates. Monsignor Daniel Haye, general secretary of the United States Catholic Conference, said his organization would not comment on specific candidates but he believed that "it's very likely that one or more individual bishops will feel compelled to comment specifically on Mrs. Ferraro's position on abortion." In their public statements bishops normally clustered issues such as abortion, nuclear war, and poverty into a "seamless garment."

The topics were clustered because speaking out strongly on one issue might cause other equally important issues to be ignored.[24]

In breaking the seamless garment, Archbishop O'Connor argued that Ferraro had "given the impression . . . .that the Catholic teaching on abortion is not monolithic . . . .that you can be a good Catholic and believe in abortion." In reality, O'Connor claimed, "there is no variance, there is no flexibility, there is no leeway . . . . It is the task of the church to reaffirm that abortion is death. It is the killing of an innocent creature." Bishop Law of Boston admitted that Catholics could disagree with church policy but added, "that to say they held a Catholic position was a contradiction in terms. 'A Catholic believes as a Catholic.'" The bishops began to explain church beliefs. As Archbishop O'Connor explained: "It is my responsibility to spell out for Catholics what the Church teaches. . . . If anyone in public office wished to differ, wished to say that it is not Catholic teaching, then that individual ought to prove it wrong."[25]

The bishops made it clear that Catholics should support politicians who accepted the Catholic view on abortion. O'Connor stated that he could understand how Catholic politicians would have a problem reconciling their Catholic beliefs and government duties. "Nevertheless," he added, "I cannot see how, in good conscience, a Catholic who believes the teaching of the Catholic Church can vote to fund abortion." Bishop Law named abortion as the crucial issue of the campaign: "We are not saying that you must vote for a particular candidate. . . . But we are saying that when you make up your mind this is the crucial issue." The message was clear — Ferraro supported abortion so Catholics should not vote for her.

Besides the charges by Catholic leaders that she was proabortion, Ferraro faced what she believed was an organized campaign to disrupt her appearances by antiabortion groups. Hecklers tried to interrupt her and she faced signs proclaiming slogans such as "Ferraro-A Catholic Judas" and "I'm Glad Ferraro Wasn't My Mother."[26]

FERRARO'S APOLOGY ON ABORTION

Ferraro was not prepared for the depth of feeling and bigotry that abortion would unleash. She was stunned by hecklers who continually tried to interrupt her speeches and rallies. The protestors caused her to make her first campaign mistake. The day after her nomination an antiabortion protestor held up a sign stating "Ferraro, what kind of Catholic are you?" In response to a question about the sign she implied that Reagan was not a good Christian. The press immediately pounced on the issue. She tried to explain that she was talking about the unfairness of Reagan's policies but the press refused to accept the explanation.

Ferraro preferred that religion not be an issue in the campaign. She said her religion was private, and reaffirmed her faith in the church. However she recognized abortion was the most difficult subject a Catholic woman must face.

Ferraro saw Archbishop O'Connor as a leader who focused on one issue while ignoring other equally important ones. For example, Ferraro believed he was ignoring the real suffering of the living while expressing concern for potential problems of the unborn.

Ferraro apologized in a speech at Scranton, Pennsylvania on September 12. A large crowd was on hand and the bishop of Scranton had scheduled a press conference immediately following her speech. She told her staff that she was going to talk about religion and public policy. She reiterated her belief that religion was a private matter so she was upset because others were using religion as a means of gaining political advantages. She quoted John F. Kennedy in his Houston Ministerial speech: " 'I do not speak for my Church in public matters, and the Church does not speak for me.' That's exactly my position today."[27] She believed that the bishops had a right to speak out but that as a public official she had the duty to maintain freedom of religion. She felt that the imposition of her religion on others was a violation of her private duty.

She faced criticism by the bishops on her supposed statements that Catholic teachings on abortion are not monolithic. The disagreement was over the wording of the letter that was sent to fifty Catholic members of Congress before a briefing on "The Abortion Issue in the Political Process." Ferraro argued that the letter referred to beliefs of individual Catholics not church doctrine. She stated that the letter did not claim that the church's teachings were not monolithic but the church's position on abortion could not be monolithic because many American Catholics did not agree with church leaders on the issue. She argued that she had never misrepresented the church's teachings in her public statements.

CONCLUSION

The accusations by the press had a profound effect on the Ferraro campaign. Although Ferraro proved she could endure a great deal of pressure, the controversy over finances took its toll. Ferraro was transformed from "Joan of Arc to just another politician."[28]

The argument could easily be made that Ferraro never really had a chance in either debate because of the power of her opponents. The press virtually controlled the form and content of the debate. Ferraro could not get her message to the public without cooperation by the media and the members of the media were her accusers. The debate over abortion was based on an issue on which people's positions were so hardened that little persuasion could occur.

The motives for the actions by members of the press and Catholic hierarchy in this case are not as clear as one might hope but their effect was significant. Ferraro's image was so tainted that she decided not to run for the U.S. Senate in 1986.

A study of accusations by the press and Ferraro's apologies make it clear that the theory of accusation and apology can be extended into studies broader than "speech acts." Critics can use the theory as a means of discovering the motives and arguments in discussions of the broader issues of American life, issues such as those surrounding Ferraro's campaign, that focus on the basic religion and moral beliefs in the United States.

NOTES

[1]The author read the *New York Times'* coverage of the 1984 election beginning with Ferraro's nomination. The *New York Times* was chosen because Ferraro was from New York so it was assumed that the coverage would be very thorough. The author often found himself extremely frustrated with the unfairness of the coverage by that paper and the weekly news magazine.

[2]Howell Raines, "Mondale Decision: Praise Ignores Risks," *New York Times*, July 13, 1984, pp. A-1, A-11; Steven V. Roberts, "Few in Poll Expressing Confidence," *New York Times*, July 16, 1984, p. A-9; and Geraldine Ferraro, *My Story* (New York: Bantam Books, 1985), p. 73.

[3]Ferraro, *My Story,* p. 162.

[4]Walter Shapiro, "Furor Over Ferraro Finances," *Newsweek*, August 27, 1984, p. 21, and John Herbers, "Activism in Faith: Big Shift Since '60," *New York Times*, September 12, 1986, p. B-9.

[5]Frank Lynn, "Tristate Democrats Agree 'Ferraro Factor' Helps," *New York Times*, July 23, 1984, p. A-12.

[6]"So Who's That in the Gray Suit," *Time*, August 13, 1984, p. 18, and Maureen Dowd, "Goodbye Male Ticket, Hello Etiquette Gap," *New York Times*, July 18, 1984, p. A-20.

[7]William Safire, "The Unhappy Family," *New York Times*, July 20, 1984, p. A-27; Shapiro, "Furor Over Ferraro Finances," p. 21; Kurt Andersen, "Letting Ferraro be Ferraro," *Time*, August 6, 1987, p. 118; and Kurt Andersen, "Spotlight on the Seconds," *Time*, October 15, 1984, pp. 25-26.

[8]Jane Perlez, "Ferraro Staff Has Troubles in Midst of Financial Ordeal," *New York Times*, August 27, 1984, p. A-10.

[9]Tom Morganthau, "Ferraro in the Limelight," *Newsweek*, August 6, 1984, p. 16; Steven V. Roberts, "Law Firm Files a Complaint Over Ferraro Finance Forms," *New York Times*, August 8, 1984, p. B-6; and Ralph Blumenthal, "Rep. Ferraro's Financial Status Starts To Emerge," *New York Times*, July 18, 1984, p. A-20.

[10]Jane Perlez, "Ferraro to Disclose Her Tax Forms, But Husband's Will Remain Private," *New York Times*, August 13, 1984, p. A-16, and "Caesar's Husband," *New York Times*, August 14, 1984, p. A-22.

[11]Jane Perlez, "Ferraro Says She Is Hoping Spouse Will Disclose Taxes," *New York Times*, August 15, 1984, p. B-7.

[12]Kurt Andersen, "Show and Tell," *Time*, September 3, 1984, p. 14; Jonathan Alter, "Is the Press Fair to Ferraro?" *Newsweek*, November 24, 1985, p. 55; and William Safire, "Patterns of Deceit," editorial, *New York Times*, August 20, 1984, p. A-23.

[13]Sam Roberts, "Ferraro Denies Any Wrongdoing But Admits Some Mistakes Were Made," *New York Times*, August 22, 1984, p. B-5; "Getting Off Sleazy St.," *Commonwealth*, September 21, 1984, p. 485; Charles Krauthammer, "Pietygate: School for Scandal," *Time*, September 10, 1984, p. 76; and Andersen, "Show and Tell," p. 18.

[14]"Ferraro Recounts Second Thoughts On Her Nomination, Citing Scrutiny," *New York Times*, August 25, 1984, p. A-29.

[15]Ferraro, *My Story*, 168, 274.

[16]*Ibid.*, p. 156.

[17]*Ibid.*, pp. 167-68, 173.

[18]Jane Perlez, "Husband Plans to Join Ferraro in Disclosing Tax Forms Tomorrow," *New York Times*, August 19, 1984, p. 30; Ferraro, *My Story*, pp. 242-43 and 276-77; and Sandra Salmens, "Abortion Foes Assail Mondale Ticket," *New York Times*, August 4, 1984, p. A-6.

[19]"The Ferraro File," editorial, *New York Times*, August 22, 1984, p. A-22; and Roberts, "Ferraro Denies Any Wrongdoing," p. B-5.

[20]Jane Perlez, "Ferraro Returns To Campaign Trail," *New York Times*, August 23, 1984, p. B-10.

[21]Jeff Gerth, "Ferraro Disclosure Data Amended to Fix Errors," *New York Times*, October 3, 1984, p. A-25, and Melinda Beck, "The Ferraro Finances," *Newsweek*, September 3, 1984, p. 22.

[22]Ferraro, *My Story*, p. 234-35.

[23]Robert D. McFadden, "Archbishop Calls Ferraro Mistaken On Abortion Rule," *New York Times*, September 10, 1984, p. A-1.

[24]Salmans, "Abortion Foes Assail Mondale Ticket," p. A-6.

[25]John Herbers, "Archbishop Explains Abortion Stand," *New York Times*, September 23, 1984, p. 34; and Michael Oreskes, "Archbishop Cites Duty to Correct Politicians on Church Teachings," *New York Times,* August 25, 1984, p. A-1.

[26]McFadden, "Archbishop Calls Ferraro Mistaken," p. B-9; Fox Butterfield, "Archbishop of Boston Cites Abortion as 'Critical Issue,'" *New York Times*, September 8, 1984, p. B-13; and Ed Magnuson, "Pressing the Abortion Issue," *Time*, September 24, 1984, p. 18.

[27]Ferraro, *My Story*, pp. 213, 219, and Jane Perlez, "Ferraro Says Religion Won't Influence Policy," *New York Times*, September 13, 1984, p. B-16.

[28]Quoted in Jack W. Germond and Jules Witcover, *Wake Us When It's Over* (New York: Macmillan, 1985), p. 447.

INFORMATION SOURCES ON THE SPEECH SET

The Accusations

The media's accusations were printed in numerous newspapers and newsweeklies. For the most significant ones see: Geraldine Ferraro, "Nomination Acceptance Address, July 19, 1984," *Vital Speeches of the Day*, August 15, 1984, pp. 644-46; Geraldine Ferraro, "Why I Believe Women Must Exercise Their Political Clout," *Glamour*, November 1984, p. 134.; Jonathan Alter, "Is the Press Fair to Ferraro?" *Newsweek*, November 24, 1984, p. 55; Kurt Andersen, "Letting Ferraro Be Ferraro," *Time*, August 6,

1984, p. 18; Kurt Andersen, "Show and Tell," *Time*, September 3, 1984, p. 18; Kurt Andersen, "Spotlight on the Seconds," *Time*, October 15, 1984, pp. 25-26; Melinda Beck, "The Ferraro Finances," *Newsweek*, September 3, 1984, p. 22; Jeff Garth, "Ferraro and Husband Release Tax and Financial Data," *New York Times*, August 21, 1984, p. B-8; "Getting Off Sleazy St.," *Commonweal*, September 21, 1984, p. 485; Jane Perlez, "Ferraro Says She is Hoping Spouse Will Disclose Taxes," *New York Times*, August 15, 1984, p. B-7; Jane Perlez, "Ferraro to Disclose Her Tax Forms, But Husband's Will Remain Private," *New York Times*, August 13, 1984, p. A-16; Howell Raines, "Mondale Decision: Praise Ignores Risk," *New York Times*, July 13, 1984, p. A-1; Walter Shapiro, "Furor Over Ferraro Finances," *Newsweek*, August 27, 1984, p. 21; and "So Who's That in the Gray Suit," *Time*, August 13, 1984, p. 18.

For transcripts of the accusations by Catholic leaders see: "O'Connor Interview Excerpts," *New York Times*, September 10, 1984, p. B-9.; "Boston Prelate on the Issue of Abortion," *New York Times*, September 23, 1984, p. A-34; and "Text of Statement by Bishop On Church Role in Politics," *New York Times*, October 14, 1984, p. 30.

Ferraro's Apology

For incomplete transcripts of Ferraro's apologies see: "Excerpts From Interview on Religion With Ferraro on Campaign Plane," *New York Times*, August 14, 1984, p. A-21.; "Text of Ferraro Statement on Loans and Zaccaro's Properties," *New York Times*, August 21, 1984, p. B-8.; "Excerpts From Ferraro's News Conference About Finances," *New York Times*, August 22, 1984, p. B-6; "'82 Letter Signed by Ferraro," *New York Times*, September 11, 1984, p. A-26; and Geraldine Ferraro, *My Story* (New York: Bantam Books, 1985).

Selected Bibliography

Drew, Elizabeth. *Campaign Journal: The Political Events of 1983-1984*. New York: Macmillan, 1985.

Germond, Jack, and Jules Witcover. *Wake Us When It's Over*. New York: Macmillan, 1985.

Goldman, Peter, and Tony Fuller. *The Quest for the Presidency 1984*. New York: Bantam Books, 1985.

Henry, William A. *Visions of America: How We Saw the 1984 Election*. Boston: Atlantic Monthly Press, 1985.

Elie Wiesel vs.
President Ronald Reagan:
The Visit to Bitburg

Robert V. Friedenberg

On June 6, 1944, allied forces under the command of General Dwight David Eisenhower came ashore at Normandy. During the months that followed, as the allied armies fought their way across Europe, the horrors of Nazi Germany were revealed to all the world. Auschwitz, Buchenwald, Bergen-Belsen, Dachau, Treblinka, and the sites of other concentration camps were transformed from mere places on a map to haunting names that evoked nothing so much as the remembrance of man's inhumanity to man.

In June of 1984, allied leaders, including President Ronald Reagan, commemorated the fortieth anniversary of the D-Day landing at Normandy. The ceremonies also hailed four decades of peace and the economic recovery of Europe. But the nation that had experienced the most remarkable recovery in the four decades since the war, the Federal Republic of Germany, was not invited to participate.

Five months later, in November of 1984, during his state visit to Washington, West German Chancellor Helmut Kohl, evidently disturbed by the lack of German involvement in the prior anniversary celebrations, urged President Reagan to visit a German military cemetery during Reagan's forthcoming European visit. Kohl is also reported to have suggested a visit to Dachau to the president.

In January and February of 1985, White House staff, primarily under the direction of Michael Deaver, working closely with German officials, developed plans for the president's European trip. The advance team approved a visit to Kolmeshohe military cemetery at Bitburg, West Germany. On April 11, the White House announced the itinerary for the president's eleven-day trip to Europe. Reagan, accompanied by Kohl, was scheduled to lay a wreath at the German military cemetery at Bitburg. Within twenty-four hours of the announcement of the president's itinerary, vigorous protest over the wreath-laying ceremony, primarily from veterans' and Jewish groups, caused the White House to announce that the president's plans were subject to review. The controversy grew intense four days later, on April 15, when widespread news reports revealed that the Bitburg cemetery contained not only the graves of German soldiers, but also the graves of German Waffen SS troops.

The SS, whose members were entirely volunteers prior to 1940 and about two-thirds volunteers throughout its existence, was officially defined as a criminal organization by the international military tribunal at Nuremberg. Its criminal actions, according to the Nuremberg tribunal, included "shooting of unarmed prisoners of war.... widespread murder and ill-treatment of the civilian population of occupied territories. . . . guarding and administration of concentration camps. . . . brutal treatment of the inmates of the concentration camps which was carried out as a result of the general policy of the SS which was that the inmates were radical inferiors to be treated only with contempt. . . . many massacres and atrocities in occupied territories."[1] Moreover, the graves of the SS members buried at Bitburg were those of an SS unit charged both with the massacre of over six hundred civilians in one incident and the December 17, 1944, massacre of over one hundred unarmed American prisoners of war.

Throughout late April the controversy grew. On April 16, the White House, responding to the controversy, announced that the president's itinerary would also include a visit to the Bergen-Belsen concentration camp. On April 17, fifty-three members of the Senate, under the leadership of Senators Arlen Spector of Pennsylvania and Howard Metzenbaum of Ohio, petitioned the president, suggesting that his visit "would be most unfortunate." They "strongly urged" that he cancel his visit to the cemetery and replace it with an activity that better commemorated the holocaust. On April 25, the House of Representatives joined the controversy, as 257 members signed a letter to German Chancellor Kohl urging him to release the president from his obligation to visit the Bitburg cemetery. The following day, eighty-six members of the Senate served as cosponsors of a resolution appealing to the president to "reassess his planned itinerary." On April 30, one day before the president's departure for Europe, 390 members of the House voted to ask him to pay tribute to more appropriate symbols of current democracy in Germany and cancel his visit to Bitburg.[2]

ELIE WIESEL'S ACCUSATIONS

The two most notable speeches of accusation during this controversy were delivered by Elie Wiesel. Chairman of the United States Holocaust Memorial Council, the preeminent scholar and chronicler of the holocaust, one of the major literary figures of the twentieth century, winner of the 1986 Nobel Peace Prize, and a holocaust survivor, Wiesel first spoke on April 18. On that afternoon, Secretary of State George Schultz preceded Wiesel as one of the principle speakers in a ceremony honoring the fortieth anniversary of the American liberation of the concentration camps. The ceremony was held in the rotunda of the Capitol, attended by numerous members of Congress, the cabinet, and other dignitaries, and hence was exceptionally well reported. The following day, April 19, in a White House ceremony, Wiesel was presented the Congressional Gold Medal by President Reagan. Wiesel utilized the opportunity in accepting this award to deliver his second speech of accusation. This speech was also exceptionally well reported.

The occasion clearly influenced Elie Wiesel's speech of April 18. A ceremony honoring the victims of the holocaust and their American liberators in the Capitol rotunda suggested a rhetorical situation that demanded a commemorative speech of tribute, not a speech of accusation. Nevertheless, this occasion presented Wiesel with an opportunity to focus national attention on the propriety of the president's Bitburg visit. Hence, Wiesel had to balance the demands of a commemorative speech of tribute with the demands of a speech of accusation.

Wiesel opened his address by utilizing a series of balanced sentences to remind his audience of those who were killed in the holocaust. He found that they "shared one dominant obsession: to be remembered." "Forty years later," Wiesel continued, "we know what they, then, could not know, that they were alone outside society and civilization, outside time." Throughout the first half of his address, Wiesel delivered a speech of commemoration. He directed his audience's attention to the essential evils of the holocaust, not only that Nazi Germany attempted genocide and killed millions, but also that the victims were "forgotten by humankind."[3]

"Why," asked Wiesel as he made the transition from commemoration to accusation, "was so little done to save them?" Wiesel noted that this remains an extremely painful question for it demonstrates the insensitivity of ourselves and our allies "to Jewish agony and death." However, Wiesel took some comfort from the fact that Americans "are now endeavoring to serve the noble cause of memory." In honoring the memory of those who perished in the holocaust, Wiesel claimed, we do not seek revenge or humiliation. "We seek, however, a commitment to memory and true reconciliation, one based upon historical truth."

Wiesel opened the accusatory section of the speech by observing that the holocaust should teach us many lessons, one of which "is to be sensitive to other people's feelings." But Wiesel believed that Reagan had not remembered, had not been sensitive to that memory: "We look with under-standing upon our government's efforts to deal delicately with German sensitivities. But what about American sensibility? Why is that not a fac-tor in the high-level decision process? Did no one consider the pain and shame some, if not most, Americans would feel upon learning that the presi-dent of the United States plans to visit a cemetery in which there are a good number of SS graves."

Wiesel argued that the president's impending wreath laying at Bitburg was an act that would bring shame to all Americans by dishonoring the memory of those who died in the holocaust. Moreover, he pointed out that the SS killed thousands of Americans, particularly at the Battle of the Bulge, and they "slaughtered defenseless American war prisoners at Malmedy." "Why," Wiesel asked in poignant anaphora, "did no one at the decision-making level think of what all those Americans who lost a son, a father, a brother, might feel as they watched their leader — our leader — visit such a cemetery? Mr. Secretary [Schultz] please be our emissary. Tell those who need to know that our pain is genuine, our outrage deep and our perplexity infinite."

Wiesel elegantly concluded his remarks with balanced antitheses and parallel sentences characteristic of his style throughout his remarkable address: "We invoke the past for the sake of the future: not to dwell on our pain, but to exorcise it. We remember what has been done to the victims, not to spite the world, but to enlighten it. If we forget, we too will be forgotten; but if we remember, we too will be remembered."

Wiesel's *kategoria* of April 18 demonstrated many characteristics of the accusatory rhetoric generated by the president's visit to Bitburg. First, Wiesel presented an accusation against a policy, the decision to lay a wreath at the Bitburg cemetery. He then defined the wreath-laying ceremony as an act of homage to Nazi Germany and the SS. This was most evident in the passages where Wiesel questioned "American sensibility," implying that many Americans would suffer because they would interpret Reagan's act as one of homage. It might be noted that other accusatory rhetoric, particularly that found in the American Jewish press coverage of this affair, utilized the stasis of definition to a far greater extent than did Wiesel.[4] Wiesel also hinged his argument on the classical stasis of quality (see Glossary). For an American president, the one figure who best symbolizes the entire nation, to lay a wreath at the grave of German soldiers who defended Nazi Germany and particularly SS members, would be an act that shamed all Americans by dishonoring the memory of all those who were both victimized by, and who fought against, Nazi Germany. Wiesel's accusations were not focused simply on President Reagan. Rather, he spoke of "high level decision makers," "policy planners," "those who need to know," indeed, all who may have forgotten the lessons of the holocaust. This was not an accusation directed entirely at Ronald Reagan. The president simply served to represent all of those who may have forgotten the lessons of the holocaust. While Wiesel indicted Reagan, the charge was intended for all of those in power who had forgotten the holocaust. Finally, it should be observed that Wiesel's use of language — his word choice, parallelism, balance, and rhythm — lifted this speech to a high level of rhetorical eloquence. The following day, April 19, in a White House ceremony, President Reagan presented Elie Wiesel with the Congressional Gold Medal. This rhetorical situation constrained Wiesel's opportunities at accusation, but it certainly did not eliminate them. The rhetorical situation called for a speech of acceptance. In the body of the address, Wiesel thanked those who granted him the award and those who helped him to earn it. Nevertheless, in the body of the address he also laid the groundwork for the accusations that were made in the conclusion. This award belonged, said Wiesel, "to all those who remember what SS killers have done to their victims. It was given to me by the American people for my writings, teaching, and for my testimony. When I write, I feel my invisible teachers standing over my shoulders, reading my words and judging their veracity." Wiesel additionally observed in the body of his speech that his feelings for the American liberators of the concentration camps "nourishes me to the end of my days and will do so." He also praised the United States as the principle force for moral authority and compassion among all the world's nations. Having praised those who helped him gain the award, all those who remembered the holocaust, and those who granted him this award, the American people, Wiesel then moved to the conclusion of his address where he shifted into an accusatory tone.

Speaking directly to the president, Wiesel opened his conclusion by claiming that his Jewish heritage commands him "to speak truth to power": "So may I speak to you Mr. President with respect and admiration. . . . We have met four or five times. And each time I come away enriched for I know of your commitment to humanity. And therefore I am convinced as you have told us earlier when we spoke that you were not aware of the presence of SS graves in the Bitburg cemetery. Of course you didn't know. But now we all are aware. May I, Mr. President, if it's possible at all, implore you to do something else, to find a way, to find another way, another site. That place, Mr. President, is not your place. Your place is with the victims of the SS." Wiesel then noted that "we know there are political and strategic reasons" for the president's actions; nevertheless, "the issue here is not politics, but good and evil."[5]

Like his accusation the preceding day, Wiesel's accusation of April 19 was muted by the rhetorical situation in which it was delivered. Hence, his accomplishments were all the more impressive, for he fulfilled the rhetorical demands of the acceptance situation while at the same time fulfilling his own agenda of delivering his accusation. Wiesel argued definition by implication. When Wiesel addressed the president directly, he implied that the president's wreath laying would be defined as an act of homage to those buried in the cemetery. He implored the president to avoid Bitburg, urging the president, "your place is with the victims of the SS." If a presidential visit were defined as an act of homage, as Wiesel felt it would be, clearly that act of homage should be paid to the victims. Wiesel also centered on the classical stasis of quality. "The issue here," he claimed, "is not politics, but good and evil." The president's proposed policy was evil, for to honor evil is to do evil.

Though Reagan still served for Wiesel as a representative of all those who may have forgotten the lessons of the holocaust, this speech did focus directly on the president. Wiesel accused not "high level decision makers or policy planners," but Ronald Reagan. While the accusations were focused more specifically on the president in this speech than in the speech of April 18, Wiesel explicitly acknowledged the president's "commitment to humanity." The fact that this speech was delivered with president Reagan in the audience, that parts of it were addressed directly to the president, and that it was given in the White House, all made it a more personal accusation than the one delivered the previous day. Yet, Wiesel clearly and appropriately remained respectful and deferential to the president.

Finally, as in his previous address, Wiesel's April 19 speech again illustrated his eloquence. Wiesel's word choice, sentence structure, use of concrete imagery, use of balance, parallelism, and rhythm, all combined to make this an eloquent address. This eloquence and the drama inherent in the White House situation made a memorable rhetorical event.

RONALD REAGAN'S APOLOGIA

The first observation that should be made about the president's responses to the accusations of Wiesel and others concerns the timing of his remarks. The first direct response made by the president was forced on him by questions in a press conference. The second response was forced on him by the necessity to present an award to his principle accuser. Both of these responses were generated primarily by the rhetorical situation. It was not until after he laid the wreath at Bitburg that the president actually delivered a major address on this affair. Clearly, the president sought to downplay this controversy by avoiding it.

In his press conference of April 18, the president was asked about his impending visit to Bitburg. Rhetoricians have identified a variety of strategies utilized in successful apologies.[6] Reagan drew upon several of them in this press conference. First, apologies are often most successful if delivered in a rhetorical situation where individuals other than the apologist seem to be in control. A good performance in a risky situation, such as a press conference, often seems to enhance public acceptance of the apologia.[7] It was not necessarily an accident that Reagan's first response was made in a press conference.

A second common strategy utilized in apologies is to deny intent, arguing that a statement or action has been misunderstood. This was the heart of President Reagan's press conference apologia. He utilized the classical stasis of definition to suggest that the wreath-laying ceremony at Bitburg was not an evil act, nor an act of homage to the soldiers of Nazi Germany. Rather, he defined it as an act of reconciliation between two staunch allies, marking "the day that 40 years ago the world took a sharp turn."[8] Throughout his answer, the president labored to define his impending actions as an act of reconciliation.

The president also used a third strategy that is characteristic of successful apologies. Bolstering strategies are attempts by the apologist to identify with something viewed favorably by the audience in order to "bolster" his image. In this press conference, the president announced that he would visit Dachau, and that "I am more than happy to do it." Subsequently, for logistical reasons, the concentration camp actually visited was Bergen-Belsen. Nevertheless, the linking of a visit to the German military cemetery with a visit to a concentration camp was a bolstering strategy the president used to identify with something his audience would view favorably.

Ronald Reagan's overall effectiveness in this press conference was badly diminished when, speaking of the German soldiers and SS troops buried at Bitburg, he claimed they "were victims just as surely as the citizens in the concentration camps." The president had preceded this statement with the observation that most of the men buried at Bitburg were drafted and had little choice but to serve Nazi Germany. His characterization of both German military personnel and concentration camp inmates as "victims" badly undermined his attempt at redefinition. His comment suggested that the Nazi soldiers buried at Bitburg were worthy of the homage paid the concentration camp victims, and that was just what Reagan's critics asserted his visit would demonstrate. It weakened his efforts to have his visit defined as an act of reconciliation, and strengthened the perception his critics fostered—that his visit was an act of homage toward Nazi Germany.[9]

The following day, April 19, President Reagan presented the Congressional Gold Medal to his principle accuser, Elie Wiesel. The rhetorical situation clearly called for a speech of presentation. However, Wiesel's presence made it impossible for the president to ignore the accusations concerning his Bitburg visit. The president's remarks tactfully, but forcefully, defended his position.

Again, Reagan relied primarily on the classical stasis of definition and on bolstering strategies. He never spoke directly about his impending actions. Rather, he repeated his theme of "a spirit of reconciliation, even between former soldiers who fought each other on the battlefields," and stressed the desirability of fostering the growth of that spirit. This rhetoric, though, must be interpreted with Bitburg in mind. Reagan tried to argue that his Bitburg visit should be defined as an act of reconciliation, taken in the context of a growing "spirit of reconciliation between the peoples of the allied nations and the peoples of Germany." This speech also evidenced a heavy reliance on bolstering strategies, more so than the preceding day's press conference. Reagan tried to associate the United States, and by implication his own actions, with the establishment of Israel, the continued defense of that nation, the humanitarian rescue of Ethiopian Jewry, and the campaign on behalf of Soviet Jewry. His record on these issues was a strong one. Moreover, his emphasis on Soviet Jewry was consistent with some of his most publicized speaking, in which he had characterized the Soviet Union as an evil empire. Although this was ostensibly a speech of presentation, it attracted attention primarily because of the president's attempts at apologia.[10]

Reagan's remarks on April 18 and 19 were constrained by the rhetorical situations in which they were made. His substantial apologia was delivered minutes after he had visited the German war cemetery on May 5, at Bitburg air base. Addressing an audience of German and American officials and American servicemen, Reagan repeatedly attempted to define his action as one of reconciliation. His opening words set the tone of the entire address: "To the veterans and families of American servicemen who still carry the scars and feel the painful losses of that war, our gesture of reconciliation with the German people today in no way minimizes our love and honor for those who fought and died for our country." He continued, "To the survivors of the Holocaust, your terrible suffering has made you ever vigilant against evil. Many of you are worried that reconciliation means forgetting. Well, I promise you, we will never forget."[11] Aiming his opening at the two groups most likely to be upset by his action, Reagan clearly sought to have that action defined as an act of reconciliation.

The need to foster reconciliation between former foes became the dominant theme of this address. After directly addressing the two groups that might be most disturbed by his actions, Reagan mourned "the human wreckage of totalitarianism," but found that in the case of World War II something desirable had resulted. "Too often in the past each war only planted the seeds of the next. We celebrate today the reconciliation between our two nations that has liberated us from that cycle of destruction." Reagan then illustrated his point by citing many joint accomplishments of West Germany and the United States, and concluded this long passage by observing that our reconciliation promised "a future to be filled with hope, friendship, and freedom."

At this point the president presented an extended story, which is so characteristic of his rhetoric. The story, constituting fully 25 percent of his speech, described a German peasant woman who shared her humble home with injured German and American soldiers on Christmas Eve during the Battle of the Bulge. Reagan concluded the story by applying the obvious moral to the current situation. "Those boys," he observed, "reconciled brief-

ly in the midst of war. Surely, we allies in peacetime should honor the reconciliation of the last 40 years." Thus, throughout the first three-quarters of
this speech, Reagan consistently stressed the importance of reconciliation.
He wanted his actions to be judged in this context and his principle rhetorical strategy was to define the wreath-laying ceremony at Bitburg as an act
of reconciliation.

Reagan also bolstered in this speech. Near the end of his speech, he
noted that "the struggle for freedom is not complete, for today much of the
world is still cast in totalitarian darkness." He then deftly identified himself
with individuals and groups his audience might view favorably because of
their resistance to totalitarianism. They included John F. Kennedy, Ber-
liners, Soviet Jews, Afghans, and others.

Reagan's speech at the Bitburg Air Base was a potent apologia, far
stronger rhetorically than his previous efforts. Doubtlessly, part of the
reason was the rhetorical situation. In his prior apologies, situational constraints inherent in press conferences and speeches of presentation limited
him; moreover, by responding extemporaneously in the press conference,
he made a serious error when he likened German soldiers to the victims of
concentration camps. At the Bitburg Air Base, Reagan prepared thoroughly in advance and spoke with virtually no other purpose than to justify his
action.

By more effectively utilizing the same two rhetorical strategies as he had
in his earlier presentations, definition and bolstering, Reagan made this
speech stronger. This speech was artistically a more satisfying apologia then
those which preceded it, characterized as it was by some of the hallmarks
of President Reagan's rhetoric, including the use of stories, stock characters, and references to a bright future.[12] Reagan's use of language, which
included frequent repetition and parallelism, also lifted this speech to a
more eloquent level than his earlier efforts.

CONCLUSIONS

Interviewed two weeks after the president's Bitburg visit, Elie Wiesel
characterized the consequences of that visit. "In the long run," he observed,
"the wounds will heal. After all he is the President and we must deal with
his policies, with his staff, with his administration. But the wounds are there
and the wounds are deep."[13] Clearly Wiesel, and the president's other
critics, found his actions and speeches unresponsive to their charges and insensitive to their feelings. However public opinion polls conducted
immediately after the Bitburg visit indicated that the public had a mixed
and divided reaction. A *New York Times*-CBS poll, conducted the day after
the visit claimed that 41 percent of the public supported the president's actions, 41 percent opposed, and 18 percent had no opinion. The same poll

indicated that the Bitburg incident "did not effect President Reagan's over-all standing with the public," and that his visit to Bergen-Belsen earlier in the day "diminished the public opposition to the Bitburg visit."[14] Though the vast majority of Congress opposed the president's visit and many of them voiced their objections in Congress, it remained for Elie Wiesel, in difficult rhetorical situations, to present two eloquent accusations against the president's Bitburg visit. Wiesel's accusations, leveled at a less rhetorical-ly skilled president, might have proven far more effective, for they were both outstanding speeches. However, although the president erred badly in his press conference of April 18, he was able subsequently to deflect the harm that might have been done to him by his accusers. His use of time to downplay the entire controversy, his use of symbolic actions, such as the visit to Bergen-Belsen, and his rhetorically strong apologia of May 5, all combined, in the public's mind, to greatly minimize the accusations of his opponents.

NOTES

[1]The best single chronology of the Bitburg incident can be found in *Bitburg in Moral and Political Perspective*, edited by Geoffrey H. Hartman (Bloomington: Indiana University Press, 1986), pp. xiii-xvi, 273-79. On Kohl's suggestion, see "Kohl Says He Urged Reagan To Visit A Nazi Camp," *New York Times*, April 17, 1985, p. A14.

[2]See "Reagan Reverses His German Plans," *New York Times*, April 17, 1985, p. A1.; "53 In Senate Ask Reagan To Cancel Cemetery Visit," *New York Times*, April 18, 1985, p. A1; "257 In The House Bid Kohl Cancel Cemetery Event," *New York Times*, April 26, 1985, p. A1; U.S. Congress, Senate, 99th Cong. 1st sess., April 26, 1985, Congressional Record, 131, p. S4860. The symbols most often suggested as appropriate were the home and grave of former chancellor Konrad Adenauer. See U.S. Congress, House, 99th Cong. 1st sess., April 29, 1985, Congressional Record, 131, pp. H2680-H2690.

[3]For Wiesel's speech see U.S. Congress, House, 99th Cong. 1st sess., April 18, 1985, Congressional Record, 131, pp. H2198-H2199.

[4]See "Reagan's Waterloo," *Washington Jewish Week*, May 9, 1985, p. 18, and "Defying Logic," *The Jewish Record of Southwest Jersey*, April 26, 1985, p. 6.

[5]See Elie Wiesel, "Speech Accepting the Congressional Gold Medal," *Weekly Compilation of Presidential Documents* [hereafter *WCPD*] 21 (April

22, 1985): 478.

[6]For a concise summary of this literature see Judith S. Trent and Robert V. Friedenberg, *Political Campaign Communication* (New York: Praeger, 1983), pp. 223-27.

[7]Ellen Reid Gold, "Political Apologia: The Ritual of Self Defense," *Communication Monographs* 45 (1978): 310-12.

[8]Ronald Reagan, "Remarks in a Question-and-Answer Session with Regional Editors and Broadcasters, April 18, 1985," *WCPD* 21 (April 22, 1985): 474.

[9]This likening of the SS and German troops to holocaust victims became almost as much an issue in the American Jewish press as was the president's wreath-laying ceremony. See Kalman Sultanik, "An Overview of Bitburg," *Midstream* 31 (1985): 11-14, and the comments of Jewish leaders cited in *Washington Jewish Week*, April 25, 1985, p. 35.

[10]Ronald Reagan, Remarks at a White House Ceremony, April 19, 1985," *WCPD* 21 (April 22, 1985): pp. 447-78.

[11]Ronald Reagan, "Remarks at Bitburg Air Base, Federal Republic of Germany at Joint German-American Military Ceremony, May 5, 1985," *WCPD* 21 (May 13, 1985): 587.

[12]See Paul D. Erickson, *Reagan Speaks: The Making of an American Myth* (New York: New York University Press, 1985), pp. 32-94, for a detailed examination of Reagan's use of stories in his speaking and an examination of the importance of each of these characteristics to Reagan's rhetoric.

[13]"Americans Voice Anger on Bitburg," *New York Times*, May 6, 1985, p. A-8.

[14]"Public is Split on Bitburg, Poll Finds," *New York Times*, May 8, 1985, p. A-12. This latter conclusion was arrived at by the *Times* which compared the results of this poll with one taken on April 22 by the *Washington Post-ABC* polling service. The *Times* reported that the earlier poll found 51 percent against the Bitburg ceremony and 39 percent in favor.

INFORMATION SOURCES ON THE SPEECH SET

Elie Wiesel's Accusations

Wiesel's speeches of accusation were presented as parts of official government ceremonies. Hence, accurate texts of both speeches can be found in the appropriate government documents.

For the speech of April 18, delivered as part of an official Congressional ceremony in the House Rotunda honoring the fortieth anniversary of the liberation of the concentration camps by American soldiers, see the *Congressional Record*, Volume 131, pp. H2198-2199.

For the speech of April 19, delivered as part of a White House ceremony awarding Wiesel the Congressional Gold Medal, see the *Weekly Compilation of Presidential Documents* 21 (April 22, 1985): 478-79.

President Reagan's Apology

All of the President's comments can be found in the *Weekly Compilation of Presidential Documents*.

For his remarks in the press conference of April 18, see *Weekly Compilation of Presidential Documents* 21 (April 22, 1985): 474-76.

For his remarks awarding Wiesel the Congressional Gold Medal, see the *Weekly Compilation of Presidential Documents*, 21 (April 22, 1985): 477-78.

For his remarks at the Bitburg Air Base on May 5 see the *Weekly Compilation of Presidential Documents* 21 (May 13, 1985): 587-89.

Selected Bibliography

Bitburg In Moral and Political Perspective.   Edited by Geoffrey H. Hartman. Bloomington: Indiana University Press, 1986.

Boyarsky, Bill. *Ronald Reagan: His Life and Rise to the Presidency.* New York: Random House, 1981.

Brown, Robert McAfee. *Elie Wiesel: Messenger to All Humanity.* Notre Dame: University of Notre Dame Press, 1983.

Cannon, Lou. *Reagan.* New York: G. P. Putnam and Sons, 1982.

Cargas, Harry James. *Harry James Cargas in Conversation with Elie Wiesel*. New York: Paulist Press, 1976.

Dallek, Robert. *Ronald Reagan: The Politics of Symbolism*. Cambridge: Harvard University Press, 1984.

Erickson, Paul D. *Reagan Speaks: The Making Of An American Myth*. New York: New York University Press, 1985.

Fine, Ellen S. *Legacy of Night: The Literary Universe of Elie Wiesel*. Albany: State University of New York Press, 1982.

Roth, John K. *A Consuming Fire: Encounters With Elie Wiesel and The Holocaust*. Atlanta: John Knox Press, 1979.

Silberman, Charles E. "Speaking Truth to Power." Afterword to *A Certain People: American Jews and Their Lives Today*. New York: Summit Books, 1985.

Stern, Ellen. *Elie Wiesel: Witness for Life*. New York: Ktav Publishing House, 1982.

Sultanik, Kalman. "An Overview of Bitburg." *Midstream: A Monthly Jewish Review* 31 (1985): 11-14.

Wiesel, Elie. *Against Silence: The Voice and Vision Of Elie Wiesel*. Edited by Irving Abrahamson. 3 vols. New York: Holocaust Library, 1985.

President Ronald Reagan's Apologia on the Iran-Contra Affair

D. Ray Heisey

This analysis of how President Reagan encountered his critics in the Iran-Contra affair is tempered by the fact that the exchange is not yet finished. At the time of writing, daily disclosures and comments by principals in the affair continue to give good copy to the press. Whatever happens, no one will seriously argue with David Gergan's comment following release of the *Tower Commission Report*, "It will be impossible for the president to get back up on the mountain where he was."[1] Although this is true, the present essay is justified on the grounds that President Reagan at least recovered from his fall. How this was accomplished rhetorically as of March 1987 merits analysis as a first phase of a *kategoria-apologia* case study that will be one of the primary political communication encounters of the decade.

THE CLIMATE OF ACCUSATION AGAINST PRESIDENT REAGAN

The irony in this encounter was that the exigence that motivated the ensuing exposure was the good news of David Jacobsen's release as a hostage on November 2, 1986. Even before Jacobsen could return home, however, a small cloud, seeming no larger at first than a man's hand, appeared on the eastern horizon that eventually became a huge political storm of fury and destruction for the administration. That small cloud was a November 3 report in a hitherto unknown-to-Americans Beirut magazine, *Al Shiraa*, that American officials had covert contacts with Tehran. The *Al Shiraa* report, mediated by the American press, alleged the Middle East action by Washington, and thus was the first accusation. The next day, November 4, election day in the United States, but a celebration day in Iran — the seventh anniversary of the American embassy takeover — witnessed the second accusation. The speaker of the Iranian Majlis, Hashemi-Rafsanjani, addressing "tens of thousands" at an anniversary rally, and broadcast by Tehran radio, "disclosed details of an alleged visit to Iran by Robert McFarlane and several other special security advisers to President Reagan, claiming that the Americans arrived in a cargo plane and asked permission to deliver a message from Reagan to Iranian leaders." The request was accompanied by symbolic gifts such as a cake in the shape of a key, for opening new ties, and a Bible inscribed by Ronald Reagan. Rafsanjani claimed their proof was photographs of the visitors' passports and the Bible signed by Reagan. He further said that "McFarlane and four Americans accompanying him were detained in a hotel for five days and then expelled after offering military equipment in exchange for Iranian cooperation in curbing terrorism."[2]

The American press became the third accuser. The day after the Rafsanjani disclosure, the *Washington Post* reported as part of its front-page news story on that speech that "If the reported McFarlane visits to Tehran were linked to allowing even indirect arms or spare parts shipments to Iran, *it would represent a reversal of what had been Reagan administration policy.*"[3] This charge was the first accusation by Americans in the total sequence of the evolving *kategoria*. The force of this accusation was that it was given as a fact that built on the two previous alleged facts against a policy. This additional charge, by one of the nation's most credible newspapers, bolstered the accusation by including the stasis of definition. If the Reagan action were defined as "a reversal of policy," it suggested an inconsistency that needed to be explained. Indeed, the *Washington Post* on November 6, 1986, placed the full force of its editorial page behind the accusation when it published "The Iranian Connection," which concluded:

> The other day we criticized the French government for contemplating, according to widespread French press accounts, arms sales to Syria and preferential treatment of an accused terrorist, if Syria would assist in the return of French hostages. Nothing France was accused of is as serious as the suggestion that the United States has considered altering a principal tenet of its Middle East policy to cultivate Iranian "moderates" and reclaim American hostages. To move from formal neutrality in a war to a position facilitating some measure of resupply of the invading state would be a real departure. Is it true? What is true? We understand that there are sometimes necessary undercover diplomatic moves that cannot be explained without endangering a benign purpose or putting a negotiating partner, who has trusted one's discretion, at risk. But Mr. Reagan badly needs to report what can be reported about this business; he needs to put to rest the incredible implications of the Iranian version of the story.

The editorial politely demanded that the Reagan administration make a reply because of "the incredible implications" of making "an offer to help enable arms" to get to Iran if the Iranians would "assist in the release of Americans," and of "making political concessions" in the face of a policy that, "while professing neutrality," attempted "to tilt to Iraq and to quarantine Iran."[4] Every evening on national television the network news reported the stories of McFarlane's referring to "fanciful" reports, Reagan's saying he could not answer questions "without endangering the people we're trying to rescue,"[5] Secretary of State George Schultz's reportedly protesting the Reagan initiative on Iran, hostage Jacobsen pleading for silence in the interest of his colleagues still held, and national security adviser John Poindexter's telling key members of Congress that the administration had miscalculated on whom it could trust in Iran.

As the media tried to force some kind of official response, an issue of *Newsweek* magazine came out just five days after the *Post* editorial on the Iranian Connection. On its cover, *Newsweek* printed "Reagan's Secret Strategy: The Iran Connection" over the forehead of a close-up photograph of the Ayatollah Khomeini. The cover story, which certainly nosed out the Democrats' upset in the Senate as the feature, headlined inside, "Cloak and Dagger — Despite a vow not to deal with terrorists, Reagan secretly permits arms shipments to Iran to win the release of three American hostages in Lebanon."[6] Such a charge, accepting as true the original accusations of fact, went beyond the policy element and implied that the president had been engaged in the highly questionable behavior of trading arms for hostages. This was an attack on both his policy and his character because he had vowed never to deal with terrorists. This element of character would become more important later. On November 12, McFarlane said the release of hostages had been a precondition for better U.S. relations with Iran and Reagan told Congressional leaders for the first time that he had authorized arms shipments. There was no admission, however, of any link between hostages and arms.

In the evolution of this *kategoria-apologia* set, three accusations, each one building upon the other from November 3 to 11, emerged. *Al Shiraa*, a Syrian-backed Beirut magazine, claimed secret contacts were made in Tehran by Washington officials. Speaker Rafsanjani, in Tehran, confirmed this information but claimed the offer to ship arms by the United States was spurned. The American media, in its leading newspapers, news magazines, and on television, charged that this permission of arms shipments was really an arms-for-hostages deal made in violation of U.S. policy, of President Reagan's own promise, and of his own efforts to convince other nations to practice an arms embargo of Iran. The accusations included the stases of fact, of definition, and a beginning hint of quality because of the apparent aiding of an enemy. Although no single source served as an accuser, the corroborating sources became a most formidable *kategoria* in giving birth to a negative image of Reagan's policy and character.

THE CLIMATE OF DEFENSE

At this point, one must leave the *kategoria*, even though it is not yet finished, because additional accusations ensued as rhetorical events unfolded. They continued to unfold because of the nature of the *apologia* that President Reagan decided to give.

In all, Reagan attempted eight major rhetorical transactions during the four and a half months of the speech set. Seven of these were his speeches and press conferences over radio and television. One was not a speech but his initiative to control the discourse coming out in his defense — the *Tower Commission Report*. Each of these efforts must be discussed in turn.

Address to the Nation, November 13, 1986

As has been intimated, Reagan's initial response to the press's reports was silence. He would not comment for fear of endangering the operation still hopefully in existence. As the speculations grew even more probable in the perceptions of many, the president decided to address the nation on the evening of November 13. In the words of the Tower Commission, he "felt that a basic statement had to come out but that we needed to avoid details and specifics of the operation."[7]

That basic statement was a categorical denial of any illegality or of any swapping of arms for hostages. The address had three essential arguments: (1) the rumors, stories, and charges Americans heard were utterly false; (2) because of Iran's strategic importance, the U.S. needed to establish a better relationship with Iran; and (3) opening a dialog with Iran might help to end the Iran-Iraq war, halt state-supported terrorism, and effect the safe return of hostages.[8]

Reagan built these three arguments on an edifice of facts asserted to counter "a lot of stories the past several days" that the American people had "been reading, seeing, and hearing." In the opening paragraph he said, "Well, now you're going to hear *the facts* [italics added] from a White House source, and you know my name"; in the third paragraph, he repeated, "So, let's get to *the facts* [italics added]"; in the fifth paragraph, he claimed, "all these reports are quite exciting, but as far as we're concerned, *not one of them is true* [italics added]"; near the conclusion of the speech, he charged, "So extensive have been *the false rumors and erroneous reports* [italics added] that the risks of remaining silent now exceed the risks of speaking out. And that's why I decided to address you tonight"; and in the next to last paragraph, he expressed his belief: "As President, I've always operated on the belief that, *given the facts* [italics added], the American people will make the right decision." Reagan attempted to absolve himself of the alleged facts by denying them, by explaining what the "true" facts were, and by asserting what he did do was not what his accusers charged. Moreover, he said his actions, completely misunderstood, were motivated by strategically important geopolitical goals. He also argued jurisdiction by appealing to a different audience for a judgment — the American people, not "the American and world press." Thus, Reagan used denial, the stories are false; mitigation, since Iran is important, we need to establish a dialog; and purification, dialog might help to achieve specific and honorable objectives in the Middle East, to answer the accusation against policy. The apology denied the accusation against his policy of arms for hostages, and included as well a defense of character for his goals and motives. By including the four stases of fact, definition, quality, and jurisdiction, Reagan tried to correct the image under attack.

In the past when Reagan wanted to offer an explanation of what he had done or hoped to do, he would take his case to the American people on nationwide television. His great communicator skills usually served him well. For example, Thomas Goodnight argued that Reagan's efforts at reformulating the rhetoric of war in his first administration proved effective in the way he was able "to recontextualize public knowledge about the limits of nuclear power."[9]

But in this case, in defending against concrete accusations, Reagan was not persuasive. Whether it was because the content of a denial approach sounded too much like Nixon's answer to Watergate, or because the context of Iran made him especially vulnerable, the apology was clearly ineffective. The Tower Commission concluded in its findings: "The speech did not stem the pressure mounting in Congress and the U.S. media." A poll taken after the speech disclosed that only one in five Americans believed the president's story and 82 percent disagreed with his decision to sell arms to Iran.[10]

Presidential News Conference, November 19, 1986

Reagan decided to hold a news conference in less than a week following his TV address to the nation. Since going over the heads of Congress and the press to the American people did not bring satisfactory results, the president went this time directly to the press.[11] His advisers felt "his performance skills and popularity remain his Administration's most formidable assets" and hoped that the crisis over Iran, like the Bitburg criticism, would soon fade.

Reagan's rhetorical position in the news conference was an extension of the November 13 address. The apology was for policy and character in response to accusations against both policy and character. The news conference, in itself, was a type of *kategoria-apologia* speech set with the questions being the accusations and the answers the defense.

Reagan's accusers broke new ground in the conference. In addition to the repeated charge that his policy was wrong, accusers questioned his damaged credibility because of an apparent violation of law, and whether he timely notified Congress if secrecy were required, according to the National Security Act of 1977. The questions about this act, about duplicity, about end-running around the embargo act, and about third country involvement, addressed the first question of the evening, "How would you assess the credibility of your own Administration?"

Reagan's answer was that "I was not breaking any law in doing that," because the law had a waiver provision if "national security can be served." Further, the embargo continued even though he made an isolated exception.

In anticipating these accusations, Reagan announced in his opening statement that to eliminate the misperception that the United States was "exchanging arms for hostages," he had directed that no further sales be made and that "all information relating to our initiative be provided to the appropriate members of Congress."

A second group of accusations questioned Reagan's competence. The questions had a strong, biting, confronting tone that asked: Was it not naive to think there were moderates in Iran? Were you not in contradiction of Donald Regan's statement that there was a shipment before the January 17 intelligence finding? Even if you were not swapping arms for hostages, did it occur to you that the Iranians might see it that way? If there were no connection between the shipments and the releases, how do you explain them? Do you know what TOW's are? These charges against Reagan's competence were further substantiated when the White House had to issue a corrective within minutes of the end of the news conference that no third country had been involved.

Reagan's defense against this accusation was so inadequate that it weakened his credibility. For example, his answers to these questions were: I really cannot get into the matter of discussing the factions within Iran. Iran does not have authority over the Hezbollah and does not have hostages so how could they see it that way. We had a particular mission in mind, and we also knew that Iran could at times influence. "And so three of our hostages came home." "Well, now if I have been misinformed [about the TOW missile], then I will yield on that."

The final accusation charged the policy was a mistake. One questioner asked, since "everything seems to have gone wrong that could possibly go wrong, . . . [w]hat would be wrong with saying that a mistake was made on a very high risk gamble and . . . get on with the next two years?" Reagan's reply was categorical, "Because I don't think a mistake was made." In fact, he implied or specifically stated, no fewer than eight times in his answers that what he did was "correct," "worthwhile," "right," and "the path" would be continued. If a thesis sentence were to be selected from this press conference for his unfolding *apologia*, it could well be, "I considered the risks, but we did what was right." This press conference was an extension and rein-forcement of the rhetorical position he took in the address to the nation. In his opening statement, he mentioned the four goals of the Iran initiative two times and two additional times later in the press conference. Thus, Reagan denied wrongdoing, tried to mitigate circumstances, and tried to purify the ends as honorable.

Again, the defense did not achieve its goals. What is more, the accusa-tion that emerged from the press conference produced a third charge of questionable competence. Reagan's responses to these tough questions ac-tually reinforced this new charge. Two separate news stories in the *New York Times* the next morning centered on the "confusion" and "misleading" results of the news conference. Bernard Gwertzman provided a detailed account of how Reagan's remarks did not "mesh" with comments he had made earlier and with comments made by his own administration. Another story by Jonathan Fuerbringer claimed, "Democrats and Republicans said tonight that President Reagan's comments on Administration dealings with Iran were confusing and misleading, and Democrats said he had done fur-ther damage to his credibility." The press continued its building of the *kategoria* against Reagan. The lead editorial of the *New York Times* the next day charged, "The test now of a successful approach to Iran, or the world, will be competence — competence to focus on substance. At the moment, the President's men seem focused only on public relations." Tom Wicker, in an editorial, "Reagan on the Dodge," said, "Not since his stumbling per-formance in his first debate with Walter Mondale in 1984 have Americans seen President Reagan so uncertain, so tongue-tied and so inept as they saw him in his news conference on Iran." A CBS/*New York Times* poll on November 30 reported that the public approval rating for Reagan follow-ing the news conference was down to 46 percent from 67 percent a month earlier — the sharpest one-month drop ever in the history of polls.

Following the news conference, *Newsweek* editorialized, "The operation was the biggest blunder of the Reagan presidency, calling into question Reagan's judgment, credibility and future leadership," and it scored the results of his news conference where he stuck to the rightness of his actions: "But almost no one was won over."

Clearly the defense was ineffective. The problems for the administra-tion were compounded when Iran claimed that it had taped conversations between McFarlane and the White House to prove that Reagan had lied to the American people in the news conference.[12]

Address to the Nation, December 2, 1986

The third effort to respond to the increasing climate of accusation in the press was a brief noon address from the Oval Office that was broadcast live on nationwide radio and television. In this address, Reagan offered two basic arguments in his defense and a final appeal to jurisdiction. He said: "I've done everything in my power to make all the facts concerning this matter known to the American people," and "it is my policy to oppose terrorism throughout the world, to punish those who support it." His final appeal was to ask the American people to "be the final arbiters of this controversy." He claimed that once all "the investigative processes now set in motion are given an opportunity to work," all the facts would be made public and the people could decide.

This address was the first time that Reagan publicly took the position in his *apologia* that he wanted to get to the bottom of this and have all the facts come out. He announced that he would ask for "an independent counsel" to be appointed, and that he had met with his special review board, the Tower Commission, and promised them "the full cooperation of the White House staff and all Agencies of the executive branch." With the controversy being compared to Watergate, he used this approach to stem the rising storm of criticism about his credibility and character.

Secondly, he defended his policy. Without mentioning that he believed he did what was right, he defined his policy as opposing terrorism, not merely permitting arms sales to obtain better relations with Iran.[13]

The speech was Reagan's third national rhetorical effort to contain the damage, but it had little effect in the midst of continuing disclosures that helped to expand the *kategoria*. The newspapers and news magazines broadened the climate of accusation by headlining the implication of others in the administration and by using the word "scandal." *U.S. News & World Report* published on its December 8 cover "Reagan's Damaged Presidency: Who Else Knew?"; inside, it claimed, "Suddenly, the controversy over the secret arms shipments to Iran and the subsequent diversion of millions of dollars to the *contra* rebels in Nicaragua had mushroomed into a full-blown scandal — complete with startling White House staff departures and talk of shredded documents and tainted money from secret bank accounts." Moreover, the magazine's editorial page charged, "It is a corruption of the gifts of the Great Communicator to see him trying to pull perception on Iran. . . . In three attempts to tough it out, the President has eroded his own credibility. . . . Our national security requires the rescue of the Presidency. . . . But imagery cannot do it."

Newsweek's cover featured a picture of Donald Regan with the question, "Who Knew?" An eleven-page story on "Reagan's Worst Crisis" began with the caption, "Trapped in a widening scandal, Ronald Reagan tries to salvage his damaged presidency." The accusations were enlarged and deepened. The perception of scandal suggested an additional accusation beyond the previous attacks on policy, character, and competence. Now the accusers were saying that Reagan's presidency was threatened. The damage was so severe that the institution of the presidency was at stake. By the following week, *Newsweek* reported the president's approval rating had dropped from 64 percent in October to only 47 percent, 79 percent disapproved of supporting the contras with money from the Iran arms sales, almost one-third believed Reagan "knew and approved everything," and 58 percent felt the whole controversy has made it difficult for Reagan to be an effective president over the next two years.[14]

Radio Address to the Nation, December 6, 1986

In the midst of such perceptions and attitudes, Reagan again went to the airways to talk to the American people. His weekly radio address on December 6 was devoted entirely to the "Iran Arms and *Contra* Aid Controversy."[15]

Of this brief address, *Time* magazine said "Ronald Reagan made yet another attempt to quell the roiling scandal" as "the national uproar over the Iran-*contra* affair was at a peak." In the address, Reagan attempted Franklin D. Roosevelt's "Fireside Chat" approach. Instead of formally challenging the accusations that came from "the energetic stirrings of official investigators and the media's would-be Watergaters,"[16] the president decided to soften his siege mentality and to respond to the *kategoria* on a personal level. He attempted to rebuild his *ethos* by personalizing the challenge to the institution of the presidency:

> I'm speaking to you today from Camp David, and because the atmosphere here is a bit more informal than everyday Washington, I thought it would be a good opportunity to think and reflect with you about those crucial foreign policy matters so much in the news lately. It's also a chance to do something I've wanted to do throughout the course of these events: and that's share some personal thoughts with you, to speak to you, the American people, from the heart.

In the next eight paragraphs, his apology built again on the four stases of fact, definition, quality, and jurisdiction. He admitted to seeking an opportunity to establish a meeting with Iranians, but declared that his policies were not wrong, as critics charged, but that "the execution of these policies was flawed and mistakes were made." By arguing quality, he reinforced his December 2 address wherein he tried to build an image of "getting all the facts out." He spent two-fifths of his address asserting, "I pledge to you I will set things right. That's what I am doing now." He then itemized five things he had done. He also stressed that if "illegalities were undertaken in the implementation of the policy, those who did so will be brought to justice. . . . I will continue to make all the facts known surrounding this matter." Thus, he endeavored to place a cloak of good intentions over the policy that he steadfastly supported.

As in the December 2 address, Reagan appealed to the fourth stasis of jurisdiction — the American people. He identified with his audience by suggesting that the people will not do it alone — they, along with the president, will solve the problem together, just as "we have done" in the past six years. Reagan's motives in this address were to purify his policy and his character. This was a clear effort to respond to the mounting accusations as they threatened his credibility and possibly his presidency.

For the next month, prior to Reagan's admission to Bethesda Navy Medical Center for scheduled surgery on January 5, 1987, news reports continued to assail Reagan. *Newsweek* noted, "*Newsweek*'s reporting, based on a number of official sources, shows that the president called the shots at virtually every juncture in the making and unmaking of the disastrous Iranian policy. The contra connection, by the same token, almost certainly flows from the fact that Reagan's aides knew he was determined to support the Nicaraguan 'freedom fighters' at any cost." Various witnesses' testimony before the Congressional committees raised further questions about the president's involvement. Oliver North's and John Poindexter's refusal to testify cast a shadow over Reagan's sincerity to get to the bottom of the matter. Demands for the resignation of Donald Regan and William Casey, something Reagan refused to do, and the distancing of GOP presidential hopefuls from the once invincible president, added to the image that Reagan, even with his four national efforts to defend himself, was not building satisfactorily an *apologia*.[17]

During December, Reagan had hoped that the pressure would die down, especially over the holidays. To help, he appointed a new national security adviser, Frank C. Carlucci; endorsed a special prosecutor; assured Congress that he was not aware of the diversion of funds to the contras; and told the American people that he was doing everything he could to get all the facts out in the open.

After he returned from the hospital, the news media focused on the Senate Intelligence Committee's probe and whether it should be published. Although the committee had voted 7-6 not to publish, the *New York Times* obtained the analytical part of the report and NBC News obtained the chronology part of the arms sales to Iran and diversion of funds to the contras. The reports were made public through these news sources. Although the report showed no evidence that Reagan knew about the diversion of funds, it sharply criticized the White House for not listening to several officials who had objected to arms sales.

By the middle of January, several Republican leaders realized that Reagan's *apologia* so far was not effective. They suggested he use his State of the Union address to make a full apology. Representative Henry Hyde of Illinois told David Abshire, the White House liaison to investigations, that the January 27 speech would make a good opportunity to make his apology. White House spokesman Albert Brashear responded with a definite answer that Reagan would *not* apologize for his handling of the Iran-contra affair. James Reston, of the *New York Times*, rightly complained: "As usual, [Mr. Reagan] is being advised by some of his old California buddies never to complain, never to explain and never to apologize—the old Central Intelligence Agency motto—to stick it out, use his veto against the Democrats in Congress and go out fighting."[18]

The State of the Union Address, January 27, 1987

To the consternation of many, the president decided, for all practical purposes, to bypass an *apologia* in the important State of the Union address.[19] Even though the White House was in the eye of the storm over the Iran affair, Reagan, out of eighty-three paragraphs in total, allowed only three brief paragraphs to the Iran scandal. In this short section, only one-third the length of his introductory remarks, he managed to make only one admission. Not even mentioning the arms sales, and referring to the hostages' release, he said, "We did not achieve what we wished and serious mistakes were made in trying to do so." This was a repetition of his previous position that the policy was honorable but those who implemented it made mistakes for which he was willing to be accountable. With reference again to his four-fold purpose of the Iran policy, he said it was not wrong to try to establish contact with a strategically important country, it was not wrong to try to save lives, and it was not wrong to try to secure freedom for the American hostages. Justifying his intentions continued to be the bedrock of his *apologia*. As for the policy, he averred that although he has done nothing wrong, if there were those who did, he would get to the bottom of this and take whatever action was appropriate.

On the face of it, the above two defenses were all that he had to say on Iran. A deeper reading of the address, however, reveals another strategy was at work. By devoting major portions of the speech to other matters, Reagan "sought to divert attention from the Iran incident by praising the economic record of his Administration and advancing a legislative agenda" of many new programs. As R. W. Apple, Jr., noted, Reagan tried themes that worked in the past when times were calmer.[20] He attempted to answer his critics by pointing to positive accomplishments and to the future proposals that prove "it's morning in America." He challenged, "Now, ladies and gentlemen of the Congress, why don't we get to work?"

Reagan's *apologia* was a clear but clever attempt to transcend the accusations by focusing his audience's attention to the future and away from the troublesome past. In the closing paragraphs, Reagan returned to one of his favorite themes, "we the people are in charge." He began a litany of five successive paragraphs with "We the People." In the final one, he said,

"We the people. Starting the third century of a dream and standing up to some cynic who's trying to tell us we're not going to get any better." He closed with a story about Benjamin Franklin. Franklin, referring to the chair behind George Washington with a painted sun on a horizon, told the Constitutional Convention in 1787 that he was sure it is a rising sun. Reagan, dismissing the cynics, critics, and naysayers, said, "You bet it's rising, because, my fellow citizens, America isn't finished, her best days have just begun."

The responses to the address by Democrats were predictable. They were willing to help rebuild Reagan's presidency, but skeptical of his competence and policies. House Speaker Jim Wright responded to Reagan's handling of domestic policies: "This is the kind of gap between rhetoric and reality that we just can't tolerate and maintain people's trust in government." Senate Majority Leader Robert Byrd, speaking on foreign policy, reiterated an accusation against policy and character. He felt there was a "gathering sense of mistrust" and also "real doubts about competence" as a result of the Iran affair. In his televised reply, he said, "Without competence, and a good measure of common sense, government will have a tough time earning the nation's trust. And government without trust is government without power." Although Dan Rather of CBS Evening News characterized Reagan's speech as "a strong performance," White House reporter Bill Plante said that all key items were in the speech, except for "the most obvious omission of any kind of apology about Iran." Since Reagan had been urged by his own party to make a full apology, the media and viewers expected one. He disappointed them.[21]

The accusers and the defendant both attempted to build continually a discourse over time. In a report issued from the White House, two nights after the State of the Union Address, it was disclosed that October 3, 1986, when Reagan angrily told news reporters, "There hasn't been a day when we haven't been trying to get the hostages free," was the very same day he had signed the Bible to give to the Iranians. Reagan's motives were constantly offered to purify his soiled image. In spite of all White House efforts, the news reporters were not satisfied. On Reagan's seventy-sixth birthday, February 6, 1987, one correspondent stressed the very few times Reagan had appeared in public since election day and only once had taken questions. He closed his report emphasizing that the "Iran scandal" is "not going away." Two days later, on another major network, Sam Donaldson said, "Iran may have done it in the sense that the President can get on TV and sway the American people."[22]

Serious discrepancies in the Iran accounts continued to be reported and the question of trust persisted. A CNN/*U.S. News* poll, reported on February 14, disclosed that people trusted their auto mechanic more than the president.[23] The Iran affair was blamed for a crippled, passive, and reactive foreign policy. One news report showed that Reagan, unlike Carter who also had been damaged by Iran but who had several victories such as Camp David, was still in search of his first victory in foreign policy.

There were some voices that helped to blunt the force of the accusations against Reagan. Tip O'Neill, former Speaker of the House, said that he had been speaking to ten thousand people for six weeks and he had yet to get a question on Iran. Henry Kissinger, concerned about other foreign policy issues, played down the Iran affair: "What happens in the arms agreement with the Soviet Union is significantly more important than the minutiae of who said what to whom in the Iran affair." Larry Speakes, now a private citizen, confirmed that the Reagan administration definitely had a public relations problem, but, he said, "Our hands were tied. We didn't know what the facts were. If we had known the facts, we would have laid them out on the table and it would have been all over."[24]

The climate of accusation worsened when it was disclosed that records of the national security council suggested that "North, McFarlane and Poindexter tried to doctor the facts after the Iranian connection was exposed." Although McFarlane reportedly agreed to help prepare a chronology that showed Reagan did not authorize the arms shipments in August, 1985, he later testified that Reagan did authorize the shipment, thus contradicting Donald Regan. McFarlane's attempted suicide only added to the pressure from the Iran scandal. When word came out that Don Regan had ordered NSC staff to conceal the early approval of arms sales and that Reagan had changed his own story to the Tower Commission, *Newsweek* issued a black cover on March 2, with a one-word caption over Reagan's face, "COVERUP."

The Tower Commission Report, February 26, 1987

In substance, the Tower report concluded, "The Iran initiative ran directly counter to the Administration's own policies on terrorism, the Iran/Iraq war, and military support to Iran." It charged Reagan with a "failure in responsibility" that began with the way he did not make the NSC system work for him. The Board also reported that, although there was an immediate effort to avoid detail "out of concern for the hostages," Reagan did take actions at least by November 20 "to ensure that all the facts would come out."[25]

The media had a field day. CBS News aired a Special Report the night of the release entitled "Judgment on the White House." The report showed Senator Muskie emphasizing, "The policy was a wrong policy and it was the President's policy." When Dan Rather asked Senator Tower what Reagan must do now, he replied, "The President must make a very candid response to the report." The next morning on the NBC "Today Show" a panel of distinguished journalists discussed the situation. Jack Germane said "the picture it gave of the President was devastating"; David Broder said, "it will require more than changing staff"; and Ken Bode added: "We have a scandal; if this had happened in England, the government would have fallen. Competence is the test."[26]

As a result of this highly damaging report, the eyes of the nation turned directly on Reagan. The expectation of a rhetorical response was overwhelming. In officially accepting the Board's report, covered by the networks, Reagan announced he would carefully study it and make a response. His first response was immediate. Chief of Staff Regan, who had been under fire for months, resigned and former Senator Howard Baker was appointed. The appointment was received by both parties as a brilliant move. Hopefully, Baker would be an answer to Reagan's credibility problem growing out of accusations against character and competence, and the presidency itself. Baker, in his first official act, announced that Robert Gates had asked for his name to be withdrawn from the CIA directorship nomination. He was still under the Iran cloud since he had been Deputy Director under Casey. This made it possible for Reagan to orchestrate another wise political move by appointing FBI Chief William Webster as the new CIA Director. It likewise was received with great favor by everyone. These moves to replace key staff positions helped to address the question that was firmly entrenched in the climate of accusation — was the President in charge, could he govern? The other question that loomed large was, would Reagan apologize for his Iran policy? Jim Wright, House Speaker, said Reagan needed to acknowledge the Iran policy was a mistake, and Howard Baker said he tried to persuade Reagan to admit that the policy was a mistake but "the President still believes it wasn't wrong."[27]

Reagan announced he would respond to the Tower report on Wednesday, March 4, 1987. The speech became a media event even before it was given. The network news made the speech the opening news item on the evening of March 4, saying it was "being talked about as the most important speech of his career," it was "expected to affect the rest of his presidency," and it was "clearly terribly important" for Ronald Reagan.[28]

The Address to the Nation, March 4, 1987

Reagan's response to the Tower report was surprisingly brief in length — just twelve minutes.[29] He attempted to include in this critical segment of his unfolding *apologia* an answer to each of the issues that existed in the climate of accusation — the accusation against policy, character, competence, and the survival of the presidency itself. But he also continued in his response an argumentative synthesis that fused these issues.

Reagan made two basic arguments: (1) "This happened on my watch," so I take full responsibility for what happened, and (2) To correct the situation, "I'm taking action" in areas of personnel, policy, and process.

Knowing he had to take greater responsibility for his policy, which was expected by the people and required by the Tower report, Reagan took the linguistic tactic of saying, "My heart and my best intentions still tell me [I did not trade arms for hostages] but the facts and the evidence tell me [I did]." He acknowledged what the Tower Commission concluded: the strategic opening to Iran deteriorated into trading arms for hostages—"It was a mistake." Reagan attempted to save face by hiding behind the Tower Board. He accepted its conclusion, but he still refused to admit that he was wrong in his original Iran initiative, and that was what many people wanted to hear.

On the character issue, Reagan appealed to his honorable motives. He told the people that his compassionate concern for the hostages "spilled over," and his heart still told him he was right. As he did previously, he purified the accusation by appealing to his honest motives that the American people could understand and trust.[30]

Regarding the charges of competency and survival of the presidency, Reagan addressed them by acknowledging the Tower report's criticism of the flawed process and management style that permitted it to happen. He recited the list of actions he had taken to restore the proper functioning of his administration, and he mentioned the new personnel he brought in to change the climate of distrust and incompetence. Those appointments also helped rebuild Reagan's character because, compared to the previous persons, these persons brought credibility to the White House.

These measures were announced as evidence that Reagan was in charge and that his presidency was back on track. He concluded his speech with another appeal to the American people that his presidency was not finished. When you make a mistake, he said "You take your knocks, you learn your lesson, and you move on." He had a great deal to accomplish "with you and for you," he told his listeners. This was a clever appeal to a common denominator value—everyone makes mistakes—in an effort to establish common ground and thereby renew the credibility he once held.

The reactions to the speech were mixed. John Tower said: "A person is never more credible than when he admits a mistake"; Senator Robert Dole concluded, "The President did a good job on a tough subject. He reached the same conclusion many of us did months ago and said about everything the American people expected him to say"; and reporter Bret Hume announced that it was likely to be well received because Reagan admitted his mistake and announced new policies: "He's on the right track as far as capitol hill is concerned." However, Dick Williams of the *Atlanta Journal* said he did not like it because there wasn't enough detail; K. E. Grubbs of the *Orange County Register* said it was "a nice touch but the issue will stay alive"; "The performance was the old Reagan," declared Clarence Page of the *Chicago Tribune*; and ordinary Americans answered reporters: "Expected him to be more explicit," "as good as he could do under the circumstances," "pleasing but no substance." In a poll, 54 percent of the people said they approved of the way the president was doing his job and 63 percent believed Reagan wanted all the facts out. "Ronald Reagan is back in the saddle again," said Senator Phil Grimm on CBS News which also reported that Americans were "satisfied" on a ratio of 2-1.[31]

Even though the Tower report may be viewed as a *kategoria* in a subset of the ongoing accusation-defense speech set, the report was really a segment of Reagan's unfolding *apologia* from November 13 to March 19. Linguistically, the report was accusatory, but rhetorically and politically, it functioned as a defense. Although the language was not Reagan's, the Board was Reagan's. He commissioned it, he selected its members, he gave it its charge, and he was able to incorporate it as part of his overall *apologia* that he created over the five-month period. The report was Reagan's official answer without challenging the legislative investigations. It was written by persons of undisputed respectability and trustworthiness. Since it was his initiative, it precluded a serious charge of a cover up. It was bipartisan. It gave acceptable and respectable access to the president himself as a witness. It functioned as his defense because it concluded that there was no suspicion of illegality or deliberate wrong-doing or deception. It gave him rhetorical room in which to maneuver—"I meant well but it turned out to be a mistake which I now accept," and it was a logical extension of his way of thinking from the beginning.

The textual evidence is very clear that Reagan saw the Board as *his* probe and *his* story. When the Board was appointed, he said, "Upon its completion, I intend to share its findings with Congress and the American people." In his March 4 speech he said, "You deserved the truth." That is why he was willing to wait for it. Even though it cost him, he wanted the "trust and confidence" that would come if he waited "for the complete story." By inference, he called the Tower report "the truth" and "the complete story." The report was *his* response to his accusers. Even though the Commission was "far more aggressive and thorough in its investigation of the affair than anyone—particularly those in the White House—had expected," Reagan should have been grateful for every indictment the report contained. It contributed to his *apologia*.[32]

President Reagan seemed to have weathered the storm. Although other investigations continued, he could emphasize what he was doing on other issues and not feel that every week he would continue to be on the defensive about Iran. He cleared the air, for a time at least, satisfied the public to a reasonable extent, and allowed the government to proceed with its proper functioning. His argument—"don't judge me any longer by what happened on my watch but by what I am now doing and will do to correct matters" — helped to save his institutional presidency but there was still the question of his old power, his rhetorical presidency. Suddenly the White House announced there would be a press conference on Thursday, March 19, 1987. The White House press corps was thrilled because Reagan had not held a press conference since the one on November 19, 1986, which was viewed as a disaster for the president.

Presidential News Conference, March 19, 1987

President Reagan began with a diversionary tactic by giving an opening statement on reducing government spending and working for a balanced budget.[33] But the press did not fall for his gambit. The press wanted to know about the Iran affair. If the questions by the press may be considered accusatory speeches, the charges were the same as before. They dealt with policy, character, and competence, but not with the issue of the presidency. His survival was dropped as an issue.

Regarding the policy, the essential question was whether Reagan now believed it was arms for hostages and was it wrong. He dodged by answering that the policy deteriorated and he would not go down that road again. The metaphor was well chosen. It indicated where he intended to go but that he would not have started if he had thought it was wrong in the first place.

On the character issue, the questions concerned his honesty. He denied deceiving the people and asserted truth-telling as his personal philosophy.

Competence came up several times in the questions of his memory of McFarlane's phone call about the Iran arms sales, of the contra diversion, and of his management ability of not knowing about aid to the contras and whether his style was to blame for the trouble. He answered these charges by saying others do not remember everything, but that he was sure his memory was right on aid to the contras because he would have opposed that. On his management style, he said it had served him well and if people did not follow the right road, the investigations would bring it out.

The press reaction to the news conference was varied. Many observers felt the press conference provided an opportunity for Reagan to demonstrate that he could not only give a good speech in defense of himself, but that he also could match wits with the press corps to show he could field their questions on this complex topic without stumbling. Immediately following the news conference, analysts said: "It's show business. It isn't a press conference"; "I thought the press was tame. I'd give the press and the president a C"; "This was an international electronic physical exam of the president. He passed his test"; "Ronald Reagan is back from the standpoint of style. From the standpoint of substance, to say his slip on

November 19 was inadvertent is just trying to find an excuse." Others said it is not *what* he said but *the way* he said it: "He seemed in command, seemed to be president; he could make one liners. He made a good impression"; and Chris Wallace said it was "a first-rate performance; he was clearly ready for this. He was showing command; some answers were clever but he will have a time selling them."[34] However, others were not so sanguine.

Tom Shales said, "He was in command once again. I like to think of Ronald Reagan sometimes not so much as president of the United States but president of television land — this other kingdom. That's why he is perceived as a great president because he handles these cosmetics so well." Dick Williams of the *Atlanta Journal* concluded, "I think people feel enough is enough until the next round of revelations. It's time to get on to other things." Jimmy Breslin of the *New York Daily News* was not ready to drop the affair, "We sold arms over the bodies of these dead marines to the same people who murdered them. This is an act of disloyalty I think to last through the ages. You would expect a government to come forth in shame. Instead President Reagan comes forth unshamed. I'd like to ask why?"[35]

If members of the press felt Reagan generally deserved good marks for his performance, he should also be given high marks for his apologetic strategy. By staging this news conference when he did, he clearly demonstrated to the public that he was in command again. It represented a move by someone on the offensive. The White House decided to give the press corps what they wanted and had not had for four months. But the press was not able to capitalize on anything. They really did not have any new questions. They were perceived as being docile and tame whereas Reagan came out looking his old self. In the Iran-contra affair, the press conference was like a denouement. The press did not get any real news but Reagan had another opportunity to enlarge his *apologia*. He elaborated on his answers and on his previous positions, such as the answer explaining why he could not give out details at the beginning because he did not know "how far we could go before we could get someone killed." It had a ring of believability about it for some of his auditors.[36]

The press conference served Reagan's apologetic strategy as a maturing segment of the universe of discourse that permitted people to see that the defense had gone as far as it could go. For the time being, the rhetorical part of phase one was complete. The conference gave Reagan an opportunity to do three important things: (1) to demonstrate that he regained his competence as "the great communicator," (2) to extend the *apologia* with elaboration of only selected elements in his defense, and (3) to enlarge the universe of public discourse for people to inhabit. Thus, Reagan proved once again that he could respond adequately and even with aplomb to the White House press corps.

CONCLUSION

Phase one of the evolving *kategoria-apologia* speech set has ended. Later phases dealing with the Congressional hearings and the investigation of the independent counsel will no doubt produce additional accusations and defenses concerning Reagan.

The first important conclusion about the present analysis is that the success of Reagan's *apologia* was built on appearances. He has persuaded Americans to believe his defense. This is quite consistent with Reagan's tradition of creating appearances for his own political purposes. Whether in domestic economic policy or in foreign policy, as Kurt Ritter's early work on Reagan's rhetoric of public relations politics showed and as my work on his responses to the international crises in Beirut and Granada demonstrated, Reagan's ability to create appearances is a strength based on his political philosophy and executed by his rhetorical art.[37] In the Iran affair, he was able to create the illusion of survival by a carefully orchestrated *apologia*. In the political arena, perception is reality.

A second conclusion is that when a *kategoria* is against a president, he has available to him certain resources that many other victims of *kategoria* would not necessarily have. He has access to the media, the power to change policies, the power of appointment, the power to schedule speeches, and thus the power to create a defense that can inoculate against subsequent and more damaging accusations that might bring down the institutional presidency itself. So far, Reagan has been able to preserve his institutional presidency and perhaps even his rhetorical presidency—the power to govern by persuasion.

As evidence that Reagan's rhetorical presidency is in peril, a prevailing attitude in Washington is that the last two years of his administration will witness few accomplishments. He is characterized as "a figurehead president" who "can no longer manage things and will rely on a regency headed by his wife, Nancy, and Mr. Baker." Others, such as David Broder, believe that Reagan's rhetorical efforts have brought "modest success" and "have opened the way for a much more important breakthrough" in "refocusing the nation's attention on his agenda" and putting "his plans and programs center-stage."[38]

From this case study about Reagan's responses to accusations, a third conclusion is offered. Reagan cleverly argued the stasis of definition. His response, "I want the whole story to come out," was a definitional obfuscation. He appointed the Tower Board to invent *his* story that he presented to the country. The Tower report was a strategic apologetic device to create the *appearance* of getting to the bottom of the affair, of clearing the president of wrongdoing. When Reagan said he wanted to know, too, the whole story, he became a questionner. This was a subtle definitional shift in his role from the accused to the accuser. Thus, he tried to join the members of the press as one who was waiting to find out the whole story.

Fourth, and last, an extended speech set may favor the apologist. Reagan's apologies because of their timing, eight rhetorical transactions over four and a half months, allowed him to repeat his good intentions and to downplay his self-inflicted wounds by making the story coherent enough to satisfy many of the auditors' expectations. Whether Reagan convinced himself of his version of the facts is unknown,[39] but he was able to convince his listeners — his judges — that his story was believable. Perhaps many of his listeners did not *want* to believe another version. Perhaps they wanted their president to succeed in his defense. If so, Reagan identified correctly with his audience. His rhetorical response brought him safely, although not unscathed, through phase one of the *kategoria-apologia* encounter. What will happen in the next phase remains to be seen.

NOTES

[1]CNN Evening News, February 26, 1987.

[2]See Foreign Broadcast Information Service (FBIS) [microfiche], Middle East & South Asia Review, November 5, 1986, p. i; "The Iran Connection: Reagan's Secret Strategy," *Newsweek*, November 17, 1986, p. 46; FBIS, p. i; and "Iran Says McFarlane, Others Came on Secret Mission to Iran," *Washington Post*, November 5, 1986, p. A1.

[3]"Iran Says McFarlane, Others Came on Secret Mission," p. A26. Italics added.

[4]"The Iranian Connection," *Washington Post*, November 6, 1986, p. 18.

[5]*Weekly Compilation of Presidential Documents (WCPD)* 22:45 (November 10, 1986): p. 1545.

[6]"The Iran Connection: Reagan's Secret Strategy," p. 46. Although the issue is dated the seventeenth, the reader should remember that it is distributed the Tuesday *before* its date of publication, which would have been November 11.

[7]"The Iranian Connection," p. 18 and *The Tower Commission Report* [hereafter *TCR*] (New York: Random House, 1987), p. 502.

[8]"Iran-United States Relations," *WCPD*, 22:46 (November 17, 1986): 1559-61. All subsequent Reagan quotations are from the designated source

in each case.

[9]G. Thomas Goodnight, "Ronald Reagan's Re-formulation of the Rhetoric of War: Analysis of the 'Zero Option,' 'Evil Empire,' and 'Star Wars' Addresses," *Quarterly Journal of Speech* 72 (1986): 409.

[10]*TCR*, p. 504 and CBS Evening News, November 13, 1986.

[11]"President's News Conference on Foreign and Domestic Issues," *New York Times*, November 20, 1986, pp. A12-13.

[12]See Bernard Gwertzman, "Confusion Over Iran," *New York Times*, November 20, 1986, p. A13; Jonathan Fuerbringer, "Lawmakers Find Reagan Misleading, *New York Times*, November 20, 1986, p. A13; "Shovels in the White House," *New York Times*, November 21, 1986, p. A34; Tom Wicker, "Reagan on the Dodge," *New York Times*, November 21, 1986, p. A35; "His Biggest Blunder," *Newsweek*, December 1, 1986, p. 3; "Reagan's 'Cowboys': Out of Control," *Newsweek*, December 1, 1986, p. 27.

[13]"Independent Counsel to Investigate the Arms Sales to Iran," *WCPD* 22:49 (December 8, 1986): 1613-14.

[14]"Reagan's Damaged Presidency: Who Else Knew?," *U.S. News & World Report*, December 8, 1986, p. 16; Harold Evans, "The Beleaguered Presidency," *U.S. News & World Report*, December 8, 1986, p. 82; "Under Siege," *Newsweek*, December 8, 1986, p. 32; "Reagan's Crusade," *Newsweek*, December 15, 1986, p. 27.

[15]"Iran Arms and *Contra* Aid Controversy," *WCPD* 22:50 (December 15, 1986): 1629-30.

[16]"Breaking Up Is Hard to Do," *Time*, February 2, 1987, p. 22; "Reagan's Crusade," p. 28.

[17]See "The Roots of a Brutal Bargain," *Newsweek*, December 15, 1986, p. 31 and "Politics: Running Away from Reagan," *Newsweek*, December 15, 1986, p. 39.

[18]James Reston, "Reagan's Happy New Year?" *New York Times*, December 28, 1986, p. E11.

[19]"President's Message to Nation on the State of the Union, *New York Times*, January 28, 1987, p. 6.

[20]R. W. Apple, Jr., "Echo of Calmer Times," *New York Times*, January 28, 1987, p. 1.

[21]Linda Greenhouse, "Democratic Leaders React with Support and Warning," *New York Times*, January 28, 1987, p. 7.

[22]CBS News Special Report, January 27, 1987; CBS Evening News, January 29, 1987; Bill Plante, CBS Evening News, February 6, 1987; ABC News This Week, February 8, 1987.

[23]CNN Prime News, February 14, 1987.

[24]Larry King Weekend, CNN, February 15, 1987; Firing Line, February 15, 1987; CNN Cross Fire, February 20, 1987.

[25]*TCR*, pp. 62, 63-86.

[26]CBS News Special Report, February 26, 1987 and NBC Today Show, February 27, 1987.

[27]ABC World News Tonight, March 3, 1987 and ABC World News Tonight, March 2, 1987.

[28]ABC World News Tonight, March 4, 1987; CBS Evening News, March 4, 1987; ABC World News Tonight, March 4, 1987.

[29]"President's Address to the Nation on the Iran Arms Controversy," *New York Times*, March 5, 1987, pp. 12-13.

[30]This compares with the values appeal Nixon made to the American people in responding to the secret fund accusation. See Henry McGuckin, Jr., "A Value Analysis of Richard Nixon's 1952 Campaign-Fund Speech," in Halford Ross Ryan, *American Rhetoric from Roosevelt to Reagan* (Prospect Heights, Ill.: Waveland Press, 1983): 124-33.

[31]ABC News Special Report, "President Reagan Responds," March 4, 1987; CNN Presidential Address, March 4, 1987; ABC World News Tonight, March 5, 1987; CBS Evening News, March 5, 1987.

[32]"Special Review Board for the National Security," *WCPD*, 22:48 (December 1, 1986): 1605; "A Small But Tough Texan," *Newsweek*, February 23, 1987, p. 24.

[33]"President's News Conference on Foreign and Domestic Issues," *New York Times*, March 20, 1987, pp. 6-7.

[34]ABC News Special Report, March 19, 1987; CBS News Special Report, March 19, 1987; NBC News Special Report, March 19, 1987.

[35]CBS Face the Nation, March 22, 1987.

[36]Dick Williams of the *Atlanta Journal* said, "The president in his news conference was fairly convincing I think to a great many people in how the initiative began and what his intentions were." CBS Face the Nation, March 22, 1987.

[37]See Kurt W. Ritter, "Ronald Reagan and 'The Speech,'" in Ryan, *American Rhetoric from Roosevelt to Reagan*, pp. 290-98 and D. Ray Heisey, "Reagan and Mitterrand Respond to International Crisis: Creating Versus Transcending Appearances," *The Western Journal of Speech Communication* 50 (Fall 1986): 325-35.

[38]R. W. Apple, Jr., "A Political Convalescence Begins, Prognosis Uncertain," *New York Times*, March 22, 1987, Section 4, p. 1; David S. Broder, "Reagan Wins Points on Political Stage," *Akron Beacon Journal*, March 22, 1987, p. C3.

[39]Bill Plante reported that President Reagan has, all through his career, convinced himself "that this version of the facts is the truth." CBS Sunday Morning, March 22, 1987. For the belief that Reagan's failure in the first month of the scandal may be attributed to his "extraordinary ability to believe the illusions he himself creates," see Anthony Lewis, "Illusion and Reality," *New York Times*, November 20, 1986, p. A13.

INFORMATION SOURCES ON THE SPEECH SET

The Accusations Against President Reagan

The original accusation, the *Al Shiraa* magazine report from Beirut, and the second accusation, the speech by Rafsanjani in Tehran, were not available at the time of this writing. The third accusation, the combined press reports and the editorials, may be found in the following primary print accusations:

"The Iran Mess: His Biggest Blunder," *Newsweek*, December 1, 1986, pp. 26-37.

"The Iranian Connection," *Washington Post*, November 6, 1986, p. A18.

"Reagan's Damaged Presidency: Who Else Knew?," *U.S. News & World Report*, December 8, 1986, pp. 16-25.

"Reagan's Secret Strategy: The Iran Connection," *Newsweek*, November 17, 1986, pp. 46-53.

"The State of Reagan," *Time*, February 9, 1987, pp. 16-20.

The Tower Commission Report. New York: Random House, 1987.

Wicker, Tom. "Reagan on the Dodge," *New York Times*, November 21, 1986, p. A35.

President Reagan's Apology

The best available texts are, in chronological order:

"Iran-United States Relations," November 13, 1986, *Weekly Compilation of Presidential Documents* 22:46 (November 17, 1986): 1559-61.

"President's News-Conference on Foreign and Domestic Issues," *New York Times*, November 20, 1986, pp. A12-13.

"Independent Counsel to Investigate the Arms Sales to Iran," December 2, 1986, *Weekly Compilation of Presidential Documents* 22:49 (December 8, 1986): 1613-14.

"Iran Arms and *Contra* Aid Controversy," December 6, 1986, *Weekly Compilation of Presidential Documents* 22:50 (December 15, 1986): 1629-30.

"President's Message to Nation on the State of the Union," January 27, 1987, *New York Times*, January 28, 1987, p. 6.

The Tower Commission Report (New York: Random House, 1987). The U.S. government edition was issued on February 26, 1987; the Random House edition was issued the first week in March 1987.

"President's Address to the Nation on the Iran Arms Controversy," March 4, 1987, *New York Times*, March 5, 1987, p. 12.

"President's News Conference on Foreign and Domestic Issues," March 19, 1987, *New York Times*, March 20, 1987, pp. 6-7.

Selected Bibliography

Apple, R. W., Jr. "Reagan's Problem," *New York Times*, February 27, 1987, pp. 1 and 11.

Broder, David S.   "Reagan Wins Points on Political Stage," *Akron Beacon Journal*, March 22, 1987, p. C3. Analysis of the March 19, 1987 address.

Gwertzman, Bernard. "Confusion Over Iran," *New York Times*, November 20, 1986, p. A13. Analysis of the November 19, 1986 press conference.

Pear, Robert. "Reagan and the Report Still Differ in Key Ways," *New York Times*, March 5, 1987, p. 13. Analysis of the March 4, 1987 address.

"Reagan's Crusade," *Newsweek*, December 15, 1986, pp. 26-40.

"Reagan's Failure," *Newsweek*, March 9, 1987, pp. 16-37.

Safire, William. "Ten Myths About the Reagan Debacle," *New York Times Magazine*, March 22, 1987, pp. 21-30.

"Under Siege," *Newsweek*, December 8, 1986, pp. 32-52.

Weinraub, Bernard. "Reagan's Last Years: How Effective Can They Be?" *New York Times*, November 19, 1986, p. 13. Analysis of Reagan's predicament following his November 13, 1986 address.

Glossary of Rhetorical Terms

ACTIO. The delivery, gestures, and voice management of the speech.

AD PERSONAM. An argument to the man or person, an appeal to prejudices rather than to reason.

AFFIRMATION BY DENIAL. A rhetorical technique wherein a speaker affirms a point by appearing to deny it.

ANAPHORA. Parallelism in language, the beginning of successive words or phrases or sentences with the same word or words.

APHORISM. A pithy statement or saying.

APOLOGIA. An apology, a speech in defense.

CLASSICAL PATTERN. For the development and arrangement of an oration; *exordium*, an introduction; *narratio*, a narration of the situation at hand; *partitio*, a division of the issues in the speech; *confirmatio*, the arguments and reasons that support the orator's position; *refutatio*, refutation of opposing arguments and positions; *epilogus*, a conclusion.

CONJECTURALIS. A classical stasis, whether an action was done or not.

DEFINITIVA. A classical stasis, how an action is defined.

DELIBERATIVE ORATORY. From Aristotle's *Rhetoric*; consists of political speaking in legislative bodies, toward policy in the future, aimed at expediency; see EPIDEICTIC ORATORY and FORENSIC ORATORY.

ENTHYMEME. A rhetorical argument based on generally held beliefs without expressing the premises of the argument.

EPIDEICTIC ORATORY. From Aristotle's *Rhetoric*; consists of ceremonial speaking before the people, toward establishing virtue and honor through praise or blame, while focusing on the present.

ETHOS. One of three rhetorical appeals from Aristotle's *Rhetoric*; the orator's character in terms of good will, good sense, and good moral character; the speaker's credibility; see *LOGOS* and *PATHOS*.

FORENSIC ORATORY. From Aristotle's *Rhetoric*; consists of legal courtroom speaking, toward establishing justice, with regard to the past; see DELIBERATIVE ORATORY and EPIDEICTIC ORATORY.

GENERALIS. A classical stasis, pertaining to a class, kind, or quality.

GENRE. A kind of speech in which similarities and differences distinguish it from other kinds of addresses.

INDUCTION. Reasoning from particular examples to a conclusion.

INNUENDO. A derogatory or depreciatory reference to persons or things.

KAIROS. Ancient Greek concept of the right or propitious time to act.

KATEGORIA. A speech of accusation, a charge.

LOGOS. From Aristotle's *Rhetoric*; a rhetorical appeal to reason; the facts and reasoning presented by the orator to prove the case.

METHOD OF RESIDUES. A rhetorical use of the disjunctive syllogism: either A, B, or C; not A, not B, therefore C; the orator eliminates alternatives until the audience is left with only the orator's alternative.

PATHOS. One of three rhetorical appeals from Aristotle's *Rhetoric*; the orator stirs the audience's emotions to persuade them.

PERSONA. The rhetorical role or character assumed by the orator for persuasive purposes.

QUALITAS. A classical stasis, the quality, nature, or degree of an action.

REDUCTIO AD ABSURDAM. An argument in which the orator takes a position, usually an opponent's, and runs the position to an absurd conclusion, thus negating the entire position or argument.

RHETORICAL QUESTION. A persuasive question with the answer implicit; the orator phrases the question to elicit the desired response from the audience.

STASIS. An ancient Greek concept of where the argument stands; see *CONJECTURALIS, DEFINITIVA, QUALITAS,* and *TRANSLATIO.*

TRANSLATIO. A classical stasis, an appeal to a different jurisdiction or audience.

TU QUOQUE. You also, a device whereby the orator charges opponents with doing or saying the same thing.

VOX POPULI. The voice of the people, a speaker who speaks for or in behalf of the people.

About the Contributors

WILLIAM L. BENOIT, Assistant Professor of Communication, University of Missouri, Columbia, teaches courses in rhetoric, argument, and persuasion. He has published in the *Quarterly Journal of Speech*, *Southern Speech Communication Journal*, *Western Journal of Speech Communication*, *Communication Education*, *Philosophy and Rhetoric*, and *Journal of the American Forensic Association*. He is writing a book with Alex Moore on John C. Calhoun's oratory, and editing a book of readings on argumentation theory with Dale Hample and Pamela Benoit.

BERNARD L. BROCK, Professor of Speech Communication, Wayne State University, Detroit, teaches courses in rhetorical criticism, political communication, and contemporary public address. He coauthored *Methods of Rhetorical Criticism: A Twentieth-Century Perspective*, coedited *Current Criticism*, and contributed to *American Orators of the Twentieth Century: Critical Studies and Sources*.

CARL R. BURGCHARDT, Assistant Professor of Speech Communication, Colorado State University, Fort Collins, teaches courses in American public address and critical methodology. He has published in the *Quarterly Journal of Speech* and contributed to *American Orators of the Twentieth Century: Critical Studies and Sources*.

RONALD K. BURKE, Associate Professor of Speech Communication, Syracuse University, Syracuse, teaches courses in American public address. He has published articles in speech communication journals and is writing a book on Frederick Douglass for the series of books on Great American Orators published by Greenwood Press.

GEORGE N. DIONISOPOULOS, Assistant Professor of Speech Communication, San Diego State University, San Diego, teaches courses in rhetoric, communication and politics, and argumentation. He has published in *Central States Speech Journal*. He contributed to *New Perspectives in Political Advertising* and *Progress in Communication Series*.

BERNARD K. DUFFY, Professor and Coordinator of Speech, Department of English, Clemson University, Clemson, teaches courses in American public address, rhetorical theory, and persuasion. He has published in *Philosophy and Rhetoric, Southern Speech Communication Journal, Communication Education, Journal of American Culture*, and *Essays in Theatre*. He is coeditor with Halford Ryan of *American Orators of the Twentieth Century: Critical Studies and Sources* and *American Orators Before 1900: Critical Studies and Sources*, and coeditor with Halford Ryan for a series of books on Great American Orators published by Greenwood Press.

ROBERT V. FRIEDENBERG, Professor of Communication, Miami University, Hamilton, teaches courses in American public address and political campaign communication. He has published approximately sixty books, chapters, articles, reviews, and scripts in a wide variety of scholarly and popular journals. He is a former communications consultant for the Republican National Committee, and coauthor of *Political Campaign Communication: Principles and Practices*.

G. JACK GRAVLEE, Professor and Chair of Speech Communication, Colorado State University, Fort Collins, teaches courses in British and American discourse. He has published in *Communication Monographs, Quarterly Journal of Speech*, and *Central States Speech Journal*. He contributed to *America in Controversy: Speaking on Issues in American History, History of American Public Address, The Oratory of Southern Demagogues, A New Diversity in Contemporary Southern Rhetoric, American Orators of the Twentieth Century: Critical Studies and Sources*, and *American Orators Before 1900: Critical Studies and Sources*. He coedited with James R. Irvine *Pamphlets and the American Revolution: Rhetoric, Politics, Literature, and the Popular Press* and *The Whores Rhetorick (1683)*.

LAWRENCE W. HAAPANEN, Associate Professor of Communications, Lewis-Clark State College, Lewiston, teaches courses in persuasion and political communication. He contributed to the *Handbook of Intercultural Communication*. He conducted research in the Dwight D. Eisenhower Library, Abilene, Kansas.

D. RAY HEISEY. Professor and Director, School of Speech Communication, Kent State University, Kent, teaches courses in the history and criticism of public address and international communication. He has published in *Communication Monographs, Quarterly Journal of Speech, Western Speech Communication Journal, Southern Speech Communication Journal,* and *Acta Symbolica.* He contributed to *America in Controversy: Speaking on Issues in American History, Preaching in American History: Selected Issues in the American Pulpit, 1630-1967,* and *Intercommunication Among Nations and People.* He served as president of Damavand College, Tehran, Iran.

DAVID HENRY, Professor of Speech Communication, California Polytechnic State University, San Luis Obispo, teaches courses in rhetorical theory, public discourse, persuasion, and argumentation. He contributed to *American Orators of the Twentieth Century: Critical Studies and Sources, American Orators Before 1900: Critical Studies and Sources,* and *In Search of Justice.* He is writing a book with Kurt Ritter on Ronald Reagan for the series of books on Great American Orators published by Greenwood Press.

RACHEL L. HOLLOWAY, doctoral student and teaching assistant in Communication, Purdue University, West Lafayette, teaches courses in public relations and issue management. She has presented papers at the annual meetings of the Speech Communication Association and the Central States Speech Association.

SUSAN SCHULTZ HUXMAN, Assistant Professor of Speech Communication and Theatre Arts, Wake Forest University, Winston-Salem, teaches courses in American public address and rhetorical criticism and theory.

RICHARD J. JENSEN, Professor of Speech Communication, University of New Mexico, Albuquerque, teaches courses in public address, rhetorical criticism, and rhetorical theory. He has published in *Western Journal of Speech Communication, Central States Speech Journal,* and *Communication Quarterly.* He coauthored with John C. Hammerback and Jose Angel Gutierrez *A War of Words: Chicano Protest in the 1960s and 1970s* and coedited with John C. Hammerback *In Search of Justice.*

THOMAS M. LESSL, Assistant Professor of Speech Communication, University of Georgia, Athens, teaches courses in rhetorical criticism and theory. He has published in the *Quarterly Journal of Speech.*

WIL A. LINKUGEL, Professor of Communication Studies, University of Kansas, Lawrence, teaches courses in American public address. He has published in *Quarterly Journal of Speech, Communication Monographs,*

Philosophy and Rhetoric, and *South Atlantic Quarterly*. He is coeditor with R. R. Allen and Richard L. Johannensen of *Contemporary American Speeches*, coeditor with Donn W. Parson of *The Ethics of Controversy: Politics and Protest, Militancy and Anti-Communication, and Television and the New Persuasion*, and coauthor with Cal W. Downs and David M. Berg of *The Organizational Communication* and with E. C. Buehler of *Speech: A First Course*.

HALFORD R. RYAN, Professor of Public Speaking, Washington and Lee University, Lexington, teaches courses in presidential rhetoric and American public address. He has published in *Quarterly Journal of Speech*, *Southern Speech Communication Journal*, and *Presidential Studies Quarterly*. He edited and contributed to *American Rhetoric from Roosevelt to Reagan: A Collection of Speeches and Critical Essays*, authored *Persuasive Advocacy: Cases for Argumentation and Debate*, and coedited with Bernard K. Duffy *American Orators Before 1900: Critical Studies and Sources* and *American Orators of the Twentieth Century: Critical Studies and Sources*.

CRAIG ALLEN SMITH, Associate Professor of Speech Communication, University of North Carolina, Chapel Hill, teaches courses in political communication, deliberation, and presidential rhetoric. He has published in *Presidential Studies Quarterly, Southern Speech Communication Journal, Communication Quarterly*, and *Central States Speech Journal*. He is coauthor of *Persuasion and Social Movements* and coeditor of *The President and the Public: Rhetoric and National Leadership*.

STEVEN L. VIBBERT, Associate Professor of Communication, Purdue University, West LaFayette, teaches courses in public relations, issue management, and rhetorical criticism. He has published in *Quarterly Journal of Speech, Communication Monographs*, and *Public Relations Review*. He coauthored *Public Relations as Communication Management* and contributed to *Handbook of Organization Communication*.

Speaker and Speech Index

Subject Index

Page numbers of actual entries appear in **boldface**.